HISTORICAL

SOUTHERN FAMILIES

VOLUME IX

HISTORICAL

SOUTHERN FAMILIES

VOLUME IX

BY

JOHN BENNETT BODDIE

Edited by Mrs. John B. Boddie

GENEALOGICAL PUBLISHING CO., INC.

BALTIMORE   1971

Originally Published
Genealogical Publishing Company
Baltimore, 1965

Reprinted
Genealogical Publishing Company
Baltimore, 1971

Library of Congress Catalog Card Number 67-29833
International Standard Book Number 0-8063-0035-3

TABLE OF CONTENTS

FAMILIES   PAGE

DEDICATED TO ALL GENEALOGISTS
WHO SEARCH FOR THE TRUTH
AND RECORD IT

"This shall be written for the generation to come."

McELROY OF NORTH CAROLINA, TENNESSEE, MISSISSIPPI, TEXAS, 1743-1965

The first documentary proof of ARCHIBALD McELROY's residence in North Carolina is 1743. From the Colonial Records of N.C., this land grant was found:

His Excellency Gabriel Johnston, Esq.: His Majesty's Captain-General, and Governor in Chief, in and over the said Province,
To the Surveyor-General, Greeting-----

You are forthwith to admeasure and lay out, or cause to be admeasured and laid out unto ARCHIBALD MACKILROY a plantation, containing 250 acres of land, lying in Craven County on the northside of Nuese upon a creek called Falling Creek on the eastside running up both sides of a branch of said creek for the complement. The said land to be seated according to right's proved within three years in _____, the delivery hereof to the surveyor.

Observing his Majesty's instructions, for running out of lands; and a Plat and certificate thereof, to return unto the Secretary's office, within 12 months from the date hereof, and for so doing, this shall be your warrant; which warrant may not be assigned. Given at Edenton under my hand, the 16th day of November, Anno Domini 1743.

Gab Johnston

At a Council held at Newbern 22d November 1744 Present His Excellency Gabriel Johnston Esq.Gov'r Read the following petitions for Warrants,Viz't:

William McIlroy	100 acres	Craven County
John McIlroy	76 acres	Johnston County
John Mackilroy	100 acres	Johnston County

File #297 George the Second: Know ye that we have given unto ARCHIBALD MACKILROY two hundred and fifty acres of land in Craven County on the northside of Neuse River on a branch of a creek called Falling Creek beginning at a red oak running thence S 62, E180 poles to a red oak thence S 40, W 220 poles to a pine, thence N 62, -W180 poles thence with a direct

1

line to the first station to hold. Dated the 20th
day of April 1745.

Gab Johnston

File #526 George the Second: To all Know ye that we have
granted unto William McKelroy one hundred acres of
land in Craven County on the northside of Neuse river,
beginning at a red oak standing on Groundnutmarsh and
runs S 56 degrees, W 50 poles, S 32 degrees, E 180
poles, N 58 degrees, E 100 poles thence with a direct
line to the first station. To hold--dated at NewBern
the 6th day of April 1750.

Gab Johnston

File # 42 George the Second: To all: Know ye that we have
granted unto John McKelroy 76 acres of land in Johnston County on the northside of Neuse river on Falling,
being the land he now lives on, beginning at a white
oak on a branch of said creek and runs N 200 poles,
then W 120 poles to a stake in a Marsh, then with a
direct line to the first station to hold. Dated at
NewBern 6th April 1750.

Gab Johnston

File #736 William McIlroy--one hundred and eighty one acres
of land in Johnston County on the northside Crabtree
Creek beginning at a pine on the northside of the
creek thence north 240 poles to a pine then West 100
poles to a pine thence south 40 poles to a hickory
shrub then W 72 poles to a white oak on the bank of
the creek thence south down the creek 100 poles to a
red oak thence E 20 poles to the bend of the creek
then down the creek to the first station. Dated 27th
day of April 1753.

File #737 William McIlroy 340 acres of land in Johnston
County beginning at an ash on the bank of the Crabtree Creek running thence S 40 poles to a hickory
shrub then W 260 poles to a white oak then N 200
poles to an ash on the bank of the creek then E 280
poles to Thomas House's line then along that line S 37
degrees W 140 poles to the creek then down the creek
to the first station. Dated 27th day of April 1753.

Book I p.8, Cross Index to Johnston County, N.C. Deeds
1746-1755, 1-140 Hartsfield, Paul from McIllroy, Archibald
p.10, McIllroy, Archibald.
Book III, Cross Index to Johnston County, N.C. Deeds August 1754-1755, MUCKELROY, ARCHIBALD from House, William 3-
374.

The next proof of ARCHIBALD McELROY's residency in

Johnston County, North Carolina is his will. A copy was
obtained from the records of Johnston County, N.C. Some
words were not legible to the reader so blank spaces were
left. It follows:

  Will of <u>ARCHIBALD McELROY, Sr.</u>

IN THE NAME OF GOD, I, <u>ARCH MACKLEROY</u>, of the County of
Johnston, in the province of North Carolina, gunsmith ____
& body & ____ is ____ for all man once to die. I hereby
make & ordain this my will & testament in ____following,
that today 1st & principally, I give & bequeath my soul
into the hands of Almighty God that gave it to me, nothing
doubting but that I shall receive the same again from the
hands of my ____ blessed Redeemer at the Day of General
Resurrection & my body to the earth from whence it came to
be buried after a Christian decent manner at the discretion
of my executors whom I shall hereafter appoint, & as for
what worldly goods it hath been pleased God to bestow on
me. After my just debts & funeral expenses are paid I
give & bequeath as followeth Viz:

IMPRIMIS: I give & bequeath to my beloved wife <u>CATHARINE</u>
    <u>MACKLEROY</u> 3 negroes named Cesar, Jane, & Doll,
    & 1 stallion called Bull, & the plantation
    whereon I now live during her life.

ITEM: I give & bequeath to my beloved grandson <u>MICA-</u>
    <u>JAH MACKLEROY</u>, the plantation & tract of land
    on Crabtree Creek whereon James Childres for-
    merly dwelt & 1 negro boy named Cook to him &
    his heirs forever.

ITEM: I give & bequeath to my beloved son named <u>AVON-</u>
    <u>TON MACKLEROY</u>, my mill & all the land adjoining
    to it as low as Polk's branch, & 1 negro boy
    named Buck, to him & his heirs forever.

ITEM: I give & bequeath unto my beloved son, <u>JOHN</u>
    <u>MACKLEROY</u>, the plantation & part of the tract
    of land I now live on after the decease of my
    wife Catharine, & 1 negro boy named Peter, to
    him & his heirs forever.

ITEM: I give & bequeath to my beloved son, <u>ANDREW</u>
    <u>MACKLEROY</u>, 100 acres of land taken out of the
    tract I now live on lying on Marsh Creek & not
    coming nearer the plantation than the red hill,
    & 1 negro boy named Will, to him & his heirs
    forever.

ITEM: I give & bequeath to my beloved daughter, Sal-
    ley, 100 acres of land out of the tract I now
    live on adjoining the land left to my son Andrew,
    at the lower end of his land, & 1 negro girl
    named Cloe, to her & her heirs forever, & also,

1 mare called Poll.

ITEM: I give & bequeath to my beloved daughter,
Frankey the upper end of the North Creek land
called the hog farm, & a negro boy named Dick,
to her & her heirs forever.

ITEM: My will & desire is that if it should please
God any of my children above mentioned or my
grandchild, MICAJAH, should die before they
come to age, the boys 21 & the girls 16, or
married, having lawfully _____ that then his or
her part to be equally divided among the sur-
vivors.

ITEM: My will & desire is that all the remainder of
my estate, both real & personal, may be equally
divided between my wife & children at the discretion of my executors for my desire is that
my estate may be inventoried but not appraised.

I do hereby appoint my beloved wife, CATHARINE
MACKLEROY, executrix, & my brother William & my
friend, Andrew Heartsfield, executors of this
my last will & testament, revoking all the wills
formerly by me made. Allowing this & no other
to be my last will & testament, Thos. Hunter &
Nathaniel Jones to assist in dividing the
estate. In witness whereof I do _____ unto set
my hand & seal this 9th day of December of 60
(1760).
Signed & sealed in   HIS
presence of Joseph Chatwin ARCH   MACKLEROY
John Polk   Fran Chatwin   MARK
                              (died by January 1761)

From: N.C. State Dept. of Archives & History, Johnston
County Court Minutes 1759-1783 Part I
Jan. 1761--ARCHIBALD McELROY's will was proved by
James Chatwin, Catharine, widow, & William McElroy
& Andrew Hartsfield, exers & extrix. (The follow-
ing item shows why Archibald McElroy named his
grandson, Micajah, as a legatee in his will.)

April 1761 SARAH McELROY, widow of ARCHIBALD McEL-
ROY, Jr., dec'd, returned inventory of her husband's
estate.
STATE RECORDS of N. C. -- Militia Returns 1754-1755
p 331. Johnston Regiment--Lewis De Rosset, Colonel:

Simon Bright, Lt. Col.
Samuel Smith, Major
Subaltern Officers: ARCH'D McILROY, quartermaster
SARAH McELROY, widow of ARCHIBALD McELROY, Jr.dec'd,
granted admn. on the estate with James Linn & John
Rench, securities.
Ordered that SARAH McELROY, widow of ARCHIBALD
McELROY, Jr., dec'd, be appointed guardian to her
child, MICAJAH McELROY, orphan of said dec'd.
WAKE COUNTY, N. C.   June Term 1776
Inventory of the estate of CATHERINE MACKLEROY,dec'd:
to wit _____ 1 negro fellow named Seasor, 1 negro
woman named Jane, 22 head of cattle, 8 head of mares
& horses, 2 feather beds, 3 sheets, 1 blanket & 1
bag of feathers, 4 dishes, 4 basins, 12 plates, 6
spoons, 1 pint pot, 1 small mugg, some knives &
forks, 5 iron potts, 3 pr pott hooks, rings & boxes
for pr cast wheels, 10 old hoes, 1 iron wedge, 1 box
iron & heaters, 1 hackel (?) & plough hoe, 3 b_____
(?), 4 axis, 1 grubing hoe, 1 mallock, 1 frying pan,
1 cotton wheel, 2 flax wheels, 1 real hook, 1 real,
1 large chest, 2 boxes, 1 trunk with papers, 1 pr
shears & chearner, 1 tub, 1 pail, 2 piggins, 2 meal
sifters, parcell of old casks, 1 side saddle & bridle,
3 old chairs, 4 hides, parcell of cotton, 1 small
cooking _____(?), 2 geese, 4 ducks, 2 pr of old cards,
1 bofat (?), 2 old b _____(?), 1030 Wt. pork, 4 old
books, 1 pr flesh (?) forks, 1 pr spoon molders, 1
stack of flax, some oates & some wheat & hogshead,
5 or 6 bushells flaxseed, a debt due from Mr. John
Shaw of 100 lbs. Virginia money, a parcell of corn,
1 meal bag, 2 ewes, some fallow, 1 old rug, 1 gallon
jug, 1 basket, 1 meal bag, 2 bread trays, 29 head of
hogs, 1 old table, 1 butter pott, 1 inch auger, some
soap, a piece of a side of leather & some salt _____.
Abington Mackleroy
This was the within inventory of the estate of CATH-
ERINE MACKLEROY, dec'd, in open Court duly proved by
the Oath of Abington Mackleroy, and ordered to be
recorded.
John Rice, Clk.
The within inventory was recorded in the Clerk's
office of Wake County in Book A pp. 89/90 this 11th
day of June 1776.
John Rice, Clk.
Wills & Inventories of Estates 1771-1797 Wake County,
N. C. p. 7. Inventory of the personal estate of
John Macleroy, dec'd, rendered by John B. Shaw,admnr.

Wake County March Term 1794, Book D.
Wake County Marriages 1770-1800 April 1929 by
Caswell-Nash
Chapter, D.A.R.
Raleigh, N. C.

FRANCES MACKLEROY to John Baptist Shaw Dec. 3, 1771.
Bondsman: AVONTON McKILROY.

Avonton McElroy, son of ARCHIBALD McELROY and Catherine, married Sarah Dawson on 3-7-1770, daughter of William Dawson and wife, Martha. Frankey (or Frances), daughter of Archibald and Catherine Mackleroy, married John
Baptist Shaw.

A copy of the will of John Baptist Shaw was obtained
from the County Clerk's office of Wake County, N. C. This
is what it shows:

Will made 16th day of September 1815 names wife
FRANKY SHAW, names sons: Simpson Shaw (married Mary High)
John Shaw (died 1848)
Willie Shaw
Capt. James Jones m Charity Alston
daughters: Elizabeth Perry
Caty Jones (m Thos. Jones)
Polly Morgan (m Samuel Morgan)
Fanny High (wife of Peyton High)
Sally Warren (m Nathaniel Warren)
Allie Brasfield

MACKLEROY to Chatwin

This indenture made this 20th of April in the year
of our Lord God 1762 & in the 2nd year of the Reign of our
Sovereign Lord George the Third, by the grace of God of
Great Britain, France & Ireland, King defenders of the
faith and between KATHERINE MACKLEROY, of the County of
Johnston & province of N. C., of the one part and Joseph
Chatwin, of the County and province of the other part.

Witnesseth, that the said KATHERINE MACKLEROY, for
and in consideration of the sum of fifteen pounds current
money of Virginia to her in hand paid by the said Joseph
Chatwin, before the ensealing and delivery of these presents, the receipt whereof this the said KATHERINE, doth
hereby acknowledge, hath given, granted bargained and sold,
and by these presents doth give, grant, bargain, sell,
alien, in fee of and confirm unto the said Joseph Chatwin,
his heirs and assigns, forever, a certain tract or parcel
of land containing two hundred acres, be the same more or
less, lying and being in the County and province above
mentioned on the northeast side of Marsh Creek, it being
part of a tract of land containing 240 acres lately granted
by the Right Honorable John, Earl of Granville, to the said

KATHERINE, where the above Joseph Chatwin now dwelleth and bounded as followeth, viz: beginning on Marsh Creek on the lower line of said tract and running east 111 poles to a white oak corner tree on Fall Branch; thence West 250 poles to a red oak corner tree on the Jumping Branch; thence West 122 poles to Marsh Creek, thence down the several meanders of said creek to the place of beginning.

TO HAVE AND TO HOLD the said granted and bargained premises with all the appurtenances, privileges and commodities to the same belonging or in anywise appertaining to him, the said Chatwin, his heirs and assigns forever, to his and their only proper use and behoof forever; and I, the said KATHERINE MACKLEROY, for my heirs, executors, administrators do convenant, promise and grant to and with the said Joseph Chatwin, his heirs and assigns, that before the ensealing hereof I am true, sole and lawful owner of the above mentioned land and premises, I am lawfully possessed herewith as my own proper right as a good estate of inheritance in fee simple, and have in myself good rite, full power and lawful authority to grant, bargain, sell, convey, and confirm the said bargained premises in manner above mentioned and the said Joseph Chatwin, his heirs and assigns, shall and may from time to time forever hereafter by power and virtue of these presents lawfully, peaceably and equally have hole use occupie, possess and enjoy the above mentioned premises with the appurtenances thereunto belonging, freely and discharged from all other gifts, grants, bargains, sales, deeds, mortgages, wills intails joynters dowery, judgments, execution, incumbrances and extents furthermore and the said KATHERINE MACKLEROY, for myself, my heirs, executors and administrators do covenant and engage the above mentioned premises to him, the said Joseph Chatwin, his heirs and assigns, agent the lawful claim or demand and of any person or persons whatsoever, I do warrant and defend unto the said Joseph Chatwin, his heirs and assigns forever, only the land Joseph Chatwin, paying to his Majestie and his successors the yearly rent of 4 shillings province money, 240 acres as in the said patent is received according to the true intent and meaning of these present.

In witness whereof, I the said KATHERINE MACKLEROY have hereunto set my hand and seal the ____ day of April 1762.

Signed, sealed & delivered in   her
the presence of: Tho.Haughton KATHERINE   MACKLEROY
                 John Belk   mark

North Carolina: Johnston County, April Court 1762.
Present his Majesties Justices then was the within Deed

acknowledged by <u>KATHERINE</u> <u>MACKLEROY</u>, ordered to be
registered.

Teste: Robert Rainey, C C

Ensealed by: Lord Tanner
&
Aaron Haskins Recorded in Book B I P. 200.

From: N.C. State Department of Archives & History - -
Johnston County Court Minutes 1759-1783 Part I

April 1759 William McElroy app'td overseer of the road
from the Falls of Neuse to Crabb Tree Creek.

July 1760 on application of Rebecka Mackleroy, admnr,
granted to her on the estate of her late husband
John Mackelroy, Jr., who died intestate - with William Mackelroy and <u>ARCHIBALD</u> <u>MACKELROY</u>, securities.

January 1761 <u>ARCHIBALD</u> <u>McELROY's</u> will was proved by James
Chatwin, Cathrin, widow, and William McElroy and
Andrew Hartsfield, exx and exers qualified.

July 1761 <u>CATHRINE</u> <u>McELROY</u>, exx and William Mackelroy and
Andrew Hartsfield, exers., returned inventory of the
estate of ARCHIBALD McELROY, dec'd.

January 1762 an account of the sales of the estate of
<u>ARCHIBALD</u> <u>McELROY</u>, Jr., dec'd returned by the
Sheriff.

April 1762 <u>SARAH</u> <u>McELROY</u>, admx., of the estate of <u>ARCHIBALD</u>
<u>McELROY, Jr.</u>, dec'd, returned an inventory of such
part of the estate as came into her hands since last
inventory.
Commissioners appointed to value a negro belonging
to the estate of <u>ARCHIBALD</u> <u>McELROY</u>, Jr., dec'd and
make return to next Court.
Deed from Cathrin Mackelroy to Joseph Chatwin for
200 acres ack'd.

July 1762 Account of sales of the estate of <u>ARCHIBALD</u>
<u>MACKELROY</u>, dec'd.

From: General Services Administration, The Nat'l Archives,
January 19, 1950, Arthur H. Leavitt, Chief Veterans'
Records Branch:
McELROY, MICAJAH S 2 785   Pension Record
Revolutionary War

Parents: Names not mentioned

Birth: September 20th or 30th, 1760, in Wake County
North Carolina.

Family: No data given

Residence: Veteran was born in Wake County, N. C.,
and resided there during his service.
He then moved to Lincoln County, Tenn.
He was still residing there in 1832 at
which time he stated that he had lived

in Lincoln County for about 23 or 24
years.

Death: Date and place not shown (died in Lincoln
County, Tenn.)

Service: When the veteran applied for pension, he
stated that he enlisted sometime in 1780
and served at various times until some-
time during the fall of 1781, amounting
to 7 months in all, under Captains Cato
Bryant, Joseph Peoples, Henry Pope, Mathew
Calems or Colems and Lewis Bledsoe and
Colonels Colier, Hardy Sanders and John
Humphreys. He was in some skirmishes
with the Tories. He was pensioned as
Private.
Certificate 7 679--Act of June 7, 1832.

State of North Carolina - Department of State
Secretary of State - Thad Eure
p. 236

N 52 CATHARINE McILROY --- 517 acres of land in Johnston
County beginning at a pine in William McIlroy's line
then along the line W 38 poles to a white oak on
Crab Tree Creek then S 30 poles to a black jack in
Colonel Hollan's line then along the line N 60
degrees W 172 poles to the corner, a hickory, then
along Judge Smith's line N 30 degrees, W 252 poles
to a hickory on Crab Tree Creek then down the Creek
and James McElevian's line S 52 degrees E 310 to a
corner white on the northside of said creek, then
along the other line N 20 -- E 320 poles to the corner, a pine then along the other line N 30 degrees
W 80 poles to a red oak in the said line, then E 188
poles to a red oak then 300 poles to a white oak on
Fall Branch then W 188 poles to a red oak then S to
the first station. Dated 28th day of February 1761.

Early Records of Georgia, Vol. I, p. 253/54.
Deed Book B B 1787-1789, p. 46.

Lamar, Zachariah and wife Sarah to John Smith-- 200
acres on Marsh Creek, original grant to Abington
McIlroy, December 20, 1789.

From: N. C. Dept. of Archives & History, Johnston County
Andrew Hartsfield made will 11-18-1761. Wife: Sarah
Children: Godfrey Hartsfield, Richard Hartsfield,
John Hartsfield, Jacob Hartsfield, Andrew
Hartsfield, Berry Hartsfield, Mary Harts-
field, Rebecca Hartsfield, Sarah Harts-
field, William McElroy, executor.
John Smyth, Jr., admn. of James McElroy.

1761 Deed of Sale--Earl Granville to John McElroy -
365 acres proved by Theophilus Hunter.

1762 Thomas Smith & Jacob Hartsfield

Book I, p. 8 Cross Index to Johnston County, N.C. Deeds
1746 - 1750, 1-140 Hartsfield, Paul, from
McILROY, ARCHIBALD.

Book III Cross Index to Johnston County, N.C. Deeds
August 1754 - 1755, MUCKELROY, ARCHIBALD
from House, William, 3-374.

May 5, 1745, Wm. Fipps sells to Adam McCoy,
a tract of 100 acres on the NW prong of Bay
River, patented 2 Nov. 1739, by the said Wm.
Fipps. B 2 Witnesses: James Mackleroy
William Carruthers

December 2, 1751 Moses Prescott sells James Mackleroy 330
acres on NS of Bay River; patented Mar. 1,
1722, B 3. Witnesses: William Mackleroy
Richard Bush

April 1764 Ordered that William McIlroy build a bridge
over Crabtree Creek at or near the road upon
his own land.

October 1766 William McIlroy on jury, to lay off a road
to meet the road from Bracewell's ferry upon
Cape Fear that extends to this county line
and from Crabtree Creek Road to Orange line.

November 1769 William McIlroy and Aberton McIlroy appt'd
patrolers from Falls of Neuse to Walnut
Creek including Joel Lane's and Abram Hill's
plantations and from thence to the mouth of
Walnut and Crabtree Creeks.

May 1770 Ordered that a road be laid out from the County
line that divides this County and Orange on
Bryer Creek and thence into the main road
that crosses Neuse River at the Sand Bar -
and that Richard Hartsfield, Constable, sum-
mon the following jury to lay out same.
Godfrey Hartsfield
William McLeroy
Abington McLeroy

August 1770 Godfrey Hartsfield is appt'd overseer of the
road from near Simpses Creek to the Road
that leads to the Sand Bar at Isaac Hunter's
and that all the hands on the lower side of
Turkey Creek and upper side of Mine Creek
work on same.

Ordered that Abington McLeroy be Constable
in room of Richard Hartsfield.

1790 Census North Carolina--Hillsborough District, Wake

County, p. 105, <u>MUCKLEROY</u>, <u>MICAJAH</u> - 1 male over 16
2 males under 16
3 females

1800 Census North Carolina--Wake County, p. 16,
<u>MUCKLEROY</u>, <u>MICAJAH</u> - 3 males to 10
1 male to 16
1 male to 26
1 male to 45

    <u>MICAJAH</u> <u>McELROY</u> moved from Wake County, N. C., to Lincoln County, Tennessee by 1810. We have documentary proof of this fact by the Court records.

<u>TENNESSEE</u>--Records of Lincoln County
Historical Records Project II
Will Book 1827-1850

p. 21   Taxes unpaid for 1810 (not listed for taxation so-doubled). <u>MICAJAH</u> <u>MUCKLEROY</u>--400 acres, entry 89, location Cane Brook. Dolls 1 cents 50.

p. 66   An indenture and sale between <u>MICAJAH</u> <u>MUCKLEROY</u> of the one part and William Polk of the other part for 400 acres of land was acknowledged in open Court by the said <u>MICAJAH</u> <u>MUCKLEROY</u> and ordered to be registered.

p. 78   Commissioners of the County of Lincoln and Town of Fayetteville have procured 100 acres of land of Ezekiel Norris divided it and lot #16 at $90.00 to ourselves which we offer to the County for the purpose of building a meeting house and on the 22nd day of last November let contract to <u>MICAJAH</u> & <u>WILLIAM</u> <u>MUCKLEROY</u> at $3,935 & the bond we took from them for the performance of the work will show the size and description of the house which is to be completed on or before the 1st day of November 1813 --let 27th May 1811.

p. 91   Reuben Washburn against <u>MICAJAH</u> <u>MUCKLEROY</u>. Jury decided that <u>MICAJAH</u> <u>MUCKLEROY</u> was not guilty and Reuben Washburn must pay costs, etc.

<u>LINCOLN</u> <u>COUNTY</u>, <u>TENNESSEE</u> Deeds, Book B, p. 154
<u>MICAJAH</u> <u>McELROY</u>--bill of sale. Know all men by these present, that we, <u>MICAJAH</u> <u>McELROY</u> & Daniel Summer, both of Lincoln County, Tenn., have sold & delivered to Robert Hairston, of same county, & State, a negro boy, 24 May 1813. Signed: <u>M</u>. <u>MUCKELROY</u>
Daniel Summers

p. 380 Deed Book E. M. McELROY. <u>MICAJAH</u> <u>MUCKLEROY</u> signed this deed 19 Oct. 1818. <u>MICAJAH</u> <u>MUCKLEROY</u> of Lincoln County to Charles Tooly of same. Consideration $1200.00 paid by Charles Tooly, 175 acres on north bank of Elk River, thence up river to mouth of

branch above where Daniel R. Summer now lives up to
John Younts' line. Proved April, 1819.

> Witnesses: T. W. Booth
> William Smith

Federal Census, 1820 <u>LINCOLN</u> <u>COUNTY</u>, <u>TENNESSEE</u>
Vol. 9, p. 336

McELROY, Henry: 1 male 18 to 26   1 fe 26 to 45
                 1 male 45 up   1 fe 45 up
McELROY, J. H.: 1 male 18 to 26   1 fe 16 to 26
McELROY, ARCH: 3 males to 10   1 fe to 10
                 1 male 16 to 18   1 fe 10 to 26
                 1 male 26 to 45   1 fe 26 to 45

Federal Census, 1830 <u>LINCOLN</u> <u>COUNTY</u>, <u>TENNESSEE</u>
Vol. 17, p. 113

McELROY, MICAJAH, Jr.: 1 male 20 to 30
                        1 male 15 to 20
                        1 male 30 to 40
McELROY, William: 3 males 5 to 10   1 fe 40 to 50
                        1 male 10 to 15
                        1 male 15 to 20
                        1 male 40 to 50
McELROY, MICAJAH, Sr.: 1 male 60 to 70   1 fe 60 to 70
p. 239   1 male 20 to 30

Federal Census, 1840 <u>LINCOLN</u> <u>COUNTY</u>, <u>TENNESSEE</u>
Vol. 8, p. 95, Dis't 23

McELROY, ELIZABETH (widow of <u>Archibald</u> McElroy who died
          1839):   2 males 5 to 10   1 fe to 5
                       1 male 10 to 15   1 fe 10 to 15
                       1 male 15 to 20   3 fe 15 to 20
                                          1 fe 30 to 40

Information received from David Sloan, County Clk., Fayetteville, Tenn. Wills recorded and proven in Fayetteville,
Tennessee:

> J. R. McElroy, 8/27/1909
> R. C. McElroy, 5/11/1912
> Sanford M. McElroy, 1/26/1877
> Louisa A. (Smith) McElroy, 7/25/1894
> William McElroy, February, 1856
> Mary McElroy, 11/3/1856
> <u>ARCHIBALD</u> <u>McELROY</u>, 10/8/1841

Fayetteville, LINCOLN COUNTY, TENNESSEE
Newspaper: "<u>OBSERVER</u>"
6-23-1859: Looking Back:

> JURY: <u>MICAJAH</u> <u>McELROY</u>: to view & report to our next
>   Court the damage that Ezekiel Norris hath sus-
>   tained.
> JURY Report: 16 May 1812 - Joseph Commons, Andrew
>   Smith, Robert Buchanan, V. Hartgrove, Joseph

Jenkins, and <u>M</u>. <u>MUCKELROY</u>.

7 Feb. 1814 - Contracted the building of the
Courthouse to WILLIAM & <u>MICAJAH</u> <u>MUCKELROY</u> at
$3,935.00. Amount paid MACKELROYS for court-
house $3,472.62½.

Monday, Feb. 6, 1815 - William Muckelroy appt'd
a constable, took oath of office and entered into bond.

Tuesday, 9 o'clock, 1816 - The Court received
the Courthouse in Fayetteville from <u>MICAJAH</u> &
<u>WILLIAM</u> <u>MUCKELROY</u> & further allowed them the sum
of $500.00 in addition to the sum first contrac-
ted for the building said house. Issue 2/8/1816.

Tuesday, May 2, 1816 - Ordered by the Court,
that an additional allowance of $250.00 be made
to <u>MICAJAH</u> <u>MUCKELROY</u>, undertaker of the Courthouse in Fayetteville, to be paid out of any
monies in the treasury of this County, not
otherwise appropriated.

Newspaper: THE <u>VILLAGE</u> <u>MESSENGER</u>--published from 3-11-1823
       --6-20-1828

9-30-1824 List of letters in the Postoffice
      . MICAJAH M'ELROY   Ramsom M'Elroy

1-9-1825   <u>ARCHIBALD</u> <u>M'ELROY</u>

1-19-1825 <u>ARCHIBALD</u> <u>M'ELROY</u>

"THE <u>VILLAGE</u> <u>MESSENGER</u>"

8-2-1826   SHERIFF SALE

By virtue of a writ of venditioni exponas that issued
from the Circuit Court of Lincoln Co., at March Term, 1826,
& in ___ directed. I shall sell at the Courthouse door in
the town of Fayetteville on the 16th day of Sept., next,
all the right, title claim & interest that <u>MICAJAH</u> <u>M'ELROY</u>,
sen., has in & to 213 acres of land, lying on the west side
of Cane Creek, where John Cox & Henry Davis now live;
bounded by land of Elbridge & Hiram Buchanan on the south,
William McElroy on the east, John Crawford on the north,
& Mathew <u>M'Clure</u> on the west; sold by virtue of said writ,
to satisfy a judgment that Alexander Greer & Mathew M'Clure
recovered against said M'ELROY. Sale within lawful hours.

                    July 29, 1826.
                    A. Smith, Deputy Sheriff

1-27-1827 Letters in postoffice: Barney L. McElroy

7-6-1827   Taken up by <u>ARCHIBALD</u> <u>M'ELROY</u>, on Elk river near
      Hannah's ford, 1 black mare.

4-7-1824   Letters in postoffice: Sarah McElroy

7-14-1824 Barney McElroy

                    *****

14

General Services Administration
Nat'l Archives & Records Service
Washington 25, D. C.   April 28, 1959

Mrs. John R. Barnett
2301 Southmore Blvd.
Houston 4, Texas

Dear Mrs. Barnett:
        Your letter of March 20th requested information con-
cerning the last payment of record made to <u>MICAJAH</u> <u>McELROY</u>
& whether it continued to be paid his widow. We regret
the delay in reply.
        We have found an entry in the pension payment volumes
showing that the last payment of record was made to <u>MICA-
JAH</u> <u>McELROY</u> by the West Tenn. pension agency the third
quarter 1833. It is indicated in this volume that his
name was transferred to the Pulaski Tenn. agency pension
rolls. However, no payments were made to him from this
agency. We have found no claim for pension made by the
widow of <u>MICAJAH</u> <u>McELROY</u>.

                            Sincerely yours,
                            Harry Schwartz
                    For: W. Neil Franklin
                            Archivist in Charge
                            General Reference Branch
Reference: <u>TENNESSEE</u>, <u>LINCOLN</u> <u>COUNTY</u> Will Book 1827-1850
pp. 112/13 #189
Will of <u>ARCHIBALD</u> <u>McELROY</u>
        This is my last will & testament made this 3rd day
of December, 1839. I give to my beloved wife, <u>Elizabeth</u>,
my negro Harry & his wife Lucy; negro boy Cook, & girl
Malinda, during her lifetime. I, also, give my wife the
house that I now occupy for 5 years, the balance of my
property to be equally divided amongst my children, after
paying my debts. I appoint my wife & Amos Hurley, guard-
ians for the children, and I, also, want them to administer
upon my estate.
Witnesses: (signed) <u>ARCHIBALD</u> <u>McELROY</u>
  W. Bonner
  John M. McGaugh   Proven at the October Term, 1841 of
  May Buchanan   the Lincoln County Court. Recorded
  Anthony Delaney   8th Oct., 1841.
<u>TENNESSEE</u> <u>RECORDS</u> Vol. 4 (1933)--K. P. Jones & P.J.Gundred
p. 85 (76)   Amos Hurley states that <u>ARCHIBALD</u> <u>McELROY</u>
              died December 1839 having made a will. Wife,
              <u>ELIZABETH</u> (<u>HURLEY</u>) <u>McELROY</u> & Amos Hurley,
              executors. Elizabeth subsequently married

Lewis Shipp & departed this life last winter
or spring. Said testator left 8 children.
Reference: 1812 Pension Records--Nat'l Archives Bldg.
#20   1812   McELROY, ARCHIBALD Wt 37942
      Private--Tennessee 2nd Regiment, Mounted Volunteer,
      Capt. John Doak
STATE of TENNESSEE)
LINCOLN COUNTY   )   On the 4th day March, 1856, William
                       B. Rhea, guardian of Thomas Benton
McElroy, minor heir of ARCHIBALD McELROY, makes application for bounty land. Land warrant for 80 acres. No widow
living. William B. Rhea, guardian of Elizabeth McElroy,
William McElroy, Benton McElroy, & Perry McElroy.
ARCHIBALD McELROY died sometime in 1839. Widow died in
early part of 1855--guardian for William J. McElroy, about
19 yrs. old; Thomas B. McElroy, about 17 yrs. old; & Elizabeth L. McElroy, about 14 yrs. old. ARCHIBALD McELROY
volunteered at Fayetteville, Tennessee, September or Oct.,
1814 for 6 months.
TENNESSEE Records of Lincoln County
p. 58 ARCHIBALD MUCKLEROY to work on roads under Alexan-
       der Meeks, overseer.
    BIOGRAPHICAL & HISTORICAL MEMOIRS of MISSISSIPPI
    1891   Goodspeed Publishing Company
                    Volume I
Dr. J. C. McELROY, physician & surgeon, of Newton County,
Mississippi, born Lincoln County, Tennessee, 1825, son of
ARCHIBALD & ELIZABETH (HURLEY) McELROY, natives of North
Carolina. The father was a planter by occupation & fol-
lowed this calling all his life. He died 1839 at age 55.
Served in War of 1812 & was an ardent admirer of General
Jackson. His father, MICAJAH McELROY, was a native of
N. C. & was a soldier in the war of the REVOLUTION.
     Dr. McELROY was reared & educated in the place where
he was born. In 1842, he came to Mississippi & settled in
Lauderdale where he resided 7 years. There, he became a
student of medicine under the preceptorship of Dr. L. A.
Ragland. In 1846/48 he attended medical lectures in Lexington, Kentucky, & graduated in the Spring of 1848. He
then came to Decatur, Newton County, Mississippi & entered
upon the practice of medicine. This he continued until
the year 1871 when he removed to Newton. Here he built up
an extensive practice. One of the oldest families in East
Mississippi & widely known throughout the surrounding
counties. Conscientious & skillful & perfectly fitted for
the numerous demands made on the family physician.
     He served in the War against Mexico in 1846 being a
Lt. of a company from Tennessee. First a private, then

physician & surgeon & afterwards promoted to Lt. Term of service was from early in 1846 until the treaty of peace was issued. Married the Fall of 1848 to Miss CYNTHIA ANN SMITH, daughter of MIJAMIN SMITH of Lincoln County, Tenn. She died July, 1869, leaving a family of 9 children, 7 of whom are still living.

Dr. McELROY's 2nd wife was Mrs. Ridgeway, daughter of Joshua Shuptrine, of Decatur, Mississippi. When the late war broke out in 1863, Dr. McELROY was a captain of a company. He was discharged in 7 months on account of disability & returned to his home. He & his family are members of the Methodist Episcopal Church South, & are active workers for the upbuilding of the cause of Christianity. He is a member of A.F. & A.M., belonging to Blue Lodge & Chapter. In 1861, the people of his County testified to the confidence which they reposed in the doctor by electing him to represent them in the legislature of the State. This honor was 3 times conferred upon him. He is an excellent gentleman of untarnished reputation. Has a high rank in his profession & is a loyal, patriotic gentleman.

A paper dated January 24, 1848, concerning his service in War against Mexico. Was at Camp El Molina, Del Rey. Certifying JACKSON C. McELROY, 1st Lt., Company E. 3rd Regiment Tennessee Volunteers. Resigned 16 May 1848. An affidavit by him concerning his service.

AFFIDAVIT: May 14, 1851)
STATE of MISSISSIPPI)
COUNTY of NEWTON) State he was 26 & resident of Newton County. Made application for Bounty Land.

AFFIDAVIT 21 June 1852--state he was 27. Applied for Bounty Land--received it. Statement regarding his physical disability & was dated Nov 1, 1897, Newton, Miss. He had been receiving $8.00 per month & asked for increase. Said he was 5' $6\frac{1}{2}$", weight 130 lbs., age $72\frac{1}{2}$. Long statement regarding his ailments. Also, mentioned riding horseback to attend his patients.

AFFIDAVIT: Mar. 24, 1914, from Mrs. M. M. Johnson, of Harrison Co., Miss., stating that her mother, CYNTHIA, was the 1st wife of Dr. J. C. McELROY. She remembers the death of her mother & to the best of her knowledge, her mother was b. 6/3/1824, & d., 1870, age 45.

AFFIDAVIT: by Dr. McELROY at age 73, called himself feeble & that he had a wry neck. A paper stating the location of the property & that it was placed under a deed of trust to A. L. Hoye, March 16, 1894 for $1396.15 for means for the support of himself & family & that he had been unable to pay anything more than the interest since it was executed. His personal property, he said, amounted to 2 horses & 2 mules, valued at $35.00 a head. That his dwelling in the town of Newton belongs to his wife as well as all furniture contained therein. This statement was made 8 November 1897.

May 13, 1897 Dr. McELROY made a statement regarding his infirmities. Soldier stated he had a prior marriage to CYNTHIA ANN SMITH & that she, CYNTHIA ANN, died July 14, 1869 at Decatur, Mississippi. He named 7 children by his 1st wife, born during the years 1851/67 & 4 children by his 2nd wife born during years 1873/85.

Some of the persons who made affidavits were: J. E. N. Huddleston, son of the minister of that name; T. M. Scanlon; Mrs. M. M. Johnson, daughter of the soldier & 1st wife; C. H. Doolittle; J. B. McAlpin & J. M. Payne. Dated March 13, 1926.

VICKSBURG, MISSISSIPPI 8-9-1926. To Commissioner of Pensions: Nat'l Archives--Bounty Land Files Act of 1847 Wt 75957

Veteran: JACKSON C. McELROY "Company E" 3rd Regiment TENN. VOLUNTEERS 1847 Grade Corporal Service under Captain Williams; Entitled under Act of 1850 Sept. 28; Warrant #75957--issued April 26. Claimant c/o of B. F. Williams--Lancaster, Newton County, Mississippi.

Applicant: 10 April 1849. JACKSON C. McELROY--noncommissioned officer in Company E, commanded by Captain G. S. Colier in 3rd Regiment Tennessee Volunteers, commanded by Colonel B. T. Chithem, entered about 1 October 1847, for term of war with Mexico & was honorably discharged at the City of Mexico 17 May A. D. 1848 by reason of disability as will fully appear from the order of discharge (exhibit A). And the soldier, JACKSON C. McELROY, says he was promoted to rank of 1st Lt., when they reached Mexico to fill vacancy in Company E, occasioned by the promotion of 1st Lt. Sherel Williams to the rank of captain of said company as will appear from the certificate hereunto annexed & marked Exhibit B.

(signed) JACKSON C. McELROY

EXHIBIT A
Camp El Molener, Del Ray
January 24, 1848

In pursuance of an order issued to me I hereby certify that JACKSON C. McELROY was elected 1st Lt. of Company E, 3rd Regiment Tennessee Volunteers, to fill the vacancy occasioned by the promotion of Lt. Sherel Williams to Captain.

John W. Whitfield
Lt. Col. Comdg. 3rd Regt.

18

EXHIBIT B

Tennessee Volunteers
Mead Quarters, Army of Mexico
Mexico April 17, 1848

Special Orders:
#39   Extract:
1st Lt. J. C. McELROY, 3rd Rgt. Tennessee Volunteers having
tendered his resignation, is hereby honorably discharged
on the 17th May to which time he has leave of absence.
           By order of: Major General Battles
                      L. Thomas, Ass't Adj. General
                 NATIONAL ARCHIVES
Pension: Mary A. F.--widow   Cert. #16164
Veteran: McELROY, JACKSON C.   Mexican War
Can 793 Bundle 10   W. C. #16064
Rank: 1st Lt.   Rate: $20.00 per month
Company E Regiment 3rd Tenn. Vols.   From: Sept. 5, 1916
Address: Newton, Newton County, Miss.
Soldier & Service: JACKSON C. McELROY, was born about
1827, in Lincoln County, Tennessee, served as 1st Lt. Com-
pany E, 3rd Tenn. Vols., from Sept. 1847 to May 17, 1848,
War with Mexico. He stated he, also, had Confederate ser-
vice in Civil War in Company D, 39th Mississippi Volun-
teers. He was pensioned at $8.00 from 1887. Death of
soldier: died December 7, 1913 at Newton, Mississippi.
MISSISSIPPI, Newton County. Applied April 14, 1851.
Residence at date of application: Newton County, Miss.
Age: 26 years.
JACKSON C. McELROY, aged 26, was a private, afterward promoted to 1st Lt., under Sherod Williams, successor to T.
Collier, dec'd--noncommissioned officer in company commanded by Colonel B. F. Cheatham, in the War with Mexico;
that he volunteered about 1 Oct. 1847 for term "during the
war with Mexico", & continued in active service about 7
months--volunteered at Winchester, Franklin County, Tenn.,
& was honorably discharged at Mexico City on or about 25
April 1848, as shown by muster rolls of said company &
makes this declaration for the purpose of obtaining land
he may be entitled to under Act granting county land to
certain officers & soldiers who have been engaged in the
military service of the United States, passed 28 September
1850.

                    (signed) J. C. McELROY
A 2nd application was made 21 June 1852 by JACKSON C. Mc-
ELROY, age 27 years. Time of service given as 7 months,
24 or 25 days. Bounty Land: Act of '47--160--Wt 75957.
Soldier's Affidavit:
Married: Yes--to Mary Frances Shuptrine.
When & by whom married: Dec. 19, 1869, Decatur, Miss., by

Rev. J. F. N. Huddleston.
Were you previously married: Yes, to <u>CYNTHIA</u> <u>ANN</u> <u>SMITH</u>,
            who died at Decatur, Miss., July 14, 1869.
Children, name & birthdate:
1st wife: Kanon A. McElroy, Nov. 4, 1851
           Ransom Mijamin McElroy, Feb. 13, 1854
           Felix Perry McElroy, Dec. 28, 1855
           ELIZABETH CORDELIA McELROY, Feb. 9, 1858, m.
                              3-27-1879, W. H.
                              Seitzler
           Mary E. McElroy, Sept. 14, 1861, m. M. M. John-
                   son
           Henry E. McElroy, April 27, 1864
           Sanford Mason McElroy, May 8, 1867
2nd wife: Glover H. McElroy, June 10, 1873
           Sallie R. McElroy, Oct. 7, 1874, m. ___ Myers
           Lelah B. McElroy, Sept. 19, 1877, m. W. E.Phelps
           Jackson C. McElroy, Jr., Dec. 19, 1883, d. 1907
                      (signed) <u>JACKSON</u> <u>C</u>. <u>McELROY</u>
Date of reply: February 17, 1898
Special examiner: W. A. Gamon 6-28-1911
Case: <u>JACKSON</u> <u>C</u>. <u>McELROY</u>
Born where: Lincoln County, Tennessee
Age at enlistment: 20 yrs. Date of enlistment: Spring of
Date of discharge: 1847.   1846.
Confederate service: Yes--Company D 39th Miss. Volunteers.
Personal description: 5 ft. 6 inches, gray eyes, dark hair,
                 fair complexion, 86 yrs. old.
                      (signed) <u>JACKSON</u> <u>C</u>. <u>McELROY</u>
<u>HISTORY</u> <u>of</u> <u>NEWTON</u> <u>COUNTY</u>, <u>MISSISSIPPI</u>--A. J. Brown
     <u>Dr</u>. <u>J</u>. <u>C</u>. <u>McELROY</u> was a physician who has probably
done more practice than any other doctor who ever lived in
the county. He started in Decatur after his return from
the Mexican War, to which he went from Tennessee, his
native state and continued until 1862, when he took a company into the service of the Confederate States. He was
Captain of Company D, 39th Mississippi Regiment, served
Newton County in the Legislation from 1861-66. He practiced
in the town of Newton & vicinity for more than 25 years.
The doctor was a small man, able to undergo great hard-
ship--always made his calls on horseback. He was considered a fine doctor & has the confidence and practice of
some of the best people of the county. He had his practice
and, also, a farm. He has many friends and has done much
for the poor of the county. He was still alive in 1894.
He was named, also, as one of the most prominent men at
Decatur. Member of the Methodist Episcopal Church South.
Charter member of A.F. & A.M.--Blue Lodge & Chapter, Newton

County, Mississippi, #57 in 1874. He attended the Medical
College of Transylvania University, Lexington, Kentucky--
matriculated for the year 1846/47. The information sent
to me was that the record showed he was from Marion, Miss.,
enrolled as a first year student and that his preceptor
was Dr. Ragland. He is, also, listed in the catalogue of
the Medical College for 1846/47. He was one of seventeen
students from Mississippi.

HOUSE DOCUMENTS--Volume 71 Series 4 McELROY
39th Regiment: Colonel: W. B. Shelby
                Lt. Col. W. E. Ross
                Major: W. Monroe Quin
                CAPTAIN: J. C. McELROY
                        ****

                        Hattiesburg, Mississippi
                        March 20th, 1898

Mr. H. C. McElroy
My Dear Brother,
        I have thought for a long time I would write to you
but I am always doing something that kept me (busy all the
time). You must excuse this paper as it is all there is
here and I don't want to put off writing you. You don't
know just how glad I was to hear from you and to get your
picture. I think you look some older, that is you look
more settled. Henry, you don't know how bad I want to see
you and have a long talk with you, and you don't say a word
about coming here, but I am glad you are doing so well in
your business, hope you well, Henry. I think my letter is
long enough for this time. Now don't you wait so long before you write again. I don't think you have any room to
quarrel with me for I have answered all your letters. Tell
Felix and Jennie I was so sorry to hear about their losing
their nice house and hope it won't be long before they will
have them another one built. Give them all our love and
tell them I would be so glad to hear from them once in a
while. Tell Felix I didn't think he would ever forget me
so completely as to never write to me sometimes. Well,
Will continues to be well. Johnny Watts is here with us.
He's an operator now and stands a chance to get work on
the Gulf and Ship Island Railroad. Well, I guess you
heard of Carrie Watt's death and Eva Watts, also. It was
so sad, both of them dying so near together. Eva Watts
didn't want to die, but she finally became reconciled. She
died in her Pa's arms. Well, Henry, I have some boarders,
have six regular boarders, only three that pay anything,
two work for Mr. Seitzler and Johnny. It is a hard life
to live. I am tired nearly to death when night comes but´
it looks like there is nothing else I can do to help along.

I never have a chance to go anywhere. I have been in
Hattiesburg nearly a year and have been in one store so
you know I don't buy much. I haven't bought any of the
children a thing since I have been here. Mr. Seitzler
stopped Waddell from school and put him to selling the
Meridian Herald and he is staying in a little store, gets
a dollar a week and the man gives him time to sell his
papers, but I hate it so bad for him to stop school. The
Professor in the school here said Waddell and Henry both
were leaders in their grade. Sanford and Henry are both
going to school all the time. I know you would like to
know how I am pleased with Hattiesburg. I am not very
well satisfied though I try to be contented. I am not
very well satisfied. I received a letter from Mollie several days ago. Marshall has been out of business ever
since Christmas and none of them got anything. Mollie
said their neighbors had been mighty kind, looked like
they tried to do all they could to help along. You know
they have five children and will soon have six, so you can
just know how things are with them. It nearly kills me to
know they are in such circumstances and I am not able to
give them anything to help along, but I am going to do my
best to have some soon to send if I have to do without myself. They want to come to Hattiesburg but I can't advise
them to come for Hattiesburg is a tight place to live in
unless you have plenty of money. So my dear Brother, let
me give you a piece of advise, don't every marry a poor
girl unless you have something to start with, as it is a
hard life to try to make your fortune after you marry and
you and wife both have to work all the time. Where is the
pleasure? My best days are gone and I never expect to
have anything more than a scant living and it is hard, and
some nights when I lie down to sleep after I have said my
prayers, I pray for all, my dear sister and brothers and
poor dear Pa. I think over them all and mine, and Mollie's
life, has been the hardest of all. Mr. Seitzler seems to
be doing very well with his paper but by the time he pays
his expenses of his office there is but little left. They
all want me to come home this summer but I guess I won't
go. I got a letter from Sallie about a week ago and all
was well at home. Mack ran away about three weeks ago and
they found him about five or six miles from home, but
didn't find him until the next morning about five o'clock,
so I heard. Sallie said they hadn't heard from you in
some time. Mollie said they were going to send patterns to
Lelah and Mrs. Johnson to make her children some clothes.
Said that Lelah's husband wrote that if they moved to send
Ethel. He would send her to school and give her music

lessons. Sallie talked like she was coming to see us in
June. Mr. Seitzler was at Newton about three weeks ago
and he said Pa was looking so well.

Well, while I was writing Miss Maggie Vail came in
so it is now after supper and I will try to finish my letter. I showed her your picture and she said it was not as
good looking as you. She said tell you "howdy" and give
you her best regards. I told her about your girl and she
said "Oh pshaw, I thought Mr. Henry was waiting for me."
Viola is in Newton now on a visit and Mag is at home with
all the children. She, Viola, certainly has a good time.
I thought when I commenced on the ninth page I would close
but seems as if I can't close. When you write to Mollie,
which you must do right soon, don't let on that I said anything about their circumstances. I will close hoping to
hear from you at an early date. Children all send love to
you all and accept lots of love from your dear Sister.

Lizzie Seitzler

(Letter written on March 20, 1898 by ELIZABETH CORDELIA
McELROY SEITZLER to her younger brother, Henry C. McElroy)

**

IN THE NAME OF GOD, AMEN, I JOHN B. SHAW, of the County of
Wake, State of North Carolina, being sick and weak in body
but of perfect mind & sound memory (blessed be God) do
make and ordain this & no other to be my last will & testament this 16th day of Sept. 1815 in & ___ following:
ITEM: I lend to my wife FRANKY SHAW during her natural
life or widowhood, the tract of land I purchased of
Cary Warren adjacent the lands of Lewis Moore &
others containing 108 acres, more or less. I do
lend her & like manner as above mentioned 10 negroes:
Otho, Dick, Cato, Billy, Lucy, Isabel, Tom, Young,
Beck, Isabel's children--Violet, Tempey's child, __,
Nina's child; 1 bay horse called Dirk, 1 bay filly
called Phosnea, 1 saddle & bridle, 3 feather beds &
furniture, all my household & ___ furniture not here
after devised. 25 gallons of ___, my cart & 2
young ___. 1/3 part of my stock of cattle, including the work ___, 1/3 part of my stock of sheep, &
1/6 part of my stock of hogs & as much of the corn,
wheat & bacon on hand & as many of my working _____
as shall be thought sufficient by my executor for
the use of the plantation. I, also, devise her the
use of the plantation whereon I now live until it be
sold and not to be ___ ____ ___ until the crops be
finished or the 25th of December after. I, also,
lend her 3 (?) of my ___ hogshead & cask until the
land is _____.

ITEM: I give & devise unto my son SIMPSON the _____ 2
negroes; Jack & Dick, called little Dick & his heirs
forever.

ITEM: I give & devise unto my son John Shaw 3 negroes:
Nathan, Richard, & Daniel to him & his heirs forever.

ITEM: I give and devise unto my son Willie Shaw 5 negroes:
Harry, Kitt, Billy, Blanch, Beck & his child Peter,
to him & his heirs forever.

ITEM: I give & devise unto my daughter Elizabeth Perry 1
negro man named ____, 1 negro woman named Patt & all
her increase to her & her heirs forever.

ITEM: I give & devise unto my daughter Caty Jones 1 negro
man named Phil, 1 negro woman named Esther & all her
increase to her & her heirs forever.

ITEM: I give & devise unto my daughter Polly Morgan 1 negro
man named ____, 1 negro woman named ___ Beck & all
her increase. I, also, give her after the death or
marriage of my wife FRANKY SHAW, 1 negro woman named
Isabel, to her & her heirs forever.

ITEM: I give & devise unto my daughter Fanny High, 1 negro
man named Ned, 1 negro woman named _____.

ITEM: I give & devise unto my daughter Sally Warren, 1 negro boy Mingo, 1 negro woman named Hannah & all her
increase, 1 negro woman named Tempy to her & heirs
forever. I, also, give her, after the death, or
marriage, of my wife FRANKY SHAW, this tract of land
I purchased of Cary Warren, lying & being in the
County aforesaid on the waters of Little Barton Creek
adjacent the lands of Lewis Moore & others containing
108 acres, more or less, her husband Nathaniel Warren,
her heirs to pay unto each of my other children the
sum of $33 1/3--SIMPSON SHAW, JOHN SHAW, WILLIE SHAW,
ELIZABETH PERRY, CATY JONES, POLLY MORGAN & FANNY
HIGH.

ITEM: I give & devise unto my daughter Allie Brasfield 5
negroes.

ITEM: My wish & desire that my negro woman Phobe, Nina &
Selah, 3 feather beds, bedsteads & furniture be sold
together without the residue of my stock of hogs,
horses, cattle & sheep, crop of every description,
1 waggon, & 4 pairs of geese, ___ chair & ____ ____
walnutt chairs, 1 large ___ shott (?) hogsheads &
casks & all the rest of the perishable part of my
estate, etc. ____
John McElroy, Sr. M _____ of Wake County, N. C.

William McElroy

James McElroy
Elizabeth McElroy
John McElroy, m. Rebecca Jones, d by 1761

/

Elizabeth McElroy (guardian of these children
John McElroy   was WILLIAM McELROY)
Mary McElroy
Rachel McElroy
Henry McElroy

Court Records of <u>Lincoln</u> <u>County</u>, <u>Tennessee</u>
January 4, 1826
     The due execution of a deed of conveyance from Bar-
ney L. McElroy to John Yount for 55 acres of land in this
County was proven in open Court by the oaths of the sub-
scribing witnesses thereto & ordered to be certified for
registration.
April 1826   <u>MICAJAH</u> <u>McELROY</u>, Plaintif
                    vs
              Henry David, Deft.
This day came the parties by their attorneys & a
Jury of good & lawful men, to wit: James Curay,
James Calhoon, Dailey Griffis, Robert Meek, John
Lane, Jr., Bartlet Woolen, Britton Phelps, Drury
Conley, Thomas Witt, John Burus, Wilson Frost, &
Wm. Parker, who being elected, tried & sworn the
truth to speak upon the issues joined upon their
oath do say that they find the issues in favor of
the Deft. It is therefore considered by the Court
that the said Deft. go hence without & recover
against said Plaintiff his costs by him about his
defense in this behalf expended.
1826   WILLIAM McELROY, Plaint.
                 vs
              Robert Dickson, Deft.
This day came the parties by their attorneys & a
Jury of good & lawful men, to wit: James Calhoon,
James Curry, Dailey Griffis, Robert Meek, John
McMillen, Samuel S. Holding, David A. Greer, William
P. Pulliam, James M. Myrick, Christopher R. Witt,
Joseph B. Hill & Warren Calhoon, who being elected,
tried & sworn the truth to speak upon the issue
joined. But by consent of the parties & with the
assent of the Court, James Calhoon, one of the Jury
is withdrawn & the rest of said Jurors from render-
ing their verdict are discharged.
July 1826
     Ordered by the Court that Amos Reed, an orphan boy,

14 or 15 yrs. old be bound to <u>MICAJAH</u> <u>McELROY</u>,
until he arrives at the age of 21 yrs. to learn
the art of carving. Whereupon the said <u>McELROY</u>
appeared & entered into bond & security to treat
him well, school & give him a horse, etc.

1827

The due execution of a deed of conveyance from
<u>MICAJAH</u> <u>McELROY</u> & B. L. Muckelroy to E. G. Buchanan
for 65 acres of land was acknowledged in open Court
by the said <u>MICAJAH</u> & B. L. Muckelroy & ordered to
be so certified for registration.

1827

Ordered that MICAJAH McELROY, Jr., be overseer of
the public road & that the order of this Court at
the April term 1826 be renewed for a jury of men
upon said road.

1828

The due execution of a deed of conveyance from
<u>ARCHIBALD</u> <u>McELROY</u> to William F. Mason for 353
acres of land was proven in open Court by the
open oaths of John M. Bell & Thos. H. Finney the
subscribing witnesses thereto & ordered to be so
certified for registration.

1828

The due execution of a bill of sale from <u>MICAJAH</u>
<u>McELROY</u> to Lynn McElroy, a negro boy was acknow-
ledged in open Court by the said <u>MICAJAH</u> <u>McELROY</u>
& ordered to be so certified.
The due execution of a Bill of Sale from John B.
Buchanan to <u>ARCHIBALD</u> <u>McELROY</u> for sundry property
of different kinds was proven in open Court by the
oaths of James Sweet & Leander Buchanan, the subscribing witnesses thereto & ordered to be so certified.

1830   CASE

William C. Kennedy
        vs
<u>MICAJAH</u> <u>McELROY</u>

This day came the parties by their attorneys &
thereupon came a jury of good & lawful men to wit:
Littleberry LeSure, I. Gray, P. Wills, H. Harris,
A. B. Nicks, H. E. Davis, J. Broadway, W. B. Sharpe,
R. H. Halcomb, I. West, Abram Burns & E. Pruitt, who
being elected, tried & sworn the truth to speak upon
the issue joined between the parties upon their oaths
do say that they find the issue in favor of the
plaint & assess his damages occasioned by the breach
of the premises of the deft. to $42.25 besides his

costs. It is, therefore, considered by the Court that the Plaintiff recover against the deft. his damages aforesaid by the jury assessed & his costs by him about his suit in that behalf sustain. Let execution issue.

1835

William McElroy vs Garner, McConnell & Weaver
It is ordered by the Court that the Sheriff of this County expose to sale according to law all the right, title, claim & interest which Robert M. Weaver has in & to the following lots in the Town of Fayetteville, #1, 22, 16, 109, 115, 116, 72, 123, 124, 125, & 126, also a tract of land lying on Cane Creek containing about 200 acres, bounded by John Crawford on the West, Stephen Clayton on the N, & Wm. McElroy on the S. Also, 26 acres bounded by George A. Wilson on E & W & Martha Shivery, on the N, also, about a 15 acre tract lying on the southside of Fayetteville adjoining the land of John Greer on the W & John M. Norris on the S levied on by B. W. D. Carty, a constable of this County on the 19th day of Feb., 1835 to satisfy a judgment which Wm. McElroy recovered against the said R. M. Weaver & N. B. Garner & F. G. McConnell on the 8th day of February, 1834, before A. I. Blakemore, Esq., a Justice of the Peace for this County, for the sum of $74.21 debt & $1.25 costs & also, the costs of this motion.

"LINCOLN JOURNAL"
A newspaper published in Lincoln County from 1-30-1840 to 6-27-1861.

4-1-1845   Letters in P. O.: Miss Sarah McElroy
7-3-1845   Letters in P.O.: William McElroy
6-25-1846   Lincoln Guards: Sherrod J. McElroy, 2nd Sgt.
7-1-1846   Letters in P.O.: William McElroy
7-30-1846   Departed this life at his residence in Lauderdale County, Mississippi, on the 7th of July 1846, BARNEY LINN McELROY, in the 44th year of his age; a native of Wake County, N. C., and for many years a citizen of Lincoln County, Tennessee, leaving an affectionate wife & 5 children, & numerous friends to lament his death. (See 1850 census of Lauderdale County, Miss., for list of wife & children.)
10-1-1846   Letters in P.O.: Miss Sarah A. McElroy
1-28-1847   Dr. S. M. McElroy, late of Alabama, would inform the citizens of Fayetteville & vicinity, that he has located in this place, & solicits a liberal share of their patronage in the

various branches of the profession.
Office: southside Public Square--2 doors east
of the old Bell Tavern.

4-1-1847   Letters in P.O.: Dr. JACKSON B. McELROY

7-1-1847   Letters in P.O.: Micajah McElroy
                           Miss L. McElroy
                           William McElroy

1-1-1848   Letters in P.O.: I. M. McElroy

4-18-1860   Dr. S. M. McElroy, having returned from New
Orleans, where he has been during the past
winter, with his health restored desires us
to give notice to his old patrons & the public
that he has taken an office on the southside
of the Square where he may be found by those
wishing his professional services. While in
New Orleans for the benefit of his own health,
Dr. McElroy availed himself of the benefits
of a course of lectures at the medical school,
from which he received a Diploma of M. D. from
the faculty with all the honors of the profession.
Letters in P.O.: W. S. McElroy

Lincoln County, Tennessee newspaper "OBSERVER"

2-7-1856   Died Wed. Jan. 30, of typhoid fever, Mr. William McElroy, age 75 (b. 1781). Deceased had
lived in county 50 years & was one of our most
esteemed citizens.

6-26-1856   Died 22nd Mrs. Mary McElroy, relict of Mr. Wm.
McElroy, age 60.

9-3-1857   Married Mr. Thos. B. McElroy & Miss Frances E.
Smith. (m. 8-19-1857)

9-15-1859   LINCOLN COUNTY COURT RECORDS Friday 28 Feb.
1812. Jury: MICAJAH McELROY: to view &
report to our next Court the damage that
Ezekiel Norris hath sustained.

11-7-1867   Lincoln County Fair
Fine Arts: Carpeting-----Mrs. S. G. McElroy
                Blankets------ "   "   "   "
                Coat---------- "   "   "   "
Model pony:---------------David McElroy
Horsemanship-------------- "   "
Equestrian boys un 12-----Willie McElroy
                              Alfred McElroy
Equestrian boys un 16-----Arch McElroy
Equestrian-ladies---------Miss Mary McElroy

2-20-1868   Real Estate Transfer--A. J. McElroy to Jas.
Ellis, title bond, 84 acres.

4-9-1868   Jasper Ellis & wife to R. C. McElroy, interest in 38 acres.

1868   LINCOLN COUNTY FAIR

A & M Society: Vice-Pres.: Sherrod G. McElroy

4-16-1868   Real Estate Transfer: Ellis & McElroy to John B. Hamilton--60 acres.

Ellis & McElroy to W. S. Buchanan--103 acres.

6-4-1868   Democratic meeting: Resolution Committee: S.M. McElroy.

11-5-1868   LINCOLN FAIR

Prizes: cake--------Miss Mary McElroy

              butter------Mrs. S. G. McElroy

              blanket-----Mrs. S. G. McElroy

Tournament--1st Maid of Honor: Miss Mollie McElroy.

6-10-1869   Married Thurs. 3rd inst. Mr. David S. McElroy & Miss Lou Hoskins.

6-24-1869   A call (petition) for L. P. Bright to be a candidate for legislature. Signed: S. M. McElroy.

6-9-1870   Advertisement: Blake & McElroy, Drugs (N. of the square).

10-27-1870   Real Estate transfer: A. J. McElroy to F. E. Dobbins--84 acres in 9th district $2520.00.

11-3-1870   J. W. & Thos. M. Goodwin to M. A. McElroy--- interest in land in 14th district $1500.00.

3-30-1871   SHERIFF's SALE   4-22-1871

All claim Jesse R. Marshall has in tract of land in C. D. #8 bounded thus:

N by lands of Wm. Connaway

E by lands of Amos Anderson

S by the lands of S. M. McElroy & Martha Smith's dower

W by the lands of S. M. McElroy & David Buchanan

112 acres   H. B. Morgan, Sheriff

11-23-1871   Real Estate transfer: J. M. Smith to S. M. McElroy, int. in land.

2-1-1872   NOTICE: the unsettled notes & accounts of the firm of McElroy & Hester have been left in the hands of Dr. G. W. Blake & McElroy's drugstore, who alone is authorized to settle & receipt for the same. Dr. Blake is instructed (which instructions will be carried out to the letter) to sue on every claim unsettled the 1st day of March next.

McELROY & HESTER

5-16-1872   Petition to call W. W. Wilson, Esq. as candidate to represent Lincoln County in the next

General Assembly of Tenn:
S. M. McElroy
A. B. McElroy
also, Colonel D. W. Holman: S. M. McElroy
                                     A. B. McElroy

1-16-1873   Dr. S. M. McElroy--offers his professional services to the public. He has removed his office to the southside of the Square, next door to the tin shop.

5-22-1873   Died Tues. 20th inst. of consumption, Dr. Arch B. McElroy, son of Dr. S. M. McElroy, aged about 22 yrs.
2 lots for sale fronting on College or Market St., running W from Fayetteville, being W of Dr. S. M. McElroy.

12-18-1873   Real Estate transfer: S. M. McElroy to B. L. Towery, 54 3/4 acres in 19th district.
A grange of the patrons of husbandry: S. M. McElroy.

4-23-1874   Ad: Dr. S. M. McElroy

5-21-1874   Mon. 5-25-1874--All right & claim Martha M. Smith has in tract of land in Civil Dis't #8 on the NS of the lands of Jessie Marshall, on the E by Amos Anderson & the lands belonging to the heirs of Jos. Bright, dec'd, on the S by the lands of John Bright, & on the W by the lands of S. M. McElroy.

11-3-1874   Real Estate Transfer: Mary A. Gray to Rufus C. McElroy, land in 8th Dist. for $51.52 2/3.

7-16-1874   Died at Bailey Springs, Alabama, Sat. 11 inst. after a lingering illness, Mr. Sanford McElroy, Jr., of this place, aged about 18 yrs. His remains were brought home Monday last & interred in Rose Hill Cemetery the same day.

10-8-1874   Real Estate Transfer: S. M. McElroy & wife to J. B. Hamilton, 19½ acres in 8th Dis't. -- $650.00.

10-22-1874   Married in this County Wed. 14th inst. by Rev. J. B. Tigert, Mr. James B. Morgan & Miss Mary, daughter of Mr. S. G. McElroy.

10-29-1874   Real Estate Transfer: R. C. McElroy to P. Halbert, 2½ acres in 8th Dis't. $75.00.
Ad: Drs. M'Elroy & Barbee.

11-12-1874   Real Estate Transfer: J. B. Watson & wife to M. L. McElroy, interest in dower in 10th Dis't $320.00.

11-19-1874   Married Jno. L. Buchanan & Mattie McElroy.

8-12-1875   Ad: The firm of Drs. McElroy & Barbee has been

	dissolved.
3-2-1876	Real Estate Transfer: S. M. McElroy & wife to Wm. McElroy, 200 acres in 8th Dis't. $2993.55.
10-26-1876	Tax sales: S. M. McElroy resident lot on Market St.
11-30-1876	Wm. McElroy to A. J. Cowan, 49½ acres in 8th Dis't. $1197.00. George J. Stonebraker, exer., to Wm. McElroy, 200 acres in 8th Dis't. -- $1756.80.
1-18-1877	Died Dr. S. M. McElroy, a well known physician of this place, died last Monday (Jan. 16). A few years ago he was stricken with paralysis, & since then has been a sufferer until relieved by death. He leaves a family & many friends. He was buried by the Masonic fraternity.
1-25-1877	TRIBUTE OF RESPECT At a called communication of Jackson Lodge #68 A.F. & A.M., held in their Hall, Fayetteville, Tenn., Jan. 17, A. D. 1877, A. L. 5877, the following resolutions were adopted: Whereas, it hath pleased the Grand Master of the Universe to remove from our midst our worthy brother S. M. McElroy, therefore, RESOLVED, that in the death of Brother McElroy, the Lodge has lost a worthy member, the community a good man, & his family a kind & affectionate husband & father. RESOLVED, that we deeply & sincerely sympathize with the bereaved family of our deceased brother. RESOLVED, that in testimony of our respect for the deceased, we wear the usual badge of mourning for 30 days. RESOLVED, that a copy of this resolution be furnished to the family of the deceased, & their publication requested in our town papers.

C. C. McKinney)
T. J. Gray   ) Committee
G. W. Morgan)

5-31-1877	CHANCERY SALE of house & lot Monday 6-11-1877 In obedience to a decree of sale pronounced at the April term 1877 of the Chancery Court at Fayetteville, Tenn., in the cause of W. T. Moyers against S. M. McElroy, wife, et als, I will attend at the Courthouse door in the town of Fayetteville, Tenn., & offer for sale to the highest bidder the following described house & lot, situated in Fayetteville, Civil Dis't. #8, Lincoln County, Tenn., & bounded as follows:

	N by College St. S by a street

N by College St.   S by a street
E by an alley   W by W E woods lot

4-4-1878   Estate of S. M. McElroy. Admnr.: J. W. Goodwin.

9-6-1877   Mr. Mike McElroy, W of town, is not yet over a
painful attack.

11-22-1877 The thoughtful landlady of the McELROY HOUSE
favored the "OBSERVER" with a magnificent
dinner on Thurs. last. The waiter was heaped
with good things--meats, potatoes, pickles,
jelly, preserves, cakes, pie, custard, & other
articles in profusion. If the regular table
is usually supplied with $\frac{1}{2}$ as good feasting &
cooking, the traveler & boarder cannot say too
much in its praise. Mrs. McElroy is the right
lady in the right place, when in charge of a
hotel.

1-24-1878   LINCOLN GUARDS ROSTER--company left Fayette-
ville on Sunday 5-31-1846 for Mexico. It was
in the Battle of Monterey.
Pryor Buchanan; Captain
Sherrod J. McElroy, 2nd Sgt.
White Buchanan, pvt.

4-25-1878   Ad: FAYETTEVILLE HOTEL: W. R. McElroy, Proprietor. This hotel (formerly Saffold House)
has been reopened to the public & refurnished.
Accomodations the best & prices moderate.

6-6-1878   Mrs. S. G. McElroy, of this place, has been
quite sick but her many friends are glad to
know that she is recovering.

11-7-1878   JURY: M. L. McElroy

1-2-1879   Real Estate Transfer: W. H. Crawford to R. C.
McElroy, int. in 38 3/4 acres in 8th Dis't.
$25.00.

8-14-1879   Real Estate Transfer: W. B. Ellis to Mattie V.
McElroy, et als, 34 acres in 8th Dis't. ---
$1000.00.

9-21-1879   Died Thurs. 4th inst. of flux, at the residence of her daughter, Mrs. Dr. McElroy, Mrs.
Martha, widow of Alfred Smith, dec'd., age 86.
Died Monday 19th inst. of hemorrhage of the
lungs, Charles, son of Mrs. S. M. McElroy,
aged about 18 yrs. He was buried by the Good
Templars.

12-18-1879 (Thurs.) S. G. McElroy, Jr., arrived from
Mississippi Friday night.

3-25-1880   Mrs. Dave McElroy is sick with fever.

4-1-1880   Died Thurs. 25th ult after a long illness,

	Mrs. Lou, wife of David McElroy, age 30 yrs.
6-22-1882	Miss Lucy McElroy returned from Nashville last week, accompanied by Miss Lou Dickinson, her cousin.
9-14-1882	A reunion of the Mexican War Veterans is now in progress in Nashville, & will continue over tomorrow. Messrs. S. G. McElroy & John H. Kay went down on Tues. to take part in the exercises.
1-25-1883	Sherrod McElroy, a well known young man, & son of Mr. S. G. McElroy, committed suicide in this place yesterday (Wed) morning. He took laudanum, & death resulted in a short time thereafter. He was about 24. We sympathize with the stricken family.
2-8-1883	W. S. Buchanan & wife to R. C. McElroy, $23\frac{1}{2}$ acres in 8th Dis't. $387.90.
5-24-1883	Represented Fayetteville at the Nashville drill: Rob't McElroy.
6-7-1883	Miss Fannie Russell, of Petersburg, was in town several days this week, the guest of Miss Sina McElroy.
7-3-1890	Miss Laura McElroy, who has been attending school in Kentucky for 2 yrs., returned home last Thursday.
12-24-1903	Thos. B. McElroy & John Price arrived from Texarkana on a visit to kin. Real Estate Transfer: E. L. McElroy et al, to J. R. Hamilton, 132 acres in 8th Dis't. --- $5265.00
8-13-1903	Misses Vicki Parten & Mattie Short, of Memphis, are the guests of Mrs. E. L. McElroy.
8-20-1903	Ed L. McElroy is raising tomatoes & utilized the public square for his patch.
8-6-1903	Married in Fayetteville at the residence of her father, Mr. Wm. Williams at 5 o'clock P.M. on Thurs. 7-3-1903, Reverend M. P. Wood officiating: Mr. James E. McElroy & Miss Julia Williams.
9-10-1903	McElroy & Wallace--Grocers.
10-22-1903	Married Mr. M. C. Ledbetter & Miss Victoria Partain, of Memphis, on 10-15-1903, at the residence of Mr. E. L. McElroy.
11-19-1903	Mrs. Sherrod McElroy, formerly of Fayetteville, is dangerously sick in Nashville.
12-26-1903	Died: Mrs. Ann McElroy, wife of Mr. S. G. McElroy, formerly of Fayetteville. Died in Nashville Wed. night at 9 o'clock, 11-11-1903. The

remains were brought to Fayetteville Friday afternoon & interred at Rose Hill Cemetery after funeral services at the grave by Rev. G. H. Hogan. She was 73 yrs. of age. Mrs. S. G. McElroy, J. S. Alexander & wife (Sina McElroy), J. B. Morgan (m. Mary McElroy), & William Mc-Elroy came to Fayetteville Sat. with the remains of Mrs. Ann McElroy, who died in Nashville.

1-21-1904   Ed. L. McElroy is on a prospecting tour to southern towns looking for a place to locate.

2-4-1904   E. L. McElroy is at Gadsden & Atalla this week.

3-31-1904   Mr. R. C. McElroy, we regret to learn is very seriously sick.

Real Estate Transfer: H. L. Moore, clk & special commissioner, to E. L., J. E. & A. A. McElroy & J. R. Hamilton, 132 acres in 8th Dis't. $6732.00.

4-24-1904   Mrs. E. L. McElroy left last week for Florence to join her husband, who with Arthur A. McElroy, has a splendid shoe business in that place.

7-7-1904   Mr. S. G. McElroy, of Nashville, has been in Fayetteville, during the past week visiting relatives & renewing old acquaintances.

7-28-1904   Mrs. C. N. Bates & Mrs. James E. McElroy (Julia) have been visiting their mother, Mrs. Wm. Williams the past week.

10-20-1904   Arthur McElroy, of Florence, was in town the past week, a witness in Court.

2-2-1905   Ed L. & Arthur McElroy have closed out their shoe business at Florence & are now in Fayetteville.

2-9-1905   Arthur McElroy is at the Spon Hotel battling with a case of pneumonia.

3-2-1905   McElroy Bros. have opened a new grocery store on the southside of the Square.

5-18-1905   Mr. S. G. McElroy came out from Nashville last week to visit relatives in Fayetteville & vicinity.

7-20-1905   Dr. J. C. McELROY & son, of Meridian, Miss., are visiting relatives & friends in Fayetteville & vicinity. The Dr. is a native of this County but removed from here 46 yrs. & now sees few things that are familiar, the very appearance of the country has undergone a change.

8-10-1905   R. M. (Erb) McElroy is visiting in town after

	a several yrs. absence. He now lives at Paris, Texas.
8-24-1905	Election of officers of Rose Hill Cemetery: E. L. McElroy was elected to fill the vacancy caused by the resignation of J. I. Pearce, who, under the postal regulations, of the U. S. government, is not allowed to hold a public office of any sort.
9-7-1905	Neal Smith is clking for McElroy Bros. & asks his friends to call.
2-22-1906	David McElroy, of Athens, is in town this week. Arthur McElroy has been kept at home during the past week with rheumatism.
3-15-1906	Jas. E. McElroy.
3-22-1906	Arthur McElroy left Monday for Hot Springs, hoping to get rid of the rheumatism with which he is troubled.
4-5-1906	D. L. McElroy, of Elkmont, is in town this week.
5-3-1906	A. A. McElroy has returned & was benefitted by the trip to Hot Springs.
8-9-1906	"OBSERVER" subscriber for 56 yrs.: R. C. McElroy.
8-16-1906	Mr. S. G. McElroy & Robert Morgan (his grandson), of Nashville, arrived yesterday on a visit to Mr. R. C. McElroy & other kin.
9-20-1906	Real Estate Transfer: Annie Lee Johnson & husband to E. L. McElroy & wife, house & lot in 8th Dis't. $750.00.
10-4-1906	Confederate Graves: Rose Hill--M. L. McElroy.
3-7-1907	Confederate soldiers now living in 22nd Dis't. of Lincoln Co.: Jack McElroy 1st Tenn. age 67 S. S. Smith (m. Cynthia McElroy) R. C. McElroy (8th Dis't.)
5-16-1907	Mr. S. G. McElroy arrived from Nashville Sat. on a visit to relatives.
7-4-1907	Died Mr. Sherrod G. McElroy, age 81 yrs., in Decatur, Alabama, at the home of his daughter, Mrs. John S. Alexander, at 2 o'clock, Tues. morning, July 2, 1907. Buried in Rose Hill Cemetery beside his wife. Leaves 2 bros.: R. C. & A. J. McElroy & one sister: Mrs. S. S. Smith, a daughter & 2 sons.
7-4-1907	Messrs. Will & Robert McElroy, of Nashville, & Mr. John Alexander & wife, of Decatur, attended the funeral of their father, Mr. S. G. McElroy.
8-22-1907	Mr. Tom McElroy, of Texarkana, Arkansas, is

here visiting his brothers.

8-29-1907   R. H. Pitts & wife to J. E. McElroy, 103½
acres in 7th Dis't. $2000.00.
Minnie Beddingfield & husband to E. L. McElroy,
house & lot in 8th Dis't $1500.00.

4-9-1908   Mr. R. C. McElroy, who lives 4 miles NW of
Fayetteville, resides on the farm on which he
was born 78 yrs. ago & where he has always
lived. The floor of his kitchen is of elm
planks which were worked out with a whipsaw in
1807. He is the owner of a pair of steelyards
which draws 80 lbs. that is of historical interest. The steelyard was brought to Lincoln
County from N. C., in 1807 & was found during
the Revolutionary War in an abandoned camp of
Lord Cornwallis, the British general.

5-21-1908   Mr. J. P. Ellis died in Fayetteville, Sun.
Night 5-17-1908, at the residence of his daughter, Mrs. John Henson, aged 79 yrs. Was in
32nd Tenn. Regt. & 4th Cavalry. Born & reared
here, member of Presbyterian Church, buried
beside his wife in Rose Hill.
Children: Mrs. William Fletcher, Floyd, Texas.
          Mr. Jas. Ellis, Minneola, Texas.
          Mrs. J. L. Buchanan, St.Cloud, Minn.
          Mrs. John Henson, Fayetteville,Tenn.

6-4-1908   E. L. McElroy to L. B. Cologne, lot in 8th
Dis't. $200.00.
Confederate Reunion: A. A. McElroy.

6-3-1909   Died Mrs. Sina M. Alexander, wife of John S.
Alexander, in Decatur, Alabama, Sunday 5-30-
1909, age about 42 yrs. Reared in Fayetteville, daughter of Mr. Sherrod G. McElroy.
Burial Tuesday.

8-19-1909   Mr. Jas. R. McElroy died at the home of his
father Mr. R. C. McElroy, near Howell, on Fri.
8-12-1909, age 40 yrs. Services by Elder E.
T. Hampton, burial at the Buchanan graveyard.

3-10-1910   "Early Times in Lincoln County"--John M. Bright
The citizens of lower Cane Creek deserve
more than a passing notice. These were the
McELROYS, the Hamiltons, the McGaughs, the
Masseys, the Dismukes, the Woodards, the
Peterson Smiths & others of equal merit,
were all as worthy as their neighbors high-
er up the creek.

6-13-1910   Real Estate Transfer: J. E. McElroy to Mrs.
Louella Holly, house & lot in 8th Dis't.$4.05.

	Mrs. Louella Holly to J. E. McElroy, house & lot in 8th Dis't., $2500.00.

8-25-1910 Tues.: Mrs. Julia McElroy, wife of Mr. Jas. E. McElroy, was in Fayetteville & at 6 o'clock started alone in a buggy to her home 1 mile E of town. On reaching the residence of Mr. Robert L. Moyers, one of the tugs broke letting the horse forward so that the shafts fell, striking the animal's leg. The horse began kicking, overturned the buggy which fell on the unfortunate lady. She died at 9 o'clock, age 28 yrs. Survived by husband, a son & a daughter, & father Mr. Wm. Williams, buried in Rose Hill Cemetery.

4-13-1911 Married: Mr. Jas. E. McElroy & Mrs. Ellie Russell in Fayetteville by Rev. R. K. Morgan on Thurs. 3-30-1911.

9-11-1911 Ad: McELROY BROS.--grocery
Telephone: 295 S. W. Corner Square

2-6-1913 Mr. Arthur McElroy left on Tues. for Rochester, Minn., for examination & treatment by Dr. Mayo.

2-13-1913 A dispatch from Rochester, Minn., stated Mon., that Mr. Arthur McElroy had that day undergone a successful operation for a diseased bone.

3-13-1913 Mr. A. A. McElroy has returned from Rochester, Minn., where he was operated on by the Drs. Mayo.

4-17-1913 Mrs. Henrietta Hamilton, widow of Mr. J. B. Hamilton, died at the home of her daughter, Mrs. E. L. McElroy (Mary) age 74 yrs. Buried in Rose Hill beside her husband.
2 daughters: Mrs. E. L. McElroy
     Mrs. J. R. Stephenson
2 sons: Robert & William Hamilton, of Calif.

7-3-1913 McELROY BROS.--dealers in Groceries & County Produce.
Letters in P.O.: B. F. McElroy.

1-1-1914 Mr. Arthur A. McElroy & Mrs. Carrie Glass married by Rev. I. S. Caldwell on Thurs. 12-18-1913. Groom is a member of the grocery firm of McElroy Bros.

2-19-1914 Mrs. Wallace McElroy is at Kelso this week visiting relatives.

3-5-1914 Mr. A. A. McElroy left Monday for California to be with his sister, Mrs. Robert Hamilton, who is very seriously sick.

4-2-1914 Mr. Arthur McElroy has returned from Los
Angeles & brings the welcome news that his
sister, Mrs. Robert Hamilton, is much improved.

4-9-1914 Mr. E. L. McElroy left Saturday for Los Angeles, California, to be with his sick sister,
Mrs. J. R. Hamilton, who is reported to be
taking a turn for the worse.

4-23-1914 Mr. Thos. B. McElroy, of Texarkana, is in town
to see his brothers. He reports himself as
getting along well & is satisfied with Texas.
Died: Kathleen Hamilton, age 10 yrs., daughter
of Mr. & Mrs. J. R. Hamilton, of spinal menin-
gitis, in Los Angeles, Calif., at 4:40 A. M.,
Friday 4-17-1914. Body brought to Fayetteville by her uncle, Mr. E. L. McElroy for
burial.

4-30-1914 Mr. Thos. B. McElroy has returned to Texarkana
after a visit to relatives.

7-9-1914 Mr. Benjamin McElroy, aged 82 yrs., died at
Taft on Wed. 7-1-1914. He was a Christian
gentleman & esteemed by everyone. Funeral by
Rev. W. J. Malone & Eb. Stewart, buried at the
Shearen graveyard.

7-30-1914 Mr. & Mrs. J. R. Hamilton arrived Tues. from
Los Angeles, Calif., & now are visiting Mr. &
Mrs. E. L. McElroy.

3-25-1915 Died: Mrs. Fannie Hamilton, wife of Mr. J. R.
Hamilton, and sister of Messrs. Ed L. McElroy
& Arthur McElroy, at the residence on Lincoln
Avenue at 12:10 o'clock Friday afternoon, Mar.
19, 1915. Member of Methodist Church. Funeral
services at home of Arthur McElroy, by Rev. J.
W. Cherry. Burial in Rose Hill Cemetery.

4-22-1915 "Looking Back"
    7-22-1852 Married Thurs. 15th by H. C. Cowan,
        Esq.: Mr. Jasper Ellis & Miss
        Elizabeth McElroy.

9-23-1915 Died Mr. S. S. (Brooks) Smith (m. Cynthia A.
McElroy) on Thurs. 9-16-1915 at the residence
near Fayetteville, of his daughter, Mrs. S. H.
Turney, age 86 yrs., 8 mos. & 8 days. Member
of Company K, 4th Tenn. Starns Regt. Member
of Methodist Church. For a number of years
lived at New Market. Funeral service by Elder
T. C. Little. Burial in McElroy graveyard. A
number of children & aged wife of 64 yrs. marriage.

10-21-1915 Died: an infant of Mr. & Mrs. Con McElroy (m.

Molly Bowers), at their home at Hamwood, 10-13-1915. Burial in family graveyard.

12-2-1915 "Looking Backward" 12-2-1852--Military Election: On the 24th ult Col. George Gant was elected Col. Commandant, Major J. T. Hester, Lt. Colonel: M. L. McElroy, Major of the 72nd Regt. Tenn. Militia.

1-13-1916 "Looking Back" 1-13-1853--All persons indebted to the firm of McElroy & Crawford are notified to settle by 1st of February. Mr. Crawford is preparing to move to Texas.

12-21-1911 Mr. Jack McElroy, aged about 73 yrs. was found about 1 o'clock Tuesday afternoon lying with his head & arm in the fireplace & badly burned. He was never married & occupied alone a small house on the farm of his brother, R. C. McElroy, 3 miles N.W. of Fayetteville. The unfortunate man had been in declining health for a year or more & had become weak & feeble. It is not known why he fell, but it is supposed to have resulted from heart failure. He enlisted in Turney's 1st Tenn. Regt. & the "hog drivers" did not have in its ranks a braver man & more loyal follower of the Confederate banner.

5-9-1912 Mr. Rufus C. McElroy, aged 82 yrs., died at his home $3\frac{1}{2}$ miles N E of Fayetteville at 4 o'clock Tues. afternoon May 7, 1912. He had been in failing health for some time which announced to his friends that the end was near & when the summons came it was as one who pulled the drapery of his couch about him & laid down to pleasant dreams. Mr. McElroy spent his life in this County & everyone knew of his splendid worth. During the war he was with Forrest's Invincibles & was one of the most intrepid followers of the "wizard of the saddle." He was a member of the Primitive Baptist Church & was prepared when the summons came. Funeral service by Elders E. T. Hampton & T. C. Little. He is survived by 3 sons: T. T. McElroy of Lampsas, Texas, Con & Clyde McElroy. Burial at McElroy graveyard by the Masons.

6-13-1912 Mr. J. B. Hamilton, aged 83 yrs., died at the residence of his daughter, Mrs. E. L. McElroy, in Fayetteville at 7:30 o'clock Tues. evening 6-11-1912. Buried in Rose Hill Cemetery.

Fought for the Confederacy.

9-1-1912 Confederate Graves at Rose Hill:
M. L. McElroy----4th Tenn. Cavalry.
S. G. McElroy----8th Tenn. Infantry.
S. M. McElroy----8th Tenn. Infantry.

4-6-1916 Mr. E. L. McElroy left Wednesday for Texas to visit his brothers.

5-4-1916 Mr. E. L. McElroy is at home after an extended trip to his bros., Messrs. James & Tom McElroy, living in Texas.

8-10-1916 "Looking Back" 8-11-1853--Married: Mr. Theodore G. Smith & Miss Elizabeth McElroy.

***

1-17-1884 Letters in P.O.: Miss Louisa McElroy.

8-14-1884 Letters in P.O.: Malinda McElroy.

12-30-1886 Married in this County Thurs. 23rd Dec. at the residence of the bride's father M. L. McElroy, 3 miles W of Fayetteville, Mr. T. G. Moyers & Miss Jennie McElroy.

8-19-1886 Robert McElroy returned Monday to Nashville, after spending a week with his parents.

4-7-1887 Mrs. David McElroy returned from Alabama last Sat.

6-23-1887 Messrs. J. C. & F. M. Kelso & David McElroy left last Monday for Anniston, Alabama with a lot as fine mules as were ever taken out of this County.

8-25-1887 Messrs. Robert Fletcher & Robert McElroy, of Nashville, are in town.

4-18-1889 Mr. S. G. McElroy, of Nashville, is in town.

6-27-1889 Circuit Court--in the case, State vs R. M. McElroy, charged with killing W. H. McCown, the jury found the defendant guilty of unintentional manslaughter & gave a sentence of 3 mos. in the County jail. A petition to Governor Taylor asking a pardon was immediately circulated & numerously signed. Mr. T. J. Bruce took the papers to Nashville to deliver them to the Governor, but he being absent, action was deferred & the defendant gave bond for his appearance at the next term of Court.

8-22-1889 Died at the residence of Mr. M. L. McElroy, Monday 8-19-1889, of teething, William, son of Mr. & Mrs. T. G. Moyers, aged about 18 months. Mr. & Mrs. S. G. McElroy & daughter, Miss Sinai, are visiting Fayetteville kin.

12-15-1887 Yerb McElroy returned from Kentucky Saturday.

10-13-1887 Mr. & Mrs. David McElroy are visiting his

mother.

11-17-1887   Mr. D. S. McElroy & sister, Miss Lucy, went to Nashville yesterday to attend the marriage of their cousin, Miss Dickinson (Lou).

10-25-1888   Married in this County Wednesday 10-17-1888 at the residence of the bride's father, Mr. J. B. Hamilton, 2 miles W of Fayetteville, by the Rev. J. B. Tigert, Mr. E. L. McElroy & Miss Mary Hamilton.

11-1-1888   Yerb McElroy, age 18, (grandson of Dr. Sanford M. McElroy), stabbed chief of Police W. H. Mc-Cowan.

11-8-1888   The entire day last Friday was taken up in the trial of R. M. McElroy, before Esqrs. McKinney, Bruce & Whitaker. He was bound over to the Circuit Court under a $3000.00 bond. Great sympathy is manifested for both sides of this sad affair.

11-29-1888   Miss Lou Dickinson, guest of Miss Lucy McElroy, returned to her home in Nashville, last Friday.

6-7-1888   Miss Laura McElroy (granddaughter of Dr. S. M. McElroy) is the guest of Chattanooga friends.

8-30-1888   Miss Mattie Dickinson, one of Nashville's fair daughters, is the guest of Miss Lucy McElroy (her cousin).

10-18-1888   Miss Lou Dickinson (daughter of Frank Dickinson & Amanda Smith), of Nashville, is visiting Fayetteville relatives.

1-5-1888   Messrs. Will McCollum, Tom Kimes, Dave Clark & Tom McElroy came in on an excursion from Texas to spend Christmas with relations & friends.

1-19-1888   Miss Lucy McElroy has returned home after a pleasant visit to Nashville.

2-3-1889   The McElroy House, when the addition is completed, will be 2 times its present size & will contain 34 rooms.

2-7-1889   Visitor to paper: R. C. McElroy.

9-11-1890   Yerb McElroy is on a visit to friends in Alabama.

10-23-1890   Miss Laura McElroy left last Tuesday morning for a visit to relations in Daville, Kentucky.

8-2-1890   Roll of Lincoln Co. Company in the Mexican War, 1st Tenn. Regt. Non-commissioned officers: S. G. McElroy, 2nd Sgt.

11-5-1891   Mrs. Lou McElroy has had her residence recently overhauled & repaired & its appearance is much improved.

7-9-1891	Mr. S. G. McElroy, of Nashville, is visiting Fayetteville friends & relatives.
7-23-1891	Mr. S. G. McElroy & Mr. J. S. Alexander & wife went to Nashville yesterday.
9-3-1891	Mrs. S. G. McElroy returned to Nashville last Saturday accompanied by Mrs. Jno. S. Alexander (her daughter) & Mrs. Claud Alexander.
1-22-1891	Monday: Mr. E. L. McElroy called.
12-4-1890	Mr. Thomas McElroy was the subject of a very narrow escape & almost serious accident the other night. Returning from Fayetteville last Wednesday night his horse became unmanageable & ran with him against the railing of the bridge across Buchanan's Creek, throwing the rider over the embankment, bruising him terribly & inflicting other injuries. Mr. Dave McElroy left Tues., for Atlanta. Mrs. McElroy is visiting her father near Athens, Alabama.
1-7-1892	Miss Lou Dickinson, of Nashville, is the guest of her cousin, Miss Lucy McElroy.
4-13-1893	Yerb McElroy has returned from Atlanta.
3-16-1893	Messrs. Dave McElroy & Morgan Eslick were here Friday. Miss Julia Whitty, of Athens, is the guest of her sister, Mrs. David McElroy, north of town.
3-30-1893	Mr. Dave G. McElroy was in Atlanta last week selling mules.
12-21-1911	Mr. Jack McElroy, aged about 73 yrs. was found about 1 o'clock Tuesday afternoon dead.

***

LINCOLN COUNTY, TENNESSEE
McELROY MARRIAGES

p 16	ELIZABETH McELROY to Lewis Shipp 10-26-1841, Pleasant Halbert, J.P.
p 53	Mary McElroy to John M. Commons 11-2-1841, Benj. F. Clark, J.P.
p 54	Sanford M. McElroy to Louisa A. Smith 10-29-1844, A. G. Gibson, M.G.
p 150	Solomon B. Smith to Martha J. McElroy 9-16-1847, Sam'l J. Bland, J.P.
p 169	J. C. McELROY to Sinthy S. A. Smith 10-2-1848
p 178	Allen McElroy to Luticia Mayfield 7-15-1849, A. J. St. Clair, J.P.
p 191	Mary J. McElroy to E. M. Crawford 1-17-1850, H. C. Cowan, J.P.

p 198	Cintha M. McElroy to Samuel S. Smith 8-22-1851, A. G. Smith, M.G.
p 212	Elizabeth McElroy to Wm. W. Woodward 4-5-1851
p 237	Elizabeth A. McElroy to Jasper Ellis 7-15-1852, H. C. Cowen, J.P.
p 253	Theodore G. Smith to Elizabeth McElroy 7-28-1853, R. Farquharson, J.P.
p 288	Rufus C. McElroy to Amanda A. Smith 9-18-1855, A. G. Smith, M.G.
p 322	Thos. B. McElroy to Frances E. Smith 4-20-1857, Rev. R. D. Hardin
p 378	Micajah L. McElroy to Martha Whitaker 10-30-1860, A. G. Smith, J.P.

**

LINCOLN COUNTY, TENNESSEE   1820 Census

		M			Fe
MUCKLEROY, WILLIAM	1	45 up	1	26-45
	1	10-16	1	16-26
	3	to 10	1	to 10
McELROY, WILLIAM	1	26-45	1	26-45
	2	to 10	1	10-26

1830 Census

		M			Fe
McELROY, MICAJAH	1	30-40		
	1	20-30		
	1	15-20		
McELROY, WILLIAM	1	50-60	1	40-50
	2	10-15	1	5-10
	1	5-10		
McELROY, THOMAS	1	20-30	1	20-30
	1	5-10	1	un 5
	1	un 5		
McELROY, MICAJAH	1	60-70		
	1	20-30		
McELROY, JAMES	1	20-30	1	20-30
	1	un 5		

1840 Census

		M			Fe
McELROY, ELIZABETH (Hurley)	1	15-20	1	40-50
	1	10-15	1	15-20
	2	5-10	1	un 5

LINCOLN COUNTY, TENN.   1850 Census

McELROY, JESSE	44
Gemina	44
Elizabeth	18
Susan	16
John W.	14
William L.	10
Jas. K. P.	5

```
McELROY, ALLEN              21
        Lutecia            18 (Mayfield)
        Rufus              18
McELROY, SANFORD            29
        Louisa             24 (Smith)
        David S.            2
        William M.
        Sanford, Jr.
McELROY, SHERROD G.         24
        Lucy Anne          19
        William R.
McELROY, WILLIAM           69
        Mary               56 (Hunter)
        Micajah L.         23
        Eliza              16 (m. Jasper Ellis on
                              7-15-1852)
        Mary Jane          19 (m. Ezekiel Crawford)
        Jackson            12
        Thos. H. B.        10
        John A.             8
        Cynthia            17 (m. S. S. Smith)
McELROY, WILLIAM           19 (brother to Sherrod)
McELROY, DAVID B.          34
        Martha             26
        Mary Ann            9
        Alexander           7
        Elsepa              5
        John

                        1860 Census
McELROY, BENTON            26
        Frances E.         19 (dau. of MIJAMIN & BETSY
                              SMITH)
                        1870 Census
McELROY, R. C.            40
        Amanda             36 (Smith)
        Constant           12
        Mattie             11
        Thos.               9
        Clyde               7
        James R.            4
McELROY, D. J.            21 (Alabama)
        Lou (Hoskins)      19
McELROY, JOHN             26
        M. A.
        Laslor             21
        Walter              1
                        1850 Census
p 102 McELROY, SANFORD M.  29 (Doctor)
```

	Louisa	24	
	David	2	
p 103 McELROY,	RUFUS C.	18	(Clerk, living with family of John McPhail)
p 111 McELROY,	S. G.	24	
	Lucy Anne	19	
Clark,	Thos.	17	

1860 Census

p 77 #1564

McELROY,	S. M.	39	(d. 1-16-1877)
	Louisa	34	(dau. of Alfred Smith & Martha Buchanan)
	David	12	
	William	10	
	Archibald	6	
	Alfred	5	
	Sanford	3	
	Lucy L.	1	
p 84 McELROY,	SHERROD G.	34	
	Lucy Ann	29	
	Mary	9	
	William	4	
	Sherrod, Jr.	2	
	JOHN	19	
#1703 McELROY,	R. C.	30	
Amanda		24	(dau. of Constant Smith & Margaret (b. 1805) Keys Buchanan)
	Constant	3	
	Martha	1	
	THOMAS	21	

LINCOLN COUNTY, TENN.   1870 Census

p 274 McELROY,	S. M.	50
	L. A.	45
	William	19
	Arch	17
	Alfred	15
	Sanford	13
	L. L.	11
	C. D.	7
p 284 McELROY,	S. G.	44
	L. A.	39
	M. L.	19
	W. R.	14
	S. J.	12
	R. D.	4
	S. L.	2
Clark,	Fanny	11

COPY:

MISSISSIPPI STATE BOARD OF HEALTH

Jackson 5, Mississippi
December 10, 1963

From: A. L. Gray, M. D., M.P.H.
Executive Officer

Dear Mrs. Barnett:

We note in the Jackson Daily News of Nov. 21, that
you are interested in information with regard to
Dr. J. C. McElroy.

We are glad to give to you information as contained
in records on file in this office.

Dr. J. C. McElroy was licensed to practice medicine
in Newton in 1882 when the medical practice act was
first passed.

Dr. J. C. McElroy died on December 7, 1913, at the
age of 89--death certificate #23180--1913. Mrs. M.
F. McElroy gave the information for the certificate.
At the time of his death, it was noted that he was
married. He was attended by Dr. A. M. Harrelson of
Newton, who signed the death certificate. The
undertaker was E. E. Powe, of Newton. It is under-
stood that the present funeral home is Hudson
Funeral Home, Newton. It is possible that they
might have additional information. It is stated on
the death certificate that Dr. McElroy was buried
in Newton. His place of birth is given as Tennessee.
According to our records, he was a graduate of Transylvania Medical College.

We wish that we could furnish to you additional
information but perhaps it may help you to have
this.

Sincerely yours,
A. L. Gray, M. D.

MINUTE RECORD BOOK 1849--1853
State of TENNESSEE
County of LINCOLN
p 482 The heirs at law of ARCHIBALD McELROY, deceased
petition
For the sale of Land Warrant #46598

It appearing to the Court that William B. Rhea is
the legally appointed guardian of <u>William</u> <u>McElroy</u>,
<u>Benton</u> <u>McElroy</u>, <u>Perry</u> <u>McElroy</u> & <u>Elizabeth</u> <u>McElroy</u>,
minor children of <u>ARCHIBALD</u> <u>McELROY</u>, deceased a
private in Captain Doak & Dobbins' Company, Tennessee Militia, War of 1812, & it further appearing to
the Court that the said William B. Rhea, guardian
as aforesaid, hath given bond & security, according
to law. Said William B. Rhea, guardian, as aforesaid, is authorized & empowered to sell & dispose
of land Warrant #46598, of 80 acres for the benefit
of said minor children of ARCHIBALD McELROY, dec'd.

<u>1790</u> <u>Census</u> North Carolina Hillsborough Dis't. Wake County
p 105 <u>MUCKELROY, MICAJAH</u>   1 male over 16 (head of family)
                               2 males un 16
                               2 females un 16
                               1 female over 16 (wife)

Pension Record, Archives Bldg., Washington, D.C.

REVOLUTIONARY WAR

Date of application 19 October 1832   Certificate #7679
<u>MICAJAH</u> <u>McELROY</u>, <u>SR</u>.   Act of June 7, 1832
Residence: Lincoln County, Tenn.   Issued: 11 May 1833
Age at date of application: 72 years
Residence at date of service: North Carolina
From: 4 March 1831   Ar: $26.00 per annum
Rank: PRIVATE   West Tenn. Agency N.C. Service
<u>MICAJAH</u> <u>McELROY</u>, being duly sworn deposed: that he entered
service in the fall of the year in N. C. under Capt.
Bryant, Major Sharpe, Colonel Cafur, Colier (or Colyar),
Lt. Joseph Peoples, & Ensign Henry Pope: that he lived in
Wake County, N. C., & was drafted there; went to Hills-
borough, to Salisbury at which place he remained 3 months--
time for which drafted; that he was born year 1760 on 30th
of September (family Bible burned) in Wake County, N. C.
That he removed to Lincoln County, Tenn., where he has
resided about 23 or 24 years.

                        Signature: <u>M</u>. <u>MACKELROY</u>
Summary of service on which pension was allowed.

<u>LINCOLN</u> <u>COUNTY</u>, <u>TENNESSEE</u> <u>RECORDS</u>
Court House, Fayetteville, Tennessee
Will Bk 2, p 128 Will of <u>WILLIAM</u> <u>McELROY</u> (Abstract)
                  (d. Wed. Jan. 30, 1856, of typhoid fever)
To sons: Sanford McElroy
          Sherrod G. McElroy--have given him 100 acres of
                               land on which he resides now.
          Micajah L. McElroy--a negro boy whom he has in
                               his possession & 90 acres of
                               land on which he resides now,

which I purchased of Leander
& Jiney Buchanan.
Rufus C. (Cooley) McElroy--94 acres adjoining
Sherrod.
To daus.: Jane Crawford--a negro girl.
Cynthia A. Smith--a negro girl (m. S. S. Smith,
son of Constant Smith).
Elizabeth C. Ellis--a negro girl.
To son: Jackson--a negro & 86 acres of land.
To son: Thos. H. B.--a negro boy & $1000.00.
To son: John A.--2 small negroes.
My wife: Mary--property for life.
To my grandchildren: David, William & Archibald McElroy,
children of my son Sanford McElroy.
Appoints Reuben A. McDonald & Constant Smith, executors.
7 June 1854.

LINCOLN COUNTY, TENN. DEEDS

Bk B, p 154   MICAJAH McELROY. Bill of Sale. Know all men
by these present that we, MICAJAH McELROY &
Daniel Summer, both of Lincoln County, Tenn.,
have sold & delivered to Robert Hairston of
same county, & State, a negro boy.
24 May 1813.
Signed: M. MUKELROY
Daniel Summers

Bk B, p 197   Deeds INDENTURE 17 Jan. 1820. Between Charles Bright, of Lincoln County, & William Mc-
Elroy, of said county, 55 acres adjoining
Cullen Campbell, boundary being 5000 acres
tract in name of Thomas Polk.

Bk D, p 78   Deeds INDENTURE 21 Jan. 1813. William Muckleroy of Lincoln County, to Patrick O. Cal-
laghan of same. Consideration $300.00 paid.
Land in Lincoln County, lot #9 & lot 87 in
Fayetteville.

Bk E, p 380   Deeds M. McELROY. MICAJAH MUCKLEROY signed
this deed 19 Oct. 1818. MICAJAH MUCKLEROY,
of Lincoln County, to Charles Tooly, of same.
Consideration $1200.00 paid by Charles Tooly,
175 acres on north bank of Elk River, thence
up river to mouth of branch above where Daniel R. Summer now lives, up to John Younts
line. Proved April 1819.
Witnesses: T. W. Booth
William Smith

Bk H, p 85   Deeds ARCHIBALD McELROY, of Lincoln County,
of Jno. B. Buchanan, of same county, land on
waters of Cane Creek, 120 acres. Consideration

48

$780.00. Jan. 26, 1821. Indent: 1-26-1821.

Bk H, p 84   Deeds ARCHIBALD McELROY to Wm. F. Mason --2
tracts of land on Elk River--352 acres 21
April 1828. INDENTURE 21 April 1828. Consideration $2294.00. One tract of land in
Lincoln County on southside of Elk River containing 109½ acres, it being a part of the
tract of land that MICAJAH McELROY purchased
of Brice M. Garner & George Coalter, adjoining dividing line of William & ARCHIBALD Mc-
ELROY.

Bk F, p 619   Deeds ARCHIBALD McELROY to Wm. F. Mason--
tract on Elk River--182 acres 19 Oct. 1833.

Bk C-2, p 74 Deeds A. J. McElroy to J. A. McElroy,
interest in estate of Thomas B. McElroy.
Mortgage 18 Aug. 1866.

Bk C-2, p 188 Deeds A. J. McElroy & others to B. C. Mc-
Elroy, interest in 38 acres, 120 poles,
Dis't. #8, Dec. 8, 1866.

Bk D-2, p 201 Deeds A. J. McElroy to Jasper Ellis, tract
of land--84 acres. Dis't. #8, Feb. 11,1868.
A. J. McElroy to T. E. Dobbins--2 tracts
land on waters of Cane Creek--84 acres, Oct.
21, 1866 (?).

Bk A-2, p 46 Deeds A. J. McElroy to Amanda A. McElroy--
tract of land--84 acres, Dis't. #8, April
19, 1892.

Bk A-1, p 338 Deeds MICAJAH McELROY to Wm. Polk--tract of
land on Cane Creek, 400 acres, April 30,
1810.

Bk D-1, p 88 Deeds MICAJAH McELROY to Thomas H. McGaugh,
interest (record torn away). May 11, 1816.

Bk E-1, p 374 Deeds MICAJAH McELROY, et als to Thos. H.
McGaugh--tract of land northside of Elk
River.--100 acres, Mar. 20, 1817. INDENTURE:
20 Mar. 1817. MICAJAH McELROY & Robert
Buchanan, or either of them, both of Lin-
coln County, to T. H. McGaugh, of same, for
$500.00 paid--land in Lincoln County on
waters of Elk River on northside--100 acres
being part of 1200 acres of Samuel & R
(Rachel) Buchanan & adjoining Wm. Edmiston.
(Rachel died 11-19-1857, age 70.)

Bk E-1, p 380 Deeds MICAJAH McELROY to Charles Tooly, 19
Oct. 1818.

Bk I-1, p 555 Deeds MICAJAH McELROY, Sr. to William Mc-
Elroy--tract of land on waters of Cane
Creek, Mar. 19, 1823.

Bk H-1, p 570 Deeds MICAJAH McELROY--to Daniel Barksdale
--tract of land on southside of Elk River--
110 acres Feb. 5, 1829. INDENTURE 5 Feb.
1829. MICAJAH McELROY, Sr., of Lincoln
County, to Daniel Barksdale of same. Consideration $550.00--tract of land in Lincoln
County, southside Elk River on dividing line
between McElroy & James Franklin, along
Franklin's line to Martin's line, adjoining
Thomas Polk's line.

Signed: M. MUKELROY

Witnesses:

ARCHIBALD McELROY
WILLIAM McELROY

LINCOLN COUNTY, TENNESSEE RECORDS

Marriages 1823-1828 1838-1860

p 16   Elizabeth McElroy to Lewis Shipp
10-26-1841, Pleasant Halbert, J.P.
(She was widow of ARCHIBALD McELROY, who died
1839.)

p 53   Mary McElroy to John M. Commons
11-2-1841, Benjamin F. Clark, J.P. for L.C.

p 54   Sanford M. McElroy to Louisa A. Smith
10-29-1844, A. G. Gibson, M. G.

p 150   Solomon B. Smith to Martha J. McElroy
9-16-1847, Sam'l. J. Bland, J.P.

p 169   J. C. McELROY to SINTHY S. A. SMITH
10-2-1848

p 178   Allen McElroy to Luticia Mayfield
7-15-1849, A. J. St. Clair, J.P.

p 191   Mary J. McElroy to E. M. Crawford
1-17-1850, H. C. Cowan, J.P.

p 198   Cintha A. McElroy to Samuel S. Smith
8-22-1851, A. G. Smith, M.G.

p 212   Elizabeth McElroy to Wm. W. Woodward
4-5-1851

p 237   Elizabeth A. McElroy to Jasper Ellis
7-15-1852, H. C. Cowen, J.P.

p 253   Theodore G. Smith to Elizabeth McElroy
7-28-1853, R. Farquharson, J.P.

p 288   Rufus C. McElroy to Amanda A. Smith
9-18-1855, A. G. Smith, M.G.

p 322   Thos. B. McElroy to Frances E. Smith
4-20-1857, Rev. R. D. Hardin

p 378   Micajah L. McElroy to Martha Whitaker
10-30-1860, A. G. Smith, J.P.

ALABAMA RECORDS, Vol. 98, Madison County

p 3   MICAJAH McELROY to Rachel Simpson

Aug. 24, 1814.

WAKE COUNTY, N. C.   Record Bk #1 1771-1782--by Frances
                    Burkhead.

p 212   Sales of estate of Edmund Bird, dec'd 1-9-1782
            1 hatt to MICAJAH McKLEROY   L2
p 221   Sales of estate of Jas. Tate, dec'd
            1 pr horse flums to John McKleroy ..5..
            1 barrell   " "   "   8
            2 stands   " "   "   ..6..3
            1 cask   " "   "   ..3..6
            1 lott of old iron "   "   ..5..6

WAKE COUNTY Marriages 1770-1825
            Nedeham Freeman & Polly Moore, Oct. 29,1785.
            Bondsman: MICAJAH MICKLEROY

WAKE COUNTY, NORTH CAROLINA
            Transfer of land, p 13, Oct. 27, 1783, between God-
            frey Hartsfield, of County of Wake & MICAJAH MICK-
            LEROY--200 acres.
            pp 25/26, Oct 7, 1783--Transfer of land from God-
            frey Hartsfield to MICAJAH MICKLEROY. This land
            had been part of a tract granted to Andrew Harts-
            field, filed by deed from Lord Carteret, Earl of
            Granville, dated Jan. 13, 1761 & left said Andrew
            Hartsfield's last will & testament, dated Nov. 18,
            1761, to Godfrey & Richard Hartsfield.

MINUTE DOCKET VOL. I 1811-1812 #58
STATE OF TENNESSEE, County of LINCOLN
p 19   Robert Buchanan, overseer from his own house to
           Major Smith, gives up the hands here named to work
           under Alexander Meeks as overseer, viz: Andrew
           Buchanan, John Nixon, MICAJAH, William & ARCHIBALD
           MUCKLEROY, issued 6-1-1811.
p 5   The following tracts of land were not listed for
           taxation for the year 1810, therefore liable to
           double tax (to wit):

Reputed Owners	Acres	Entry	Situation	Dollars	Cents
MICAJAH MUCKLEROY	400	89	Cane Creek	1	50

p 21   Article 66--An INDENTURE of bargain & sale between
           MICAJAH MUCKLEROY of the one part & William Polk of
           the other part for 400 acres of land was acknow-
           ledged in open court by the said MICAJAH MUCKLEROY
           & ordered to be registered.
p 24   Article 78--The COMMISSIONERS for the County of
           Lincoln & town of Fayetteville made return to the
           Court as follows: to wit: That they have procured
           100 acres of land of Ezekial Norris & taken a deed
           of conveyance to themselves & successors in office
           as the law directs & causing the same to be laid

off in lots as the annexed plot will shew, &
agreed to allow Ezekial Norris $150.00 for
shrubbing the said 100 acres of land & we have
sold off the said lots at 12 months credit
from the 1st Monday in last September & the
amount of sale is $1672.00 & we received lot
#47 for the use of the jail. Also received
lot #112 being the lot that includes the
spring for the use of the public; also, bid
off lot #16 at $90.00 to ourselves which we
offer to the County for the purpose of building a meeting house on the 22nd day of last
November to MICAJAH & WILLIAM MUCKLEROY for
$3935.00 & the bond that we took from them for
the performance of the work will show the size
& description of the house which is to be completed on or before the 1st day of November
1813 & we give them our bonds to be paid in 3
equal annual installments from the day of
letting the building.
Witness our hands 27th May 1811.

> John Whitaker
> Eli Garret
> Early Holman
> William Edmiston

Copy of MINUTE DOCKET in D.A.R. Library,
Washington, D. C.

MINUTE DOCKET   p 18, #55

Barnes Reuben Washburn Plaintiffs

vs

MICAJAH MUCKLEROY   Defendant

p 50, #91, 1811   Reuben Washburn

vs

MICAJAH MUCKLEROY

This day came the parties, by their attorneys & a
jury of good & lawful men, to wit: Abner Wells,
James Sims, John Porter, William Street, Amos Small,
John Newberry, Daniel Koonce, Joshua Owins, Frederick A. Burns, Joseph Campbell, George W. Higgins
& Andrew McCartney, who, being elected & tried &
sworn to tell the truth, to speak upon the issue
joined upon their oaths, do say that the said
MICAJAH McKLEROY is not guilty in manner & form as
the said Reuben, in declaring, hath complained
against him. To be considered, therefore, by the
Court that the said MICAJAH go therefore without day
& recover against the said Reuben his costs by him
about his defense for that behalf expendes & the

said Reuben for his false claim be not mercy, etc.
Summary of service on which <u>REVOLUTIONARY PENSION</u> was
allowed for MICAJAH McELROY, Sr.

<u>DRAFTED</u>	<u>Time</u>	<u>Rank</u>	Officers	State	<u>Age now</u>	Proof
1780	3 mos.	PVT.	Capt.Bryant	N.C.	72	Tradition
1781	2 mos	"	Col. Colier	"	"	"
			Capt. Peoples	"	"	"
			Col. Sanders			
Light horse	"	"	Col. Humphrey	"	"	"
			Lt. Bledsoe			

Statement by Aaron Alexander, clergyman.
<u>ALABAMA RECORDS</u> Vol. 39, Marengo County, p 71 (p 141)
   MICAJAH McLEROY, of Limestone County to Samuel
   Elliott, Oct. 9, 1821. Witnesses: Robert Elliott
                                    MICAJAH McLEROY
      Huntsville, Alabama Democrat, 7-7-1826:
      MICAJAH MUCKLEROY & wife Rachel.
Last Will & Testament of <u>MARY</u> (HUNTER) <u>McELROY</u>
(NOTE: daughter of Reuben Hunter and Cynthia)
      I, MARY McELROY, do make & publish this my last will
         & testament:

1st: I will that if there is any money lacking to pay the
       bequests made by my husband's last will to be paid
       in cash that my Estate make up the deficiency.

2nd: I will that my 3 daughters: Mary Jane Crawford,
       Cynthia Smith, & Elizabeth Ellis, have each $2200.
       worth of my negroes, the same to be set apart by 2
       or more disinterested men & said negroes so set
       apart are to be theirs for their sole & separate
       use during their natural life & then go to their
       children, heirs of their body.

3rd: I will to my son, THOMAS, $600.00, to be paid him
       in cash or negro property, set apart & valued to
       him at cash valuation by 2 disinterested men; I,
       also, will him my roan horse.

4th: I will to my daughter CYNTHIA SMITH, my bay mare.

5th: I will to my sons: ALEXANDER, MICAJAH, JACKSON,
       THOMAS & JOHN, each a bed & furniture.

6th: I will that my son JACKSON have the use & control
       of all my property of every description the present
       year, except my negro men, Bob & Anthony; my said
       son, JACKSON, is to make a crop & for his services,
       after payments for his part of the land, he is to
       have 1/3 part of all the crops raised.

7th: I will all the balance of my property, not hereto-
       fore willed, to be equally divided between my sons,
       SANFORD, JACKSON, THOMAS, & JOHN, if it should con-
       sist in negroes, I wish them valued & divided, if

not susceptible of division, I wish someone, or
more of my sons, to take them at valuation & pay
the other or others for their share. I do not want
any of my negroes sold out of the family. I appoint
my sons SANFORD & MICAJAH as my executors.
Signed, sealed & delivered in the presence:
1856   MARY McELROY (sealed)
Testators: Pleasant Halbert
            David Buchanan
Proven in open Court: 3rd November 1856
Will Book #2, pp 164/165   Eli L. Hodge, Clerk

****

Direct Line of MRS. LEE SEITZLER BARNETT
(COMPILER)
Present Address: 106 MacTighe Drive
                  Bellaire, Texas

ARCHIBALD McELROY, b. ca 1710, d. ___ .
ARCHIBALD McELROY, JR., b. ca 1738, d. ca 1760.
MICAJAH McELROY, b. 9/20/1760, d. 1834.
ARCHIBALD McELROY, b. 1780, d. December, 1839.
Dr. JACKSON CARROL McELROY, b. 4/28/1825, d. 12/8/1913.
ELIZABETH C. McELROY, b. 2/9/1858, d. 10/17/1898, m. Wm.
                H. Seitzler, b. 1849, d. 3/18/1925.
SANFORD M. SEITZLER, b. 9/16/1888.
LEE SEITZLER, b. 6/1/1915, at Houston, Texas, m. 6/1/1939,
            John Ruckman Barnett, son of Robert Lee
            Barnett, Jr., and Mary Jane Ruckman.
            Children: John Ruckman Barnett, Jr.,
                      b. 10/5/1940.
                      Jerrold Lee Barnett, b. 5/27/1947.
                      William Dickson Barnett,
                      b. 9/24/1950.

****

EZELL of KENTUCKY, TENNESSEE & TEXAS

I. GEORGE EZELL and wife, Elizabeth.
II. TIMOTHY EZELL and wife, Mary.
III. THOMAS EZELL (Sr.) and wife, Anne.
(For records on these generations, refer to
HISTORICAL SOUTHERN FAMILIES by John Bennett
Boddie, Vol. V, page 265.)
IV. BALAAM EZELL (Sr.) and first wife, Liddy (?) who
d. prior to 1803. He was b. 7 Oct. 1756, Sussex
Co., Va. Christened 6 Mar. 1757, Albemarle Parish,
Sussex Co., Va., d. 1844, Trigg Co., Ky. Will
dated 22 Aug. 1844 and probated 11 Nov. 1846,Trigg
Co., Ky. One of the founders and a minister of
the Muddy Fork Primitive Baptist Church in Cerulean
(Cerulean Springs), Trigg Co., Ky., in the early
1800's. Church still standing, more than 135 yrs.
old, July 1963.

Revolutionary Soldier, serving in Captain
Gray Judkin's Company of Virginia Troops. Allowed
pension in Sept. 1832, Pension No. S-31016. His
name appears on the bronze plaque on the monument
to Revolutionary Soldiers in Cadiz Cemetery,Cadiz,
Ky. In the Spring of 1964, a Revolutionary Soldier marker was placed at his grave in Thomas Cemetery near Cerulean, Trigg Co., Ky.

After the War, he moved the family to Bruns-
wick Co., Va., for 7 years; then to Mecklenburg
Co., same state, for 14 years; and finally to Trigg
Co., Ky., where he resided for the balance of his
life.
(Reference: THE EZELL FAMILY IN AMERICA, DESCEN-
DANTS OF GEORGE EZELL OF OLD COLONIAL SURRY CO.,
VA., 1692-1961, by Christine W. Sheldon,pp.23-26.)
Children by this first marriage:
1. Jeremiah Ezell, b. 9/27/1775,Sussex Co.,Va.
2. BALAAM EZELL, Jr., (see later)
3. Jeptha Ezell, b. 1784-5, Virginia.
See U.S. Population Census, 1820 Trigg Co., Ky.

MUDDY FORK PRIMITIVE BAPTIST CHURCH
in
Cerulean (Cerulean Springs), Trigg County, Kentucky

V. BALAAM EZELL, Jr., and wife, Keziah Tarkington, b. 4/11/1783, Brunswick Co., Va., m. 7/18/1805, Williamson Co., Tenn. (Mar. Bk. 1, p. 16) The marriage bond was for $1,250.00, signed by Balaam Ezell and Jesse Tarkington to the Governor of Tennessee, issued 7/17/1805, married the following day.) d. 6/21/1833, Williamson Co., Tenn. Will dated 1/1/1832, and probated in Williamson Co., Tenn., in July, 1833.

His wife, Keziah Tarkington, was b. 8/11/1778, N. C. (?), and d. 6/2/1850, Williamson Co., Tenn. She was a daughter of Zebulon Tarkington and wife, Mary Hassell.
(Reference: LIFE & TIMES OF EDWARD SWANSON by William H. McRaven, 1937, p. 223.)

Balaam Ezell, Jr., and wife are buried in Flat Creek Cemetery, Williamson Co., Tenn., near Chapel Hill, with markers at their graves.
Children by this marriage:
1. MARY SAUNDERS EZELL, (see below).
2. Littleberry R. Ezell, b. 7/19/1807.

   3. L. B. Ezell, b. 3/12/1809.
   4. Joseph D. Ezell, b. 3/15/1810.
   5. Jeptha Ezell, b. 5/16/1811.
   6. Deborah Ezell, (?).
   7. Emeline Ezell, b. 3/1/1815.
   8. William C. Ezell, b. 4/10/1816.
   9. Balaam H. Ezell, (?).
  10. Nancy E. Ezell, b. 9/24/1820.
  11. Burket M. Ezell, b. 11/6/1821.
  12. George W. Ezell, b. 4/10/1823.

(Reference: Bible of Orren Vincent owned in Feb. 1961, by Odell Burnette, Corinth, Miss.)
See U.S. Population Census, 1820 and 1830, Williamson Co., Tenn.

VI. MARY SAUNDERS EZELL and husband, Orren Vincent, b. 8/8/1806, Williamson Co., Tenn., m. 11/5/1828, same county; (The marriage bond was for $1,250.00 to Samuel Houston, Esq., Governor of Tennessee, issued on 10/30/1828, with marriage on the following 5th of November.), d. 7/8/1878, Weakley Co., Tenn.

      Her husband, Orren Vincent, was b. 7/1/1788, in N. C., and d. 8/17/1861, Weakley Co., Tenn. He was son of Ozias Vincent and wife, Susanna (?). (1800 census, Wake Co., N. C.) He was a soldier in the War of 1812, listed in MUSTER ROLLS OF SOLDIERS OF THE WAR OF 1812 FROM NORTH CAROLINA, p. 35. An 1812 marker was placed in 1964 at his grave in Sandy Branch Cemetery near Ruthville, Tenn.

Children by this marriage:
   1. ELIZABETH CAROLINE VINCENT,(see later).
   2. MINERVA ANN VINCENT, b. 3/11/1831. (" ").
   3. Mary Saunders Vincent, b. 1/23/1833.
   4. Martha Kezia Vincent, b. 11/22/1834.
   5. Sarah Emeline Vincent, b. 7/12/1836.
   6. Orren Balaam Vincent, b. 10/1/1838.
   7. William Harvey Vincent, b. 9/10/1840.
   8. Margret Eleanor Vincent, b. 6/1/1843.
   9. John Ozias Vincent, b. 4/17/1845.
  10. Nancy Livonia Vincent, b. 11/2/1850.

(Reference: Bible of Orren Vincent.)
See U. S. Population Census:
   1830, Williamson Co., Tenn.
   1840, Weakley Co., Tenn.
   1860, same county - occupation "farmer".
   1870, same county - Mary S. Vincent, widow.

VII. ELIZABETH CAROLINE VINCENT and husband, John P.

Andrew Hays, b. 12/13/1829, Williamson Co., Tenn., m. 12/17/1846, Weakley Co., Tenn., (Mar.Bk. 1849-54, p. 174), d. 8/20/1872, Weakley Co., Tenn.

Her husband, John P. Andrew Hays, was b. 5/10/1824, Weakley Co., Tenn., and d. 3/6/1887, Gleason, Tenn. He was a son of William Abram Hays and wife, Virginia Adams. (U.S. census, Weakley Co., 1830, 1840, and 1850 when he was listed as a "farmer" 53 years of age.) The Office of the Adjutant General, Frankfort, Kentucky, lists John P. Andrew Hays as a soldier in Co. K, 8th Regt. Inf., Ky. Vols., C.S.A., enlisted on 3/1/1862 at Memphis, Tenn. He was taken prisoner at Camp Douglas, Ill.; took oath of allegiance to the United States after his release. The grave marker for John and Elizabeth Vincent is 7 feet high in Old Salem Primitive Baptist Church cemetery near McKenzie, Tenn.

Children by this marriage:
1. George Augustus Hays, b. 10/10/1847.
2. William Abram Hays, b. 12/4/1848.
3. Mary Jane Hays, b. 12/26/1849.
4. Thomas Daniel Hays, b. 6/10/1852.
5. John Almus Hays, b. 12/10/1853.
6. Orren Vincent Hays, b. 2/12/1855.
7. Martha Ann Elizabeth Hays, b. 10/10/1856.
8. NANCY TENNESSEE HAYS, (see later).
9. John Gilbert Hays, b. 5/18/1860.
10. Sallie Hays, b. 6/27/1863.
11. Theodocia Adella Hays, b. 4/16/1866.
12. Westwood Bowden Hays, b. 11/19/1867.
13. Little Fain Hays, b. 7/5/1872.

(Reference: Hays family Bible owned in 1965 by Hermann H. Seele, San Antonio, Texas.)

See U.S. Population Census:
1850, Weakley Co., Tenn. - occupation"farmer".
1860,   "   "   " "wagon maker".
1870,   "   "   " "farmer".
1880,   "   "   "   " & mechanic".

VIII. NANCY TENNESSEE HAYS and husband, Thomas Daniel Scott, b. 8/18/1858, Weakley Co., Tenn., m. 10/17/1882, same county, (Mar. Bk. 1878-86-B, p. 301), d. 12/1/1931, Corpus Christi, Texas, buried: Rose Hill Park Cemetery, Corpus Christi, Texas.

Her husband, Thomas Daniel Scott, was b. 9/24/1860, Metropolis, Ill., d. 3/11/1894, Gleason, Tenn., and buried, with marker at his grave, Hopewell Cemetery in Gleason. He was a son of William

Harrison Scott and wife, Nancy Jane Bond. There
is one large marker in Mt. Zion Missionary Baptist
Church Cemetery, Buncombe, Ill., at the graves of
the parents of William H. Scott, who were Thomas
D. Scott and Elizabeth A. Henderson.
Children by this marriage:

    1. Bessie Irene Scott, b. 7/15/1883.
    2. Aurora Scott, b. 12/9/1885.
    3. Thomas Drewry Scott, b. 1/20/1887.
        (In 1965, resides in San Antonio, Texas.)
    4. Fain Scott, b. 7/16/1889.
    5. Ida Jessie Scott, b. 8/20/1891.
    6. GRACE SCOTT,(see later).

(Reference: Hays Bible.)
See U.S. Population Census, Weakley Co., Tenn.:
1870, Thomas D. Scott, age "9 years", listed in
household of George W. Phelps.

IX. GRACE SCOTT and husband, Hermann Hugo Seele, b.
6/13/1894, Gleason, Weakley Co., Tenn., m. 7/6/1918,
San Antonio, Texas., d. 11/28/1964, San Antonio,
Texas., buried: Mission Cemetery #1, San Antonio,
Texas. COMPILER: First part of this Chapter.

    Her husband, Hermann Hugo Seele, was b.
7/29/1894, San Antonio, Texas, and resides at 318
Tophill Road; San Antonio, Texas, in 1965. His
parents were Harry C. Seele and wife, Hulda Wetzel.
During WW-I, he served as 1st Lt., in the Infantry,
165th Depot Brig., enlisted May, 1917, at A & M
College, Texas.
Child of this marriage:

    1. HERMANN HAYS SEELE, (see later).

X. HERMANN HAYS SEELE and wife, Mildred Jim Kaderli,
b. 5/12/1920, San Antonio, Texas, m. 2/10/1945,
San Antonio, Texas, and in 1965, resides in San
Antonio, Texas.

    His wife, Mildred Jim Kaderli, was b. 10/4/
1920, Brownwood, Texas, a daughter of James Nicholas Kaderli and wife, Alta Williams.
Children by this marriage:

    1. James Hermann Seele, b. 7/10/1946.
    2. William Hays Seele, b. 11/18/1948.

                 ****

MINERVA ANN VINCENT, (p.56), dau. of Orren Vincent
and his wife, Mary Ezell, was b. 3/11/1831, d. 11/12/1875.
She was the second wife of Rev. Reuben Ross, b. 2/8/1807,
in N. C. They m. 11/7/1860, and had four children. (The
first wife of Rev. Reuben Ross was Mary Ann Henderson, b.
ca. 1817, in Ky.; they had nine children, (Authority: "Our

(Grace Scott)
MRS. HERMANN SEELE

HERMANN HUGO SEELE

Pioneer Heritage", by Pauline Johnson McDonald, great
granddaughter of Rev. Reuben Ross and Mary Henderson). His
third wife was listed in Weakley Co., Tenn., Census 1880,
as Louisa Ross, age 65. No issue of this marriage.

The Rev. Reuben Ross was the son of Rev. Thomas Ross,
who is listed in the "History of the Kehukee Primitive
Baptist Association," by Elder Cushing Biggs Hassell,1885,
p. 852, as a member of Conetoe Primitive Baptist Church,
(a branch of the Church at Flat Swamp, Edgecombe Co., N.C.).
In July, 1803, Thomas Ross was called to take the pastoral
care of Conetoe Church, in which office he officiated until
he removed to Tenn., about 1814. He was ordained by Elders
Joseph Biggs, Jonathan Cherry and Luke Ward. Goodspeed's
"History of Tennessee", (1887 Edition, p. 841), names Thomas Ross as among the pioneer preachers of Weakley Co.

The Weakley Co. Court Register lists a "Deed of Gift"
from Thomas Ross to Reuben Ross, recorded Nov. 3, 1828.
Rev. Thomas Ross organized the old Middle Fork Primitive
Baptist Church near Como, Tenn., in 1818. His great-grand-
son, Rev. A. B. Ross, preached the centennial service there
in 1918, b. 1874, d. 1962.

THE REV. REUBEN ROSS

The Rev. Reuben Ross was ordained into the Ministry in Blooming Grove Primitive Baptist Church, Weakley Co., in 1837, by Elders William Hays, Fleming Cayce, Silas ___, and Jeremiah Sheldon. (The original hand-written "Record of Ordination", is owned by the granddaughter of the Rev. Reuben Ross, Mrs. Nell Ross Morris.) The Sandy Branch Primitive Baptist Church, near Dresden, Tenn., was organized by Rev. Reuben Ross in 1840, and he served there as pastor until his death in 1884. He is buried beside his second wife, Minerva (Vincent) Ross, in the Sandy Branch Primitive Baptist Church Cemetery. The Centennial of this church was celebrated in 1940, and the Rev. A. B. Ross preached the sermon, having served as pastor for 36 years. He retired in 1942, age 68. Children of the Rev. Reuben Ross and Minerva Ann (Vincent) were born in Weakley Co., Tenn.

Children:

I. Reuben Thompson Ross, (see later).
II. Ida Ross, b. 1863, m. ___ Spence, buried in Sandy Branch Cemetery.
III. Cordelia Ross, b. 3/4/1866, d. 9/5/1907, m. Sam Moss, buried at Union City, Tenn.
IV. Eva Lou Ross, b. 1868, d. ca. 1902, m. A. B. Mitchell, 10/8/1891, buried at Union City, Tenn.

Reuben Thompson Ross was b. 11/17/1861, d. 3/11/1912, buried at Cedar Lawn Cemetery, Jackson, Miss., m. 2/3/1889, in Union City, Tenn., Janie C. Dalton, b. 10/23/1870, d. 8/17/1954, of Robertson Co., Tenn., dau. of Rev. Thomas Berryman Dalton, a Civil War Veteran, b. in Logan Co., Ky., and his wife, Miriam Jane (Grymes), b. in Dickson Co., Tenn. Reuben Ross and his wife were active members of the Baptist Church, where he served as a deacon for many years. He helped to organize the building of the Griffith Memorial Baptist Church, Jackson, Miss., in 1907. He was a Mason.

SANDY BRANCH
PRIMITIVE BAPTIST CHURCH

Children:
1. Bertie Ross, (dau), b. 8/26/1890, Union City, Tenn., M. Sydney F. Berry, b.Grenada, Miss., son of Edgar Ford Berry and Minnie Kettle, 11/4/1923. They have been active members of the Baptist Church for many years. No issue.

2. Bessie Lee Ross, b. 8/18/1892, Union City,
Tenn., m. in Griffith Memorial Baptist
Church, Jackson, Miss., 3/18/1920, Fred
Reber Langley, b. 11/9/1891, Jackson, Miss.,
son of James W. Langley, Sr., and Sue Reynolds. Fred Langley served as Quartermaster
Sergeant in WW I; honorable discharge, 3/22/
1919, Camp Shelby, Miss. He is a member of
the Masonic Order, The American Legion, and
the Sons of the Confederacy. He and his
wife are members of the Alta Woods Baptist
Church, Jackson, Miss.
Child:
(1) Betty Jane Langley, b. 2/13/1925, B.A.
Degree at Miss. College, Clinton, Miss.,
in 1947, taught school in Albemarle Co.,
Va., and at the University of Va., m.
12/16/1944, Atley A. Kitchings, Jr., b.
6/10/1925, in Miami, Fla., son of Dr.
Atley A. Kitchings, Sr., Baptist minister and Professor of Foreign Languages,
Miss. College, Clinton, Miss., (now
retired) and his wife, Marian B. Mudd.
Atley A. Kitchings, Jr., received B.A.
Degree at Miss. College, 1947, LLB Degree
in 1950, at University of Va, served as
acting District Attorney for the Northern District of Ala., began his career
as general attorney for the Miss. Southern Bell Telephone Co., in Jackson, in
1957, and is in the Naval Air Intelli-
gence Reserve.
Children:
a. Jane Marlea Kitchings, b. 5/22/1955,
Birmingham, Ala.
b. Atley Langley, b. 8/21/1960, Jackson,
Miss.
3. Nellie (called Nell) Ross, b. 10/3/1894, in
Dyersburg, Tenn., m. 2/1/1920, in Griffith
Memorial Baptist Church, Jackson, Miss.,
William Henry Morris, b. 8/3/1892, son of
Allen Lemuel Morris and his wife, Lula May,
of Brandon, Miss. William H. Morris volun-
teered in WW I, on Dec. 15, 1917, in New
Orleans, La. He served in the 6th Regiment
Marines in France, Battle of St. Mihiel and
Meuse Argonne. He remained in Germany with
the Army of Occupation for six months. He

received honorable discharge at Quantico,
Va., 8/13/1919. He is a member of the Sons
of the American Revolution, a 32nd degree
Scottish Rite Mason, and Shriner, Bahia
Temple, Orlando, Fla. He spent 43 years in
the Variety Chain Store Business, and was in
the New York Office for 19 years. He and
his wife are members of the First Baptist
Church, and now live in DeLand, Fla. MRS.
NELL ROSS MORRIS IS THE COMPILER OF THIS
RECORD OF ROSS GENEALOGY.
Child:
(1) Martha Janelle Morris, b. 10/4/1922, in
New Orleans, La., graduated, Garden Country Day School, Jackson Hts., N. Y.,
1941, Harcum Jr. College, Bryn Mawr, Pa.,
1943, and attended Miss. College, Clinton, Miss., m. 10/7/1944, in Community
Church, Jackson Hts., N. Y., 1st. Lieut.
Herman John Harjes, b. 1/12/1923, in New
York, son of Herman D. Harjes and Meta
D. Boymann. He volunteered for service
in the U.S. Infantry, received his commission at Camp Davis, Wilmington, N.C.,
served from Feb., 1942, to Sept., 1946.
He graduated from Massachusetts Institute
of Technology, Cambridge, Mass., 1947,
with B.A. Degree in Engineering Administration, and is now employed as Management supervising Engineer with the Port
of N. Y. Authority, N. Y. He and his
wife are active members of the Community
Church, East Williston, Long Island,
N. Y., where they live.
Children:
a. Herman William Harjes, b. 12/11/1950.
b. Ross Boymann Harjes, b. 10/28/1953.
4. Robert Bryan Ross, b. 1/26/1897, at Fulton,
Ky., d. 12/31/1959, in Jackson, Miss., m.
6/26/1921, in Jackson, Miss., Zula Mae Dunn,
b. 12/16/1901, of Johnston Station, Miss.,
d. in Jackson, 6/16/1962, dau. of Andrew
Jackson Dunn and May Coney. Robert Bryan
Ross volunteered for service in WW I, and
served as sergeant, Battery B, 140th Field
Artillery in U. S., and in Europe. Honorable
discharge, 6/19/1919. He was a member of the
Baptist Church, active in Boys' Clubs of

America, Veterans of Foreign Wars, was a
32nd Degree Scottish Rite Mason, and a
Shriner, member of the Wahabi Temple, Jackson, Miss. He and his wife are buried in
Cedar Lawn Cemetery, Jackson, Miss.
Child:
(1) Robert Bryan Ross, Jr., b. 4/11/1924, m.
6/16/1946, in Griffith Memorial Baptist
Church, Jackson, Betty Lou Mize, b. 8/
26/1926, of Logan, West Va., dau. of
Richard Rieser Mize and Lee Armstrong.
Robert B. Ross, Jr., volunteered in WW
II, in Army Air Force, 12/2/1942, Camp
Shelby, Miss., served as Staff Sergeant
in U. S., one year, and in South Pacific,
two years. Honorable discharge, 1/1/
1946, at Camp Shelby, Miss. Graduated
Miss. College, Clinton, Miss., June,
1949, B. A. Degree. He and his wife are
members of the Alta Woods Baptist Church,
where he serves as a deacon.
Children:
a. Rebecca Ann Ross, b. 4/10/1952.
b. Betty Lynn, b. 8/27/1955.
5. Miriam Cordelia Ross, b. 10/22/1902, at
Batesville, Miss., d. 10/8/1904, Jackson,
Miss.
6. Reuben Thompson Ross, Jr., b. 10/22/1907, d.
2/27/1908, at Jackson, Miss.

*****

DICKENS OF HALIFAX, NORTH CAROLINA

Tradition in the Dickens family of Halifax County,
N.C., is that the ancestor of this family came to Halifax
County from England, and that the family was not seated in
Virginia before coming to North Carolina as so many families were. A search of the existing records of Virginia
has shown that there were early settlers of that name in
that colony. However, nowhere has it been possible to
connect the Dickens family of Halifax with one of these
families. Nothing so far has been found to disprove tradition indirectly. Therefore, until further discoveries
are made tradition must be accepted as fact in the light
of research previously conducted.

The progenitor of the Dickens family of Halifax Co.,
N.C., was one William Dickens. Other than his name, little
else is known about the founder of this family. It is
with uncertainty that the statement is made that he ever
came to America, but the fact that his name was William
Dickens is proven. (D.B. 16, p.349) William Dickens was
born in England about 1700-1710, and was married about
1733. He either died in England or if he came to North
Carolina he died before 1782, the year the first existing
tax list was taken for Halifax County. The name of his
wife has not been preserved but it is possible that her
name was Elizabeth or Temperance. Only two of his children are known.

Children of William Dickens, b. ca 1700-10.
I. Joseph Dickens. (See later)
II. William Dickens. (See later)

Joseph Dickens, son of William Dickens was born in
England according to tradition about 1737, emigrated to
America about 1755, and settled first in Northampton Co.,
N.C., about 1758. (Pension Record of William Dickens;
Washington, D.C.) Before September 9, 1769, he moved to
Halifax Co., N.C., where he witnessed a deed of Lyman
Lunsford and wife, Mary, to William Dickens. (Id.D.B.11,
p.167.) On March 2, 1771, Joseph Dickens and his wife,
Hannah, sold half of this land to William Dickens. (Id.

65

66

D.B.12, p.103.)

The history of this tract of land is very interesting and must be given here in order to explain why later William and Joseph purchased their respective portions of it from Erasmus Brewer of St. Paul's Parish in the state of Georgia. On Oct. 26, 1765, Beverly Brewer of Halifax Co., gave a deed of lease for the land to Lyman Lunsford. (Id. D.B.9, p.345.) The deed stated that it was to be Lyman Lunsford's during the life of Thomas Brewer and that it was the same land which Thomas Martin gave his daughter, Mary, the wife of Thomas Brewer. Therefore, on November 9, 1773, Joseph Dickens purchased his remaining share of the land from Erasmus Brewer. (Id.D.B.13, p.106.) William Dickens did the same.

On August 6, 1796, Joseph Dickens purchased a tract of land from John Tumblin. (Id. D.B.18, p.53.) On Jan. 18, 1798, he sold this land to James Parker of Halifax Co., for Ł. 52. (Id. p.306.) On July 24, 1801, William Lovall and wife, Mary, sold to Joseph Dickens a small plantation which had been granted the said William Lovall on May 20, 1769. (Id. D.B.14, p.505.) This land was adjacent to William Edward's line and that of Gill Long's and the Marsh Swamp.

On October 11, 1802, Joseph Dickens made his will and the same was probated in the November Court for Halifax, N.C., for that year. (Id. W.B.3, p.279.) In it is mentioned all his children and his wife, Hannah Dickens.

From the ages of his children, it is believed that Joseph Dickens was twice married. The name of his first wife whom he married about 1756 is not known but his second wife was named Hannah _____; whom he married between 1763 and 1766. She survived him.

Joseph Dickens was a man of education. He signed all his deeds and all his original signature may be seen on a Revolutionary Voucher, a copy of which follows:

No. 3557. State of North Carolina, Halifax District. This certified that Jos.Dicken was allow[d] Eighteen Shillings Specie as pr.Report of Board of Auditors 10th Jan., 1782.

Joseph Dicken.   J.Bradford
Wm. Wooten, Clk.-F.C.   W. Branch
(Archives, Raleigh, N.C. Dickens Vouchers)

The above voucher and several others in the collection show that Joseph Dickens was a Revolutionary patriot and sold provender to the Revolutionary Army.

Children of Joseph Dickens:

I. William Dickens was born in Northampton Co., N.C., in 1758 according to his petition for a pension for his services in the Revolutionary War. He died in Halifax County, N.C., on March 19, 1837. He married (1) before 1794, Lucy Brown, daughter of William Brown of Brunswick County, Va., who died in 1797 in Halifax County. (W.B.3, p.280) He married (2) Elizabeth (Smith) Dickens, widow of his cousin Mathew Dickens on Dec. 18, 1826. (Id. Minutes, 1832, p.165.) Elizabeth (Smith) Dickens-Dickens was born in 1781, and after the death of her husband in 1847, she, with members of her family moved to Maury Co., Tenn., and is shown residing there in 1850 (Census), but in 1856, she was residing in Hickman Co., Tenn. (Pension Records of Elizabeth Dickens, Washington, D.C.) During the Revolutionary War, William Dickens was at the Battle of Guildford Court House.

Children of William Dickens and wife Lucy (Brown)

1. Martha Dickens, b.ca 1784; m. Elias Brown, d. 1815.
2. Pink(ton) Dickens, b. 1786; m. Jan. 3, 1829, Susan Dickens.
3. Evaline Dickens, m. Gilderoy Tucker.
4. Elias Dickens, b.ca 1793; m. Dec. 15, 1821,Polly Dickens.
5. Ann Dickens, m. Elisha Dickens. She received in 1854 her dower right from Elisha Dickens' estate. (D.B.33, p.533.)
6. Frankey Dickens, a daughter, m. ___ Dickens.
7. Chapell Dickens, b. 1802; m. Dec. 25, 1829, Mary Brown.

II. Thomas Dickens, b. ca 1761; m. in 1789, Molly Stevens. (Anderson's Marriages, Hal. Co.) He with his family moved to Chatham Co., N.C., before 1800.

Children by second marriage:

III. John Dickens, m. 1786, Elizabeth Stevens (Id.) and moved to Chatham, N.C.

IV. Bennett Dickens, m. Hannah Footman Lovell in 1789. (Id.) (See later)

V. Jesse Dickens, m. Nancy ___. In 1813, he sold his lands and moved.

VI. Benjamin Dickens, left Halifax Co.

VII. Temperance Dickens, b. 1780; m. Capt. Rhodam Barnes and had 8 sons, 2 daughters.

Bennett Dickens, fourth child of Joseph and Hannah Dickens, was born in Halifax Co., N.C., about 1769, and died there between June 19, 1842, and the November Court of that year. (W.B.4, p.213.) In 1789, he married Hannah Footman Harrison Lovell, daughter of William Lovell and his wife Mary Harrison who were both born in Westmoreland Co., Va. (W.B.3, p.408.) Hannah was born in 1770, and was living in 1850.

Children of Hannah (Lovell) and Bennett Dickens:

I. Charles T. Dickens, b. 1789-90; m. Polly, daughter
of Margaret (Purnell) and Levy Browning.

> Children:
> 1. Daughter
> 2. Calvin Dickens, b. 1823; m. (1) Nancy_____.
>   m. (2) Amanda Herbert.
> 3. Frances Dickens, m. William H. Barnes, her
>   cousin, son of Capt. Rhodam Barnes and his
>   wife, Temperance Dickens.
> 4. Holly Y. Dickens, m. Sept. 7, 1848, her cou-
>   sin, Oscar Faulcon Dickens, son of Bennett
>   E. and Nancy Dickens-Dickens.
> 5. Hardy Dickens, b. 1830; dsp. 1860.

II. Hester Dickens, b. 1792; m. 1817, Julius Hieronymous Zollicoffer, (1786-1854). (See later)

III. Bennett E. Dickens, b. Feb. 4, 1794; m. Dec. 18,
1818, his cousin Nancy, daughter of James and Martha
Dickens.

IV. Malachi Dickens, m. his cousin, Nancy Dickens. (See
later)

V. Harriet Dickens, m. her cousin, Guilford Dickens,
son of Elizabeth (Smith) and Matthew Dickens. (Children
under father.)

Hester Dickens, daughter of Hannah (Lovell) and Bennett Dickens, was born in 1792. She married in 1817,
Julius Hieronymous Zollicoffer, son of Ann (Lindsay) and
Capt. George Zollicoffer, who was born in 1786, and died
in 1854.

> Children:

I. Jerome B. Zollicoffer (1820-1884); m. Mary Ann Hawkins (1820-1876). He was a Colonel in the CSA; after the
war, he became Baron Zollicoffer, head of the family by
right of male descent and entitled to returns from the
Castle and lands at Altenklingen, Switzerland. He m. (2)
Sally Cheek. His first wife was mother of all his children.

> Children:
> 1. Mary Ann Zollicoffer, b. 1843.
> 2. Dr. Augustus R. Zollicoffer, b. 1854.
> 3. Eugenia Zollicoffer, b. 1850.
> 4. Dr. Dallas C. Zollicoffer, b. 1853.
> 5. Alison C. Zollicoffer, resided in Henderson,
>   N.C.
> 6. Marion Zollicoffer, dsp.

II. Emily Caroline Zollicoffer, b. June 24, 1824, d.
Nov. 16, 1872; m. Mar. 5, 1844, John Dorman Weeks, b. Dec.

25, 1810, d. Mar. 13, 1892.
Children:
1. Thomas Weeks, dsp.
2. Laura Ellen Weeks, b. June 1, 1849, d. Nov.
30, 1922, m. Nov. 13, 1867, John Eppes
Anderson, son of Joseph John Anderson.
Children:
   (1) James Redmond Anderson, b. Nov. 29,1867,
   m. Willis Mitchell and had issue: Wier,
   Robert, Russell, Redmond, Maurice,Harry,
   and Soloman Mitchell.
   (2) Susan Caroline Anderson, b. Dec. 6,1870,
   m. J. K. Dickens.
   (3) David Robert Anderson, b. Mar.25, 1873,
   d. Dec. 1, 1948, m. Nov. 15, 1899,Daisy
   E. Jenkins and had Mary and Jack Anderson.
   (4) Louis Anderson, b. July 24, 1875, m.
   Margaret Williams and had 3 children.
   (5) Malcolm Anderson, b. 1877, m. Annie
   Mitchell and had: Mary Emily, Annie
   Mitchell, and Frances Anderson.
   (6) Beatrice Anderson, b. 1879, m. Arthur
   Gibson Sloan and had 6 children.
   (7) Leonhardt Weeks Anderson, b. Aug. 27,
   1881, m. Mrs. Susie (Brickell) Grimmer,
   widow of Wm. I. Grimmer of Wilson Co.,
   N. C., on Aug. 16, 1911. Mrs. Anderson
   is a genealogist of note on Halifax Co.
   families.
   Children:
   a. Leonhardt Weeks Anderson, b. May
      24, 1912, d. Apr. 19, 1951, m. Dec.
      5, 1936, Ruth Booth at Branchville,
      Va.
      Children:
      (a) Leonhardt Weeks Anderson, b.
          Sept. 15, 1938.
      (b) Jacqueline Ruth Anderson, b.
          Nov. 15, 1940.
      (c) Laura Marine Anderson, b. Dec.
          9, 1942.
      (d) Sarah Brown Anderson, b. June
          15, 1944.
   b. Edward Johnston Anderson, b. Aug.
      4, 1914, m. Oct. 8, 1938, Mary W.
      Chapman.
      Children:

          (a) Edward Johnston Anderson, b. May 14, 1940.

          (b) Robert Chapman Anderson, b.Sept. 19, 1942.

          (c) Susan Nichols Anderson, b. Oct. 22, 1945.

      c. Sarah McGregor Anderson, b. Jan.22, 1916, m. Linwood Braddy Windley at Raleigh, N. C., Nov. 28, 1945. Children:

          (a) Linwood Braddy Windley, b. Aug. 12, 1946.

    (8) Hugh C. Anderson, b. 1883, m. Ada Glasgow and had: Hugh C., Paul, and Susie Anderson.

    (9) Irene Anderson, residing 1954 in Charlotte, N. C.

    (10) Helen Anderson, m. Willis Dickens. No issue.

  3. Delia Weeks, m. Bradford Jenkins. Issue: 4 children.

  4. John Dorman Weeks, Jr., m. and had issue.

  5. George Cary Weeks, m. (1) Lizzie Johnson, (2) Cora Worsley. Issue: 11 children.

  6. Mollie Weeks, dsp.

III. George Zollicoffer, b. 1828, son of Julius H. Zollicoffer, was unmarried in 1850. No further record.

    Bennett Dickens, son of Hannah (Lovell) and Bennett Dickens, was born in Halifax County, N. C., Feb. 3, 1794. On Dec. 18, 1818, he married his cousin, Nancy Dickens, born June 2, 1804, daughter of James and Martha Dickens. Both Bennett and Martha were living in 1850, but were deceased by 1860.

    Children:

  I. Sophia Vester Dickens, b. Dec. 5, 1819, d. post 1860, m. Benjamin Browning, b. 1800, son of Levi Browning and his wife Margaret (Purnell).

    Children:

    1. Nathaniel Browning, b. Jan. 22, 1843.

    2. John Franklin Browning, b. Jan. 28, 1844, d. Nov. 24, 1862.

    3. W. Daniel Browning, b. Jan. 22, 1847.

    4. Caroline Virginia Browning, b. Sept 1, 1849, m. Jan. 23, 1867, Robert Calvin Rogers.

  II. Wyatt Harrison Dickens, b. Sept. 9, 1821, d. May 20, 1890.

  III. Harriet Temperance Dickens, b. Jan. 24, m. March 12, 1859, her cousin, Redding Anderson Dickens, son of Lunsford

James Dickens. No issue.

IV. Lucy Hellen Dickens, b. Feb. 4, 1826; m. Dec. 1, 1848, Benjamin Cullen, son of Joel Cullen. Issue: 9 children.

V. Alexander Harrison Dickens, b. May 2, 1828; m.Frances Jane Moore of Dinwiddie Co., Va. Issue: 1 child.

VI. Oscar Faulcon Dickens, b. May 7, 1830; m. Sept. 7, 1848, his cousin, Hollie Y. Dickens, daughter of Charles T. Dickens. Issue: 9 children.

VII. Laura G. Dickens, b. May 26, 1833; m. Isaac Glasgow, as his 2nd wife. Issue: 6 children.

VIII. Isaac Faulcon Dickens, b. Apr. 26, 1836, k. Battle of Gold Harbor in the War between the States, m. Louise Browning. Issue: 3 children.

IX. Henry Kemper Dickens, b. Mar. 3, 1841, m. Rebecca Johnson.

X. Hyder David Dickens, b. Feb. 3, 1842, m. Dec. 12, 1860, Frances Jane (Moore) Dickens, widow of his brother. No issue.

XI. Haywood B. Dickens, b. Dec. 24, 1843, k. in War between the States.

Malachi Dickens, son of Hannah (Lovell) and Bennett Dickens, was born in Halifax County, N. C., near Ebenezer Methodist Episcopal Church about 1796, and died there about 1846. He was a member of that church. About 1816, he married his cousin, Nancy, daughter of Rebecca (Green) and Samuel Dickens. She was born in 1805, and died in 1861. Nancy (Dickens) Dickens was familiarly known as "Nancy Mack" to distinguish her from her cousin, wife of Bennett Dickens, who was known as "Nancy Ben." Nancy, wife of Malachi Dickens was also a member of Ebenezer Church, and it was her grandfather, George Green, who gave the land for the church. This church is one of the oldest Methodist Churches in Halifax County.

Children:

I. Margaret Dickens, b. 1820, m. Egbert W. Lewis as his 2nd wife, his first wife having been Lucretia Green, daughter of George Green.

Children:
1. Thomas M. Lewis, b. 1846, m. Rebecca Sledge. No issue.
2. Eugenia Atkins Lewis, b. 1848.
3. William Dudley David Lewis, b. 1850.

II. Enoch Dozier Dickens, m. Frances John Bass. (See later)

III. Rebecca Elizabeth Dickens, b. 1826, d. 1870-80, m. Jan. 8, 1857, John J. Keeter, b. 1825, d. 1857, son of James, b. 1790, and Sally Keeter. They were Methodists.

After Rebecca's death, he m. Martha (Neville) Ramsey, but there were no children by this marriage.

Children:

1. John Long Keeter, b. 12/25/1857, d. 6/21/1919, m. Lydia Ann Gibson, dau. of Wm. Henry and Sophia Gibson. Issue: 4 children.

2. Fletcher Joyner Keeter, b. 1860, m. Cora Johnson, dau. of Lovett D. Johnson and his wife, Ann M. (Branch), dau. of Eliza (Bass) and Willie Branch, who was the son of Olivia (Holden) and Jesse Branch. They had issue.

3. Rebecca Jane Alice Keeter, b. 1862, d. 2/12/1933, m. her cousin, Joseph E. Dickens, son of Balaam Dickens and his 2nd wife, Susan Ann Branch. (Children under father)

4. Margaret Ann Keeter, m. her cousin, Robt. Patrick Dickens.

IV. Iley N. Dickens, b. 1828, m. 8/5/1853, Mary R. Britt, dau. of Richard Britt and his wife, Louisa Eliza (Mills), his cousin. Iley N. Dickens was killed in the War, 7/4/1864, at Gettysburg. Children:

1. Martha A. Dickens, m. 3/25/1872, her cousin, Wm. A. Barnes, son of Wm. Barnes and his wife, Frances (Dickens), dau. of Charles T. Dickens. Wm. Barnes was the son of Temperance (Dickens) and Capt. Rhodam Barnes.

2. Richard Dickens, d.s.p.

3. Netty Dickens.

V. Long Dickens, left Halifax Co., for Texas in 1850's. All traces lost.

VI. Louise Agatha Ann Dickens, b. 1837, d. 1913, m. (1) her cousin, Edmund Jacob Dickens, son of Elizabeth (Taylor) and Edmund Dickens. Children under father; m. (2) Wm. Branch, m. (3) Burton Lewis; no issue by last two marriages.

VII. James Dickens, b. 1848, k. in the War on 7/4/1864, d.s.p.

VIII. Virginia D. Dickens, b. 1848, m. Augustus Harlow, son of John and Jane Harlow. Issue: 7 children.

Enoch Dozier Dickens, son of Malachi and Nancy (Dickens) Dickens, was b. 12/10/1823, d. 10/18/1892, m. 1/1/1841, Frances John Bass, dau. of Margaret (Pugh) and Simon Bass. Enoch Dickens was an extensive land owner. He and his family were Methodists. Children:

I. Mary Jane Dickens, b. 1/28/1842, m. Samuel Warren Branch, b. 1839, k. in War, son of Wm. and Elizabeth Branch.

Children:
1. Josephine E. Branch, m. Franklin Luther
   Pitts.
   Children:
   (1) Martha Irene Pitts.
   (2) Mary Gooch Pitts, m. Alexander Morse
       Atkinson. She resides in Enfield, N.C.
       Children:
       a. Jane Cary Atkinson.
   (3) Erma Pitts, m. Charles Henry Pegram.
       Children:
       a. Joan Pegram.
II. Munge Dickens, dsp.
III. Rebecca Elizabeth Dickens, b. 1846, m. (1) her
cousin, Matthew Britt, son of Eliza (Mills) and Richard
Britt, m. (2) her cousin, Benjamin Hux. Children under
fathers.
IV. Sarah Eliza Dickens, b. Dec. 25, 1848, m. Feb. 1,
1867, James W. Allen, son of Elizabeth Mason (Johnson) and
James V. Allen, who resided near Littleton, N.C.
   Children:
   1. Florence Allen.
   2. & 3. Adelaide and Cassie Allen (Twins).
   4. Ellen Allen, m. her cousin, Wm. Harlow, son
      of Virginia (Dickens) and Augustus Harlow.
   5. Mattie Allen, m. Nathaniel Collier. Issue:
      5 children.
V. John Wesley Dickens, b. Feb. 1, 1850, m. Dec. 22,
1870, Roberta Butts, daughter of Joseph M. and Mary Butts.
Issue: 14 children.
VI. Laura Frances Dickens, b. Aug. 28, 1853, d. June
22, 1914, m. Dec. 26, 1871, her cousin, Wm. J. B. Smith,
son of Wellington Jackson Smith and Rebecca R. (Kilpatrick)
daughter of Nancy Elizabeth (Barnes) and Albert (?) Kilpatrick. Issue: 11 children.
VII. Thomas Howard Dickens, b. Sept. 25, 1855, d. Feb.
29, 1932, m. Mar. 8, 1882, Lucy Susan Henderson, b. Sept.
23, 1859, d. May 8, 1907, at Heathsville, N. C., daughter
of Mary Elizabeth (Partin) and Andrew Jackson Henderson.
   Children:
   1. Ester Weymouth Dickens, b. Apr. 4, 1884, m.
      James Newton Crumpler, b. Nov. 14, 1881,
      son of Irvin Ashley Thomas Crumpler and his
      wife, Martha Frances Guthrie of Germantown,
      N. C.
      Children:
      (1) James Newton Crumpler, Jr., m. Margaret
          E. Dunn.

Children:
a. Cary Dunn Crumpler.
b. Bruce Crumpler.
(2) Thomas Dickens Crumpler.
(3) Weymouth Bridgers Crumpler, m. Mary Ellen Putzinger.
(4) Nelson Collingwood Crumpler, m. Evelyn K. Copeland.
Children:
a. Gail M. Crumpler.
b. Ellen A. Crumpler.
(5) Julia Esther Crumpler, m. (1) C. A. Greganus, (2) Thomas Giles.
Children:
a. Susan Lee Giles.
b. A daughter.

2. Ruby Elizabeth Dickens, b. Jan. 6, 1886, m. Feb. 24, 1911, Oliver Harold Carper, b. Feb. 23, 1885, son of Emma J. (Williams) and Benjamin F. Carper.
Children:
(1) Elizabeth (Betty) Hunter Carper, b. May 8, 1915, m. June 2, 1942, Dr. Wm. F. Grigg, Jr., son of Lenore (McClees) and Wm. F. Grigg of Richmond, Va. Mrs.Grigg is a graduate of Westhampton College, University of Richmond and of the Medical College of Virginia, and has had additional training at Walter Reed Hospital, Washington, and Veteran's Hospital at Oteen, N. C.
Children:
a. William Franklin Grigg, III.
b. Harold Carper Grigg.

3. Enoch Dana Dickens, b. Aug. 29, 1887, m. Maude Sturdivant. He is one of the outstanding Republican leaders of his district. He and his family are Methodists.
Children:
(1) Mirium Dickens, m. Leonard Black, Jr.
Children:
a. Martha Sue Black.
b. Name not recorded.
c. Mirium Black.
(2) Thomas Howard Dickens, m. Lucile Rook, daughter of Sadie M. (Clements) and Lewis W. Rook. Issue: 2 children.
(3) Enoch Dana Dickens, Jr., m. Louise

Edwards, daughter of John Lee Edwards.
Issue: 2 children.
    (4) Alice Dickens, m. her cousin, Austin
A. Dickens, son of Agnes T. Hux and
Charles M. Dickens. Children under
father.
    4. Lucy Henderson Dickens, b. May 5, 1889, m.
Alexander Rollins Brinkley, b. 1883.
Children:
    (1) Francis H. Brinkley, b. 1911, m. Mar-
garet Jane Lynn.
Children:
    a. Reed Brinkley.
    b. Lynn Brinkley.
    c. Alexis Jane Brinkley.
    5. Annie Bell Cason Dickens, b. Aug. 20, 1891,
m. Sept. 24, 1913, Milton Johnson, b. Jan.
20, 1871, d. Aug. 8, 1951, son of Rebecca
(Hollan) and John A. Johnson. No issue.
VIII. Margaret Ann Dickens, b. Dec. 9, 1857, d. Feb. 26,
193-, m. her cousin, Cicero Julius Smith, b. Apr. 20, 1855,
d. Feb. 26, 1907, a brother of W.J.B. Smith mentioned
above. Issue: 8 children.
    IX. Maria Alice Dickens, b. 1861, m. Fletcher White-
head.
Children:
    1. Lila Frances Whitehead, m. (1) John Timber-
lake, m. (2) John Christian. Resides in
Enfield, N. C.
Children:
    (1) Francis Timberlake.
    2. Alice J. Whitehead, dsp.
    3. Edith Harrison Whitehead, m. Gilbert Neal.
    X. Edward Crittenden Dickens, b. Sept. 24, 186-, m.
(1) Sarah J. Barham, m. (2) Blanche Dunn. No issue.

      William Dickens, son of William Dickens (b. ca 1700-
10) was born in England according to tradition about 1743
and emigrated to America about 1755, with his brother
Joseph Dickens. (ante) His first appearance in Halifax
County was in the County Court, versus Richard Pemberton,
May 1768. (Trial Docket 1766-1770) Also on Sept 9, 1769,
he witnessed the deed of Lyman Lunsford and wife, Mary, to
Joseph Dickens. (D.B.10, p.514.) On March 2, 1771, Joseph
Dickens and his wife, Hannah, sold William Dickens a tract
of land located on Marsh Swamp. (D.B.12, p.103.) This
tract of land was near the Ebenezer Methodist Episcopal
Church, as were many other tracts in district number five
which he bought through the years (D.B.17, pp. 500, 671,

732; D.B.18, p.404) until by 1800, he is shown as the largest in the county. (Tax list 1802.)

During the Revolution, William Dickens sold provender to the Continental Army, for which he received vouchers. Thus, it makes him a Revolutionary Patriot. Several of these vouchers are in the N. C. Archives.

William Dickens was married twice; first to Mary ____ (last name unknown), although it is thought that she was the daughter of William Kinchen, Jr., and his wife, Elizabeth Dawson. She died prior to Feb. 18, 1805, as she did not sign the deed that William Dickens gave Jacob Dickens on that date. (D.B.19, p.460.) Nor did his second wife, Susanna _____ sign the deeds William Dickens made his sons, Matthew, Edmund, James, William, Jr., and John Dickens, in June 1809. (D.B.21, pp.331, 319, 313, 318.) As Susanna Dickens' son, Christopher, was born in 1811 (he gave his age as 69 in Census of 1880), it seems that William Dickens was settling upon his sons their portion of his estate before he remarried. Susanna survived him and was living in Feb. 1831. (D.B.28, p.230.)

William Dickens made his will April 21, 1827, probated November Court 1830. He lends his wife, Susanna, the plantation he lived on to support herself and son; at her death to go to son, Christopher Dickens. He divised to Susanna all the property she owned at their marriage; ordered the land on which his son Ephraim lived to be sold to pay his debts and gave to all his children five shillings with what he had given them before. His two sons, Jacob and William Dickens, were executors. Since he did not name his children, his daughters are not known. However, the names of his sons have been proven from the following: Census, Halifax Co. 1790-1860; all the Dickens deeds and wills; William Dickens estate settlement; information from Miss Ann Pruitt of Franklin Co., N. C.; and from Mr. and Mrs. Edward W. Dickens, Halifax Co., N. C.

Children of William Dickens:

I. A daughter, b. 1771.

II. Joseph Dickens, Jr., b. 1772-3, m. Elizabeth ____. In his will dated Dec. 1, 1805, probated Feb.1806, he mentions "children" but not by name.

III. James Dickens, b. 1774, m. Patsy (Martha) Brantley (?). His will dated Dec. 10, 1813, probated Feb. 1814, (W.B.3, p.547) gives the names of his four children who reached maturity.
Children:
1. Lunsford James Dickens, b. 1806, m. Apr. 27, 1827, Malicia, daughter of Abner Mills and wife, Rebecca (Green) Dickens, d.1833. (W.B.3,

p.314.)

Children:

(1) James W. Dickens, b. 1829, m. Feb. 27,1850, his cousin, Sarah Elizabeth, daughter of Emsley and Melissa Jane Dickens.

(2) Louise P. Dickens, m. June 24, 1850, Albert G. Smith. Issue: 3 children.

(3) Redding Anderson Dickens, b. 1833, m. Mar. 12, 1859, his cousin, Harriet T., daughter of Bennett E. Dickens. No issue.

(4) Martha E. Dickens, b. 1837, dsp.

(5) Angelin Dickens, b. 1840, dsp.

(6) Asbury Dickens, k. in CSA during the War.

(7) Rebecca M. Dickens, b. 1846.

(8) Lundy L. Dickens, m. Oct. 14, 1873, Wm. M. Cullum. Issue: 7 children.

2. Nancy Dickens, b. June 2, 1804, m. her cousin, Bennett E. Dickens, son of Hannah (Lovell) and Bennett Dickens. Children under father.

3. Mariah Temperance Brantley Dickens, b. 1810, d. after 1890, m. Wm. Hux, son of Wm. and Nancy Hux.

Children:

(1) Alexander Austin Hux, b. Mar. 18, 1841, d. Nov. 16, 1897, m. Oct. 12, 1866, Sarah E., daughter of Louise E. (Mills) and Richard Britt, m. (2) Sarah, whose father was also a Richard Britt. She d. April 18, 1917.

Children:

a. Alexander Samuel Hux, b. Nov. 17, 1868, d. March 3, 1919, m. his cousin Odessa Onessa Odora Barnes Smith, sister of Wm. J. B. Smith, mentioned before. Issue: 5 children.

b. Willis Richard Hux, b. July 7, 1870, m. (1) Maggie, m. (2) Daisy (Hux) Lewis, daughters of Emily (Dickens) and T. R. Hux, m. (3) Annie Sledge. Issue: 8 children.

c. Frances Lula Hux, b. July 11, 1872, m. her cousin, Mont(ford) Hux, brother of Maggie, above. Issue: 7 children.

d. Eliza Donna Brantley Hux, b. Sept. 18, 1874, m. her cousin, Edward Walter, son of Susan (Branch) and Balaam Dickens. Children under father.

e. George Alphos Hux, b. Sept. 11, 1876, m. his cousin, Adelia, daughter of

Lewis K. Dickens and Elizabeth (Hux),
daughter of Benjamin Hux and Annie
Barnes, daughter of Rhodam Barnes and
Temperance (Dickens), m. (2) his cousin
Ethel, daughter of Cicero J. Smith.
Children: (second marriage)
(a) Leonidas Hux.
(b) George Austin Hux, Clerk of Supe-
    rior Court for Halifax, N. C.
(c) Mable Hux.
(d) Bertha Hux.
(e) Undine Hux, m. Guy Caudle.
(f) Sarah Hux.

  f. Sarah E. Hux, m. Barzilla Hux. Issue:
14 children.

  g. Mathew W. Hux, b. May 20, 1881, m. (1)
Belva Crawley, m. (2) Annie (Bonds?).
Issue: 9 children.

  h. Myra R. Hux, b. Aug. 19, 1883, m. Dod-
(son) Hux. Issue: 10 children.

  i. Leonore A. Hux, b. Feb. 28, 1886, m.
Ellis Crawley. Issue: 8 children.
Children by second marriage.

  j. Agnes T. Hux, b. Nov. 22, 1888, m.
Charles Dickens, son of Johnnie (Arrington) and Mecum Dickens. Children under
father.

(2) Wm. Henry Hux, m. Jan. 1, 1868, (1) Margaret W. Britt, m. (2) Sophia M. Dickens.
Issue: 13 children.

(3) Benj. G. Hux, called "Yankee Ben", b.1844,
m. June 3, 1869, Rebecca E. (Dickens)
Britt. Issue: 10 children.

(4) Gardner H. Hux, b. 1846, m. April 21,1871,
Martha O. Dickens. Issue: 5 children.

(5) Sarah M. Hux, dsp.

(6) James Austin Hux, b. Mar. 18, 1849.

(7) Elizabeth Hux, b. Aug. 11, 1851, m. Sept.
19, 1871, John Burt, son of S. F. and Margaret Burt. Issue: 2 daughters.

(8) George C. Hux, b. Mar. 11, 1854, m. (1)
Lucy Dickens, m. (2) Anna Keeter. Had
issue.

4. Kinchen Dickens, b. 1805-6, m. Sarah _____.
Children:
(1) Caroline Dickens.
(2) Raven Dickens, a son.
(3) Josephine Dickens, b. 1855.

IV. Henry Dickens, b. ca 1776, m. Penelope _____, d.
1807. (W.B.3, p.469.) His widow m. Wm. Dickens. (D.B.
28, p.266.)
Children:
1. Wilson Dickens, b. 1805, m. Dec. 17, 1827,
Elizabeth Dickens. Issue: 6 children.
V. Matthew Dickens, b. ca 1777-8, m. Elizabeth Smith
who after his death, m.William Dickens, d. 1802, moved to
Tennessee and was living in Maury Co., in 1850.
Children:
1. Guilford Dickens, m. Harriet Dickens. Issue:
5 children.
2. Angeline Dickens, m. Wm. Jackson and was living
in Maury Co., Tenn., in 1850. Had issue.
3. Mary Dickens, m. Elias Dickens in 1832.
4. Barsheba Dickens, dsp. in Tenn.
5. Bradford Dickens, m. Sylvestra _____. Issue: 7
children.
6. Sarah Dickens, b. 1812.
7. Andrew J. Dickens, m. Susan Smith, daughter of
Elizabeth and Matthew Smith. In 1850, he was
in Maury County, Tenn.
VI. Samuel Dickens, b. 1779 (ca), d. before 1809, m.
Rebecca Green, daughter of George Green.
Children:
1. Nancy Dickens, b. 1805, d. 1861, m. Malachi
Dickens. Children under father.
VII. Daughter, name unknown, b. ca 1781.
VIII. Jacob Dickens, b. ca 1783, m. (1) _____ Smith, sister of James Smith and Elizabeth Smith, m. (2) Sally,widow
of Jesse Green.
Children:
1. William Dickens.
2. Mary Dickens, m. Ransom M. Shearin.
3. Mecum Dickens.
4. Warren Dickens, b. 1812, m. May 25, 1835, Eva-
lina Dickens. Issue: 9 children.
5. Littleton Dickens, b. 1815, m. Frenetta Kilpatrick. Issue: 4 children.
6. Bryant Dickens, m. Mar. 1, 1860, Frenetta Kilpatrick (Dickens). No issue.
7. Emsley Dickens, b. ca 1810, m. Melissa J. _____.
Children:
(1) Jacob D. Dickens, b. 1830, m. June 2,1853,
Melissa J., daughter of Egbert and Lucretia (Green) Lewis. Issue: 9 children.
(2) Sarah E. Dickens, m. James W. Dickens.
(3) Mary J. Dickens, b. 1832.

(4) Matthew R. Dickens, b. 1837.

IX. William Dickens, Jr., b. ca 1785, d. 1836, m. Penelope, widow of his brother, Henry Dickens.

Children:

1. Charlotte Dickens, m. James H. Barnes.

X. John Dickens, b. ca 1787, m. and had issue. Untraced.

XI. Edmund Dickens, b. ca 1780, d. post 1870, m. Elizabeth Taylor. (See later.)

XII. Ephraim Dickens, b. ca 1793, m. Feb. 17, 1815, in Franklin County, N. C., Silvia Perry.

Children:

1. William Dickens.
2. Obediah Dickens, m. (1) Rebecca Perry, Feb. 1, 1841, m. (2) Nancy Perry, Dec. 18, 1850.
   Children:
   (1) Benjamin Dickens, b. 1842-3.
   (2) James or Jones Dickens, b. 1844.
   (3) Perry Dickens, b. 1846.
   (4) Rebecca Dickens, b. 1849.

XIII. Christopher Dickens, b. 1806, m. Dec. 18, 1830, Lucy Liles.

Children:

1. William B. Dickens, b. 1832, m. Sept. 16,1854, Sylvestra W. Jordan. Issue: 2 children.
2. Adelia Dickens (Mary on Census records), b. 1838, m. May 28, 1856, Wm. Keeter. Issue: 9 children, possibly more.
3. Charles Augustus Dickens, b. ca 1840.
4. Virginia J. Dickens, b. 1847, m. Oct. 16,1869, Richard H. Moore, son of Mary and Richard Moore. Had issue.

Edmund Dickens, son of William and Mary (Kinchen?) Dickens, was born in Halifax County about 1785, and died there after 1870. In 1820, he married Elizabeth Taylor, daughter of John and Lucy Taylor. John Taylor was born about 1740, in Lancaster County, Va., and died in Halifax, N. C., 1819-20. (W.B.3, p. 653.) He was the son of James Taylor who died in Halifax Co., N. C., 1771-2, (W.B.1, p. 304) and his wife, Dorcas Walters. (35V. pp.211-218; 309-312; 36V. pp.388-389; 47V. pp.81-84; Family Records.) Edmund Dickens and his family were Methodists.

Children:

I. Christiana Dickens, b. ca 1821, m. Jan. 18, 1845, Eli Cook, grandson of Joseph and Nancy Holt. Eli Cook was k. in the War. Issue: 5 children.

II. Hiram Dickens, b. 1824, m. Susan Powers. He was a soldier of the CSA. Issue: 8 children.

III. Minerva Dickens, b. 1831, m. James M. Dickens.
Children:
1. Mecum Dickens, b. 1857, d. 1907, m. Dec. 9,
   1875, Johnnie Arrington.
   Children:
   (1) Dora Dickens, m. Ezra Dickens, her cousin.
   (2) Edward Dickens, m. Lena Arrington. Issue:
       3 children.
   (3) Willis Dickens, m. Alice Barham.
   (4) Charles Dickens, m. his cousin, Agnes T.
       Hux. Issue: 8 children.
   (5) Lonnie Dickens, m. _____.
   (6) Raleigh Dickens, m. Lucy Warren. Issue: 8
       children.
2. Sarah E. Dickens, b. 1861, m. Lewis Hux. They
   moved to Missouri.
3. Julius K. Dickens, m. his cousin, Susan Anderson. No issue.
4. Jacob B. Dickens, b. 1865, d. 1933, m. Sarah
   Hamill. Issue: 5 children.
IV. Balaam Dickens, b. near Darlington, N. C., 1828,
d. there, 1874, m. (1) Margaret Partin, b. 1820, m. (2)
Mar. 6, 1860, Susan Ann Branch, b. 1839, d. June 9, 1912.
Balaam enlisted in the CSA, Oct. 1, 1862, and served
during the entire War.
   Children:
1. Joseph E. Dickens, b. 1851, m. (1) Mittie Cook,
   m. (2) Dec. 21, 1880, Rebecca Jane Alice Keeter,
   he moved to Hendersonville, N. C. All his
   children were born to his second wife.
   Children:
   (1) Eugenia Dickens, m. Walter G. Smith. No
       issue.
   (2) Morton Dickens.
   (3) Joseph Dickens, m. _____. Had issue.
   (4) Avis Dickens, m. Willis M. Guill. Issue:
       3 children.
2. Margaret Dickens, b. 1853, m. Dec. 22, 1868,
   Francis M. Hux. They moved to Missouri.
3. Emily Jane Dickens, b. 1855, m. (1) Thomas
   Rhode Hux, m. (2) George Arrington. Issue: 7
   children by 1st marriage.
4. William B. Dickens, b. 1857, m. Jan 7, 1881,
   Ida T. Green, b. 1862. Issue: 3 children.
5. Robert Patrick Dickens, b. at Darlington, N. C.
   Feb. 7, 1866, d. at Latta, S. C., Jan. 18,1934,
   m. (1) Jan.25, 1885, Margaret Ann Keeter, b.
   near Darlington, N. C., Aug. 24, 1865, d. in

Latta, S. C., May 28, 1910, m. (2) Alice
Rogers of Dillon, S. C.
Children: (All by 1st marriage)
(1) Minnie Dickens, d. 1912, dsp. She was a
noted beauty.
(2) Robert Dallas Dickens, dsp., 1915.
(3) Willie Alice Dickens, d. 1935, m. Walter
Driggers.
Children:
a. Teresa Bell Driggers, m. Raymond B.
Perry. She graduated from Winthrop
College. Resided in Watchung, N. J.,
in 1955.
(4) Cora Bell Dickens, m. as his 2nd wife,
Walter Driggers.
(5) Ida Estell Dickens, dsp.
(6) Armond Joyner Dickens, Apr. 5, 1895, dsp.
(7) Joseph Numa Dickens, unmarried.
(8) Teressa Hope Dickens, b. in Dillon Co.,
S. C., Oct. 6, 1902, graduated from Coker
College for Women, Hartsville, S. C., in
1923, on June 5, 1927, m. William Marion
Mann, son of Mary Elizabeth (Parker) and
Benjamin Denton Mann. Children under
father.
6. Edward Walter Dickens, b. 1868, m. his cousin,
Eliza Donna Brantley Hux, b. Sept. 18, 1874,
daughter of Alexander Austin Hux and his first
wife, Sarah E. Britt. It is to Mrs. Dickens
that the author is indebted for much of this
material. From her remarkable memory, she
gave material containing more than 450 names,
all of the people mentioned being connected
with the Dickens and Green families. This was
done after she was 78, and no mistake has been
found. She resides at her home in Darlington,
Halifax Co., N. C. (1955)
Children:
(1) Ann Elizabeth Dickens, dsp.
(2) Wesley McKeva Dickens, m. Lucretia Barnes.
Children:
a. Balaam Dickens, m. Annie Harlow. Child:
Linda Dickens.
b. Frances Dickens, m. Calvin Dickens,
son of Mack and Mary A. E. Dickens.
Issue: 2 children.
c. Mary Donna Dickens, m. Lewis Tanner.
(3) Alexander Balaam Dickens, m. Blanche,

daughter of Sally (Lee) and William Wood,
and had issue: Horace, Caroline, Marion
and Marvin, twins, and Christene Dickens.

(4) Lou Ella Dickens, m. Eugene S. Jenkins.
Children:
a. Edward Jenkins, d.s.p.
b. Ella Davis Jenkins, m. Samuel Dickens,
son of Calvin Dickens and 1st wife,
Naomi Hux. Child: Samuel Dickens, Jr.
c. Carlton Dickens, m. Mack Bradley.

(5) Myra Tabitha Bartheny Dickens, m. A. Herman Poole. No issue.

(6) Eliza Jane Davis Dickens, m. Ferdinand H.
Clarke. His ancestry is given in Grove's
"Alstons and Allstons of North and South
Carolina." No issue.

(7) Edward Walter Dickens, Jr., m. Ruth Jes-
sup. Child: Edward Walter Dickens, III.

7. Willie Dickens, b. 1870, moved to S. C., where
he died.

8. Ella Jemima Dickens, b. 1874, d. 1/30/1930, m.
Willis Henry Butts. Issue: 6 children.

V. Edmund Jacob Dickens, son of Edmund and Elizabeth
(Taylor), m. 1/4/1856, Louisa Agatha Ann Dickens, b. 1837,
d. 1913. He was killed in the War in 1863.

1. Millard L. Dickens, b. 1858, m. Martha Hux,
dau. of Lydia (Neville) and John M. Hux. Had
issue.

2. David B. Dickens, b. 1861, m. (1) 3/2/1884,
Emma Dickens, b. 1866, sister of Robert W.
Dickens, m. (2) _____, and had issue.

3. Mary Jane Dickens, b. 2/20/1864, m. Thaddius
L. Branch, b.1845, son of Jemima (Powell) and
Patrick H. Branch.

****

(Reprinted from SOUTHSIDE VIRGINIA FAMILIES, Vol. II)

BIBLE RECORDS
of
WILLIAM B. BODDIE

Original owner: William Bennett and Eliza Ann Alston
                 Boddie, of Jackson, Mississippi.
Copied from the original Bible, now owned by: Mrs. Ben
                 Hamlet Jones, of Canton, Madison Co.,
                 Mississippi. (Date Copied: 1959.)
NOTE: Nathaniel Boddie, Revolutionary ancestor of Mrs.
Ben H. Jones,(b. 1732, Isle of Wight Co., Va.: d. 1797, at
Rosehill, Nash Co., N. C.) married in 1762, Chloe Crudup,
daughter of John & Mourning Dixon Crudup. Their son,
George Boddie,(b. 1769, in Nash Co., N. C.: d. 1842) mar-
ried, 2nd, Lucy Williams, daughter of John & Frances
(Bustin) Slatter Williams. Four of their sons moved to
Mississippi.

   One son, John Boddie, died 1864, on his plantation,
"Tougaloo," north of Jackson, Hinds Co., Mississippi. He
had built a lovely home, which is still standing and is
now known as "The Mansion," on the grounds of what is now
Tougaloo Christian College, in preparation for marriage,
but for some reason his fiancee "jilted" him. He never
married. Another son, William Bennett Boddie,(b. 1814, in
Nash Co., N. C.: d. 1854, in Jackson, Miss.) married in
Halifax Co., N. C., Eliza Ann Alston, (b. 1814, in Hali-
fax Co., N. C.: d. 1888, in New Orleans; buried at Jackson,
Miss.). They were the grandparents of Mrs. Ben H. Jones.
   Nathaniel Boddie, (b. 1732) represented Edgecombe Co.,
Va., in the Provincial Congress of N. C., which met at
Halifax, April 4, 1776, and declared for Independence.
Ref: Wheeler's "History of North Carolina," p. 78.
   John Williams, father of Lucy Williams, who married
George Boddie, was a Major in the Revolutionary Army.
Ref: (1) Revolutionary Army Accounts, Vol. 12, Secty. of
State., N. C.: (2) John B. Boddie's "Historical Southern
Families," Vol. I, p. 345.
   Col. Willis Alston, grandfather of Eliza Ann Alston,
was a Colonel of Militia, Halifax District, N. C., and a

member of the Constitutional Convention. Ref: Groves' "The
Alston and Allstons," (1901), p. 149.

Benjamin Sebastian, (b. 1739, in Va.: d. 1832, in Ky.)
Rev. ancestor of George C. Sebastian, although an ordained
minister of the Episcopal Church, served as a private in
the 1st Va. Regiment under Patrick Henry. His original discharge papers (1783) are on file in the Va. State Library,
Richmond, Va. After he took up his land grant in Ky., after
1783, he gave up preaching and became a prominent judge.
(See Benjamin E. Jones Bible.)

MARRIAGES

William B. Boddie and Eliza Ann Alston were m. on 20th
Dec., 1830.

George C. Sebastian and Laura Boddie were m. in Jackson, Miss., on the 14th day of March, 1865.

BIRTHS

Mary Fielding Sebastian was b. in the city of New
Orleans on the 12th day of Mar., 1866 at 4 o'clock 45 min.
A.M.

Lillie Stuart Sebastian was b. in the city of New
Orleans on the 12th day of Mar., 1866 at 4 o'clock 45 min.
A.M.

Charles William Sebastian was b. at 357 Rampart St.,
New Orleans on the 23rd day of Sept., 1867.

George Garner Sebastian was b. in the city of New
Orleans on the 1st day of April, 1870, on Calliope St., between Dryades and Baronne.

Annie Fearn Sebastian was b. on the 25th day of Sept.,
1871, on Grand Route St. John near the Bayou St. John.

Clara Lee Sebastian was b. corner Second and Caronde-
let Streets on the 30th day of April, 1873.

John Tobin Sebastian was b. on Dorgenois St., between
Barracks and Hospital on the 20th day of June, 1875.

Odile Vredenburg Sebastian was b. on Dorgenois St.,
on the 5th day of Jan., 1877.

Amelia Broadwater Sebastian was b. on Dorgenois St.,
on the 5th day of Jan., 1879.

Juanita Preston Sebastian was b. on Dorgenois St., on
the 20th day of March, 1883.

George Sebastian West, son of William A. West and
Lily Stuart Sebastian, was b. Jan. 25, 1889, at 4:30
o'clock at residence of Major G. C. Sebastian, corner of
Hospital and Dorgenois Streets, New Orleans, La.

DEATHS

Laura M. W. Boddie, August 5, 1841.
Joseph J. Boddie, September 19, 1841.
Nathan W. Boddie, August 17, 1841.

Margaret Boddie, August 10, 1841.
William G. Boddie, January 5, 1854.
George C. Sebastian, August 7, 1897.
****

BENJAMIN E. JONES BIBLE

Original owner: Benjamin Edward and Ellen Hay Boddie
Jones of Canton, Madison Co., Mississippi.
NOTE: William B. Jones, father of Benjamin Edward Jones,
married in Maury Co., Tenn., Martha D. (maiden name not
known). In 1832, he had migrated to Mississippi and pur-
chased that year land in Vernon (now Kearney Park), Madi-
son County, Mississippi. Benjamin Edward Jones, son of
Wm. B. and Martha D. Jones, married in 1868, Ellen Hay
Boddie, daughter of William Bennett & Eliza Ann Alston
Boddie of Jackson, Mississippi.

MARRIAGES

B. E. Jones to Ellen Boddie, March 8, 1868.
Bessie Philips Jones to Al Kennedy, December 14,1904.
Willye Boddie Jones to Walter Gill Kirkpatrick.
Ben Hamlet Jones to Laura West, September 14, 1914.
Camille Morgan to Stanley Ruddiman, March 1, 1916.
DuAine Boddie Morgan to Primrose Thompson.
Laura Boddie Jones to Earle Bowers, Jr., May 9, 1944.
Edsel Ruddiman to Dorothy Chubbock, March 1, 1942.

BIRTHS

Mallie Baughn Jones, February 6, 1869.
Annie Bartels Jones, January 25, (year not given).
Willie Boddie Jones, March 30, 1874.
Bessie Phillips Jones, June 30, 1877.
Ben Hamlet Jones, October 13, 1879.
Georgia Harvey Sebastian (Jones), April 28, (year not
given).
Camille Morgan, July 13, 1891.
DuAine Morgan, February 21, 1894.
Benjamin Edsel Ruddiman, January 10, 1917.
William Boddie Ruddiman, January 9, 1928.
Laura Boddie West Jones, June 24, 1915.
George William Jones, July 11, 1922.
Ellen Sebastian Jones, February 6, 1927.
Barbara Jean Morgan, January 30, 1927.
Catherine Ruddiman, November, 1942.
Earle Cooper Bowers, III, November 17, 1944.

DEATHS

Mrs. Eliza Boddie, February 27, 1888.
Willie B. Boddie, April 17, 1889.
Mallie Baughn Morgan, September 3, 1897.
Ben Edward Jones, November 4, 1910.

Ellen Boddie Jones, May 3, 1912.
Willye Jones Kirkpatrick, May, 1925.
Mrs. Malvina Baughn, September 1, 1912.
Earle Cooper Bowers, Jr., September 27, 1944.
George Harvey Jones, June 13, 1944.
Bessie Jones Kennedy, 1947.
Annie Bartels Jones, September 1, 1947.
Walter Gill Kirkpatrick, May, 1925.

****

HILLIARD OF VIRGINIA

"Think of your ancestors and your posterity."
                                        -Tacitus.

A re-evaluation of the records pertaining to the
early history of this family of Hilliard in Virginia
published in SOUTHSIDE VIRGINIA FAMILIES in conjunction
with other records pertaining to that family of the period
leads one to conclude that Thomas Ballard did not marry a
"step-daughter" of William Thomas as has been previously
stated but that Thomas Ballard was himself a step-son of
William Thomas. This conclusion effects the Hilliard
lineage in that it means that the surname of Jane Hillard,
the wife of John Hilliard (father of Jeremiah) was Ballard
and that she was a sister of Thomas Ballard. The proof
seems most conclusive and will be summarized below.

Thomas Ballard, who was apparently the brother of
Jane, wife of John Hilliard, was born about 1630 and was
buried March 24, 1689. He was Clerk of York County, Va.,
in 1652 and many years later, a Burgess from James City in
1666, member of the council in 1675, speaker of the House
of Burgesses in 1680, and High Sheriff of James City in
1660. During Bacon's Rebellion, Thomas Ballard's wife was
captured by Bacon and placed with other ladies who were
also wives of members of the council upon the brestworks
before Jamestown where their white aprons warned Berkeley
from Attack. Capt. Robert Baldry (J. P. of York, came to
Virginia in 1635, age 18, and died in 1675) left his
estate to the following children of Col. Ballard: John,
eldest son, Thomas, Lydia, Elizabeth, and Margaret. In
1694, Capt. Thomas Ballard, son of Col. Thomas Ballard,
was sheriff of York County and his brother, Francis (probably born after 1675) was sub-sheriff. (William and Mary
Quarterly, Vol. 2, p. 276; Calendar Virginia State Papers,
Vol. 1, p.6).

About 1664, William Thomas of York County, Va., made
his will and mentioned wife, Anne, son-in-law, Thomas
Ballard, daughter-in-law, Sarah Herman, and daughter-in-

law, Jane Hilliard, wife of John Hilliard. In that day, son-in-law and daughter-in-law also meant step-son and step-daughter. Therefore, it appears that Thomas Ballard, Sarah Herman, and Jane Hilliard were related in the same degree to William Thomas, and for this to be so, they must have been children of Anne, the wife of William Thomas, by a former marriage to ___ Ballard. What records exist which support these conclusions?

There is in Surry Co., a record dated April, 17, 1664, in which John Hilliard acknowledged that the cattle in his possession were the "cattle and estate of my wife, Jane Hilliard, and that I have no power to sell or dispose of them" . . . as appears by a deed of gift from William Thomas, which deed remains "in the custody of my brother, Thomas Ballard". (Surry Co., Va., Book 1, p. 240) Furthermore, the following record also has been found: Thomas Ballard consents to the sale of a heifer by his sister Hilliard, from her estate to Francis Gray, and sow and pigs, for her own and her children's use; but not to be disposed of as by ye deed of gift made by William Thomas to my said sister. August 31, 1667, (Surry Co. Records, 1652-1684, p. 83, by Davis). That Thomas Ballard calls Jane Hilliard "sister" and John Hilliard calls Thomas Ballard "brother" apparently means that John Hilliard had married Jane Ballard, "sister" of Thomas Ballard; for it is doubtful that these terms of relationship would have been used had John Hilliard and Thomas Ballard married sisters. Also, in this interpretation of the records, there is perfect agreement with the relationship expressed in the will of William Thomas.

Therefore, John Hilliard married before 1664, Jane Ballard, sister of Thomas Ballard and daughter of Anne, wife of William Thomas by a former marriage to ___Ballard; and at the time the "consents" were made by Thomas Ballard on August 31, 1667, Jane (Ballard) Hilliard was the mother of "children." Thus, the next question which arises, is, who were these children?

Jeremiah[2] Hilliard and John[2] Hilliard were residing in James City in 1704, and the Quit Rent Rolls show that Jeremiah held 225 acres and John 200 acres.

It has been shown that John[2] Hilliard died in York in 1706. He held no property in York in 1704. Since it has been shown in a previous book that his children and grandchildren resided in James City, it is very probable that he is the John[2] Hilliard who held 200 acres in that county adjoining Jeremiah[2] Hilliard. William Buckner, a lawyer who had married Katherine Ballard, granddaughter of Thomas Ballard whom John[1] Hilliard had called "brother," was the administrator of John[2] Hilliard's estate. There can be but little doubt that John[1] Hilliard was the father of John[2] Hilliard who died in 1706.

Since John[1] Hilliard and Jane Ballard were married previous to April 17, 1664, their son, John, probably was born about that time and may have been about 42 or 45 years of age at his death. His son, John[3] Hilliard was over 21 in 1706, when he recorded the deed of gift of his aunt, Sarah Jones, in that year. (W.B., 12-423) John was, therefore, born not later than 1655.

This brings us to Jeremiah[2] Hilliard who held 225 acres in James City Co., near John[2] Hilliard's plantation in 1704. There is no further record of this Jeremiah Hilliard. However, it is shown that the name "Jeremiah" was a very prevalent name among the descendants of John[3] Hilliard in James City. The name was also conspicuous among the Hilliards of North Carolina. There can be but little doubt that they were related and that Jeremiah[2] Hilliard of James City, probably born about 1666, was a son of John[1] Hilliard of York and James City, and that Elizabeth Hilliard of James City was his widow. There was no other person unaccounted for in this family.

Elizabeth Hilliard, a widow of James City Co., m. (2) Simon Jeffries, a Lawyer and Official Surveyor of that County. ——

*****

HILLIARD OF NORTH CAROLINA
by
J. Byron Hilliard

Mrs. Elizabeth Jeffreys, who made her will in Northampton County, N. C., June 20, 1742, probated February
Court 1742, was first married to Jeremiah[2] Hilliard of
Virginia, son of John[1] Hilliard, bv whom she had four
sons, John[3], Robert[3], Jeremiah[3], and William[4]. She married
second time, probably in Virginia, Captain Simon Jeffreys,
and had issue: Elizabeth Jeffreys who married John Boddie, and Osborne Jeffreys. (See her will Vol. 1, p. 251.)

John[3] Hilliard, son of Jeremiah[2] and Elizabeth Hilliard made his will in Northampton County, N. C., Nov. 6,
1748, probated November Court 1748 and names sons, Robert
and John Hilliard, daughter Sarah Hilliard, wife and
executrix Mary Hilliard.

Robert[3] Hilliard, son of John and Mary (probably
Bridger) Hilliard of Northampton County, N. C., died before 1790. He married Mary, daughter of Dugald McKeithan
and wife Mary of Bladen County, N. C. (Dugald McKeithan
made his will January 1, 1750, probated March Court 1751
in Bladen County, N. C.)

Robert and Mary (McKeithan) Hilliard had issue:

I. Mary[4] Hilliard, born in Northampton County, N.C.
d. unmarried at the home of her sister, Pharaby
Hilliard Barrow, in Louisiana.

II. Martha "Patsy" Hilliard, m. Norfleet Harris of
Halifax County, N. C., and had issue: one son,
Robert Hilliard Harris, who d. in 1799 under age.
Martha Hilliard Harris d. in 1793, and Norfleet
Harris married second time and d. Oct. 22, 1807.

III. Pharaby Hilliard, b. Feb. 10, 1775, d. ___1827.
She married June 26, 1792, William Barrow, son
of William Barrow and wife Olivia Ruffin, dau.
of Robert Ruffin of Northampton County, N. C.,
and his wife Anne, dau. of Captain William Bennett and his wife, Grace of Northampton County,
N. C.

Children of Pharaby Hilliard and William Barrow,
Jr., born at "Highland" plantation near St.
Francisville, Louisiana:

1. Robert Hilliard Barrow (1795-1823) married
   Eliza Pirrie (1805-1851), pupil of the famous Auduborn and who he complimentarily
   referred to as "the beautiful Eliza Pirrie."
       Robert Hilliard Barrow II (1824-1878),
   married his cousin, Mary Eliza Barrow (1825-
   1920), the first daughter of "Afton Villa"
   plantation, built by her father.
       Robert Hilliard Barrow III (1859-1929),
   married Carrie R. Reeves.
       Robert Hilliard Barrow IV, married
   Nellie Norman.
       Robert Hilliard Barrow V.
2. Nancy Ann Ruffin Barrow (1795-1856).
3. William Ruffin Barrow (1800-1862).
4. Bennett Barrow (1803-1805).
5. Martha Hilliard Barrow (1809-1899).
6. Bennett Hilliard Barrow (1811-1854).
7. Eliza Eleanor Barrow (1814-1885).
8. James Barrow (1817-1819).

John[4] Hilliard, son of John[3] and Mary Hilliard of
Northampton County, N. C., married Margaret Duke, daughter
of John Duke, who made his will in Northampton County,
N. C., dated Jan. 30, 1783, proved June Court 1787, and
his wife Sarah. John Hilliard, husband of Margaret (Duke)
Hilliard, probably died about 1778. Margaret (Duke) Hilliard made her will in Halifax County, N. C., 1786, mentions sons, John[5] and William Hilliard; daughters Christian Judge and Sarah Throwe; granddaughter Charlotte
Thrower. July 22, 1786. Feb. 1787.

John[5] Hilliard, son of John[4] and Margaret (Duke) Hilliard, made his will in Northampton County, N. C., March
16, 1790, recorded June 1, 1797. He married Priscilla,
daughter of David Dickinson, who made his will in Northampton County, N. C., 1783. By her marriage to John Hilliard, they had issue: John D. James, and David Hilliard.
Priscilla Hilliard married second time, Jeremiah Hilliard,
son of Jacob and Sarah (Battle) Hilliard of Edgecombe Co.,
N. C. After the death of Jeremiah Hilliard, she married
third time, Robert Blick. Priscilla Blick died in Halifax
County, N. C., about 1819. According to court records,
her three Hilliard sons died under age without issue.
Robert Blick married second time, Polly Kearney Williams,
daughter of Major William Williams and his wife, Elizabeth
Alston Kearney. Robert Blick died without issue 11/9/1825.

Robert[3] Hilliard, son of Jeremiah[2] and Elizabeth Hilliard, made his will in Edgecombe Co., N. C., April 13, 1743, same probated May Court 1751.

Hilliard, Robert   Edgecombe County, N. C.
April 13, 1743   May Court 1751.
       (Grimes Abstract of Wills 1690-1760, p. 166)
            Devisees and Legatees:

Jacob Hilliard, Robert Hilliard, Jeremiah Hilliard ("Plantation on the Falls of Tar River"); Sampson Hilliard, Mary Hilliard (all children of Jeremiah Hilliard); William Hilliard, James Hilliard (sons of William Hilliard). Wife Chariety. Executors: William Hilliard and Osborne Jeffreys.

Robert[3] Hilliard married Chariety Alston, daughter of John Alston of Chowan County, N. C. (This marriage is proven in a deed made in Halifax County, N. C., by Chariety Hilliard.)

       On April 14, 1752, Edward Brown sold to Chariety Hilliard of Edgecombe County for ten pounds current Virginia money 454 acres on Cypress Swamp, Conneho Creek, Beaver Dam Branch, witnessed by John Dawson and Thomas (t) Doles. (Halifax County, N. C. Deed Book 4, p. 264)

       On April 3, 1754, Chariety Hilliard of Edgecombe County made an agreement with John Dawson, Gent. of Northampton County, planter, witnessed by William Hilliard, Robert Hilliard and Samuel Whitney; being about to marry said Dawson, she conveyed to the two Alstons her interest in certain lands, slaves, stock, etc., after the death of herself and John Dawson. (Halifax County, N. C. Deed Book 2, pp. 25/28.)

Robert and Chariety (Alston) Hilliard left no issue.

       The will of John Alston of Chowan County on Feb. 20, 1755, names daughter, Chariety Dawson and sons Joseph John Alston and James Alston. (Grimes, p. 6)

       Jeremiah[3] Hilliard, son of Jeremiah[2] and Elizabeth Hilliard died in Edgecombe County, N. C., in 1741/42. He married Mourning Pope, daughter of Jacob Pope and wife Jane (Edgecombe Co., Book "A", p. 189) Inventory of the estate of Jeremiah Hilliard, Sr., taken in Edgecombe County 1742, "by his widow Mourning Hilliard Adminrs." (Edgecombe County Inventories & Accounts of Estates 1733-1753, p. 79, pp. 145/146, p. 10, pp. 37/38.)

       On May 14, 1743, Joseph Howell, Elias Fort, and Robert West divided the estate of Jeremiah Hilliard among the five children, and the report was submitted to the Edgecombe County Court in the same month, under the oath of Joseph Thomas in the right of his wife Mourning Thomas, late the wife of the said Jeremiah Hilliard. (Ibid., p. 17, pp. 65/68 & p. 24 & pp. 92/94.)

> Jacob Hilliard received a list of goods valued at 275/15/4.
>
> Robert Hilliard received a list of goods valued at 280/2/8.
>
> Jeremiah Hilliard received a list of goods valued at 271/18/8.
>
> Mary Hilliard received a list of goods valued at 236/3/8.
>
> Sampson Hilliard received a list of goods valued at 276/16/0.

Mourning Pope Hilliard, widow of Jeremiah Hilliard is illustrative of a feature of colonial life. No one in those days remained single very long. Life was too hard and too lonely. She married (2) Joseph Thomas and had five children by him. He died in 1758 and she married (3) William Prigen who lived about a year. She then married (4) George Wimberley, Sr.

Jacob[4] Hilliard, son of Jeremiah and Mourning (Pope) Hilliard of Edgecombe County, N. C., died in Edgecombe in 1764. (See will) He married Sarah Battle, daughter of Elisha Battle. Jacob and Sarah (Battle) Hilliard had issue:

I.   Jeremiah Hilliard, born about 1760, d. 4/21/1810. He married first, Anne (Nancy) Hilliard, dau. of Capt. Isaac Hilliard and wife Leah Crafford of "Woodlawn" plantation, Nash County, N. C. Jacob Battle Hilliard, only child of Jeremiah Hilliard and wife Anne (Nancy) Hilliard died under age without issue. After the death of Anne (Nancy) Hilliard, Jeremiah Hilliard married Mrs. Priscilla Hilliard, widow of John Hilliard of Northampton County, N. C., and daughter of David Dickinson, who made his will in Northampton County, N. C., 1783.

II.   Elizabeth Hilliard, b. 9/6/1763, died in Tenn., 10/4/1819. She married March 6, 1782, William Fort, b. 6/23/1759, d. 1/8/1802. William Fort and his family removed from Edgecombe County, N. C., to Robertson (then Cumberland) County, Tenn. He was the son of Elias Fort and Sarah Suggs of Edgecombe Co., N. C.

Children of Elizabeth Hilliard and William Fort:
1. Jacob Hilliard Fort, b. 1/13/1783, d. 9/13/1785.
2. Jeremiah Hilliard Fort, b. 8/28/1784, d.

2/23/1806. He married Temperance Battle, daughter of Jethro Battle and Martha Lane.

3. Sarah Coleman Fort, b. 9/6/1786, m. Orren D. Battle.
4. James Fort, b. 10/18/1788, d. 7/9/1819, m. (1) Jane Vernon Hampton, (2) Miss Ewing.
5. William Anthony Fort, b. 12/21/1790, d. 6/5/1817, unmarried.
6. Jacob Hilliard Fort, b. 11/29/1792, d. 12/22 /1833, Cynthia Copeland.
7. Josiah W. Fort, b. 6/25/1795, m. (1) Diana Coleman Ligon, (2) Miss Montgomery.
8. Mary Smith Fort, b. 10/24/1797, m. 4/22/1817, John William Nicholas Arthur Smith.

Robert Hilliard (3), son of Jeremiah and Mourning Hilliard of Edgecombe County, N. C., untraced.

Jeremiah Hilliard (3), son of Jeremiah and Mourning Hilliard of Edgecombe County, N. C., married and settled in Granville County, N. C. He has many descendants living in Texas.

Mary Hilliard (3), daughter of Jeremiah and Mourning Hilliard of Edgecombe County, N. C., is said to have married Rev. Jonathan Thomas of Edgecombe County, N. C.

Sampson Hilliard, son of Jeremiah and Mourning Hilliard of Edgecombe County, N. C., untraced.

WILLIAM[3] HILLIARD (2), (Jeremiah[2], John[1]) was probably born in Virginia and died in Northampton County, N.C. He made his will in Northampton County, N. C., dated July 4, 1754, probated May Court 1756. (See Will, Vol. 1, pp. 256-57)

WILLIAM HILLIARD married ANNE, daughter of JOHN and SARAH (CRAFFORD) NEWSOM of Surry County, Virginia. ANNE HILLIARD died in Northampton County, N. C., in 1771. ANNE (NEWSOM) HILLIARD (d. 1771), mother of Capt. Isaac Hilliard was the daughter of John Newsom (1674-1723/24) and his wife Sarah Crafford, daughter of Robert and Elizabeth (Carter) Crafford. John Newsom was the son of William Newsom II (1648-1691), and his wife Anne Sheppard Hart, widow of Thomas Hart, and daughter of Major Robert Sheppard of Surry. Burgess in 1646-47-48. Major Robert Sheppard married Elizabeth, daughter of William Spencer. William Spencer "yeoman and ancient planter" is noted as a member of the first expedition which arrived in Jamestown, 1607. (See Hart)

WILLIAM AND ANNE (NEWSOM) HILLIARD HAD ISSUE:

I.   William[4] Hilliard, Jr., d. unmarried before 1771.
II.   James[4] Hilliard made his will in Northampton Co., N. C., in 1764.

III.   Elias[4] Hilliard, d. in Granville County, N. C.,
       before 1790. He m. (1) Lydia (probably Hart),
       by whom he had issue:
       1. Henry Hilliard, d. unmarried in Franklin Co.,
          N. C. (His will dated 1789.)
       2. Elizabeth Hilliard, m. 12/16/1797, William
          Green of Franklin Co., N. C. (Franklin
          County Marriage Bonds)
       3. Mary Ann Hilliard, m. Major Jacob Durden and
          settled in Emanuel County, Georgia. (See
          Darden-Durden, S.V.F., Vol. II.)
       4. Martha Hilliard, m. 1/9/1790, William Green
          of Franklin Co., N. C. (Franklin County
          Marriage Bonds)
       5. Sarah Hilliard, d. between 1772 and 1789.
          She is mentioned in the will of her grand-
          mother, Anne Hilliard, 1771, but is not
          mentioned in the will of her brother, Henry
          Hilliard, 1789.
       Elias Hilliard m. (2) Sarah Norfleet, daughter
       of Mary (Battle) and James Norfleet. Sarah (Nor-
       fleet) Hilliard m. (2) Col. William Horne.

IV.   Anne[4] Hilliard m. _____ Ricks; daughter Anne
       Ricks.

V.   ISAAC[4] HILLIARD, m. LEAH CRAFFORD. (See later)
          ISAAC[4] HILLIARD, son of William[3] and Anne (Newsom)
Hilliard married Leah Crafford and settled in Edgecombe
County, N. C., on land devised to Isaac Hilliard in his
father's will, 1754-56. (The western half of Edgecombe
County was made into Nash County in 1777.)
       "Woodlawn" plantation, the county seat of the family
in Nash County, N. C., was established by Isaac Hilliard
and his wife, Leah Crafford about 1765. "Woodlawn" plantation embraced over twenty thousand acres and was situated
about ten miles from Rocky Mount, N. C. The mansion house
at "Woodlawn" was a large Georgian Colonial house, built
on a bluff over-looking Swift Creek, and faced the old
stage coach road that ran from Halifax to Fayetteville.
       Isaac Hilliard was born in Northampton County, N. C.,
7/28/1738, and died at "Woodlawn" plantation, Nash County,
N. C., 6/25/1790. He m. 4/20/1765, Leah Crafford of
Surry County, Virginia, daughter of Carter Crafford, Jr.,
and his wife, Elizabeth, daughter of Captain Barnaby Kearney and his wife, Elizabeth Godwin of Nansemond County, Va.
Leah Crafford was born in Surry County, Va., 8/27/1749,
and died at "Woodlawn" plantation, Nash County, N. C.,
10/20/1823. According to old letters in possession of the
family, Isaac Hilliard was educated at William and Mary

College. At his death in 1790, he was the largest land
and slave owner in Nash County. (Federal Census for N. C.
1790.)

Children of Isaac and Leah (Crafford) Hilliard
born at "Woodlawn" plantation Nash County, N. C.:

I. Elizabeth (Betsey) Hilliard (1766-1816), m.
    Archibald Davis of Franklin Co., N. C., son of
    Thomas and Hartwell (Hodges) Davis of Isle of
    Wight Co., Virginia and Halifax Co., N. C. After
    the death of Thomas Davis 1764/65, his widow m.
    James Drake of Nash Co., N. C. (See later)

II. JAMES HILLIARD (1768-1832), m. Mourning Boddie,
     daughter of Nathan and Chloe (Crudup) Boddie of
     "Rose Hill", Nash Co., N. C. (V.H.G. 299) (See
     later)

III. Anne (Nancy) Hilliard (1769-1797), m. her cousin,
      Jeremiah Hilliard, son of Jacob and Sarah (Bat-
      tle) Hilliard of Edgecombe Co., N. C. After the
      death of Anne (Nancy) Hilliard, Jeremiah Hilliard
      m. Mrs. Priscilla Hilliard, widow of John Hil-
      liard of Northampton Co., N. C.

IV. Robert Carter Hilliard (1771-1828), m. Amaryllis
     Hunt, daughter of Capt. John Hunt and his wife,
     Mary Jeffreys of Franklin Co., N. C. (See later)

V. John Hilliard (1773-1814), m. Elizabeth (Betsey)
    Barker Tunstall, daughter of Edmund and Ann
    Eliza (Nancy) Tunstall, (first cousin). Edmund
    Tunstall was the son of Thomas Edmund Tunstall.
    Ann Eliza (Nancy) Tunstall was the daughter of
    Lt. Col. William Tunstall, who married Betsy
    Barker, daughter of Hon. Thomas Barker of Eden-
    ton, N. C. (See later)

VI. Isaac Hilliard (1775-1832), m.Mary Moore Murfree,
     dau. of Col. Hardy Murfree and wife, Sally Bric-
     kell of Murfreesboro, N.C. and Tenn.(See later)

VII. Henry Hilliard (1771-1797), was drowned in the
      Miss. River while rescuing people from a burning
      steam boat on which he was a passenger. A monu-
      ment was erected to his memory near the spot.

VIII. Mary (Polly) Hilliard, b. 1783, d.s.p.

IX. William Hilliard, b. 1785, d. young unmarried.

X. Martha Hilliard,(1788-1847), m. (1) James Branch
    of Halifax Co.,N.C. After his death, she m. her
    cousin, Nathaniel Macon Hunt of Franklin Co.,
    N.C., brother of Amaryllis Hunt who m. Robert
    Carter Hilliard. Nathaniel M. Hunt and his family
    removed from Franklin Co., N.C., and settled in
    Haywood Co., Tenn., about 1828.(See Hilliard-Hunt)

Elizabeth (Betsy) Hilliard, daughter of Captain Isaac
Hilliard and his wife, Leah Crafford, was born at "Wood-
lawn" plantation, Nash Co., N. C., 8/27/1766, and died at
"Columbia Farm", Franklin Co., N. C., 8/25/1816. She m.
1789, Archibald Davis, b. 4/14/1763, d. at "Columbia Farm",
Franklin Co., N. C., 2/22/1821, son of Thomas and Hartwell
(Hodges) Davis. Hartwell Hodges, daughter of Benjamin
Hodges and his wife, Constance Goodrich (widow of John
Harrison), and daughter of Capt. John Goodrich and his
wife, Anne Bechinoe, of Isle of Wight Co., Virginia.

Archibald Davis represented Franklin Co., in the N.C.
House of Commons 1795-96-98-99.

Mrs. Thomas Davis m. (2) 1766, James Drake (ca. 1725-
1791) of Nash Co., N. C., and had by him two sons: (1) Maj.
John Hodges Drake (1769-1859), who married Frances Williams,
sister of Lucy Williams, who married George Boddie of "Rose
Hill", Nash Co., N. C., (2) Benjamin Drake who married
Cecilia Taylor.

Mrs. Hartwell Drake d. in Nash Co., N. C., 1796.

Archibald Davis was a private in Taylor's Co. 6th N.C.
Regiment, under Col. Gideon Lamb, enlisted for 2½ years,
omtd 1778, enlisted as musician drummer, August, 1782,
became a private in Dec. 1782. Re-N.C. Genealogical
Register Vol. 2, #4, p. 584. Certificate from War Department State Records of N. C., Vol. 16.

    Children of Elizabeth (Hilliard) and Archibald
Davis:

I.   Anne Maria Davis, b. 9/30/1790, d. 3/27/1822, m.
(1) B. F. Brickell; no issue. She m. (2) 11/16/
1813, Josiah Crudup, b. 1/13/1791, and d. 5/19/
1872. Josiah Crudup m. (2) Mary Boddie, daughter
of George and Lucy (Williams) Boddie of "Rose
Hill", Nash County, N. C. (See later)

II.   Elizabeth Crafford Davis, b. 1/21/1792, d. 1/17/
1872, m. 7/20/1812, Nicholas Faulcon Alston, b.
7/31/1787, d. in 1818, son of Thomas Whitmel
Alston and wife Lucy Faulcon, daughter of Nicholas Faulcon of Surry Co., Virginia, and his wife
Lucy Wyatt. (See later)

III.   Harty Hodge (Hartwell Hodges) Davis, b. 4/27/1793,
d. ca. 1870, m. 10/10/1812, Robert Webb Williams,
b. 2/27/1792, d. 11/1/1822, son of Maj. William
Williams and his second wife, Elizabeth (Betsy)
Alston Kearney. (See later)

IV.   Leah Hilliard Davis, b. 8/27/1795, d. 9/26/1796.

V.   James Hilliard Davis, b. 7/21/1797, d. July,
1798.

VI.   Archibald Hilliard Davis, b. 6/3/1799, d.11/18/

1854, m. (1) Lucy Massenburg; no issue. (2)
Caroline Cornelia Kearney, daughter of William
Kinchen Kearney and his wife, Maria Alston. (See
later)

VII.   Martha Hilliard Davis, b. 2/22/1801, d. 5/16/1876,
m. Edward Alston, brother of Nicholas Faulcon
Alston, who married Elizabeth Crafford Davis.

VIII.   Mary Kearney Davis, b. 12/13/1802, d. 2/27/1887,
m. Joseph John Williams, III, son of Joseph John
Williams, Jr., and wife Elizabeth Norfleet Hunter Williams, daughter of Elisha Williams of
Roanoke who married Sarah Josie.

IX.   Temperance Williams Davis, b. 9/26/1804, d.
8/6/1854, m. William Williams Thorne, son of Dr.
Samuel Thorne and wife, Mrs. Martha Whitmel (Williams) Hill, widow, and daughter of Col. Joseph
John Williams and wife, Elizabeth Alston, dau.
of Maj. Phillip Alston and his wife, Winifred
Whitmel.

X.   Dr. Thomas Davis, b. 4/3/1806, d. 11/3/1862, m.
(1) Mary Ann Slade, m. (2) Martha E. Batchelor.

XI.   John Calvin Davis, b. 6/19/1808, d. 3/10/1889,
m. Lucy Faulcon Alston, dau. of Maj. Alfred
Alston and wife, Mary Plummer of Warren Co.,
N. C.

XII.   Lucy Henry Davis, b. 10/11/1811, d. 9/26/1896,
m. 12/8/1831, Nicholas Bryar Massenburg, b.
4/5/1806, d. 10/25/1867, son of Dr. Cargill Massenburg and wife, Ann Bryar.

Anne Maria Davis, daughter of Elizabeth (Hilliard)
and Archibald Davis, was b. at "Columbia Farm", Franklin
Co., N. C., 9/30/1790, and d. in Wake Co., N. C., 3/27/
1822. She m. (1) B. F. Brickell, no issue. She m. (2)
11/16/1813, Josiah Crudup, b. in Wake Co., N. C., 1/13/
1791, and d. there 5/19/1872, son of Josiah and Elizabeth
(Battle) Crudup. He m. (2) Mary Boddie, dau. of George
and Lucy (Williams) Boddie of "Rose Hill", Nash Co., N.C.

Children of Anne Maria (Davis) and Josiah Crudup
born in Wake County, N. C.:

I.   Archibald Davis Crudup, b. 8/8/1814, d. 6/6/1896,
unmarried. Lt. Col. C.S.A.

II.   James Henry Crudup, b. 5/19/1816, d. at Greensboro, Alabama, 1838, unmarried.

III.   Martha Alston Crudup, b. 4/12/1818, d. Nov.1843.
She m. Joshua Perry of Franklin Co., N. C. He
moved to Texas after the death of his wife. One
son, Edward Crudup Perry, lived in Texas.

IV.   Edward Alston Crudup, b. 8/1/1820, d. 4/1/1876.

He m. Columbia Jones of Wake Co., N. C. (See later)

Edward Alston Crudup, son of Anne Maria (Davis) and Joshua Crudup, was b. in Wake Co., N. C., 8/1/1820, and d. in Franklin Co., N. C., 4/1/1876. He m. 6/25/1856, Columbia Jones, b. in Wake Co., 2/13/1831, and d. in Franklin Co., N. C., 12/29/1900, dau. of Seth Jones of Wake Co., N. C.

Children of Edward Alston and Columbia (Jones) Crudup, born in Franklin Co., N. C.:

I. Edward Alston Crudup, b. 3/8/1857, d. 12/20/1915, unmarried.

II. Seth Jones Crudup, M.D., b. 8/27/1858, d. in Julian, Nebraska, 8/19/1919, unmarried.

III. Sallie Alston Crudup, b. 3/9/1860, d. 2/6/1931. She m. (1) 11/4/1879, Dr. Bennett Boddie Perry, son of Dr. Algernon Sidney and Leah (Hilliard) Perry, of "Cascine", Franklin Co., N. C. She m. (2) Robert P. Taylor of Granville Co., N. C. One child by her second marriage.
Sallie Alston (Crudup) and Dr. Bennett Boddie Perry had issue:
1. Bennett Boddie Perry, b. 9/7/1880, m. Kate Clifton, dau. of J. B. and Annie (Smith) Clifton of Louisburg, N. C. Issue: one son, Willie Clifton Perry, M.D., of Louisburg, N. C.
2. Edward Crudup Perry, b. 11/1/1881. He m. Elinor Lois Tucker of Louisburg, N. C., and had issue:
   (1) Elinor Lois Perry, b. 5/19/1904.
   (2) Edward Crudup Perry, b. 9/17/1906.
   (3) Sallie Taylor Perry, b. 3/21/1909.
   (4) Josephine Ellis Perry, b. 12/17/1915.

IV. Annie Davis Crudup, b. 3/4/1862, d. 7/15/1865.

V. Archibald Henry Crudup, b. 12/12/1864, d. 7/24/1865.

VI. Susan Lillie Crudup, b. 10/24/1865, unmarried, lived at Wake Forest, N. C.

VII. Charles Perry Crudup, b. 6/18/1868, unmarried, lived at Nebraska City, Nebraska.

VIII. Josiah Crudup, b. 3/5/1870. Baptist Minister. B.S., 1890, Wake Forest College. Law student at University of N. C., 1892. He m. 11/15/1893, Antonio Carelli Bristowe Remfry, b. Wales, 6/22/1870. Issue:
1. Elizabeth Bristowe, b. 10/30/1894.
2. Antonio Carelli Crudup, b. 12/17/1896.

3. Josiah Crudup, b. 3/17/1901.
4. Edward Alston Crudup.
5. William.
IX. Columbia Crudup, b. 3/3/1873, lived in New York
City, unmarried.
X. Anne Davis Crudup, b. 12/24/1875, lived at Wake
Forest, N. C., unmarried.

Elizabeth Crafford Davis, daughter of Elizabeth (Hilliard) and Archibald Davis, b. at "Columbia Farm", Franklin Co., N. C., 1/21/1792, d. 1/17/1872, m. 7/20/1812, Nicholas Faulcon Alston, b. 7/31/1787, d. in 1818, son of Thomas Whitmel Alston and wife, Lucy Faulcon, daughter of Nicholas Faulcon of Surry Co., Virginia, and his wife, Lucy Wyatt.

Children of Elizabeth Crafford (Davis) and
Nicholas Faulcon Alston:
I. Thomas Nicholas Faulcon Alston, b. 2/15/1815, m.
(1) Ruina Brodie, (2) Elizabeth Boddie Perry.
(See later)
II. Archibald Davis Alston, b. 6/11/1817, m. Missouri Florida Alston. (See later)

Thomas Nicholas Faulcon Alston, son of Elizabeth Crafford (Davis) and Nicholas Faulcon Alston, b. at "Cleveland", Warren Co., N. C., 2/15/1815, d. Sept., 1872, at "Alston Place", Warren Co., N. C. He m. (1) Ruina Brodie and (2) Elizabeth Boddie Perry, daughter of Bennett Boddie Perry and wife, Martha Boddie.

Children of Thomas Nicholas Faulcon Alston and
his first wife, Ruina Brodie:
I. John Alston, d.s.p.
II. Lucy Faulcon Alston, m. Julian Valencourt Perkins of Pitt Co., N. C. (See later)
Children by second marriage to Elizabeth Boddie
Perry:
III. Bennett Perry Alston, b. 3/27/1847, m. Caroline
Matilda Williams. (See later)
IV. Bryan Grimes Alston, m. Virginia Temperance
Arrington.
V. Pattie Boddie Alston, b. 6/22/1854, m. James S.
Yarborough.
VI. Thomas Nicholas Faulcon Alston, Jr., d.s.p.
VII. Ada Alston, b. 8/30/1858, m. Solon Augustus
Foster.
VIII. Walter Alston, d.s.p.

Lucy Faulcon Alston, daughter of Thomas Nicholas Faulcon Alston and his first wife, Ruina Brodie, m. Julian Valencourt Perkins of Pitt Co., N. C.
Children:
I. Margaret J. Perkins, b. 12/21/1860, m. Charles

Warburton Tayloe. (See later)
II.   Ruina B. Perkins, d.s.p.
III.   Churchill Perkins, d.s.p.
IV.   Florence T. Perkins, m. Harry Webb.
V.   Alston Perkins, m. Annie Yarborough.
VI.   David Perkins, d.s.p.
VII.   Faulcon Perkins, d.s.p.
VIII.   Valencourt Perkins, d.s.p.

Margaret J. Perkins, daughter of Lucy Faulcon (Alston) and Julian Valencourt Perkins, b. 12/21/1860, d. at Washington, N. C., 3/1/1897, m. 12/23/1884, at Pactolus, Pitt Co., N. C., Charles Warburton Tayloe, b. 12/3/1860, d. at Washington, N. C., 2/14/1908, son of Dr. David Thomas Tayloe and wife, Mary Grist of Washington, N. C. Margaret J. (Perkins) and Charles Warburton Tayloe had issue: one child, Lucy Alston Tayloe, b. 5/26/1886, m. Benjamin Franklin Bowers. (See later)?

Lucy Alston Tayloe, daughter of Margaret J. (Perkins) and Charles Warburton Tayloe, b. at Washington, N. C., 5/26/1886, m. 12/27/1906, Benjamin Franklin Bowers, b. 2/21/1879, son of William Sheppard Bowers and wife, Catherine Boseman of Halifax Co., N. C.
Children born at Washington, N. C.:
I.   Charles Tayloe Bowers, b. 12/21/1907, m. 1/9/1939, Lillian Tennys Thornton, b. 5/25/1910, at Goldsboro, N. C., residence, Washington, N. C.
Issue:
1. Tennys Thornton Bowers, b. 6/25/1940.
2. Charles Tayloe Bowers, b. 9/17/1943.
II.   Margaret Alston Bowers, d.s.p.
III.   Lucy Tayloe Bowers, b. 5/6/1914, m. at Washington, N. C., 4/10/1937, James Marion Johnston, b. 9/25/1908, son of E. G. Johnston, Sr., and wife, Lucy Arrington of Rocky Mount, N. C., residence, 531 N. Mercer Street; Rocky Mount, N. C.
Issue:
1. James Marion Johnston, Jr., b. 1/23/1942.
2. Franklin Bowers Johnston, b. 3/6/1945.
IV.   Jarl Ellis Bowers, b. 2/24/1918.
V.   Frances Elizabeth Bowers, b. 7/13/1920, m. 11/30/1946, Tompson Dumont Litchfield, b. 9/20/1917, residence, Washington, N. C.
Issue:
1. Tompson D. Litchfield, Jr., b. 9/1/1947.
2. William Franklin Litchfield, b. 10/6/1948.

Bennett Perry Alston, son of Thomas Nicholas Faulcon Alston and his second wife, Elizabeth Boddie Perry, dau. of Bennett Boddie Perry and wife Martha Boddie, dau. of

Wm. and Martha (Jones) Boddie of Nash Co.,N.C. Bennett Boddie Perry was the son of Capt. Jeremiah Perry and his wife Temperance Boddie, dau. of Nathan and Chloe (Crudup) Boddie of "Rose Hill", Nash Co., N.C. Dr. Bennett Perry Alston, b. 3/27/1847 at "Alston Place", Warren Co., N.C., and d. 10/31/1908 at "Alston Farm", Vance Co., N.C. He m. 12/19/ 1877 at "Myrtle Lawn", Warren Co., N.C., Caroline Matilda Williams, b. 6/20/1854, d. 8/6/1922, dau. of Dr. Robert Edgar Williams and wife, Valeria Virginia Kearney, dau. of William Kinchen Kearney and wife, Maria Alston.

Dr. Bennett Perry Alston was educated at the Medical College of the University of Maryland, Class 1868, and practiced his profession in Vance Co., N. C. Dr. Bennett Perry Alston left school and enlisted in Junior Reserves Confederate Army early in 1863, at the age of 17. Having his own horse, he served as Courier first for General Bryan Grimes, later transferred to General Lee's Army in Virginia. He was at the surrender at Appomattox.

Children of Dr. Bennett Perry Alston and wife, Caroline Matilda Williams:

I. Valeria Virginia Alston, b. 1/5/1879, m. Robert Lee Bell, no issue.
II. Bennett Perry Alston, Jr., b. 2/17/1881, d.s.p.
III. Walter James Alston, b. 6/11/1883, m. Myrtle Ruth White. (See later)
IV. Carrie M. Alston, b. 6/30/1885, unmarried.
V. Pattie Boddie Alston, b. 12/10/1886, m. George Wilson Macon.
VI. Emma Jones Alston, b. 12/3/1888, m. William Gary Anderson, no issue.
VII. Bessie Lee Alston, b. 2/6/1895, unmarried.
VIII. Margaret Perkins Alston, b. 2/20/1900, unmarried.

Walter James Alston, son of Dr. Bennett Perry Alston and wife, Caroline Matilda Williams, b. 6/11/1883, m. at Bolivar, Tenn., 12/28/1920, Myrtle Ruth White, b. 10/29/ 1893, and d. at Henderson, N. C., 12/18/1942.

Mr. Alston is a large land owner in Franklin and Vance Counties, N. C., and with his son, operates Tobacco Auction Warehouses in Henderson, N. C.

Children of Walter James Alston and wife, Myrtle Ruth White, born at Henderson, N. C.:

I. Walter James Alston, Jr., b. 11/15/1925, m. 8/6/1948, Nancy Kathryn Fulton, b. 10/10/1926, dau. of George Henry Fulton and wife, Mamie Clyde Snow of Elkin, N. C. Walter James Alston, Jr., was educated at Woodberry Forest and the University of N. C., residence, Cypress Drive, Henderson, N. C.

Issue:
1. Jean White Alston, b. 4/6/1952.
II.   Myrtle White Alston, b. 2/14/1929, m. at Henderson, N. C., 6/22/1949, John Chilton Mott, b.
1/20/1921, son of Burke Wylie Mott and wife,
Ethyl May Pitt of Norfolk, Virginia. John Chilton Mott was educated at the University of Va.,
and Virginia Theological School at Alexandria,
Va. He is now Rector of Holy Trinity Episcopal
Church, Greensboro, N. C. Mrs. Mott was educated at St. Mary's School, Raleigh, N. C., and
Sweet Briar College.
Issue:
1. Mary Chilton Mott, b. 5/3/1950, d. 3/30/1953.
2. Elizabeth Lee Alston Mott, b. 2/29/1952.
3. Margaret Chilton Mott, b. 2/8/1954.

Archibald Davis Alston, son of Elizabeth Crafford
(Davis) and Nicholas Faulcon Alston, b. at "Cleveland",
Warren Co., N. C., 6/11/1817, d. at "Saxham Hall", Warren
Co., N. C., 5/4/1899, m. at "Butterwood", Halifax Co.,
N. C., 3/3/1842, Missouri Florida Alston, b. 11/2/1824, at
"Butterwood", and d. at "Saxham Hall", 2/2/1868, dau. of
(Congress) Willis Alston, II, and wife, Sarah Madiline
Potts of "Butterwood", Halifax County, N. C.

Archibald Davis Alston was educated at Hampden & Sid-
ney College and the University of N. C.
Children born at "Saxham Hall", Warren Co., N.C.:
I.   Elizabeth Ada Alston, d.s.p.
II.   Sallie Potts Alston, d.s.p.
III.   Charles Julias Alston, d.s.p.
IV.   Elizabeth Crafford Alston, d.s.p.
V.   Ella Ann Alston, d.s.p.
VI.   Archibald Davis Alston, d.s.p.
VII.   Nicholas Faulcon Alston, d.s.p.
VIII.   Willis Walter Alston, d.s.p.
IX.   Sallie Madiline Alston, d.s.p.
X.   Edward Alston, d.s.p.
XI.   William Thorne Alston, m. Caroline Thorpe. (See
later)
XII.   Frank Alston, d.s.p.
XIII.   Missouri Florida Alston, m. William Henry
Pleasants of Louisburg, N. C., no issue.

William Thorne Alston, son of Archibald Davis Alston
and his wife, Missouri Florida Alston, b. at "Saxham Hall",
Warren Co., N. C., 10/7/1862, and d. at Warrenton, N. C.,
4/29/1923, m. at Oxford, N. C., 10/20/1886, Caroline
Thorpe, b. 8/8/1857, d. 3/31/1929, dau. of Benjamin Thorpe
and wife, Anna Elizah Norman of Oxford, N. C.

Children:
I.   Archibald Davis Alston, III, b. 8/4/1893, m.
Pattie Southerland, b. 12/10/1906, dau. of Solon
Southerland.
Issue:
1. William Edward Alston, b. 11/22/1930.
2. Patricia Alston, b. 1/21/1936.
II.   Willis Faulcon Alston, b. 1/24/1896, m. Julia
Elam.
III.   Benjamin Thorpe Alston, b. 12/6/1897, d. unmar-
ried, 6/22/1926.

The third child of Archibald Davis and his wife,
Elizabeth Hilliard was named after his mother, Hartwell
(Hodges) Davis. "Harty Hodge" was a diminutive used in
family circles for the original Hartwell Hodges and for
those named after her.

Harty Hodge Davis, dau. of Elizabeth (Hilliard) and
Archibald Davis, b. at "Columbia Farm", Franklin Co., N.C.,
4/27/1793, and d. ca. 1870, while on a visit to her sister
Martha Hilliard Davis, wife of Edward Alston of Warren Co.,
N. C. She m. 10/10/1812, Robert Webb Williams, b. 2/27/
1792, d. at "Vine Hill", Franklin Co., N. C., 11/1/1822,
son of Major William Williams and his second wife, Eliza-
beth (Betsy) Kearney.
Children:
I.   Elizabeth Ann Williams, b. 12/27/1813, m. James
Yarborough and had issue:
1. Robert Yarborough.
2. Ruina Yarborough.
3. James Yarborough.
II.   Ruina Temperance Williams, b. 12/3/1814, m. Sam-
uel Thomas Alston. (See later)
III.   Robert Edgar Williams, b. 9/16/1817, m. Valeria
Virginia Kearney. (See later)
IV.   Martha Harriet Williams, b. 2/18/1819, m. Ben-
jamin Thorne Ballard. (See later)
V.   Archibald Davis Williams, b. 1/5/1821, m. Lucy
Ann Lewis.

Ruina Temperance Williams, b. 12/3/1814, dau. of Harty
Hodge (Davis) and Robert Webb Williams, m. 9/1/1831, Sam-
uel Thomas Alston, b. 10/5/1806, son of Samuel Alston and
wife, Elizabeth, dau. of Nicholas Faulcon and wife, Lucy
Wyatt.
Children:
I.   Edward Faulcon Alston, b. 9/1/1833, m. Ellen
Hendrix, no issue.
II.   Samuel Thomas Alston, Jr., killed in C.S.A.
III.   Caroline Medora Alston, m. William Kearney

Alston Williams, son of Lewis Alston Williams
and wife, Priscilla Kearney.

IV. Robert Williams Alston (Maj. C.S.A.), m. Martha
Davis, dau. of John Calvin Davis and wife, Lucy
Faulcon Alston.

V. Solomon Williams Alston (Surgeon C.S.A.) d. in
Army.

VI. John Davis Alston, b. 9/3/1841 (C.S.A.), m. Tempie Davis, dau. of Dr. Thomas Davis and his
second wife, Martha E. Batchelor.

VII. Philip Guston Alston (Capt. C.S.A.), m. Elizabeth
Williams, dau. of Capt. Archibald Davis Williams
and wife, Lucy Ann Lewis.

VIII. Susan Luella Alston, b. 10/23/1845, m. Lewis
Alston Thompson, son of Thomas Bond Thompson and
wife, Tempie Maria Williams.

IX. Elizabeth Faulcon Alston, m. George W. Alston,
Jr., son of George W. Alston and wife, Marina
Williams, dau. of Maj. William Williams.

X. Ruina Temperance Alston, b. 1851, m. Philip Kearney Williams, son of Solomon Williams and wife,
Maria Alston Kearney.

Dr. Robert Edgar Williams, son of Harty Hodge (Davis)
and Robert Webb Williams was b. at "Vine Hill", Franklin
Co., N. C., 9/16/1817, and d. at "Myrtle Lawn", Warren
Co., N. C., 11/4/1904, m. 10/20/1841, Valeria Virginia
Kearney, b. 12/7/18__, d. Nov., 1907, dau. of William Kin-
chen Kearney and wife, Maria Alston.

Children:

I. Emma Placidia Williams, b. 7/20/1842, m. 5/8/
1866, Joseph John Jones of Warren Co., N. C.

II. Charles Sydenham Williams, (1844-1854).

III. Whitmel Kearney Williams, b. 2/2/1848, d. 9/21/
1921, m. Lucy H. Davis, dau. of Archibald Hilliard Davis and wife, Charlotte Harris.

Children:

1. Charles Sydenham Williams, b. 4/24/1895, at
"Myrtle Lawn", Warren Co., N. C., m. 8/24/
1918, at Springfield, Ky., Louise Lee Thompson.

Children:

(1) Susan Whitmel Williams, b. 10/24/1920,
m. 11/24/1938, Norvin Wilford Fenster.
Child: Robert Lee Fenster, b.7/8/1947.

(2) Lucy Davis Williams, b. 9/10/1922, m.
8/9/1942, Paul E. Potter. Child: Paula
Virginia Potter, b. 5/22/1946.

(3) Charles Sydenham Williams, Jr., b.

7/13/1925, m. 11/27/1947, Doris
Marie Weise. Child: Katherine
Diann Williams, b. 9/26/1951.
(4) James Lee Williams, b. 6/30/1929,
m. 8/21/1954, Wilma Frances Pickett.
(5) Mary Ann Williams, (1931-1932).
(6) Judith Ann Williams, b. 11/13/1933,
m. 6/14/1952, William D. Patterson,
residence, Louisville, Kentucky.

2. Oscar Davis Williams, m. Cora Burns.
IV. Mary Boyd Williams (1846-1854).
V. Nicholas Alston Williams, b. 1/14/1850, m. Mary
Ellis Boyce.
VI. William Kearney Williams, b. 3/9/1852, m. Nida
Smith.
VII. Caroline Matilda Williams, b. 6/20/1854, m. Dr.
Bennett Perry Alston.
VIII. Laura Eaton Williams, b. 6/28/1856, m. James
Wesley Jones of Franklin Co., N. C.
IX. Robert Edgar Williams, Jr., b. 8/18/1858, m.
Charlotte Elizabeth Davis, dau. of Archibald
Hilliard Davis and wife, Charlotte Harris.
Children:
1. Robert Edgar Williams, III, dentist in Golds-
boro, N. C.
2. Estelle Williams, m. Irwin Lipscomb.
3. Frederick Williams, m. (1) Alma Scull and
(2) Mabel Hayes. Lives at "Myrtle Lawn",
Warren Co., N. C.
X. James Yarborough Williams, b. 1/4/1861, m. Lillie
Harden Jones.
XI. Mary Alston Williams, b. 1/12/1864, d. 8/21/1864.
XII. Valeria Virginia (Minna) Williams, b. 1/12/1864,
(twin sister of Mary Alston Williams), d. 9/11/
1904, m. 1/24/1894, Robert Southerland.
Children:
1. Robert Edgar Southerland, b. 6/14/1895, m.
Mary Alston.
2. Charlotte Anne Southerland, b. 9/14/1897, at
"Milford", Vance Co., N. C., m. 7/23/1921,
Hubert Olive, b. 8/25/1895, Randleman Ran-
dolph Co., N. C., son of Andrew Jackson
Olive and wife, Emma Beckwith. Mr. Olive was
educated at Wake Forest College. He is past
Commander of the N. C. Department American
Legion. He was appointed in June of 1955, by
Governor Luther H. Hodges, Judge of Superior
Court for his District. He resigned as Judge

          of Superior Court in 1952. Mrs. Olive was
educated at Peace Junior College, Raleigh,
N. C., residence, Lexington, N. C.
Children:
(1) Valerie Virginia Olive, b. 4/7/1924, m.
    Lewis Hartzog.
(2) Hubert E. Olive, Jr., b. 1/1/1929.
(3) Charlotte Anne Olive, b. 4/6/1939.

3. Joseph Lewis Southerland, b. 3/7/1899, m.
Mattie Belle Alston.
4. William Kearney Southerland, b. 4/13/1901,
m. Rosa Mae Stokes.
5. Nicholas Whitmel Southerland, b. 12/28/1902,
m. Lydia Culp.

XIII.   Lee Davis Williams, b. 5/20/1866, d. 11/21/1940,
unmarried.

    Martha Harriet Williams, dau. of Harty Hodge (Davis)
and Robert Webb Williams, b. at "Vine Hill", Franklin Co.,
N. C., 2/18/1819, and d. at "Rocky Hill", Franklin Co.,
N. C., 11/6/1873, m. at "Vine Hill", 2/15/1835, Benjamin
Thorne Ballard, b. 11/28/1813, d. at "Rocky Hill", 2/19/
1894, son of Dr. Benjamin Ballard and wife, Eliza Thorne.
Children:

I.   Walter Ballard (1837-1838).
II.   Robert Edgar Ballard (1839-1893), m. Sarah Agnes
Branch, (1847-1891), dau. of Washington Branch
and wife, Martha Ann Lewis. Lived in Warren Co.,
N. C.
Children:
1. Branch Ballard, (1872-1922), m. 1918, Ellen
Hayes. No issue.
2. William Henry Ballard, (1874-1894), d.s.p.
3. Anna Williams Ballard (1876- ____), m. 1903,
Samuel Williams Alston.
4. Edgar Agnes Ballard, b. 1878, m. 1899, Mack
Lee Bradley.
5. Eliza Hodges Ballard, b. 1880, m. 1920, Lawrence McDonald.
6. Nicholas Massenburg Ballard,(1882-1939), m.
1910, Maude Doyle.
7. Robert Edgar Ballard, (1885-1931), m. (1)
1908, Laura Walker, m. (2) 1918, Esther Fry.
8. Lewis Lenir Ballard, (1886-1916).
9. Van Alston Ballard, b. 1888, m. Annie Hines.
III.   William Henry Ballard, (1841-1888), m. 1869,
Elizabeth Ann Green, (1852-1926), dau. of William
Willis Green and wife, Mary Perry.
Children:

1. Mary Lavina Ballard, b. 1871, m. 1897, Alexander Henderson Cary.
2. Benjamin Thorne Ballard, (1873-1903),d.s.p.
3. Laura Burwell Ballard, (1876-1950), m. (1) 1902, Charles Macgill, d. 1910, m. (2) Erwin Allen Holt, no issue.
   Children:
   (1) Charles Richard Macgill, m. 5/24/1930, Frances Mabbett Barrow, b. 1/1/1902, dau. of Martha Ruina (Ballard) and Joseph James Barrow. Child: Charles Richard Macgill, Jr., b. 8/27/1931, educated Episcopal High School, Alexandria, Va., and University of N. C., class, 1953.
   (2) Mollie Macgill, m. Gene Hallford.
4. Elizabeth Ballard, b. 1877, m. 1904, Charles Henry Blacknall. Child: Charles Henry Blacknall.
5. William Green Ballard, (1879-1930), m. 1907, Helen Reid.
6. Wiley Perry Ballard, b. 1881, m. 1921, Helen McCary.
7. Robert Williams Ballard, b. 1883, m. Cora Childress.
8. Victor Hugo Ballard, b. 1885, m. 1913,Bessie Withers.

IV. Junius Ballard, (1843-1870), m. 1865, Laura Burwell, dau. of Blair Burwell and wife, Mary Eliza Davis, child: Junius Ballard, b. 1870.
V.   Benjamin Ballard, (1845-1846).
VI. Eugene Ballard, (1847-1848).
VII. Frank Ballard, (1849-1932), m. 1880, Louisa Mabbette Clark, (1851-1904), dau. of Gen. David Clark and wife, Anna Maria Thorne, child: David Clark Ballard, b. 1882, m. 1911, Bessie May Conley.
VIII. Eliza Hodges Ballard, (1851-1931), m. 1872,Hugh Davis Egerton, (1849-1929).
   Children:
   1. Martha Ballard Egerton, b. 1873, m. William Kearney Alston Williams.
   2. Mary Gray Egerton, (1875-1877).
   3. Charles Sidney Egerton, b. 1877, unmarried.
   4. Laura Burwell Egerton, b. 1880, m. Joseph Bromfield Jones.
   5. Benjamin Ballard Egerton, b. 1882, m. Elizabeth M. Hines.
   6. Hugh Wilmot Egerton, (1883-1930), m. Florence

White.
7. George Blount Egerton, b. 1885, m. 1906,
Mary Elizabeth Macon.
8. Robert Edgar Egerton, b. 1888, m. Annie Bell
Alston.
9. Walter Eugene Egerton, b. 1889, m. 1924,
Florence Hartley Trundle.
10. Junius Nicholas Egerton, b. 1892, m. 1914,
Lucy E.Daniel.
IX.   Benjamin Walter Ballard, (1854-1927), m. 1876,
William Eleanor Parker, (1856-1940), dau. of
Jacob Parker and wife, Elizabeth Kinchen Kearney.
Children:
1. Bettie Eleanor Ballard, b. 1877, m. 1905,
William Furnifold Joyner.
2. Walter Junius Ballard, (1878-1930),d.s.p.
3. Martha Harriet Ballard, b. 1881, m. 1916,
Dr. Richard Fenner Yarborough of Louisburg,
N. C.
4. Kate Averitt Ballard, b. 1882, unmarried.
5. Nena Parker Ballard, (1884-1918), m. 1909,
James Bullock Cheatham.
X.   Nicholas Massenburg Ballard, (1857-1930), d.s.p.
XI.   Martha Ruina Ballard, (1863-1953), m. 1890,
James Joseph Barrow. (See later)
     Martha Ruina Ballard, dau. of Martha Harriet (Wil-
liams) and Benjamin Thorne Ballard, b. at "Rocky Hill",
Franklin Co., N. C., 5/13/1863, d. at "Alston Farm",Frank-
lin Co., N. C., 5/31/1953, m. at Louisburg, N. C., 9/24/
1890, Joseph James Barrow, b. at Louisburg, N. C., 11/9/
1860, and d. there 7/7/1925, son of Jordan S. Barrow.
Joseph James Barrow was Clerk of Court for Franklin Co.,
N. C., 22 years, 1901-1923.
Children:
I.   William Ballard Barrow, b. 7/8/1891, at Louis-
burg, N. C., and d. there 8/30/1944, m. at
Louisburg, N. C., 11/29/1915, Mamie Elizabeth
Jones, b. 2/5/1888, d. 1/10/1952.
Children:
1. William Ballard Barrow, Jr., b. 9/30/1921,
graduated U.S. Naval Academy, Annapolis,
Maryland, June, 1943, m. 8/6/1946, Mary Wil-
ton, dau. of William Ogden Wilton.
2. Joseph James Barrow, b. 3/14/1925,graduated
U.S. Naval Academy, June, 1949, m. 5/2/1953,
in Christ Church, Raleigh, N. C., Cecile
Meetze Bickett, dau. of William Yarborough
Bickett and wife, Cecile Meetze, of Raleigh,

N. C., child: Joseph James Barrow.

II.   Julia Elizabeth Barrow, b. 1/1/1896, m. (1) Dr.
F. O. Swindell, no issue, and (2) 8/4/1923, Nor-
man Yates Chambliss, b. 5/17/1891, son of William
H. Chambliss and wife, Leonora Mallory of Empor-
ia, Virginia.
Children:

1. Norman Yates Chambliss, Jr., b. 2/17/1925,
m. at Louisburg, N. C., 9/3/1947, Frances
Ann Earle, b. 1/5/1925, dau. of James Roches-
ter Earle and wife, Rochelle Greene Gulley
of Louisburg, N. C.
Norman Yates Chambliss, Jr., was educated at
Louisburg College and N. C. State College,
Raleigh, N. C., vol. to A.F., 6/10/1943,
classified Pilot, Dec., 1943, Preflight
school, Maxwell Field, Ala., Dec., 1943/44,
primary flying school, Douglas, Ga., March
& May, 1944. Basic Flying School, June &
Aug., 1944, Advance Flying School, Sept. &
Nov., 1944. Graduated and received Wings
and Commission, Nov., 1944, Tyndall Field,
Fla., 1st Lt. A.F. Reserve.
Children:
(1) Martha Ballard Chambliss, b. 7/21/1948.
(2) Norman Yates Chambliss III, b. 8/28/1951.
(3) Rochelle Earle Chambliss, b. 9/6/1953.
Residence: 611 Evergreen Rd., Rocky Mount,
N. C.

2. Joseph Barrow Chambliss, b. 5/31/1929, m.
11/15/1952, at Schenectady, N. Y., Betty
Frances Halve, b. 10/27/1929, at Waco, Texas,
dau. of Max Halve and wife, Helen Frances
Glab of Waco, Texas. Joseph Barrow Chambliss
left College (University of N. C.) and
enlisted at Raleigh, N. C., 1/15/1951,
U.S.A.F., assigned to Basic training, Lack-
land A.F.B., San Antonio, Texas. Assigned
Pope A.F.B., Fort Bragg, N. C., to Staff
Judge Advocate Office Hdqs., with A.F. as
legal clerk, promoted to Cpl., 9/1/1951, Sgt.
3/1/1952. Assigned and reported to Aviation
Cadet Training - Radar Observer School, 5/5
1952, James Connally, A.F.B., Waco, Texas.
Graduated Radar Observer, 11/1/1952. Commissioned 2nd. Lt. in A.F.R., and same date,
assigned 65th Fighter Intercept Sqdn., Elmen-
dorf A.F.B., Alaska. Promoted to 1st. Lt.

> 5/1/1954. Child: Joseph Barrow Chambliss,
> Jr., b. 8/29/1954.
>
> 3. Mallory Lewis Chambliss, b. 1/27/1935, stu-
>   dent, University of N. C.

III. Frances Mabbette Barrow, b. 1/1/1902, m. 5/24/
1930, Charles Richard Macgill, son of Laura
Burwell (Ballard) and Charles Richard Macgill.
Child: Charles Richard Macgill, b. 8/27/1931.

Archibald Hilliard Davis, son of Elizabeth (Hilliard)
and Archibald Davis, b. 7/3/1799, at "Columbia Farm",
Franklin Co., N. C., and d. 11/18/1854, at "Cypress Hall",
Franklin Co., N. C. He m. (1) Lucy Massenburg, no issue,
and (2) Caroline Cornelia Kearney, b. 10/8/1820, dau. of
William Kinchen Kearney and wife, Maria Alston.
Children:

I. William Kearney Davis, b. 10/8/1838, m. Mary
Jones, no issue.

II. Thomas Whitmel Davis, b. 8/7/1840, m. Penelope
Smith Jones.

III. John Edward Davis, d.s.p.

IV. Maria Alston Davis, b. 11/3/1843, m. Edward
Alston, Jr., son of Martha Hilliard (Davis) and
Edward Alston, Sr.

V. Elizabeth Hilliard Davis, m. Richard W. Respass.

VI. Lucy Massenburg Davis, b. 2/7/1847, d. 1873, m.
Col. William Henry Yarborough, b. 3/1/1840, d.
8/3/1914, of Franklin Co., N. C.
Children:

1. Fanny Neal Yarborough, b. 10/11/1870, d.
7/2/1941, m. at Louisburg, N. C., 11/29/1898,
Thomas Walter Bickett, b. 2/28/1869, d. at
Raleigh, N. C., 12/27/1921, son of Thomas
Winchester Bickett and wife, Mary Cobington
of Monroe, N. C.; A.B. Degree from Wake
Forest College, 1890; B.L. Degree, University of N. C., 1893. Two years later, he
settled in Louisburg, N. C.; Attorney General
of N. C., 1907/1915; Governor of N. C. 1917/
1921.
Issue:

(1) William Yarborough Bickett, b. 8/30/1899;
Prosecuting Officer, 7th Judicial Dis-
trict; now Judge of Superior Court, 7th
Judicial District. He m. 11/18/1925,
Cecile Meetze, b. 12/18/1902, of Lexing-
ton, S. C.
Children:

a. Fanny Yarborough Bickett, b. 5/19/1927.

        b. Cecile Meetze Bickett, b. 5/19/1931,
          m. 5/2/1953, Joseph James Barrow.
        c. Caroline (Bill) Pinckney Bickett, b.
          2/11/1936.
        Residence: Raleigh, N. C.
    2. Richard Fenner Yarborough, M.D., b. 3/21/
        1872, d. at Louisburg, N. C., 6/22/1944, m.
        Martha Harriet Ballard, dau. of Benjamin
        Walter Ballard and wife, William Eleanor
        Parker, dau. of Jacob Parker and wife, Eliza-
        beth Kinchen Kearney.
        Children:
        (1) Richard Fenner Yarborough, graduated
            U.S. Naval Academy, m. Evelyn Peele, no
            issue.
        (2) Martha Harriet Ballard Yarborough.
VII.   Alston Davis, d.s.p.
VIII.   Martha Matilda Davis, d.s.p.
 IX.   Rebecca Brehon Davis, b. 2/27/1853, d. at
        Raleigh, N. C. M. in 1877, Hon. Marmaduke James
        Hawkins (1850-1920), graduated University of
        Virginia; atty., and partner of Gov. Bickett,
        of N. C.; State Senator, 1909, son of William J.
        Hawkins, M.D., and wife, Mary Alethea Clark of
        Warren Co., N. C., and Raleigh, N. C.
        Children:
    1. Lula Davis Hawkins, (1879-1904), m. Joel
        Whitaker, M.D., of Raleigh, N. C., no issue.
    2. Mary Alethea Hawkins, (1880-1883).
    3. Weldon Edwards Hawkins, (1881-1939), m. Mrs.
        Dorothy (Pugh) Stanley.
    4. Janet McKenzie Hawkins, (1883-1909), m.1906,
        Milo Pendleton, (1881-1911). Child: Kath-
        erine Clark Pendleton, b. 9/6/1909, m..Wil-
        liam Conway, no issue.
    5. Marmaduke James Hawkins, (1890-1942), m. (1)
        1914, Martha Bryan Parker, m. (2) 1938,
        Frona Opal Dinkins.
    Thomas Whitmel Davis, son of Archibald Hilliard Davis
and wife, Caroline Cornelia Kearney, b. 8/7/1840, at "Cypress Hall", Franklin Co., N. C., and d. at Raleigh, N. C.,
12/24/1927. He m. 12/23/1863, at "Crabtree", Wake Co.,
N. C., Penelope Smith Jones, b. 6/8/1846, d. 11/20/1919,
dau. of Kimbrough Jones and wife, Mary Webb Warren of
"Crabtree", Wake Co., N. C.
        Children:
   I.   Mary Warren Davis, m. 6/6/1903, Erwin Allen Holt
        of Burlington, N. C., no issue, son of Lawrence

Shackelford Holt and wife, Margaret Locke Erwin
of "Bellevue", Burke Co., N. C.

II. Archibald Hilliard Davis, Commander U.S.N., b.
9/22/1866, d. at Washington, D. C., 9/19/1934,
educated at Bingham School, near Mebane, N. C.,
and graduated U.S. Naval Academy, Annapolis,
Maryland, 1887, m. 11/20/1907, Emily Marion Colton.
Children:
1. Archibald Hilliard Davis, (1908-1908).
2. Emily Colton Davis, b. 6/5/1918, m. Joseph
D. Croll.

III. Cornelia Kearney Davis, b. 3/16/1868, m. Robert
Spencer Plummber, no issue.

IV. Kimbrough Jones Davis, b. 10/28/1869, unmarried.

V. Pattie Jones Davis, b. 7/8/1871, m. LeRoy Jackson of Mapleville, Franklin Co., N. C.
Children:
1. Elizabeth Ridie Jackson, b. 11/20/1902, m.
Dr. David Coles Wilson.
Children:
(1) Mary Frances Wilson.
(2) David Coles Wilson, Jr.
(3) Elizabeth Wilson.
(4) Patricia Wilson.
2. Frank Borden Jackson, b. 5/15/1907, m.
11/28/1934, Mildred Stiles of Whiteville,
N. C.

VI. William Kearney Davis, b. 2/22/1872, m. Florence
McAlister, no issue.

VII. Thomas Whitmel Davis, b. 11/10/1876, m. Frances
Conrad.

VIII. Penelope Jones Davis, b. 3/14/1878, m. Robert
Spencer Plummer, as his second wife, no issue.

IX. John Neal Davis, twin, b. 8/3/1879, d.s.p.

X. Henry Jones Davis, twin, b. 8/3/1879, d.s.p.

XI. Maria Alston Davis, b. 3/13/1883, d.s.p.

XII. Lula Yarborough Davis, b. 3/22/1885, d.s.p.

Dr. Thomas Whitmel Davis, son of Thomas Whitmel Davis
and wife, Penelope Smith Jones, b. 11/10/1876, at "Cypress
Hall", Franklin Co., N. C., m. 6/8/1904, in Winston-Salem,
N. C., Frances Conrad. Residence: Winston-Salem, N. C.
Children:
I. John Conrad Davis, b. 4/6/1905, m. 2/25/1936,
Mildred Boyd, of Richmond, Va.
Children:
1. Mildred Boyd Davis, b. 10/8/1938.
2. John Conrad Davis, Jr., b. 10/8/1940.

II. Thomas Whitmel Davis, III, b. Feb., 1908, m.
4/8/1931, Sarah Sutton, of Richlands, N. C.
Child:
1. Mollie Conner Davis, b. 2/18/1932.

III. Archibald Kimbrough Davis, b. 1/22/1911, m.
5/12/1938, Mary Louise Haywood, dau. of Thomas
Holt Haywood and wife, Louise Bonson of Winston-
Salem, N. C.

IV. William Kearney Davis, b. 8/6/1916, m. 9/20/1940,
Helen Gilmer Dickson.

 Martha Hilliard Davis, dau. of Elizabeth (Hilliard)
and Archibald Davis, b. at "Columbia Farm", Franklin Co.,
N. C., 2/22/1801, d. in Warren Co., N. C., 5/16/1876, m.
Edward Alston, b. 12/8/1797, in Warren Co., N. C., and d.
there 2/12/1856, son of Thomas Whitmel Alston and wife,
Lucy Faulcon, dau. of Nicholas Faulcon of Surry Co., Va.,
and wife, Lucy Wyatt.
 Children:

I. William Thorne Alston, m. Laura Eaton, dau. of
Hon. William Eaton, no issue.

II. Elizabeth Alston, d.s.p.

III. Nicholas Faulcon Alston, d.s.p.

IV. Alfred Alston, m. Mary (Polly) Dawson Kearney.

V. Edward Alston, Jr., m. Maria Alston Davis.

VI. Mary Davis Alston, d.s.p.

 Alfred Alston, son of Martha Hilliard (Davis) and
Edward Alston, b. 12/28/1826, d. 4/8/1894, m. 4/20/1853,
Mary (Polly) Dawson Kearney, b. 11/22/1834, d. 6/14/1910,
at Warrenton, N. C., dau. of William Kinchen Kearney and
wife, Benj. Hardee James Maria Alston.
 Children:

I. Edward Alston, (1854-1858).

II. William Thorne Alston, (1855-1858).

III. Maria Alston, (1857-1945), d.s.p.

IV. Martha Edward Alston, m. Buxton Boddie Williams,
son of John Buxton Williams and wife, Mary Temperance Hilliard, dau. of James and Mourning
(Boddie) Hilliard of Hilliardston, Nash Co.,
N. C.

V. Nicholas Faulcon Alston, (1862-1937), d.s.p.

VI. Laura Eaton Alston, (1864-1945), d.s.p.

VII. Herbert Alston, b. 4/18/1869, m. Lily Arrington.

VIII. Van Dawson Alston, b. 6/22/1872, m. Grace Virginia Jackson.

 Edward Alston, Jr., son of Martha Hilliard (Davis)
and Edward Alston, m. Maria Alston Davis, b. 11/3/1843, dau.
of Archibald Hilliard Davis and wife, Caroline Cornelia
Kearney of "Cypress Hall", Franklin Co., N. C.

Children:
I.   Cornelia Kearney Alston, m. Frank Howe Cheatham.
     Child:
     1. Frances Howe Cheatham, b. 11/30/1896, m.
        9/17/1919, James Allison Cooper of Henderson,
        N. C., b. 3/17/1894, son of David Young
        Cooper and wife, Leah Hilliard Perry of Hen-
        derson, N. C.
        Child:
        (1) David Young Cooper, M.D., b. 8/14/1924,
           (Lt. U.S.N.R.)
II.   Edward Alston, III, d.s.p.
    Mary Kearney Davis, dau. of Elizabeth (Hilliard) and
Archibald Davis, b. at "Columbia Farm", Franklin Co., N.C.,
12/13/1802, and d. in Warren Co., N. C., 2/27/1887, m.
1/31/1820, Joseph John Williams, III, son of Joseph John
Williams, Jr., and wife, Elizabeth Norfleet Hunter Williams,
dau. of Elisha Williams, of Roanoke who m. Sarah Josie.
Joseph John Williams, Jr., son of Col. Joseph John Williams,
youngest son of Samuel Williams and wife, Elizabeth Alston,
dau. of John Alston of England.
     Children:
I.   Joseph John Williams, IV, d. unmarried while in
     college.
II.   Dr. Thomas Calvin Williams, m. Virginia Pryor
     Boyd.
III.   Mary Elizabeth Williams, m. Dr. Peter B. Hawkins.
     Children:
     1. Lucy Williams Hawkins, d.s.p.
     2. Mary Hawkins, d.s.p.
     3. Elizabeth Hawkins, d.s.p.
     4. Rufus Hawkins, d.s.p.
     5. Thomas Hawkins, m. Sallie Vaughan of Mur-
        freesboro, N. C., lived at Charlotte, N. C.
        Children:
        (1) Rosa Hawkins, unmarried.
        (2) Vaughan Hawkins, m. and has one son,
           Vaughan Hawkins, Jr.
        (3) Thomas Williams Hawkins, m. Mrs. Mary
           Lineberger Wilson, widow.
           Children:
           a. Thomas Williams Hawkins, Jr.
           b. Martha Vaughan Hawkins.
        (4) Sarah Alice Hawkins, unmarried.
IV.   Lucy Eugenia Williams, m. Col. William Polk of
     Columbia, Tenn. (brother of President James K.
     Polk).
    Lucy Eugenia Williams, dau. of Mary Kearney (Davis)

and Joseph John Williams, III, b. at "Montmorenci", Warren Co., N. C., 10/10/1826, d. 1/11/1906, m. 7/14/1854, Col. William H. Polk of Columbia, Tenn., b. 5/24/1815, d. 12/15 /1862.

Children:

I.   William H. Polk, Jr., m. Miss Marable, and d. without issue.

II.   Tasker Polk, m. Eliza Tannahill Jones of Warren Co., N. C.

Tasker Polk, son of Lucy Eugenia (Williams) and Col. William H. Polk, b. 3/24/1861, at Columbia, Tenn., and d. at Warrenton, N. C., 7/5/1928. He m. at Warrenton, N. C., 1/24/1895, Eliza Tannahill Jones, b. 3/4/1869, d. 10/16/ 1939, dau. of Charles Johnston Jones and wife, Alice Harvey Tannahill of Warren Co., N. C.

Children:

I.   William Tannahill Polk, b. at Warrenton, N. C., 3/12/1896, m. 6/30/1931, Marion Campbell Gunn.
       Children:
       1. Marion Knox Polk, b. 7/30/1932.
       2. Katherine Ross Polk, b. 12/4/1939.
       Mr. Polk is Associate Editor of the Greensboro Daily News, author of "Southern Accent" and many short story articles. Residence: Greensboro, N. C.

II.   Mary Tasker Polk, b. at Warrenton, N. C., 12/15/ ___, m. 1921, Francis Herbert Gibbs, atty. of Warrenton, N. C.
       Children:
       1. Alice Harvey Gibbs, b. 1/21/1923, d. 10/19/ 1928.
       2. Mary Tasker Polk Gibbs, b. 10/11/1929, m. 2/6/1954, Barnaby Warren MacAuslan of Providence, R. I.
       3. Francis Herbert Gibbs, Jr., b. 4/9/1934, student U.N.C.

Lucy Fairfax Polk, b. at Warrenton, N. C., 12/2/1902, m. 9/6/1921, John G. Mitchell of Warrenton, N. C.

Child:

I.   Lucy Fairfax Polk Mitchell, b. 6/5/1927, m. 6/5/1954, Dr. James G. Lyerly, Jr., of Jacksonville, Fla., son of Dr. James G. Lyerly and wife, Emily McIlwaine of Prince George Co., Va.

James Knox Polk, b. at Warrenton, N. C., 5/4/1905, m. 7/27/1940, Anne Hunter Fishel, of Vaughan, Warren Co., N.C.

Children:

I.   Tasker Polk, b. 6/26/1941.
II.   Anne Knox Polk, b. 6/3/1946.

Temperance Williams Davis, dau. of Elizabeth (Hilliard) and Archibald Davis, b. at "Columbia Farm", Franklin Co., N. C., 9/26/1804, d. at "Prospect Hill", Halifax Co., N. C., 8/6/1854, m. in 1820, William Williams Thorne, (1798-1838), son of Dr. Samuel Thorne, (1767-1838), and wife, Mrs. Martha (Whitmell-Williams) Hill, (1771-1827), dau. of Col. Joseph John Williams and Elizabeth Alston, dau. of Maj. Philip Alston and Winifred Whitmell.

Children:

I. Martha Elizabeth Thorne, (1821-1897), m. 1839, Thomas Willis Nicholson, (1816-1884).

II. William Henry Thorne, (1822-1895), m. 1856, Martha Jane Alston, (1836-1888) dau. of Maj. Alfred Alston and Mary Ann Plummer.

III. Anna Maria Thorne, (1824-1899), m. 1845, Gen. David Clark, (1820-1882), lived at "Airlie" near Littleton in Halifax Co., N. C. Gen. David Clark, son of David Clark, (1772-1829) and wife, Louise Norfleet, (1789-1828), dau. of Marmaduke Norfleet and Hannah Ruffin, dau. of William Ruffin and Sarah Hill.

IV. Mary Eliza Mabbett Thorne, (1825-1872), m.1848, Kemp Plummer Alston, (1820-188_) of Warren Co., N. C.

V. Samuel Thomas Thorne, (1827-1921), m. 1872,Mary Whitmell Harriss, (1848-1933), dau. of Thomas Whitmell Harriss and Martha Helen Kearney.

VI. Dr. Edward Alston Thorne, (1828-1911), m. 1852, Alice Maria Harriss, (1834-1907), dau. of Thomas Whitmell Harriss and Martha Helen Kearney.

VII. Lucy Emily Thorne, (1831-1910), m. 1852, Blake Baker Nicholson, (1828-1910), lived in Halifax Co., N. C.

VIII. Archibald Davis Thorne, (1833-   ).

IX. John Davis Thorne, (1834-1900), m. 1865, Kate Mumford Thompson, (1848-1927), dau. of Samuel Thompson and Addeline Spicer. (Lived at St. Martinsville, St. Martin Parish, Louisiana and Halifax Co., N. C.)

X. Temperance Davis Thorne, (1836-1927), m. (1) in 1857, Samuel Johnston Clark, (1829-1859), no children, m. (2) in 1869, John Buxton Williams, (1815-1887), no children.

XI. Ozelia Eudora Thorne, (1838-1869), m. 1859, Alfred Alston, (1833-1873), of Warren Co., N. C.

Martha Elizabeth Thorne, dau. of Temperance Williams (Davis) and William Williams Thorne, (1821-1897), m. 1839, Thomas Willis Nicholson, (1816-1884). Lived in Halifax

Co., N. C.

Children:
I. Capt. William Thorne Nicholson, (1840-1865).
    (C.S.A. Killed in battle at Petersburg)
II. Guilford Nicholson, (1841-1884), m. 1870, Eliza-
    beth Winter, (1846-1916). Lived at Elliott,
    Grenada County, Miss.
    Children:
    1. Anna Statham Nicholson, b. 1872, m. 1912,
       Paul Neiswanger of Kansas City, Mo. No
       issue.
    2. William Winter Nicholson, b. 1875, m. 1907,
       Grace Rohrbough. Lives in Elliott, Miss.
       Issue: one son.
    3. Martha Elizabeth Nicholson, b. 1878, m.1905,
       James B. Keister. No issue.
    4. Edward Thorne Nicholson, (1880-1881).
III. Edward Alston Thorne Nicholson, (1843-1865).
    (C.S.A. Killed in battle at Petersburg)
IV. Thomas Willis Nicholson, (1845-1857).
V.   Emma Pauline Nicholson, (1847-1880), m. 1872,
    Capt. Sydenham Benoni Alexander, (1840-1921).
    Lived at Charlotte, N. C.
    Children:
    1. Pattie Thorne Alexander, (1873-1893).
    2. Violet Graham Alexander, b. 1874, unmarried.
    3. Julia McGehee Alexander, b. 1876, unmarried.
    4. Sydenham Brevard Alexander, (1877-1935), m.
       1899, Mary W. Robertson. Lived at Charlotte,
       N. C., issue, one daughter.
    5. Thomas Willis Alexander, b. 1879, m. 1908,
       Alice Winston Spruill. Lived at Charlotte,
       N. C., issue, four children.
    6. Dr. Emory Graham Alexander, (1880-1930), m.
       Harriet Deaver. 3 children.
VI. Sallie Lee Nicholson, (1849-1917), m. (1) 1874,
    John Morehead Hobson, (1842-1878), m. (2) 1886,
    William Prosser Nelson, (1849-1921).
    Issue of first marriage:
    1. Pattie Thomas Hobson, b. 1874, m. 1901,
       Robert Allison Moore of Jackson, Tenn. No
       issue.
    Issue of second marriage:
    2. Sallie Lee Nelson, b. 1889, unmarried.
VII. Samuel Thorne Nicholson, (1852-1933), m. 1899,
    Jennie Irene Conwill, (1865-1919).
    Children:
    1. Marie Louise Nicholson, b. 1901, unmarried.

2. Martha Elizabeth Thorne Nicholson, b. 1904,
m. James Ivan Barrett. Issue: 2 children.

VIII. ——Joseph Wright Nicholson, (1853-1916), m. 1885,
Alice Eudora Clark, (1857-1933). One son,Joseph
Wright Nicholson, (18__-1893).

IX. Mason Wiggins Nicholson, (1856-1915), d.s.p.

X. James Mann Nicholson, (1859-1878), d.s.p.

XI. Anna Thorne Nicholson, (1861-____), m. 1885,
Francis Nelson, (1853-____). Lived at Washington, D. C.
Children:
1. Lettia Thorne Nelson, b. 1886, m. 1911,
Andrew Jackson Powers, issue: 4 children.
2. Mary Prosser Nelson, (1888-1909), d.s.p.
3. Emma Paulie Nelson, (1893-1893), twin.
4. Anna Lee Nelson, (1893-1893), twin.
5. Evelyn Byrd Lee Nelson, b. 1899, m. Walter
Claud Propps of Washington, D. C., one son.

William Henry Thorne, son of Temperance Williams
(Davis) and William Williams Thorne, (1822-1895), m. 1856,
Martha Jane Alston, (1836-1888), daughter of Maj. Alfred
Alston and Mary Ann Plummer. Lived in Halifax Co., N. C.
Children:

I. Mary Mabbett Thorne, (1857-1857).

II. Lula Thorne, (1859-1942), d.s.p.

III. Pattie Davis Thorne, b. 1861, unmarried.

IV. Anna Maria Thorne, (1864-1923), d.s.p.

V. Samuel Thomas Thorne, (1865-____), m. 1891,Agnes
Roberta Patterson, (1869-1938), dau. of Dr.
Robert Atkinson Patterson and Indianna Boyd.
Lived at "Airlie", Halifax Co., N. C.
Children:
1. Indianna Boyd Thorne, b. 1892, m. Fletcher
Harrison Gregory of Halifax, N. C. 4 children.
2. William Alfred Thorne, b. 1894, m. Katie Lee
McKinnon. 1 daughter.
3. Lula Patterson Thorne, b. 1896, m. Gordon
Malone Carver. 2 children.
4. Samuel Thomas Thorne, (1898-1904).
5. Agnes Patterson Thorne, b. 1907, m. 1933,
John Suiter MacRae. 2 children.
6. Robert Patterson Thorne, b. 1909, m. Charlotte Marshall Darden. 1 daughter.
7. Samuel Thorne, b. 1910, m. 1938, Elizabeth
Norwood Boyd.

VI. William Henry Thorne, (1867-____), m. 1907,
Elizabeth Thomas Alston, dau. of George Washing-

tɔn Alston and Elizabeth Faulcon. Lived at
"Airlie", Halifax Co., N. C.
Children:
1. Elizabeth Alston Thorne, b. 1908, m. 1940,
   Alex P. Johnson. No issue.
2. Eudora Thorne, b. 1911, m. 1934, John Phillips. 1 son.
3. William Henry Thorne, b. 1914, m. 1938,
   Lilian Bell Jenkins. No issue.
4. Edgar Faulcon Thorne, b. 1918.

VII.   Eudora Alston Thorne, b. 1870, unmarried.
VIII.   Mary Plummer Thorne, b. 1872, m. 1907, George
Garland Alston.
Children:
1. George Washington Alston, b. 1909.
2. William Thorne Alston, (1911-1911).

IX.   Susan Lewis Thorne, (1881-1890).

Anna Maria Thorne, (1824-1899), dau. of Temperance
Williams (Davis) and William Williams Thorne, m. 1845, Gen.
David Clark, (1820-1882), son of David Clark and wife,
Louise Norfleet, dau. of Marmaduke Norfleet and Hannah
Ruffin, dau. of William Ruffin and Sarah Hill. Issue born
at "Airlie", near Littleton in Halifax Co., N. C.
Children:
I.   Walter Clark, (1846-1924), m. 1874, Susan Wash-
ington Graham, (1851-1909), dau. of Gov. Wil-
liam A. Graham and Susannah Sarah Washington.
II.   David Clark, (1848-1862).
III.   Samuel Thorne Clark, (1850-1854).
IV.   Louisa Mabbett Clark, (1851-1904), m. 1880,
Frank Ballard, (1849-1932), son of Benjamin
Thorne Ballard and Martha Harriet Williams, dau.
of Robert Webb Williams and Hartwell Hodges
Davis, dau. of Archibald Davis and his wife,
Elizabeth, dau. of Capt. Isaac Hilliard and
wife, Leah Crafford of "Woodlawn", Nash Co.,N.C.
Son:
1. David Clark Ballard, b. 1882, m. Bessie May
   Conley. 3 children. Lives at Richmond, Va.
V.   Anna Leila Clark, (1852-1924), m. 1890, Rev.
Joseph David Arnold. No issue.
VI.   Edward Thorne Clark, (1855-1932), m. 1880, Mar-
garet Lillington, (18__-1924), dau. of John
Alexander Lillington and Elizabeth Williams.
Lived at Weldon, N. C.
Children:
1. Alexander Lillington Clark, (1881-1934), m.
   (1) 1909, Rebecca Johnson of Weldon, no

children, m. (2) 1915, Clara Belle Foy of
Weldon, N. C. 7 children.

2. David McKenzie Clark, b. 1885, m. 1928,
Myrtle Brogden. Lived at Greenville, N. C.
2 children.

3. Mary Williams Clark, b. 1887, m. 1912,Felix
Williamson Graves of Mebane, N. C.
8 children.

VII.   Alice Eudora Clark, 1857-1933, m. 1885, Joseph
Wright Nicholson. (Mentioned before)

VIII.   Henry Norfleet Clark, (1859-____), unmarried.

IX.   Martha Thorne Clark, (1860-1937), m. 1882,Robert
Boyd Patterson, (1855-1890).
Child:

1. Henry Norfleet Clark Patterson, b. 1883, m.
1916, Sylvia Crawley. Lives at Clarksdale,
Miss. 2 children.

X.   Lucy Norfleet Clark, (1862-1936), d.s.p.

XI.   Sallie Hill Clark, (1864-1936), m. 1914, Maj. W.
A. Graham, no issue.

XII.   David Clark, (1866-1866).

XIII.   Mary White Clark, (1868-1879).

Chief-Justice Walter Clark, b. 8/19/1846, d. 5/19/
1924, was b. at "Prospect Hill", the Thorne homeplace in
northwest Halifax County, N. C., not far from Littleton.
At 14 years of age, he was appointed a drillmaster with
rank of Second Lieutenant, and at 17, he was elected a
Lieutenant-Colonel, in the Confederate States Army. He
participated in the first Maryland campaign, the capture
of Harper's Ferry, and the battles of Second Manassas,
Sharpsburg, Fredericksburg, etc., also Fort Branch and Ben-
tonville. After the war, he managed his large plantation
on the Roanoke River and practiced law at Scotland Neck and
then at Halifax. In Nov., 1873, he removed to Raleigh. In
1885-1889, he was a Judge of the Superior Court. In 1889-
1902, he was an Associate Justice, and in 1903-1924, he was
a Chief Justice, of the Supreme Court of N. C. He d. at
Raleigh and was buried there beside his wife in Oakwood
Cemetery. He married, at Hillsboro, N. C., on 1/28/1874,
Susan Washington Graham, (3/9/1851-12/10/1909), dau. of
Gov. William Alexander Graham and his wife, Susannah Sarah
Washington, dau. of John Washington and his wife, Elizabeth
Heritage Cobb. Eldest, Susan, b. Hillsboro; others,Raleigh.
Children:

I.   Susan Washington Clark, b. 6/18/1875, m. 6/30/
1908, Joseph Ernest Erwin, b. 12/24/1867, son of
Joseph J. Erwin and his wife, Elvira Jane Holt.
Mr. Erwin was a Representative from Burke Co.,

in the N. C., Legislature of 1903. Residence:
"Belevue", Morganton, N. C.
Children:
1. Susan Graham Erwin, b. 4/16/1909. She was a
   Representative from Mecklenburg Co., in the
   N. C., Legislature, 1949. She m. (1), 9/10/
   1930, Joseph Wilson Ervin, b. 3/3/1901, d.
   12/24/1945. Member of Congress. She m. (2),
   4/29/1950, Walter Harold Williamson, b. 5/19
   /1899.
2. Joseph Erwin, b. 5/5/1910, d. 6/10/1911.
3. Walter Clark Erwin, b. 7/10/1913, m. 10/8/
   1949, Helen McGill Barnhardt. Walter Clark
   Erwin was a Commander, U.S. Navy in WW II.
   Child:
   (1) Walter Clark Erwin, Jr., b. 10/31/1950.
4. Elvira Holt Erwin, b. 11/28/1921, m. 6/12/
   1943, Edgar Loren Lesh, b. 1/30/1917. He
   was a Lieutenant, U.S. Army, in WW II. He
   was in the Signal Corps and served in North
   Africa and Italy.
   Children:
   (1) Joseph Erwin Lesh, b. 3/4/1944.
   (2) Edgar Loren Lesh, Jr., b. 10/12/1946.
   (3) David Clark Lesh, b. 4/12/1949.
II. David Clark, b. 5/15/1877, m. 4/8/1916, Aileen
Butt, dau. of William Lee Butt and his wife,
Jessie Wheeler. Mr. Clark was a Captain, U.S.
Army, in the Spanish-American War. Residence:
100 Hermitage Road, Charlotte, N. C.
III. William Alexander Graham Clark, b. 8/14/1879, d.
at Washington, D. C., 1/24/1953, m. 12/6/1911,
Pearl Chadwick Heck, b. 1/28/1889, d. at Washing-
ton, D. C., 6/30/1939, dau. of Col. Jonathan
McGee Heck and his wife, Mattie Anna Callendine.
Mr. Clark resided at 3712 Morrison St., Washing-
ton, D. C. Mr. and Mrs. Clark are buried in
Cedar Hill Cemetery, Suitland, Maryland.
Children:
1. Margaret Heck Clark, b. 7/9/1915, m. 5/3/1940,
   Guy Edwin Crampton, Jr., b. 9/19/1913.
   Children:
   (1) Guy Clark Crampton, b. 3/25/1944.
   (2) Gregory Byrd Crampton, b. 8/7/1947.
      Residence: Raleigh, N. C.
2. Graham Montrose Clark, b. 3/12/1922, m.
   6/10/1943, Jane Arleigh Blue, b. 12/28/1922.
   Graham Montrose Clark, a graduate of the U.S.

Naval Academy, was a Lieutenant, U.S. Navy, in WW II. He served on a destroyer through- out the Pacific, from Kwajalein to Hokkaido: seven battle stars.

Children:
(1) Graham Montrose Clark, Jr., b. 9/5/1945.
(2) Walter Blue Clark, b. 11/24/1947.
(3) Robin Arleigh Clark, b. 10/24/1950.

IV. Anna Thorne Clark, b. 4/20/1883, d. 7/23/1884, buried in the Presbyterian Churchyard at Hills- boro, N. C.

V. Walter Clark, Jr., b. 8/1/1885, d. 2/19/1933, m. 3/2/1918, Mary Roper Johnston, dau. of Latta Crawford Johnston and his wife, Annie Lee Thorn. They live at 1326 East Morehead St., Charlotte, N. C. Walter Clark, Jr., was buried in Elmwood Cemetery at Charlotte. His widow now lives at 403 Lakeshore Drive, Asheville, N. C. Walter Clark, Jr., was a Captain, U.S. Army, in WW I; saw front-line service in France with the 30th Div. Before that, he had served under General Pershing on the Mexican Border. He was a Sena- tor in the N. C., Legislature of 1929.

Children:
1. Annie Thorn Clark, b. 6/6/1921, m. 6/16/1950, Robert Dorr Kinney, b. 10/18/1917. He was Major, U.S. Air Force, in WW II. He served in North Africa and through the "Battle of Britain" and the "Invasion of Europe." Flew pursuits: 38 confirmed victories. He received the D.S.M., D.F.C., Silver Star, Air Medal (7 clusters), Purple Heart (oak- leaf cluster).
   Child:
   (1) Robert Dorr Kinney, Jr., b. 4/28/1951.
2. Mary Johnston Clark, b. 6/18/1925, d. 2/21/ 1950, m. 3/30/1946, Harmon Miller Lee.
   Child:
   (1) Mary Latta Lee, b. 7/21/1947.
3. Sarah Hill Clark, b. 12/30/1927, m. 4/8/1951, (as his second wife), Harmon Miller Lee, b. 12/4/1917.

VI. John Washington Clark, b. 10/5/1887, m. 11/5/ 1919, Nannie Elizabeth Wright, dau. of Thomas Davenport Wright and his wife, Betty Lunsford Allen. Mr. Clark was a Lieutenant, U.S. Army in WW I. Residence: 1001 Country Club Drive, Greensboro, N. C.

Children:
1. Nancy Wright Clark, b. 9/7/1920, m. 8/25/
   1943, Alexander Dowling McLennan. He was a
   Lieutenant Commander, U.S. Navy, in WW II.
   He was executive officer of a destroyer
   escort in the Atlantic and Mediterranean
   Areas; also, executive officer of an A.P.D.
   in the Southwest Pacific: five battle stars.
   Children:
   (1) Nancy Clark McLennan, b. 5/23/1945, d.
       9/11/1946.
   (2) Alexander Dowling McLennan, Jr., b.
       9/24/1946.
   (3) Gail Clark McLennan, b. 10/12/1947.
   (4) Mary Angela McLennan, b. 4/24/1950.
2. Sudie Graham Clark, b. 10/18/1921, m. 7/18/
   1942, William Alexander Hanger, b. 12/10/
   1917. He was a Lieutenant Commander, U.S.
   Navy in WW II. He served on a carrier in
   the Pacific. Received the Bronze Star, two
   Unit Citations, five battle stars.
   Children:
   (1) Elizabeth Clark Hanger, b. 9/21/1943.
   (2) William Alexander Hanger, Jr., b. 1/12/
       1945.
   (3) John McCarthy Hanger, b. 12/30/1946.
   (4) James Edward Hanger, b. 4/26/1950.
3. Julia Wright Clark, b. 7/19/1924, m. 10/14/
   1949, Rufus Tucker Carr, b. 5/25/1922. He
   was a Private, first-class, U.S.Army, in WW
   II. He served in the Field Artillery and
   served in North Africa, Italy, France, and
   Germany. Received the Purple Heart and four
   battle stars.
   Child:
   (1) Rufus Tucker Carr, Jr., b. 1/19/1951.
4. Walter McKenzie Clark, b. 3/21/1926. He was
   a radar technician, U.S. Navy, in WW II.
5. Betty Allen Clark, b. 2/16/1933.

VII. Thorne Clark, b. 12/21/1889, m. 10/2/1913, Mabel
Bossett, dau. of James Pleasant Gossett and his
wife, Sallie Brown. Mr. Clark was Mayor of Lin-
colnton, N. C., 1931-33; a Representative from
Lincoln Co., in the N. C., Legislature of 1937;
and Chairman of the Board of County Commissioners
in 1940. Residence: 400 North Cedar Street, Lin-
colnton, N. C.
Children:

126

1. Thorne McKenzie Clark, b. 7/6/1914, m. 7/4/1936, Margaret Louis McNeely. He was in the Chemical Warfare Service and his duties took him to North Africa, England, Australia, and the Pacific Theater. Before that, he had served in the U.S. Marine Corps.
Children:
   (1) Thorne McKenzie Clark, Jr., b. 2/13/1948.
   (2) Louis McNeely Clark, b. 6/28/1949.
   (3) Margaret Gossett Clark, b. 4/18/1951.
2. Sallie Brown Clark, b. 6/17/1916, m. 9/3/1938, Thomas Francis Huguenin. He was a Lieutenant in WW II. Served in Alaska and the Aleutians.
Children:
   (1) Thomas Francis Huguenin, Jr. b. 7/15/1939.
   (2) Thomas Barksdale Huguenin, b. 2/4/1942.
3. Walter Clark, b. 1/4/1918, m. 7/14/1945, Caroline Lewis Webster. He was a Major, U.S. Air Force, in WW II. Served in Egypt, Palestine, and in the Pacific Theater. He received the Silver Star, Bronze Star, and Air Medal.
Child:
   (1) Caroline Fielding Clark, b. 9/12/1948.
4. David Clark, b. 7/4/1922, m. 4/18/1951, Kathryn King Goode. He was a Lieutenant, U.S. Air Force, in WW II. He served in the Philippines and Japan. Received the Air Medal. He was a representative from Lincoln Co., in the N. C., Legislature of 1951.

VIII. Eugenia Graham Clark, b. 2/12/1892, m. 2/9/1922, Dr. John Allen MacLean, D.D., b. 1/24/1891, son of John Allen MacLean, Sr., and wife, Mary Brown. Dr. MacLean was a Chaplain in U.S. Army in WW I. He was in the Field Artillery and served in France, through the St. MiHiel and Meuse-Argonne Campaigns, until disabled by an enemy poison-gas attack at Rogmane. Residence: 3420 Hawthorne Avenue, Richmond, Virginia.
Children:
1. Walter Clark MacLean, b. 7/10/1927, d. in infancy.
2. Duart Fitzroy MacLean, (adopted), b. 11/29/1930.

Mary Eliza Mabbett Thorne, (1825-1872), dau. of Temperance Williams (Davis) and William Williams Thorne, m.

1848, Kemp Plummer Alston, (1820-188_). Lived in Warren Co., N. C.

Children:

I. Alfred Thorne Alston, (1850-1923), d.s.p.
II. Anna Clark Alston, (1853-1892), m. 1890, Thomas Harriss Clark, (1859-1892). Issue: 2 children, d. in infancy.
III. Kemp Plummer Alston, (1856-1899), m. 1886, Virginia Standeford, (1856-1912).
   Child:
   1. Mary Erwin Alston, b. 1888, m. 1910, Louis Ludwig Maser of Kansas City, Mo. Issue: 3 sons.
IV. DuTihl Cabanna Alston, (1859-1919), d.s.p.
V. Frank Ballard Alston, (1861-1864).

Samuel Thomas Thorne, (1827-1921), son of Temperance Williams (Davis) and William Williams Thorne, m. 1872, Mary Whitmell Harriss, (1848-1933), dau. of Thomas Whitmell Harriss and Martha Helen Kearney. Lived in Warren Co., N. C.

Children:

I. Tempe Williams Thorne, b. 1874, unmarried.
II. Silas Owens Thorne, b. 1876, m. 1923, Clarissa Abbey. Lives at Charlotte, N. C.
   Child:
   1. Silas Owens Thorne, Jr., b. 1924.
III. Annie Blackwell Thorne, b. 1878, unmarried.
IV. Nena Thorne, b. 1883, m. 1911, Arthury Stanley Bussey, b. 1877.
   Children:
   1. Arthury Stanley Bussey, b. 1914, m. 1940, Wilma Johnson. Issue: one daughter.
   2. Mary Whitmell Bussey, b. 1917.
   3. Samuel Thorne Bussey, b. 1922.
V. Samuel Thomas Thorne, b. 1888, m. 1925, Nancy Ethel Cornelius.
   Child:
   1. Samuel Thomas Thorne, b. 1929.
VI. Thomas Whitmell Thorne, b. 1891, m. 1927, Carolyn Lawton.
   Children:
   1. Thomas Whitmell Thorne, b. 1930.
   2. Caroline Lawton Thorne, b. 1932.

Dr. Edward Alston Thorne, (1828-1911), son of Temperance Williams (Davis) and William Williams Thorne, m. 1852, Alice Maria Harriss, (1834-1907), dau. of Thomas Whitmell Harriss and Martha Helen Kearney. Lived in Halifax Co., N. C.

Children:
I.   Temperance Davis Thorne, (1853-1923), m. 1878,
        Joseph Townes, (1833-1893). No issue.
II.   William Thorne, (1855-1855).
III.   Martha Helen Thorne, (1858-1925), m. (1) 1885,
        Silas Owens, (1836-1889).
        Children:
        1. Nena Owens, b. 1886, m. 1903, Joseph Emmett
            Williams; issue: 2 sons.
        2. Alice Tempe Owens, b. 1888, m. 1910, John
            Melvin Bragg; issue: 2 children.
        Martha Helen Thorne, m. (2) 1895, John Henry
        Harrison, (1858-1927).
        Children:
        3. Edward Thorne Harrison, b. 1896, m. 1926,
            Clara Page. Issue: 1 daughter.
        4. John Henry Harrison, b. 1898, m. Jeanne
            Leach. Issue: 1 son.
        5. Blake Baker Harrison, b. 1901, m. 1934,Helen
            Lonon.
IV.   James Harriss Thorne, (1860-1861).
V.   Elizabeth Thorne, (1862-1930), m. 1887, George
        Dudley Able, b. 1858. Lived at Normandy, St.
        Louis Co., Missouri.
        Children:
        1. Corrie Mae Able, b. 1888, m. Robert C. Moss.
            Issue: 1 daughter.
        2. Thorne Able, b. 1889, m. 1914, Grace Shafer.
            Issue: 3 children.
        3. Helen Dudley Able, b. 1890, m. 1915, Adrian
            Woods Frazier. Issue: 3 children.
        4. Elise Able, b. 1891, m. 1914, George Doling
            Haynes. Issue: 2 daughters.
        5. Alice Mildred Able, b. 1904.
VI.   Edward Alston Thorne, (1866-1903), d.s.p.
VII.   Thomas Whitmell Thorne, (1867-1919), d.s.p.
VIII.   Mary Whitmell Thorne, b. 1872, m. 1896, Joseph
        Atkinson Patterson, b. 1873. Lived at Littleton,
        N. C.
        Children:
        1. Alice Thorne Patterson, b. 1898, m. (1) 1918,
            Leon Ashby Adams; issue: 2 children, m. (2)
            1932, Hendrix Geddie of Warrenton, N. C. No
            issue.
        2. Tempe Townes Patterson, b. 1899.
        3. Roberta Harriss Patterson, b. 1901.
        4. Robert Atkinson Patterson, b. 1903.
        5. Edward Thorne Patterson, b. 1905, m. 1936,

Irene Sutton.
6. Thomas Whitmell Patterson, b. 1909.

IX. Buxton Williams Thorne, (1874-1910), m. 1905,
Voorhies Daniel, b. 1886. Lived at Holly Springs,
Miss.
Children:
1. Edward Alston Thorne, b. 1907, m. 1935, Ruth
O'Hara.
2. Frances Thorne, (1908-1910).
3. Chesley Thorne, b. 1910, m. 1931, Augustus
Smith, Jr.

Lucy Emily Thorne, (1831-1910), dau. of Temperance
Williams (Davis) and William Williams Thorne, m. 1852,
Blake Baker Nicholson, (1828-1910). Lived at Halifax Co.,
N. C.

Children:
I. Temperance Winifred Nicholson, (1853-1939), m.
1878, Erasmus Alston Daniel, (1831-1916). Lived
in Halifax Co., N. C.
Children:
1. Erasmus Daniel, (1879-1879).
2. Erasmus Alston Daniel, (1881-1924), m. 1908,
Norfleet Owens Bryant. Issue: 4 children.
3. Blake Baker Nicholson Daniel, b. 1883, m.
1911, Ruth Whitaker. No issue.
4. Tempe Downs Daniel, b. 1885, m. 1910, Joseph
John Williams Clark, (1883-1936). Issue: 4
children.
5. Mary Long Daniel, b. 1888.
6. John Graham Daniel, b. 1890, m. 1918, Hattie
O'Brien Taylor, d. 1924. Issue: 3 children.
7. Lucy Edward Daniel, b. 1892, m. (1) 1914,
Junius Nicholas Egerton, m. (2) 1934, Robert
Scales Clark.
II. Dr. Samuel Timothy Nicholson, M.D., (1855-1930),
m. 1876, Annie Elizabeth Lucas, (1855-1937), dau.
of Jesse Lucas and Elizabeth Satchwell. Lived
at Washington, Beaufort Co., N. C.
Children:
1. David Lucas Nicholson, (1877-1883).
2. John Lawrence Nicholson, b. 1879, m. 1907,
Frances Hill. Issue: 2 children.
3. Jesse Burbage Nicholson, (1881-1883).
4. Lucile Thorne Nicholson, b. 1883, m. 1903,
Henry Clay Carter of Washington, N. C. Issue:
5 children.
5. Elizabeth Satchwell Nicholson, b. 1885, m.
1907, Louis Mann. Issue: 2 children.

6. Annie Plummer Nicholson, b. 1888, m. 1911,
   Danford Taylor. Issue: 2 children.
7. Samuel Timothy Nicholson, (1889-1889).
8. Blake Baker Nicholson, (1890-1890).
9. Thomas Wright Nicholson, (1892-1892).
10. Winifred Wiggins Nicholson, b. 1894, m.1925,
    Jacob Douthit. Issue: 1 child.
11. Carolotta Nicholson, (1896-1919), m. 1917,
    Harold Washbourn. Issue: 1 child.

III. Dr. John Thorne Nicholson, M.D., (1857-1935), m.
     1886, Katherine McNeal, b. 1869, dau. of William
     McNeal and Mary Margaret Bishop. Lived at Wash-
     ington, Beaufort Co., N. C.
     Children:
     1. Dr. Samuel Timothy Nicholson, b. 1887, m.
        1912, Carter Peyton. Issue: 2 children.
     2. Blanche Baker Nicholson, b. 1888, m. 1917,
        John Webb. Issue: 2 children.
     3. Katherine Estelle Nicholson, (1890-1898).
     4. John Thorne Nicholson, b. 1891, m. Gladys
        Snyder. Issue: 2 children.
     5. Mary Lucille Nicholson, b. 1893, m. 1918,
        Dr. Edward J. Wolfe. Issue: 4 children.
     6. Harry McNeal Nicholson, (1899-1901).
     7. Edward Harold Nicholson, b. 1900, m. 1925,
        Georgette Stephens. Issue: 3 children.
     8. Dr. William McNeal Nicholson, b. 1905, m.
        1929, Eunice Stamey.

IV. Thomas Wright Nicholson, (1860-1863).
V. Ida Mabbette Nicholson, (1861-1863).
VI. Blake Baker Nicholson, (1863-1919), m. 1902,Mrs.
    Sallie Owens Bryant, b. 1865, dau. of Silas
    Owens and Nena Harriss.
    Children:
    1. Blake Baker Nicholson, (1903-1911).
    2. Plummer Alston Nicholson, b. 1910, m. 1937,
       Charlotte Kugler. Issue: 2 children.

VII. Dr. Plummer Alston Nicholson, (1865-____), m.
     1889, Estelle Brown Hunter, (1869-____), dau. of
     Samuel Hunter and Margaret Brown.
     Children:
     1. Plummer Alston Nicholson, (1897-1897).
     2. Bernice Hunter Nicholson, b. 1898, m. 1923,
        Charles Joseph Bunn of Tarboro, N. C. Issue:
        2 children.
     3. Margaret Plummer Nicholson, b. 1905.

VIII. Mary Elizabeth Nicholson, (1866-____), m. 1884,
      Samuel Johnston Clark, (1857-1922). Lived at

Enfield and Airlie, Halifax Co., N. C.
Children:
1. Lucy Marina Clark, (1886-1887).
2. Robert Scales Clark, b. 1890, m. Mrs. Lucy
   (Edward Daniel) Egerton, issue: 1 son.
3. William Nicholson Clark, b. 1893, m. 1921,
   Julia Grace Cunningham, issue: 1 son.
4. Samuel Johnston Clark, b. 1895, m. 1919,
   Eula Jones, issue: 1 son.
5. Temperance Winifred Clark, b. 1897, m. 1918,
   John Leah Skinner of Littleton, N. C., issue:
   2 children.
6. James Thomas Clark, b. 1899, m. 1931, Edith
   Breazeale. No issue.
7. Alice Eudora Clark, b. 1901.
8. David Crocket Clark, b. 1904, m. 1933, Mary
   Traynham Wyche. Lives at Garysburg, N. C.,
   issue: 1 son.
9. Timothy Nicholson Clark, b. 1906, m. 1928,
   Alice Ledbetter.
IX.   William Edward Nicholson, (1868-____), m. 1895,
      Erma Ownes, (1878-____), dau. of Silas Owens and
      Nena Harriss. Lived at Airlie, Halifax Co.,N.C.
      Children:
      1. Helen Owen Nicholson, b. 1896, m. 1923, Le-
         roy Smith, issue: 1 son.
      2. William Edward Nicholson, b. 1897, m. 1923,
         Hazel Davis, issue: 2 children.
      3. Silas Owen Nicholson, b. 1900, m. 1926,
         Valeria DeMilhau, issue: 2 children.
      4. Blake Baker Nicholson, b. 1902, m. 1932, (1)
         Dorothy Romine, (mother of his children),
         and (2) Mrs. Harold Browder.
      5. Norfleet Nicholson, (1905-1923).
      6. Thomas Wright Nicholson, b. 1906, m. Mildred
         Scott, issue: 2 children.
      7. Cornelia Winifred Nicholson, b. 1909, m.
         1938, Thomas Wilmer Morris, issue: 1 child.
X.   Lucile Emma Nicholson, (1869-1916), m. 1891,
      James Harriss Clark, (1864-1940).
      Children:
      1. Lucy Blake Clark, (1892-1894).
      2. Garna Lee Clark, b. 1894.
      3. Ferdinand Harriss Clark, b. 1896, m. 1938,
         Eliza Jane Dickens. No issue.
      4. Plummer Nicholson Clark, b. 1900, m. 1937,
         Mary Lucile Conner.
      5. James Norfleet Clark, b. 1904, m. 1927, Mary

Shaw.

    6. Lucile Margaret Clark, b. 1909.

XI.   Kathlee Lee Nicholson, (1872-1933), d.s.p.

    Archibald Davis Thorne, (1833-1833).

    John Davis Thorne, (1834-1900), son of Temperance
Williams (Davis) and William Williams Thorne, m. 1865,
Kate Mumford Thompson, (1848-1927), dau. of Samuel Thompson and Addeline Spicer. Lived at St. Martinsville, St.
Martin Parish, Louisiana, and in Halifax Co., N. C.

    Children:

I.   Samuel Thomas Thorne, (1866-1866).

II.   Harry Hill Thorne, b. 1869, m. 1899, Ella Alston,
      b. 1871.

      Child:

      1. Crichton Alston Thorne, b. 1900, m. 1920,
         Van Kearney Davis, issue: 2 children.

III.   Addie Ashton Thorne, b. 1871, m. (1) 1904,
      Howard Alston. No issue. M. (2) 1913, Oswald
      E. Heideman of Bay St. Louis, Miss.

      Child:

      1. Kathryn Thorne Heideman, b. 1916.

IV.   William Henry Thorne, (1874-1929), d.s.p.

V.   Frank Forest Thorne, b. 1876, m. 1904, Ruth Mc-
      Graw, b. 1872.

      Child:

      1. Kathryn Eveline Thorne, b. 1905, m. 1929,
         Allen Arness.

VI.   John Davis Thorne, (1879-1902), d.s.p.

    Temperance Davis Thorne, (1836-1927), dau. of Temperance Williams (Davis) and William Williams Thorne, m. (1)
1857, Samuel Johnston Clark, (1829-1859). No issue. M.
(2) 1869, John Buxton Williams, (1815-1887). No issue.

    Ozella Eudora Thorne, (1838-1868), dau. of Temperance
Williams (Davis) and William Williams Thorne, m. 1859,
Alfred Alston, (1833-1873). Lived in Warren Co., N. C.

    Children:

I.   Mary Plummer.Alston, (1859-1892), m. 1884,
      Plummer Davis, (1848-1912). Lived in Franklin
      Co., N. C., issue: 1 son, died in infancy.

II.   Emma Pauline Alston, (1860-186_).

III.   Edward Thorne Alston, (1862-1931), m. 1883, Rosa
      Speed, (1862-____), dau. of Robert A. Speed and
      Mary Plummer Davis. Lived in Franklin and Vance
      Counties, N. C.

      Children:

      1. Julian Meredith Alston, b. 1888, m. 1922,
         Clara Alston, issue: 4 children.

      2. Eugene Speed Alston, (1890-1909).

3. Mary Davis Alston, b. 1892, m. 1920, Robert Southerland.
4. Myrta Thorne Alston, b. 1894.
5. Mattie Belle Alston, b. 1896, m. Joseph Southerland.
6. Edward Thorne Alston, (1897-1935), m. 1919, Myrtle Clark.
7. Annie Lou Alston, b. 1900.
8. Alfred Plummer Alston, b. 1901, m. 1931, Evie Riggs.
9. William Thorne Alston, (1904-1930), d.s.p.
IV. Eudora Thorne Alston, b. 1863, unmarried. Lived near Henderson, Vance Co., N. C.

Dr. Thomas Davis, son of Elizabeth (Hilliard) and Archibald Davis, b. at "Columbia Farm", Franklin Co., N.C., 4/3/1806, d. 11/3/1862, m. (1) Mary Slade, and (2) Martha E. Batchelor.

Children:
I. Elizabeth Hilliard Davis, m. General Bryan Grimes. (C.S.A.)
II. Dolphin Davis.
III. Augustus Davis.
IV. Tempie Davis, m. John Davis Alston, son of Ruina Temperance (Williams) and Samuel Thomas Alston.
V. Mollie Davis, m. William Boyd of Warrenton, N.C.
VI. Frank Davis.
VII. John Calvin Davis.
VIII. Nicholas Davis.

Elizabeth Hilliard Davis, dau. of Thomas and Mary Slade Davis, m. General Bryan Grimes.

Child:
I. Elizabeth (Bettie) Grimes, m. Samuel Fox Mordecai.

Children:
1. Elizabeth (Bessie) Mordecai, m. Desassure MacKay.
2. George Washington Mordecai, m. Mary Day Faison.
3. Henry Lane Mordecai, m. Mettie Sturdivant.
4. Edward Waller Mordecai.
5. Ellen Mordecai, m. Richard C. Kelley.
6. Alfred Mordecai, m. Elsie Hess.
7. Margaret Mordecai, m. I. L. Blomquist.
8. William Grimes Mordecai, m. Georgia Davis.

John Calvin Davis, son of Elizabeth (Hilliard) and Archibald Davis, b. at "Columbia Farm", Franklin Co., N.C., 6/19/1808, d. 3/10/1889, m. Lucy Faulcon Alston, dau. of Major Alfred Alston and wife, Mary Plummer of Warren

Co., N. C.

Children:
- I.   Hodges Davis, m. George Jones, no issue.
- II.   Mary Plummer (Mollie) Davis, m. Maj. Robert A. Speed.

  Children:
  1. Annie Jones Speed, m. (1) Capt. E. M. Clayton, and (2) Dr. E. H. Bobbitt.
  2. Robert A. Speed, m. Eva Harris.
  3. Lula Alston Speed, m. S. J. Beckwith.
  4. John Davis Speed, m. Maggie Harris.
  5. Rosa Belle Speed, m. Edward Thorne Alston.
  6. Alfred Alston Speed, d.s.p.
  7. Henry Plummer Speed, m. Addie Speed.
  8. Minnie Scott Speed, m. Robert J. Stewart.
  9. Eugene Davis Speed, d.s.p.
  10. Elmo Murry Speed, m. Julia Joyner.

- III.   Archibald Hilliard Davis, m. Charlotte Harris, dau. of Henry Harris.

  Children:
  1. Laura Davis, m. Walter Daniel.

     Child:
     (1) Archibald Daniel.
  2. Archibald H. Davis, d.s.p.
  3. Lucy Davis, m. Whitmel Kearney Williams, son of Dr. Robert Edgar Williams and wife, Valerie Virginia Kearney.
  4. Charlotte Elizabeth (Davis), m. Robert Edgar Williams, Jr.

     Children:
     (1) Robert Edgar Williams, III, dentist in Goldsboro, N. C.
     (2) Estelle Williams, m. Irwin Lipscomb.
     (3) Frederick Williams, m. (1) Alma Scull, (2) Mabel Hayes. Lives at "Myrtle Lawn", Warren Co., N. C.
  5. Minnie Davis, d.s.p.
  6. Estelle Davis, unmarried.
  7. Oscar Harris Davis, m. Bertha Webster.

     Children:
     (1) Webster Davis.
     (2) Dorothy Hilliard Davis.

- IV.   Martha (Pattie) Davis, m. Robert W. Alston, son of Samuel Thomas Alston.
- V.   Plummer A. Davis, m. Mary P. Alston, no issue.
- VI.   Lucy Davis, d.s.p.
- VII.   Alfred Alston Davis, d.s.p.

    Lucy Henry Davis, dau. of Elizabeth (Hilliard) and

Archibald Davis, b. at "Columbia Farm", Franklin Co., N.C.,
10/11/1811, and d. at Louisburg, N. C., 9/26/1896, m.
12/8/1831, Nicholas Bryar Massenburg, b. 4/5/1806, d.
10/25/1867, son of Dr. Cargill Massenburg and wife, Ann
Bryar.

Children:

I. Archibald Cargill Massenburg, b. 1834, d.s.p.,
    (C.S.A.).
II. Wiley Perry Massenburg, b. 4/30/1836, m. Panthea
    Boyd, b. 10/24/1848.
III. William Edward Massenburg, b. 10/18/1837, m.
    Sallie Moss.
IV. John Nicholas Massenburg, b. 1839, killed (C.S.A.)
V. Mariam Stamps Massenburg, b. 6/2/1840, d. 12/25/
    1900, m. 8/20/1860, William J. Norwood, b. 7/10/
    1836, d. 5/7/1909.
    Children:
    1. Lucy Norwood, (1861-1863).
    2. Bettie Massenburg Norwood, b. 11/7/1863, m.
       9/28/1881, Henry Armstead Boyd of Warrenton,
       N. C., b. 7/11/1855.
       Children:
       (1) William Norwood Boyd, b. 7/19/1882, m.
           6/4/1907, Elizabeth Burwell.
           Children:
           a. Lucy Burwell Boyd, b. 7/31/1908, m.
              12/29/1934, Robert D. Meade.
           b. Henry Armstead Boyd, b. 5/2/1912, m.
              Mary Archer Randolph of Richmond, Va.
              Residence: Richmond, Va. Atty.
              Children:
              (a) William N. Boyd.
              (b) Randolph Boyd.
              (c) Henry A. Boyd.
           c. Elizabeth Norwood Boyd, b. 12/19/1913,
              m. Samuel Thorne, son of Samuel Tho-
              mas Thorne and wife, Agnes Roberta
              Patterson of Halifax Co., N. C.
              Children:
              (a) Elizabeth Boyd Thorne.
              (b) Agnes Thorne.
           d. Mariam Boyd, b. 5/18/1920, m. Wright
              Tisdale.
              Children:
              (a) Wright Tisdale, Jr.
              (b) Norwood Tisdale.
       (2) Anne Jones Boyd, m. 6/27/1907, Major
           William A. Graham of Warrenton, N. C.

No issue.

(3) Mariam Norwood Boyd, unmarried.

3. Annie Laura Norwood, d. young.

4. Willie Bryar Norwood, m. Robert Sampson Jones.

VI. Elizabeth Crafford Davis Massenburg, b. 4/7/1842, d. 9/30/1915, m. 10/3/1866, Joel George King, M.D., b. 12/12/1841, d. at Warrenton, N. C., 4/13/1913, son of William R. King, M.D., of Louisburg, N. C., and his wife, Temperance, dau. of George Pugh Tunstall and his wife, Temperance Williams.

Children:

1. Laura June King, b. 8/15/1871, d. 10/30/1938, m. 8/15/1895, George Warren Alston, b. 10/14/1866, d. 6/19/1912, at Texarkana, Ark., son of Philip Guston Alston and wife, Jane Elizabeth Crichton.

Children:

(1) Marion Frances Alston, b. 6/25/1896, at Warrenton, N. C., m. at Raleigh, N. C., 11/30/1920, Henry Clark Bourne of Tarboro, N. C., b. 8/1/1893, at "White Oaks", Edgecombe Co., N. C., son of Henry Clay Bourne and wife, Maria Toole Clark. Residence: Tarboro, N. C. Atty.

Children:

a. Henry Clay Bourne, Jr., b. 12/31/1921, m. Margaret Barr Thomas.

b. Laura June Bourne, b. 11/24/1923, m. 6/10/1944, at Tarboro, N. C., Willie Jones Long, Jr., son of Willie Jones Long and wife, Caroline Moncure of "Longview", Northampton Co., N. C.

Children:

(a) Marion Frances Long, b. 10/6/1948.

(b) Willie Jones Long, III, b. 6/25/1950.

(c) Henry Bourne Long, b. 5/24/1952.

(d) Richard Moncure Long, b. 5/30/1953.

c. Joel King Bourne, b. 7/23/1925.

(2) Katherine Crichton Alston, b. 12/12/1901, m. Preston Edsall.

Child:

a. Hugh Crichton Edsall.

(3) Philip King Alston, b. 1/24/1910, m. Virginia Coxe. No issue.

2. Marion Norwood King, M.D., of Norfolk, Va., b. 10/15/1875, m. Melissa Payne. No issue.
3. Nora Lillington King, b. 4/3/1883,unmarried.
4. William Richmond King, d.s.p.
5. Joel G. King, d. young.
6. Marshall W. King, d. young.

VII. Mary Frances Massenburg, b. 1/23/1846, d. 11/27/1928, m. Hugh Perry of Franklin Co., N. C., b. 7/21/1842.
VIII. Lucy Cargill Massenburg, b. 10/10/1847, d.s.p.
IX. Benjamin Ballard Massenburg, b. 1849, d. 9/8/1911, m. Lillian Augusta Mangum, b. 8/28/1859, d. Jan., 1928, left a large family of sons and daughters.
X. Thomas Davis Massenburg, d. in infancy.

James Hilliard, son of Isaac and Leah (Crafford) Hilliard, was b. at "Woodlawn" plantation, Nash Co., N. C., 10/30/1768, and d. at Hilliardston, Nash Co., N. C., 7/6/1832. He m. 9/25/1798, at "Rose Hill", Nash Co., N. C., Mourning Boddie, b. 2/26/1778, and d. at Hilliardston, 2/25/1847, dau. of Nathan and Chloe (Crudup) Boddie of "Rose Hill", Nash Co., N. C. James and Mourning (Boddie) Hilliard are buried at "Woodlawn."

Children:
I. Anne (Nancy) Hilliard, b. 9/25/1799, d. 9/25/1800.
II. Isaac Hilliard, b. 2/25/1801, m. his cousin, Lucy Emily Hilliard, dau. of John and Elizabeth (Tunstall) Hilliard of "Black Jack", Nash Co., N. C. (See later)
III. James Crafford Hilliard, b. 11/3/1806, d. 4/13/1860, m. (1) Mary Ann Ruffin, (2) Martha Ann Pitts. (See later)
IV. Elizabeth Jane Hilliard, b. 2/1/1809, m. Jonas Johnston Carr. (See later)
V. Bennett Boddie Hilliard, b. 4/1/1811, d. 4/10/1826.
VI. Archibald Davis Hilliard, b. 2/15/1813, d. 10/24/1813.
VII. Elijah Boddie Hilliard, b. 1815, m. Rebecca Brown Powell. (See later)
VIII. Mary Temperance Hilliard, b. 11/16/1816, m. John Buxton Williams. (See later)
IX. Leah Hilliard, b. 5/2/1819, m. her first cousin, Dr. Algernon Sidney Perry, son of Capt. Jeremiah Perry and wife, Temperance Boddie. (See later)

Isaac Hilliard, son of James and Mourning (Boddie) Hilliard, was b. at Hilliardston, Nash County, N. C.,

2/25/1801, and d. at his plantation "Mill Brook", Halifax
Co., N. C., 3/28/1853. He inherited "Mill Brook" from his
father, James Hilliard, at his death in 1832, which was
built by his uncle, Isaac Hilliard and bought by James Hilliard in 1828, when Isaac Hilliard sold his North Carolina
holdings and settled in Williamson Co., Tenn.

Isaac Hilliard m. 11/4/1830, his cousin, Lucy Emily
Hilliard, b. 4/14/1810, and d. at "Mill Brook", 10/15/1845,
dau. of John and Elizabeth (Tunstall) Hilliard of "Black
Jack" plantation, Nash Co., N. C.

Children: (b. at "Mill Brook" Halifax Co., N.C.)

I. John James Byron Hilliard, b. 8/22/1832, m.
Maria Louisa Henning Hobbs, widow. (See later)
II. Ellen Alberta Tunstall Hilliard, d. in infancy.
III. Lucy Emily Hilliard, m. Dr. William Edward Wal-
ker, whose sister m. Dr. Robert Carter Hilliard.
Child:
1. William Edward Walker of Lafayette, La., b.
9/15/1858, d. 2/3/1948, m. 6/25/1890, Ellen
Parker Pharr. No issue.
IV. Kearney Barker Hilliard, d. in infancy.
V. Laura Virginia Hilliard, b. 12/26/1838, d.
9/11/1925, whose marriage to Hamilton Glentworth
in 1859, is noted in Virginia Clay-Clopton's
"Belle of the Fifties", as an important event in
Washington Society.
Child:
1. Clement Hilliard Glentworth, d. in Europe
without issue.
VI. Ella Hilliard, b. 8/12/1840, d. 4/10/1868, m.
Col. Thomas J. Faries of La. No issue.
VII. Tempie Leah Hilliard, d. in infancy.
VIII. Mary Roberta Hilliard, d. in infancy.

John James Byron Hilliard, son of Isaac and Lucy
Emily (Hilliard) Hilliard, was b. at "Mill Brook" plantation, Halifax Co., N. C., 8/22/1832, and d. at Louisville,
Ky., 3/22/1901. He attended Columbian College, Washington,
D. C., (now George Washington University) where he graduated
with an A.B. degree in 1850, after which he entered the
Harvard Law School, and graduated with his L.L.B. degree in
1852, being then only in his 20th year. He practiced law
in Halifax and Nash Counties, N. C., for nine years. At
the outbreak of the Civil War, he enlisted in the Confederate Army. After the war, he engaged in the cotton commission business in New Orleans. About 1870, Mr. Hilliard
moved to Louisville, Ky., and engaged in the banking business. He m. 4/25/1871, Mrs. Maria Louisa Henning Hobbs,
widow of Basil Hobbs and dau. of James W. Henning and wife,

Mildred Maupin, b. at Louisville, Ky., 5/4/1845, and d.
there 3/9/1894.

J. J. B. Hilliard and Son, Investment Securities,
established by the late John James Byron Hilliard about
1870, is now managed by his two sons, Isaac and Edward
Hobbs Hilliard of Louisville, Ky. John James Byron Hilliard
and his wife, Maria Louisa Henning Hobbs lived in Louisville, Ky.

Children:
I. James Henning Hilliard, b. 1872, d. 1883.
II. Byron Henning Hilliard, b. 8/5/1873, d. 3/10/
1922, continuing his father's business, m. at
Louisville, Ky., 11/15/1898, Aleen Lithgow Muldoon, b. at Louisville, Ky., 5/19/1877, dau. of
Michael McDonald Muldoon and wife, Alice Lithgow
of Louisville, Ky. In 1924, Mrs. Hilliard m.
Judge Robert Worth Bingham, late American Ambas-
sador to Great Britain.
Children:
1. James Byron Hilliard, b. 12/4/1899, present
owner of the Hogarth portrait of Betsy Barker Tunstall; m. 6/10/1925, Alice Gaylor
Latham.
Child:
(1) Elsie Gaylor Hilliard, b. 11/19/1933.
2. Alice Lithgow Hilliard, b. 6/14/1901, d. unmarried, 2/1/1931.
III. Mildred Maupin Hilliard, b. 10/3/1876, m. Ferdinand LaMotte, son of Ferdinand LaMotte and
wife, Ellen Newbold of Binghampton, N. Y.
Children:
1. Ferdinand LaMotte, d. in infancy.
2. Ferdinand LaMotte, b. 1/29/1910, m. 6/14/
1935, June Mitchell.
Children:
(1) Ferdinand LaMotte, IV, b. 2/18/1936.
(2) William Mitchell LaMotte, b. 9/3/1938.
(3) Nicholas Hilliard LaMotte, b. 8/14/1945.
3. Byron Hilliard LaMotte, b. 4/5/1913, m.
11/22/1941, Virginia Davis.
Children:
(1) Virginia Rankin LaMotte, b. 6/15/1944.
(2) Byron Hilliard LaMotte, b. 3/12/1947.
IV. Fanny Speed Hilliard, b. 1878, d. in infancy.
V. Isaac Hilliard, b. 10/10/1879, senior partner of
J. J. B. Hilliard and Son, m. 11/1/1910, Helen
Cochran Donigan, b. 7/23/1889, d. at Louisville,
Ky., 1/21/1932, dau. of Richard W. Donigan and

wife, Helen Cochran. Mr. Hilliard was educated
at Princeton University, Class of 1902.
Children:
1. Richard Donigan Hilliard, b. 11/5/1911, un-
    married, Second World War Service, Reserve
    F.A., 1st Armored Div., with overseas con-
    tingent to N. Ireland; three amphibious
    landings, Oran, Salerno, Anzio, served
    through N. Africa and Italian campaigns,
    with 568 days of combat, cited personally
    three times, received Bronze Star and Oak
    Leaf cluster, two unit citations, Major last
    year of War, killed in auto accident, 6/13/
    1948.
2. Helen Cochran Hilliard, b. 4/4/1914, m.
    12/28/1937, Baldwin Burnham, Lt. Col.(Staff)
    A.F.; no issue.
3. James Henning Hilliard, b. 5/25/1916, Sgt.
    Ground Forces A.F., with bombardment group
    in England two years, m. 4/8/1947, Mary G.
    Wheeler.
    Children:
    (1) Helen Donigan Hilliard, b. 5/13/1948.
    (2) Margaret Wheeler Hilliard, b. 5/25/1950.
    (3) Mary Guthrie Hilliard, b. 6/4/1953.

VI.   Edward Hobbs Hilliard, b. 8/5/1882, partner in
       J. J. B. Hilliard and Son, m. 1/28/1913, Nanine
       Shirley Irwin, b. 11/18/1883, dau. of Theodore
       Irwin and wife, Mary Craig Hobbs. Mr. Hilliard
       was educated at Princeton University. A.B. 1905.
       Children:
1. Nanine Irwin Hilliard, b. 11/1/1916, b. at
    Louisville, Ky., m. 4/26/1941, Grady E. Clay,
    Jr.
    Children:
    (1) Grady E. Clay, III, b. 5/6/1943.
    (2) Theodore Irwin Hilliard Clay, b. 3/12/
        1946.
    (3) Peter Maitland Clay, b. 10/16/1948.
2. Theodore Irwin Hilliard, b. 8/28/1918, at
    Louisville, Ky., unmarried, served in WW II,
    with 91st F.A. Bn. 1st Armored Div., and
    killed in action at Battle of San Pietro,
    Italy, 12/14/1943.
3. Edward Hobbs Hilliard, b. 10/22/1922, at
    Louisville, Ky., m. 10/20/1951, Joy Rushmore
    of Plainfield, N. Y., dau. of Murry Rushmore
    and wife, Helen Joy of Plainfield, N. Y.

Residence: 4201 Galapago St., Denver, 16,
Colorado.
Child:
    (1) Byron Rushmore Hilliard b. 4/28/1953.
    James Crafford Hilliard, son of James and Mourning
(Boddie) Hilliard, was b. at Hillardston, Nash Co., N. C.,
11/3/1806, and d. at "Woodlawn" plantation, Nash Co.,N.C.,
4/13/1860. He m. 2/10/1835, Mary Ann Ruffin, dau. of Samuel and Mary (Johnston) Ruffin. Mary Johnston was the dau.
of Col. Jonas Johnston of Rev. fame and his wife, Esther
Maund. Mary Ann Ruffin was b. at "Sycamore Grove", Edgecombe Co., N. C., 2/10/1813, and d. at "Woodlawn" plantation, Nash Co., N. C., 12/11/1843. James Crafford Hilliard
m. (2) 5/20/1845, Martha Ann Pitts, b. 11/19/1813, d. 10/
2/1889, dau. of Walter and Laura (Marshall) Pitts of Halifax Co., N. C. James Crafford Hilliard and his first wife,
Mary Ann Ruffin, had issue, born at "Woodlawn" plantation,
Nash Co., N. C.
    Children:(I-IV, 1st Marriage; V-X, 2nd Marriage)

I.   Mourning Boddie Hilliard, m. James M. Vaughan of
Warren Co., N. C. (See later)

II.   Elizabeth Maund Hilliard, b. 5/18/1838, d. in
Warren Co., N. C., 1862, m. 5/14/1861, William
T. Pegram of Warren Co., N. C.

III.   Samuel Ruffin Hilliard, m. Sarah Elizabeth Jones,
dau. of Alexander Clay Jones, M.D., and wife,
Sarah Rogers of Wake Co., N. C. (See later)

IV.   Jonas Johnston Hilliard, b. 11/14/1842, d. 6/6/
1862. Unmarried.

V.   James Cary Hilliard, b. 11/13/1846, d. 8/7/1886,
unmarried.

VI.   George W. B. Hilliard, b. 9/6/1848, d. 6/16/1888,
unmarried.

VII.   Martin Luther Hilliard, b. 1/17/1850, d. 6/22/
1850.

VIII.   Walter Scott Hilliard, b. 5/10/1851, d. 10/19/
1922, unmarried.

IX.   Laura Marshall Hilliard, b. 9/9/1853, d. 2/27/
1854.

X.   Mary Eliza Hilliard, b. 6/7/1856, d. 8/6/1936,
unmarried.

    Mourning Boddie Hilliard, dau. of James Crafford and
Mary Ann (Ruffin) Hilliard, was b. at "Woodlawn" plantation,
Nash Co., N. C., 12/21/1835, and d. at "Woodlawn", 7/29/
1917. She m. 11/14/1860, James M. Vaughn of Warrenton,
N. C., b. 11/7/1817, d. at "Woodlawn", 11/4/1886.
    Children:

I.   Mary Ann Vaughan, b. 10/2/1862, d. unmarried,

1/13/1924.

II.　　Lucy Hilliard Vaughan, b. 8/1/1864, m. 3/8/1908,
　　　　Henry A. Battle. No issue.

III.　Tempie Williams Vaughan, b. 6/25/1866, d. 11/23/
　　　　1918, m. 11/20/1897, C. F. Ellen of Nash Co.,
　　　　N. C., b. 4/5/1854, d. 11/19/1916.
　　　　Children:
　　　　1. Lucy Hilliard Ellen, b. 8/17/1899, m. 10/31/
　　　　　　1920, Charles Frederick McIntyre.
　　　　　　Children:
　　　　　　(1) Charles Frederick McIntyre, b. 10/29/
　　　　　　　　1921.
　　　　　　(2) Roderick Donald McIntyre, b. 9/5/1924.
　　　　　　(3) William Butler McIntyre, b. 7/29/1928.
　　　　　　(4) Lucy Ellen McIntyre.
　　　　2. Tempie Williams Ellen, b. 3/6/1903, m. Lewis
　　　　　　E. Roberts. No issue.

IV.　Olivia Salina Vaughan, b. 7/19/1868, d. 7/1/1870.
V.　　Samuel Johnston Vaughan, b. 9/18/1873, d. 9/8/
　　　　1898, unmarried.

Samuel Ruffin Hilliard, son of James Crafford and
Mary Ann (Ruffin) Hilliard, was b. at "Woodlawn" plantation,
Nash Co., N. C., 11/10/1840, and d. at Rocky Mount, N. C.,
10/2/1922. He attended Horner Military Academy, Oxford,
N. C. Also, Union College (now Duke University). At the
outbreak of the Civil War, he left college and enlisted at
Raleigh, N. C., in the Confederate Army, 4/12/1861, as a
member of Company "K", 15th N. C. Regiment. He was wounded
at Lee's farm near Richmond, Va., 4/12/1862, (one year from
date of enlistment). He was later Captain and Quarter Mas-
ter 2nd, Regiment N. C. State Guard. After the war, he
returned to "Woodlawn" and continued the operation of his
plantation. Samuel Ruffin Hilliard m. 1/17/1894, at Selma,
Johnston Co., N. C., Sarah (Sallie) Elizabeth Jones, who
was b. in Wake Co., N. C., 11/28/1866, and d. at Rocky Mount,
N. C., 12/9/1926, dau. of Alexander Clay Jones, M.D., of
Wake and Wilkes Counties, N. C., and his wife, Sarah, dau.
of Willie and Sarah (Whitehead) Rogers of Wake Co., N. C.
Samuel Ruffin Hilliard and his wife, Sarah Elizabeth Jones,
had issue, born at "Woodlawn" plantation, Nash Co., N. C.
　　　　Children:
I.　　Isaac Marvin Hilliard, b. 10/10/1894, m. Richard
　　　　Helen Whitnall. (See later)
II.　James Byron Hilliard, b. 1/15/1897, unmarried.
III.　Mary Ruffin Hilliard, b. 4/3/1899, unmarried.
　　　　Teacher in public schools (Lee School), Alexan-
　　　　dria, Va.
IV.　Elizabeth Rogers Hilliard, b. 10/1/1900.Unmarried.

V.   Samuel Jones Hilliard, b. 9/18/1902, m. 10/3/
      1936, at Adamstown, Maryland, Mary Hannah Patton,
      b. 11/12/1903, dau. of Fred Leith Patton and
      wife, Margaret Ann Hopkins of Charleston, Ill.
      No issue. Samuel Jones Hilliard is connected
      with the U. S. Navy Department, Washington,
      D. C., and resides near Leesburg, Va.
VI.   Foy Lynn Hilliard, b. 4/18/1907, m. Benjamin
      Robert Bostick, Jr. (See later)
     Isaac Marvin Hilliard, son of Samuel Ruffin and Sarah
Elizabeth (Jones) Hilliard, was b. at "Woodlawn" plantation, Nash Co., N. C., 10/10/1894, m. 7/8/1922, Richard
Helen Whitnall, dau. of Richard H. and Lou (Douglas) Whitnall of Fort Lauderdale, Fla. Isaac Marvin Hilliard
attended Bingham Military School at Asheville, N. C. Lives
at Miami, Fla. Issue born in Fla.
      Children:
I.   Helen Marvin Hilliard, b. 4/25/1923, m. 4/10/
      1948, Robert Earl Todd, b. 2/10/1921, at Van
      Wert, Ohio, son of Karl W. Todd and wife, Char-
      lotte Mae Gast of Van Wert, Ohio. Robert Earl
      Todd was educated at the University of Penn.,
      Carnegie Tech., and graduated at the University
      of Fla., 1949, B. of Arch. He is now in busi-
      ness at Fort Lauderdale, Fla., under the firm
      name of Todd and Wiesman, Architects.
           Second World War Service, enlisted 9/3/1943,
      at Philadelphia, Pa., discharged 1/17/1946, at
      Camp Atterbury, Ind., as T/5 in the 320th Eng.
      Bn. 95th Inf. Div. Saw action in Northern
      France, Rhineland, wounded crossing Moselle
      River at Metz, France in Nov., 1944, received
      American Theater Ribbon; EAMET Ribbon w/2 Bronze
      Stars, Good Conduct Medal, Purple Heart, and
      Victory Medal.
      Children:
      1. Richard Carey Todd, b. Fort Lauderdale, Fla.,
         10/9/1952.
      2. Gregory Brian Todd, b. 4/30/1956.
II.   William Kearney Hilliard, b. 8/6/1927, m. 4/29/
      1949, at Miami, Fla., Carol Jeanne Hendrix, b.
      11/22/1929, at Philadelphia, Pa., dau. of Wil-
      liam Wallace Hendrix and wife, Mildred Beatrice
      Davis. William Kearney Hilliard was educated at
      the University of Miami, Miami, Fla., U.S.N. WW
      II. Enlisted 5/21/1945, discharged 7/31/1947.
      Residence: 8000 S.W. 120 St., South Miami, Fla.
      Children:

      1. Patricia Gail Hilliard, b. 12/9/1950, Miami,
          Fla.
      2. Susanne Marie Hilliard, b. 6/15/1953, Miami,
          Fla.

III.   Betty Rogers Hilliard, b. 3/14/1929, m. at Miami,
          Fla., 6/26/1948, William Francis Donovan, b. at
          Lynn, Mass., 11/21/1927, son of William Ambrose
          Donovan and wife, Frances C. Dearden. U. S.
          Coast Guard, WW II. Enlisted at Boston, Mass.,
          1/5/1946, discharged June, 1947. William Francis
          Donovan was educated at Bentley School of
          Accounting, Boston, Mass. Residence: 785 Salem
          St., S. Lynnfield, Mass. Issue born at S. Lynn-
          field, Mass.
          Children:
      1. Carol Lou Donovan, b. 5/5/1949.
      2. William Michael Donovan, b. 6/16/1953.

IV.   Richard Whitnall Hilliard, b. 3/26/1932, U. S.
          Naval Reserve. Student, University of Miami,
          Miami, Fla.

    Foy Lynn Hilliard, dau. of Samuel Ruffin and Sarah
Elizabeth (Jones) Hilliard, b. 4/18/1907, m. Benjamin
Robert Bostick, Jr., Sat., 3:30 P.M., 7/23/1938, in St.
Peters, Church of England, at Valparaiso, Chile, the Rev.
Hubert S. Matthews, officiating. Benjamin Robert Bostick,
Jr., was b. 10/21/1910, son of Benjamin Robert Bostick and
his wife, Emily Ashforth of Westchester Co., N. Y. Residence:
581 Sheridan Drive, Lexington, Ky. Benjamin Robert Bostick,
Jr., is connected with the Universal Leaf Tobacco Co. Issue
born at Valparaiso, Chile.
          Children:
I.   Lynn Hilliard Bostick, b. 7/15,1939.
II.   Benjamin Robert Bostick, III, b. 11/1/1942.

    Elizabeth Jane Hilliard, dau. of James and Mourning
(Boddie) Hilliard of Hilliardston, Nash Co., N. C., was b.
2/1/1809, and d. at "Bracebridge Hall," Edgecombe Co., N.C.,
12/25/1840. She m. 9/20/1832, Jonas Johnston Carr, b.
2/15/1805, d. at "Bracebridge Hall," Edgecombe Co., N. C.,
5/16/1843, son of Elias and Celia (Johnston) Carr of Edgecombe Co., N. C. Issue of Elizabeth Jane (Hilliard) and
Jonas Johnston Carr were born at "Bracebridge Hall," Edgecombe Co., N. C.
          Children:
I.   Mary Boddie Carr, m. Major David Hinton. (See
          later)
II.   William Byas Carr, m. Elizabeth Irwin. (See later)
III.   Elias Carr, m. Eleanor Kearney.
IV.   James Hilliard Carr, d. in infancy.

Mary Boddie Carr, dau. of Elizabeth Jane (Hilliard) and Jonas Johnston Carr, was b. at "Bracebridge Hall," Edgecombe Co., N. C., 7/18/1833, and d. at "Midway," plantation, Wake Co., N. C., 7/30/1917. She m. 3/31/1852, David Hinton, b. at "The River," plantation, Wake Co., N.C., 10/1/1826, and d. at "Midway," plantation, Wake Co., N.C., 2/27/1876, son of Charles Lewis and Ann (Perry) Hinton.

Children:

I.   Charles Lewis Hinton, m. Elizabeth Tate Cain. (See later)

II.   Betsy Hinton, d. in infancy.

III.   David Hinton, d. in infancy.

IV.   Jane Hinton, m. William Randolph Watson. (See later)

V.   Mary Hilliard Hinton, unmarried, resided at the ancestral home "Midway" plantation, Wake Co., N. C., eight miles east of Raleigh, on the Raleigh-Rocky Mount Highway #64, b. 7/7/1869, d. 1/6/1961.

Charles Lewis Hinton, son of Mary Boddie (Carr) and David Hinton, was b. at "Midway" plantation, Wake Co., N.C., 6/15/1853, and d. there 11/19/1930. He m. 11/15/1882, Elizabeth Tate Cain, b. 6/15/1860, d. at "Midway" plantation, Wake Co., N. C., 7/19/1888, dau. of James Frederick Cain, M.C., and wife Julia Tate of Hillsboro, N. C. Charles Lewis Hinton was educated at the University of Va., and was a Wake Co. planter.

Children:

I.   David Hinton, b. 9/1/1883, d. 6/7/1884.

II.   James Cain Hinton, b. 2/27/1885, d. 1/6/1900.

III.   Elizabeth (Bessie) Cain Hinton, b. 12/4/1887, m. Henry Sprague Silver. (See later)

Elizabeth (Bessie) Cain Hinton, dau. of Charles Lewis and Elizabeth Tate (Cain) Hinton was b. at "Midway" plantation, Wake Co., N. C. 12/4/1887, m. at "Midway", 4/20/1920, Major Henry Sprague Silver, b. 7/7/1888, and d. at Raleigh, N. C., 11/10/1931, son of Manuel Silver and his wife, Kate Hale Sprague. Henry Sprague Silver was educated at N. C. State College, Raleigh, N. C. Major U.S.A. WW I, A.E.F. 28th Infantry 1st Div. D.S.C. (five citations). Issue born at Raleigh, N. C.

Children:

I.   Charles Hinton Silver, b. 2/18/1921, m. at Edenton, N. C., 12/18/1943, Betty Winston Wales, b. 5/2/1923, dau. of Charles Paddock Wales and wife, Duncan Cameron Winston of Edenton, N. C. Charles Hinton Silver was educated at Riverside Military Academy and N. C. State College. Commissioned

2nd Lt. Inf., 2/14/1942 (ROTC Riverside Military
Academy, Gainesville, Ga.), ordered to active
duty, 3/16/1942, South Pacific, 9/1/1942 to
12/1/1943, ETO, 9/1/1944 to 2/1/1945. Retired
1st Lt. Inf., 3/14/1946. End Terminal leave,
6/19/1946. Decorations, Combat Infantry Badge,
Bronze Star Medal, Purple Heart Medal, Asiatic
Pacific Theatre Medal, European Theatre Medal,
Victory Medal WW II. Residence: "Midway" plantation, Raleigh, N. C.
Children:
1. Charles Hinton Silver, Jr., b. 12/3/1945, at
    Ft. Sill, Oklahoma.
2. Winston Sprague Silver, b. 3/5/1948.
3. John Wales Silver, b. 4/15/1952.

II.   Henry Sprague Silver, Jr., b. 4/25/1922, m. at
        Los Angeles, California, 5/19/1946, Margret
        Elinor Meals, b. 10/5/1925, at Phoenix, Arizona,
        dau. of Ross Knight Meals and wife, Florence
        Caroline Youngberg. Henry Sprague Silver, Jr.,
        was educated at Porter Military Academy, Char-
        leston, S. C., and N. C. State College, Raleigh,
        N. C., Class of 1944. U.S.M.C., 4/4/1942, Com-
        missioned, 2nd Lt., 8/1/1945. 1st Lt., 8/1/1948,
        Captain, 12/12/1953. (Reserve status since
        6/26/1946.) Residence: P. O. Box 692, Raleigh,
        N. C.
        Children:
        1. Henry Sprague Silver, III, b. 9/18/1947.
        2. Mary Hinton Silver, b. 5/9/1952.
        3. James Cain Silver, b. 7/15/1954.

III.   Elizabeth Sprague Silver, b. 7/21/1927, m.
        4/23/1949, Godfrey Cheshire, Jr., in Christ
        Church, Raleigh, N. C. Godfrey Cheshire was b.
        7/17/1918, son of Godfrey Cheshire and wife,
        Alice C. Shiell of Raleigh, N. C., educated at
        Sewanee, Tenn., and the University of N. C., Lt.
        Commander, U.S.N., in WW II. Residence: 1300
        Park Drive, Raleigh, N. C.
        Children:
        1. Godfrey Cheshire, III, b. 6/3/1951.
        2. Sprague Silver Cheshire, b. 2/17/1953.

Jane Hinton, dau. of Mary Boddie (Carr) and David
Hinton, was b. at "Midway" plantation, Wake Co., N. C.,
7/26/1861, d. at Darlington, S. C., 6/25/1930, buried at
Warrenton, N. C. She m. at "Midway", 10/14/1891, William
Randolph Watson, b. 8/29/1859, d. 2/27/1937, son of Lewis
N. and Anna (Chritchton) Watson of Warrenton, N. C. Mr.

Watson was connected with the Export Leaf Tobacco Co., and lived at Darlington, S. C.
> Children:
>
> I.   David Lewis Watson, b. 8/11/1892, d. unmarried, 5/3/1946.
>
> II.   William Randolph Watson, Jr., b. 9/7/1894, m. 6/28/1930, Katherine Badger Johnston, dau. of Rev. David Thomas Johnston, Episcopal Minister. William Randolph Watson, Jr., graduated from the University of N. C. Served in WW I and II. Now Col., U.S.A.
> > Children:
> > 1. William Randolph Watson, III, b. 5/5/1931.
> > 2. David Thomas Watson, b. 1/20/1936.
> > 3. Katherine Johnston Watson.
>
> III.   Mary Hinton Watson, b. 6/21/1897, unmarried.

Elias Carr, son of Elizabeth Jane (Hilliard) and Jonas Johnston Carr, was b. at "Bracebridge Hall," Edgecombe Co., N. C., 2/25/1839, and d. there 7/22/1900. He m. 5/24/1859, Eleanor Kearney, b. 3/1/1840, d. 3/29/1912, dau. of William and Maria (Alston) Kearney of Warren Co., N. C. Elias Carr was educated at the University of N. C., and Va. He was elected 71st Governor of N. C., in 1892 and served four years. Issue born at "Bracebridge Hall."
> Children:
>
> I.   William Kearney Carr, m. Martina Van Riswick, no issue.
>
> II.   John Carr, M.D., d. unmarried.
>
> III.   Mary Elizabeth Carr, d. unmarried.
>
> IV.   Elias Carr, m. Maud Inge. (See later)
>
> V.   Eleanor Carr, m. Hugh Matthews, no issue.
>
> VI.   Annie Bruce, m. Douglass Sterrett, no issue.

Elias Carr, Jr., son of Elias and Eleanor (Kearney) Carr, was b. at "Bracebridge Hall," Edgecombe Co., N. C., 8/6/1866, and d. at "Bracebridge Hall," 1/9/1923. He m. 2/25/1903, Maud Inge, b. 10/22/1880, dau. of Adolphus Merriman Inge and his wife, Mary Della Cochrane of Halifax Co., N. C.
> Child:
>
> I.   Martina Van Riswick Carr. (See later)

Martina Van Riswick Carr, only child of Elias Carr, Jr., and his wife, Maud Inge, was b. at "Bracebridge Hall," Edgecombe Co., N. C., 9/3/1904, m. 7/11/1924, William Haydock Fillmore, Col. A.F., U.S.A., WW II. Col. Fillmore and his family reside at "Chosumneda," their plantation in Edgecombe Co., N. C.
> Children:
>
> I.   William Carr Fillmore, b. 8/18/1926, graduated

U.S. Naval Academy, Annapolis, Maryland, June,
1950. He m. at National Cathedral, Washington,
D. C., 12/3/1953, Joan Florence Cooke, dau. of
Dr. Francis Trowbridge Cook, D.D., and wife,
Florence Rey.

II. Martina Carr Fillmore, b. 11/19/1928.
III. Joan Kearney, b. 12/21/1930.

William Byas Carr, son of Elizabeth Jane Hilliard and
Jonas Johnston Carr, was b. at "Bracebridge Hall," Edgecombe Co., N. C., 5/25/1835, and d. in Warren Co., N. C.,
8/4/1871. He m. Elizabeth Irwin, dau. of Thomas and Caroline (Arrington) Irwin of Nash Co., N. C.

Children:

I. Caroline Irwin Carr, b. Sept., 1859, d. 7/30/
1938, buried at Warrenton, N. C., m. Don Mitchell
of Oxford, N. C., no issue.
II. Jonas Johnston Carr, b. 9/1/1861, d. at Asheville, N. C., 7/10/1918, buried at Warrenton,
N. C. He m. at Oxford, N. C., Viola Jones, b.
1/6/1862. (See later)

Jonas Johnston Carr, son of William Byas and Elizabeth (Irwin) Carr, was b. 9/1/1861, at "Fair Mount," Warren Co., N. C., and d. at Asheville, N. C., 7/10/1918, m.
3/21/1883, at Oxford, N. C., Viola Jane Jones, b. 1/6/1862.

Children:

I. William Byas Carr, b. 1/21/1884, d. at Los
Angeles, Calif., 6/24/1929, m. 9/14/1922, Bertha
McLaurin Cleveland, no issue.
II. Mary Davis Carr, b. 10/2/1885, m. Edward Z. Ray
of Asheville, N. C., no issue.
III. Elbert Carr, b. 8/15/1887, lives at Dallas,
Texas, m. 6/27/1914, Annette Cannon.
IV. Jane Carr, m. William Rogers Robertson, no issue.
V. Josephine Johnston Carr, b. 9/26/1897, m. 6/4/
1927, John Frederick Peter Tate.
VI. Edith Puryer Carr, b. 1/9/1900, m. 2/18/1928,
Thomas Pangle.
VII. Francis John Carr, b. 8/6/1903, m. Dorothy
Moller.
VIII. Hilliard Wainwright Carr, b. 3/14/1905, married.

Elijah Boddie Hilliard, son of James and Mourning
(Boddie) Hilliard, b. at Hilliardston, Nash Co., N. C.,
1815, and d. there 7/27/1862, m. 11/24/1835, Rebecca Brown
Powell, b. 8/22/1816, d. 11/18/1860, dau. of Jesse and
Mildred (Brown) Powell of Wake Co., N. C. Elijah Boddie
Hilliard and his wife are buried at "Woodlawn." He was
educated at the University of Va., and inherited Hilliard-
ston plantation from his father and continued the operation

of Hilliardston plantation until his death.
Children:
I.   Alice Hilliard, b. 8/16/1836, m. William Whitfield Carraway.
II.   Rebecca Hilliard, b. 9/9/1838, m. Gavin Hogg Clark. (See later)
III.   Elizabeth Jane Hilliard, b. 11/25/1840, m. Alexander Hamilton Hilliard, son of William Henry and Sally (Dortch) Hilliard.
IV.   Jesse Powell Hilliard, b. 11/16/1842, m. (1) Caroline B. Garrett, m. (2) Maud C. Spruill. (See later)
V.   Mary Bennett Hilliard, b. 6/26/1845, m. William Whitfield Carraway.
VI.   James Hilliard, d. in infancy.
VII. Sidney Perry Hilliard, b. 10/26/1850, m. Elizabeth Garrett. (See later)
VIII. Blanch Hilliard, b. 8/22/1855, m. Capt. (C.S.A.) Orren Williams. (See later)
IX.   Elijah Boddie Hilliard, b. 10/26/1858, d. 2/7/1894, unmarried.

Rebecca Hilliard, dau. of Elijah Boddie and Rebecca (Powell) Hilliard, b. at Hilliardston, Nash Co., N. C., 9/9/1838, d. 1/3/1897, m. 11/18/1857, Gavin Hogg Clark, (1835-1906), son of William McKenzie Clark and wife, Martha Boddie Williams of Bertie Co., N. C.
Children:
I.   Martha Rebecca Clark, (1859-1939), m. (1) George Douglas Drake, no issue, m. (2) I. B. Gardner, no issue.
II.   Kenneth McKenzie Clark, (1860-1895), d.s.p.
III.   Harriet Janet Clark, (1861-1903), m. 1880, Frederick Battle Drake, (1854-1922).
Children:
1. Elijah Hilliard Drake, (1887-1940), d.s.p.
2. Clark Battle Drake, b. 1890, m. 1912, Mary Battle.
3. Margaret Drake, b. 1893, m. 1912, John Freeman.
4. Elizabeth Drake, b. 1895, m. 1912, Neverson York.
5. Rebecca Drake, b. 1898, m. 1918, Will Fred Battle.
6. Mary Drake, b. 1900, m. 1921, Edgar Taylor
7. Tempie Buck Drake, b. 1903, m. Charles Saunders.
8. Fred Battle Drake, b. 1905, m. Lena Joyner.
IV.   Gavin Hogg Clark, (1863-1897), d.s.p.

V. Atherton Hill Clark, (1865-1939), m. (1) Sallie
Bryant, m. (2) Lucy Gay.

VI. Laura Pugh Clark, (1867-1892), d.s.p.

VII. Lucy Hilliard Clark, (1870-1941), m. 1890, Andrew Joyner Campbell, (1859-1924).
Children:
1. Andrew Joyner Campbell, b. 1891, m. 1932,
   Ethel Barker.
2. Lucy Clark Campbell, (1893-1901), d.s.p.
3. Elizabeth Hilliard Campbell, b. 1895, m.
   1918, LaVerne Pyles.
4. Caroline Rebecca Campbell, b. 1898, m. 1918,
   George N. Benoit.
5. William McKenzie Campbell, b. 1900, m. 1931,
   Josephine Phillips.
6. Gary Campbell, b. 1902, m. (1) 1926, Bessie
   V. Grimes, m. (2) 1934, Jewell Hill.
7. Frank Edward Campbell, b. 1904, m. (1) 1922,
   Ruth DeGrange, m. (2) 1928, Gladys Williams.
8. Emily Davis Campbell, b. 1911, m. 1932, Malcolm A. Edwards.
9. Jessie Roper Campbell, b. 1913, m. 1930,
   Clifton H. Ralph.

VIII. Colin McKenzie Clark, (1873-1927), m. 1898, Mrs.
Anna Eliza (Boseman) Hart, (1859-1930).
Child:
1. Rebecca Wilson Clark, b. 1899, m. 1931,
   Theodore Allen Snyder.

IX. Frances Gray Clark, b. 1875, m. 1900, David Roswell Hogan, (1870-1941), no issue.

X. Jesse McKenzie Clark, (1879-193_), d.s.p.

Jesse Powell Hilliard, son of Elijah Boddie and Rebecca (Powell) Hilliard, b. at Hilliardston, Nash Co., N. C.,
11/16/1842, and d. at Plymouth, N. C., 6/1/1902, m. (1)
8/10/1864, Caroline Belinda Garrett, b. 10/12/1841, d. at
Plymouth, N. C., 3/31/1887, dau. of Alfred Franklin Garret.
He m. (2) 1/14/1891, Maud Carstarphen Spruill.

 Children: (1st marriage)

I. Alfred Franklin Hilliard.

II. Caroline Rebecca Hilliard, b. 10/1/1867, d. at
Plymouth, N. C., 11/23/1936, m. at Plymouth,
N. C., 12/31/1890, James Henry Smith, b. 9/8/
1864, d. at Plymouth, N. C., 1/28/1940.
Children:
1. Isolind Smith, b. 3/12/1892, m. 1/17/1911,
   Sidney Ambrose Ward, b. 8/17/1887, d. at
   Plymouth, N. C., 7/8/1939.
   Children:

    (1) Sidney Alfred Ward, b. 2/24/1912, d. at
        Ft. Meade, Md., 2/12/1953, Capt. U.S.A.
        He m. 9/7/1945, Eula Bennett, b. 9/17/
        1911, dau. of Willie David and Julia
        (Pitts) Bennett, no issue.
    (2) James Harold Ward, b. 11/17/1920, m.
        Nancy Louise Bunker. Residence: Ply-
        mouth, N. C.
    (3) Rebecca Hilliard Ward, b. 1/27/1923, m.
        Percival Rudolph Ashby, b. 12/4/1920,
        son of Percival Rudolph Ashby and wife,
        Ruth Nicholson.
        Children:
        a. James Nicholson Ashby, b. 7/14/1947.
        b. Rebecca Hilliard Ashby, b. 2/24/1951.
        Residence: Greenville, N. C.
2. Carrie Garret Smith, b. 7/10/1893, m. Nicho-
    las S. Mobley, no issue.
3. Laura Meredith Smith, b. 2/14/1895, m. 4/26/
    1916, Robert Ward Johnston.
    Child:
    (1) Meredith Latham Johnston, b. 1/6/1923.
4. Mary Owens Smith, b. 9/11/1896, m. (1) 10/18/
    1923, Charles Warren Cahoon, b. 10/18/1896,
    d. 12/1/1931. She m. (2) Chester Hawkins,
    no issue. Residence: Elizabeth City, N. C.
    Children: (1st marriage)
    (1) Mary Corinne Cahoon, b. 10/22/1926, m.
        6/12/1954, Porter Graves Lea, Jr., of
        Burlington, N. C.
    (2) Anne Hilliard Cahoon, b. 12/6/1926, m.
        9/2/1950, Jack Dillard Stratton, Jr., b.
        1/8/1922.
        Children:
        a. Richard Cahoon Stratton, b. 3/19/1952.
        b. Katheryne Anne Stratton, b. 2/26/1954.
        Jack Dillard Stratton, Jr., was educated
        at University of N. C., Class, 1950.
        Residence: 23644 Schoolcraft, Detroit,
        23, Michigan.
5. Corinne Davenport Smith, b. 3/21/1899, m.
    6/27/1923, Horace Vernon Austin, no issue.
6. James Hilliard Smith, b. 1/26/1907, Plymouth,
    N. C., m. 5/6/1932, Evelyn Ward Brown, b.
    5/21/1910, Plymouth, N. C., dau. of Henry
    Ward Brown and wife, Evelyn Lee Owens. James
    Hilliard Smith was educated University of
    N. C., now in Insurance Business at Goldsboro,

N. C.
Child:
(1) James Hilliard Smith, Jr., b. 4/7/1939.

III.   Alice Cary Hilliard, b. 3/6/1869, m. 10/2/1889, William Thomas Spruill.
Children:
1. Carrie Garret Spruill, (1890-1915), d.s.p.
2. Ida Blount Spruill, b. 12/30/1899, m. Louis Latham Owens.
3. Millie Estelle Spruill, b. 4/2/1894, m. Edgar R. Boney.
4. Nathan Hilliard Spruill, b. 4/5/1896.
5. Jesse Ward Spruill, b. 11/9/1898, m. Clifton Cotton.
6. William Thorne Spruill, b. 6/8/1902.
7. Alice Cary Spruill, b. 11/3/1907.

IV.   Jesse Peace Hilliard, b. 11/13/1870, m. 1/10/1902, Fred Williams.
Children:
1. Raymond Hilliard.
2. Fred Grandy Hilliard.
3. Richard Alfred Hilliard.
4. Carl Williams Hilliard.

V.   Mary Temperance Hilliard, b. 8/11/1874, m. Louis Latham Owens.
Child:
1. Doris Hilliard Owens, b. 10/19/1906, m. 12/30/1925, Jewell C. Ayers.
Child:
(1) Mary Owens Ayers, b. 8/15/1926.
Children: (2nd marriage)

VI.   Willie Carstarphen Hilliard, b. 10/22/1893, m. 6/8/1930, Mary Grady Daniels.

VII.   Fannie Gordon Hilliard, b. 10/12/1896.
VIII.   Sidney Boddie Hilliard, b. 3/16/1899, m. Sybel Martin.
Child:
1. Rebecca Hilliard, b. 10/14/1926.

Dr. Sidney Perry Hilliard, son of Elijah Boddie and Rebecca (Powell) Hilliard, b. at Hilliardston, Nash Co., N. C., 10/26/1850, and d. at Greensboro, N. C., 12/24/1919, m. 1871, Elizabeth Garrett, dau. of Dr. Joseph J. Garrett and wife, Henrietta Mercer of Halifax Co., N. C. Twelve years later, when he was thirty-two, he begin the study of dentistry at the Baltimore College of Dental Surgery, and was an honor graduate from this institution in the Class of 1883. In his professional career, he was especially known throughout N. C., and adjoining States for his skill in

building beautifully contoured fillings from cohesive foil.
For fifteen years, he was honored as a member of the N. C.
State Board of Dental Examiners, and was also honored as
President of the Society in the year, 1889-90. In the
business and social life of his community, he was as prom-
inent as in his profession life. For a number of years, he
served as vice-president of the First National Bank of Rocky
Mount, N. C., which institution he helped to organize.
Among the fraternal orders, he stood high as a Mason and
Shriner, and was also a member of the orders, Knights of
Pythias and Odd Fellows. In his religious life, he was a
member of the First Methodist Episcopal Church (South) of
Rocky Mount, N. C. His wife died Christmas Eve night,1925.
Dr. and Mrs. Hilliard are buried in the Hilliard plot, Pine
View Cemetery, Rocky Mount, N. C.

         Children:
I.   Son, d. in infancy.
II.   Albert Sidney Hilliard, d. age, 26, unmarried.
    Blanch Hilliard, dau. of Elijah Boddie and Rebecca
(Powell) Hilliard, b. at Hilliardston, Nash Co., N. C.,
8/22/1855, and d. at Tarboro, N. C., 2/24/1934, m. 11/15/
1887, (as his second wife), Capt. (C.S.A.) Orren Williams
of Tarboro, N. C., b. 7/6/1835, d. at Tarboro, N. C.,
1/19/1904, son of John Williams and wife, Eliza Caroline
Mathewson.

         Child:
I.   Blanch Hilliard Williams, b. 7/25/1890, m. at
        Tarboro, N. C., 8/7/1918, Charles Cecil Todd, b.
        9/4/1882, son of John Casey Todd and wife, Mar-
        tha Elizabeth Younger of Weakley Co., Tenn.
        Residence: 1133 Sycamore Street, Rocky Mount,
        N. C.
        Children:
        1. Martha Cecil Todd, b. 6/11/1926, educated
           at Peace Jr. College, Raleigh, N. C., and
           Queens College, Charlotte, N. C., m. 8/19/
           1950, John Wilson Dillard, Jr., educated
           N. C. State College, Class of 1950, son of
           John Wilson Dillard and wife, Annie Mae
           Barnes of Wilson, N. C. Residence: Martins-
           ville, Va.
           Children:
           (1) John Wilson Dillard, III, b. 12/15/1953.
           (2) Charles Todd Dillard, b. 9/15/1954.
        2. Charles Cecil Todd, Jr., b. 3/3/1929, B.S.,
           University of N. C., 1950.
    Mary Temperance Hilliard, dau. of James and Mourning
(Boddie) Hilliard, b. at Hilliardston, Nash Co., N. C.,

11/16/1816, and d. at "Buxton Place," Warren Co., N. C.,
2/4/1866, m. at Hilliardston, 12/17/1834, Warren Co., N. C.,
7/17/1887, son of Henry Guston Williams and wife, Lucy
Tunstall, dau. of Lt. Col. William Tunstall and wife, Betsy
Barker, dau. of Hon. Thomas Barker of Edenton, N. C. John
Buxton Williams m. (2) Mrs. Samuel Johnston Clark, nee Tempie Thorne, cousin of his first wife, Mary Temperance Hilliard.

Children:
I.   James Hilliard Williams, b. 10/7/1835, m. Susan
      Elizabeth Lyon. (See later)
II.   Lucy Tunstall Williams, d.s.p.
III. Henry Guston Williams, killed at battle of Mal-
      vern Hill, (C.S.A.).
IV.   John Buxton Williams, M.D., m. Carrie Peters of
      Norfolk, Va.
      Children:
      1. Tempie Hilliard Williams.
      2. William Peters Williams.
      3. John Buxton Williams, M.D., Washington, D.C.
      4. Henry Guston Williams.
      5. Mary Peters Williams.
      6. Virginia Reed Williams.
      7. Laura Williams.
V.   Solomon Buxton Williams, b. 8/22/1846, m. Eva
      Douglas Thornton of Suffolk, Va. (See later)
VI.   Tempie Hilliard Williams, b. 12/17/1848, d. at
      Warrenton, N. C., 7/13/1923, m. 6/14/1876, John
      Alexander Dameron, b. 12/10/1846, d. at Warren-
      ton, N. C., 6/8/1918.
      Children:
      1. Buxton Williams Dameron, b. 3/18/1877, d.
          1/23/1923, unmarried.
      2. Julia Mangum Dameron, b. 5/28/1878. Lived
          at Warrenton, N. C., unmarried.
      3. William Henry Dameron, b. 1/21/1880, d.
          10/7/1935, at Warrenton, N. C., m. 12/21/
          1911, Mattie W. Jones.
          Children:
          (1) Mattie Wiggins Dameron, m. Thomas Kenan
              Smith.
              Children:
              a. Thomas Kenan Smith, Jr.
              b. Mildred McRary Smith.
          (2) William Henry Dameron.
          (3) Rozella Wiggins Dameron.
      4. John Alexander Dameron, b. Nov., 1881, m.
          Annie Shirley Fitts, no issue.

5. Tempie Hilliard Dameron, b. 10/21/1883, unmarried, lives at Warrenton, N. C.
6. Leah Josephine Dameron, b. 8/20/1885, unmarried, lives at Warrenton, N. C.
7. Thomas Barker Dameron, b. 5/27/1888, m. Isa Sills of Nashville, N. C. Residence: Goldsboro, N. C.
   Children:
   (1) Isa Sills Dameron.
   (2) Martha Scott Dameron.
   (3) Thomas Barker Dameron, Jr.
8. Lula Mae Dameron, unmarried, lives at Warrenton, N. C.
9. Lillie Belle Dameron, unmarried, lives at Warrenton, N. C.

VII. Jonas Carr Williams, b. 12/24/1850, m. (1) Martha (Pattie) Clark Jones, (2) Mrs. Anna Edgerton. (See later)

VIII. Romeo Williams, d.s.p.

IX. Thomas Barker Williams, b. 8/9/1855, d. 5/3/1926, M.D., m. 10/23/1877, Lucy Thweatt Jerman, b. 5/20/1854, d. ____, dau. of Dr. T. P. Jerman, of Ridgeway, Warren Co., N. C.
   Children:
   1. Palmer Jerman Williams, b. 3/25/1879, d. 10/13/1925.
   2. Buxton Barker Williams, b. 4/27/1881, d. 3/8/1930, m. Sept., 1911, Sue Prestlow, b. 12/5/1885.
      Child:
      (1) Buxton Barker Williams, b. 11/25/1912, m. 5/30/1936, Margaret Paschal.
   3. Lucy Snydnor Williams, b. 12/17/1883, unmarried.
   4. Thomas Barker Williams, (1886-1893), d.s.p.
   5. Tempie Hilliard Williams, (1888-1892), d.s.p.
   6. Julia Borden Williams, b. 11/15/1891, unmarried.

X. Buxton Boddie Williams, b. 3/18/1858, at "Buxton Place," Warren Co., N. C., and d. 10/11/1930, M.C., at Greensboro, N. C., m. 11/7/1883, Martha Edward Alston, b. 3/11/1860, d. 1/9/1931, dau. of Alfred Alston and wife, Polly Dawson Kearney. Dr. Williams was educated at University of Maryland.
   Children:
   1. William Alston Williams, d. young.
   2. Van Wyck Williams, b. 7/18/1886, m.4/17/1926,

Sarah Alberta Watkins, b. 2/23/1897, dau. of
Dr. Warren Byers Watkins and wife, Pearl
Banks of Greensboro, Ala.
Children:
(1) Dorothy Alston Williams, b. 10/4/1927,
    m. 8/22/1947, James Landon Taylor.
    Child:
    a. John Van Wyck Taylor, b. 6/17/1950.
(2) Van Wyck Williams, Jr., b. 10/30/1930,
    m. 12/10/1952, Betty Anderson Duncan, b.
    2/18/1926.

3. Rie Alston Williams, b. 5/21/1888, at Centerville, Franklin Co., N. C., m. (1) 3/29/1910,
Oscar S. Rand, b. 2/19/1885, d. 6/18/1913,
son of Jackson Rand and wife, Laura Carlock
of Huntsville, Ala., m. (2) 11/28/1925,
Robert Hunt Parker, b. 2/15/1892, son of
Romulus Bragg Parker and wife, Victoria Hunt
of Enfield, N. C., A.B. Degree from University of Va., 1912, B. L. Degree from same,
1915, F.A. Officer, WW I, Member of General
Assembly of N. C., Prosecuting Officer, 3rd
Judicial District, Judge of Superior Court,
3rd Judicial District, now Associate Justice
of the N. C. Supreme Court. No issue.
Residence: Sir Walter Hotel, Raleigh, N. C.,
and Roanoke Rapids, N. C.

4. Harry Buxton Williams, b. 6/7/1890, m. 4/20/
1918, Elizabeth Grist Carrow, b. 9/29/1898,
dau. of Harvey Carrow and wife, Annie Grist
of Washington, N. C.
Child:
(1) Elizabeth Carrow Williams, b. 7/20/1920,
    m. Owen G. Rodman, b. 1/8/1915.
    Children:
    a. Elizabeth Carrow Rodman, b. 5/16/1948.
    b. Diane Alston Rodman, b. 7/4/1952.

5. Alfred Alston Williams, b. 6/23/1892, d.
9/9/1918, unmarried.

6. Fanny Somerville Williams, b. 6/11/1895, m.
12/15/1915, at Greensboro, N. C., Fielding
Lewis Fry, b. 3/12/1892, son of Howell Lewis
Fry and wife, Mary Estelle Pepper of Greensboro, N. C. Fielding Lewis Fry was educated
at University of N. C., and is in the Insurance business at Greensboro, N. C. Was Mayor
of Greensboro, 1947-48.
Child:

(1) Martha Williams Fry, b. 10/27/1916,
m. 4/20/1940, at Greensboro, N. C.,
Richard Reed DeVane.
Children:
a. Martha Alston DeVane, b. 6/16/
1941.
b. Mary Lewis DeVane, b. 1/2/1947.

James Hilliard Williams, son of Mary Temperance (Hilliard) and John Buxton Williams, was b. 10/7/1835, at Hilliardston, Nash Co., N. C., and d. 1/15/1897, at Newton, N. J., served in signal corps (C.S.A.), at Smithfield, N. C. He graduated at the University of N. C., Class,1857. He m. 8/20/1857, in Pickens Co., Ala., Susan Elizabeth Lyon, b. there 9/23/1837, d. 1/16/1883, in Warren Co., N. C., dau. of Andrew Jackson Lyon and wife, Susan Garnett.
Children:

I. John Buxton Williams, (1858-1863).
II. Andrew Lyon Williams, b. 2/6/1860, in West Carroll Parish, La., d. 8/10/1918, at his home in Bay City, Texas., m. 5/25/1887, Elizabeth Adams, b. 10/12/1861, dau. of Thomas S. Adams and wife, Lucy Tunstall Clanton, daughter of Landon Clanton and wife, Harriet Rowena Williams.
Children:

1. Talbot Adams Williams, b. 10/13/1888, m. 6/5/1918, Josephine McCollough and lives at Bay City, Texas.
Child:
(1) Talbot Adams Williams, b. 4/22/1921.
2. Susan Lyon Williams, b. 4/12/1890, m. 9/1/1916, Thomas N. McFarlane and lives at Galveston, Texas.
Child:
(1) Barbara Gray McFarlane, b. 11/7/1917, m. 11/16/1939, Grafton Tennant Austin, Jr.
3. Jean Elizabeth Williams, b. 2/28/1895, m. 4/16/1926, Paul Spurgeon Lewis and lives at Victoria, Texas.
Children:
(1) Paul Spurgeon Lewis, b. 10/1/1930.
(2) Thomas Spencer Lewis, b. 8/17/1933.
4. Grace Williams, b. 10/21/1898, m. 1934, Firman Y. Jackson and lives in Texas.
5. Andrew Lyon Williams, b. 3/16/1902, m. 5/1/1926, Joyce Hester and lives at Laredo, Tex.
Child:
(1) Andrew Lyon Williams, b. 2/28/1931.
III. James Hilliard Williams, (1861-1868).

IV.   Harry Guston Williams, b. 7/2/1864, Warren Co.,
N. C., d. 11/2/1937, at his home near Ludowici,
Ga., m. 3/18/1886, Elizabeth Ann McDuffie, b.
2/25/1864, d. 11/6/1952, dau. of James L. Mc-
Duffie and wife, Mary Johnson of Fayetteville,
N. C.
Children:
1. Harry Guston Williams, (1887-1907), d.s.p.
2. James Lyle Williams, b. 6/14/1890, m. 8/8/
1916, Mary McDuffie of Macon, Ga.
Child:
(1) James Lyle Williams, b. 5/9/1918.
3. Lillian Lacy Williams, b. 9/27/1893, m.
11/22/1922, Pettway Boyd Burwell of Warrenton, N. C., no issue. Residence: Walterboro,
S. C.
4. Mary Fairfax Williams, b. 8/29/1895, m. (1)
8/10/1938, Charles Farmer Hendry, (2) 4/9/
1938, David Starr Owen.
Child:
(1) Mary Williams Hendry, b. 9/18/1928,
legally adopted by D. S. Owen and name
changed to Owen in 1938, m. 1/3/1952,
Amos Ryder Worth, Capt. U.S. Army of
Staten Island, N. Y.
Children:
a. Thomas Ryder Worth, Jr., b. 10/28/
1952, Savannah, Ga.
b. Elizabeth Lyon Worth, b. Munich,
Germany, 3/19/1954.
5. Susan Elizabeth Lyon Williams, b. 10/5/1897,
m. 12/27/1919, Walter W. Meeks, Jr. No
record of issue.
6. Helen Reid Williams, b. 9/14/1899, m. 5/14/
1927, Thomas Auld Coxon of Helensburgh,
Scotland. Helen William Coxon was a member
of the Lower House of the General Assembly
of Ga., 1933/1939, and a member of the State
Senate of Ga., 1941/1942. She was appointed
a member of the Ga. State Board of Pardons
and Paroles in 1943, for a seven year term
and resigned at the end of six years. No
issue. Residence: "Old Williams Place,"
Ludowici, Ga.

V.   Major Lyon Williams, b. 8/6/1866, in La., d.
6/6/1939, at his home in Grapeland, Tex., m.
1895, Warrior, Ala., Josephine Dean, b. 11/28/
1875, dau. of W. L. Dean of Warrior, Ala.

Children:
1. Harry Williams, b. 1/28/1896, of Grapeland,
   Tex., served in France in WW I, m. 9/26/
   1927, Effie Rogers.
   Children:
   (1) Ina Ruth Williams, b. 1/14/1932.
   (2) Mira Jo Williams, b. 5/23/1935.
   (3) Mary Frances Williams, b. 1/8/1939.
2. Ruth Williams, b. 3/28/1897, m. 6/2/1925,
   Edd Kastrop and lives at Houston, Tex.
3. Hilliard Williams, b. 5/10/1898, m. 1/19/
   1928, Anna Belle Walters and lives at Grapeland, Tex.
   Children:
   (1) Patsy Nell Williams, b. 7/7/1933.
   (2) Barbara Jean Williams, b. 3/14/1937.
4. Thomas Barker Williams, b. 4/1/1900, m.
   10/14/1927, Evelyn Burden and lives at
   Houston, Tex.
   Children:
   (1) Dorothy Jane Williams, b. 9/11/1928.
   (2) Shirley Williams, b. 1/21/1940.
5. Minnie Williams, b. 12/19/1901, m. 2/4/1922,
   R. J. Haynes and lives at Grapeland, Tex.
   Child:
   (1) Katherine Haynes, b. 10/26/1922, m.
       9/25/1943, William Alvis Story.
       Child:
       a. Fay Lee Story, b. 8/15/1945.
6. Edgar Williams, b. 4/10/1903, m. 12/24/1925,
   Nelda Minor and lives at Kilgore, Tex.
   Children:
   (1) Charles Harold Williams, b. 9/3/1926.
   (2) Paul Dean Williams, b. 9/8/1938.
7. Andrew Williams, b. 9/26/1904, m. 2/19/1930,
   Fay Minor and lives at Kilgore, Tex.
   Children:
   (1) Duane Williams, b. 10/21/1931.
   (2) Judith Arlene Williams, b. 8/31/1944.
8. Esther Williams, b. 5/5/1907, m. 3/4/1927,
   Elva Stockbridge and lives at Houston, Tex.
   Children:
   (1) Jo Evelyn Stockbridge, b. 1/15/1928, m.
       John Roark.
       Child:
       a. Linda Carol Roark, b. 12/1/1948.
   (2) Jeraldine Stockbridge, b. 9/5/1940.
9. Shepard Williams, b. 10/6/1908.

10. Woodard Williams, b. 4/5/1910, m. 11/13/1931,
    Olive Walters, and lives at Longview, Tex.
11. Paul Williams, b. 3/21/1912, and m. 11/4/
    1938, Delma Cheatham and lives at Grapeland,
    Tex.
    Children:
    (1) Martha Ann Williams, b. 9/18/1939.
    (2) Michael Paul Williams, b. 10/23/1941.
12. Loge Williams, b. 4/7/1915, of Grapeland,
    Tex.

Eugenia Lyon Williams, b. 11/19/1868, in Carroll Parish, La., d. 8/5/1947, at Highland Park, N. J., graduated
in nursing, 1889, at old Blockley, now Philadelphia General
Hospital. She m. 3/23/1892, at Kayser, N. C., Dr. Shepard
Voorhees, b. 10/5/1859, in Toga Co., Pa., d. 4/26/1919, at
their home in Newton, N. J., son of Dr. Charles Voorhees
and wife, Julia Ann Shepard.
        Children:
I.   Lamar Shepard Voorhees, b. 3/21/1894, Newton,
        N. J., d. there 10/31/1937, doctor in U.S. Navy
        in WW I, m. 5/11/1921, Naomi Ethel Usher, of
        Jersey City, N. J.
        Child:
        1. Harry Voorhees, b. 8/20/1929.
II.   Loyd Angew Voorhees, b. 2/19/1897, Newton, N.J.,
        in U.S. Marines in WW I, m. Oct., 1925, Mildred
        Renaud at Monroe, La.
        Children:
        1. Jacquelyn Lee Voorhees, b. 8/31/1926.
        2. Loyd Agnew Voorhees, b. 11/13/1927.
        3. Robert Roosevelt Voorhees, b. 11/10/1929.
        4. Janet Renaud Voorhees, b. 10/8/1930, m.
           7/2/1948, Almer Glenn Golson, and lives at
           Monroe.
           Child:
           (1) Almer Glenn Golson, b. 6/17/1949.
III.   Adrian Reid Voorhees, b. 1/11/1901, Newton, N.J.,
        m. 6/30/1928, Mary Elizabeth Locke, and lives at
        Rochester, N. Y.
IV.   Julia Constance Voorhees, b. 8/13/1903, Newton,
        N. J., m. 7/10/1931, Philadelphia, Pa., Dr. Carl
        Gaillard Kapp of Bloomsbury, Pa., and lives at
        Elizabeth, N. J.
        Children:
        1. Carl Voorhees Kapp, b. 4/16/1932.
        2. Elizabeth Eugenia Kapp, b. 2/21/1939.
        3. Bruce Shepard Kapp, b. 6/6/1944.
V.   Elizabeth Lyon Voorhees, b. 6/9/1906, Newton,

N. J., m. 4/17, 1931, at Philadelphia, Pa.,
Joseph Hoffman Edgar, Col. in U.S.A., served in
WW I, as 2nd Lieut., and served five years in
WW II, two years in England, France and Germany,
and now a lawyer at New Brunswick, N. J.
Children:
1. Joseph Hoffman Edgar, b. 4/19/1932.
2. James Shepard Voorhees Edgar, b. 11/1/1935.
3. John Buxton Edgar, b. 6/28/1938.
    George Clanton Williams, b. 1/17/1871, Greene Co.,
Ala., d. 2/14/1937, at his home in San Francisco, Calif.,
m. (1) Mary Campbell, in Fla., and (2) Bertha Katherine
Haase of Wisconsin, in San Francisco, Calif.
        Children: (1st marriage)
I.   Shepard Clanton Williams, b. in Fla., and now of
        San Francisco, Calif., m. Mary Matto.
        Children:
        1. Shepard Clanton Williams.
        2. Gloria Williams.
II.   Jennie Williams, b. in Fla., now of Taft, Calif.,
        m. Jack Hoffman.
        Children:
        1. Genevieve Hoffman.
        2. Helen Hoffman.
    Temperance Hilliard Williams, b. 5/23/1874, d. 4/10/
1940, unmarried.
    Jerome Clanton Williams, b. 5/23/1874, d. 7/28/1946,
at New Brunswick, N. J., and buried at Ridgeway, N. C., m.
Cora Hawkins.
        Child:
I.   Harry Clanton Williams.
    Thomas Barker Williams, b. 8/8/1879, d. 3/17/1930, at
his home in Atlanta, Ga., m. 6/30/1906, Alice Gregg.
        Child:
I.   Susan Alice Williams, b. 8/12/1907, m. 7/25/1929,
        James Baird Wilson, and lives at Atlanta, Ga.
        Children:
        1. Richard Barker Wilson, b. 6/30/1930.
        2. James Ronald Wilson, b. 7/23/1931.
        3. Charlotte Alice Wilson, b. 1/2/1933.
    Solomon Buxton Williams, son of Mary Temperance (Hil-
liard) and John Buxton Williams, b. 8/22/1846, d. 6/6/1911,
m. 6/14/1866, Eva Douglas Thornton of Suffolk, Va., b.
10/21/1847, d. 5/30/1929.
        Children:
I.   Cornelia Hilliard Williams, b. 4/6/1867, d.
        11/11/1896, m. 12/20/1893, John Leonard Hender-
        son, b. 9/23/1851, d. 1/12/1905.

Child:

1. Archibald Erskine Henderson, d. in infancy.

II.   John Buxton Williams, b. 2/25/1869, m. 6/17/1895, Emma Ward, b. 7/4/1875.

Child:

1. Hilliard Thornton Williams, b. 11/9/1898, m. (1) Harriett Dohlbier, (2) 10/24/1936, Rosa Bank.

   Child: (1st marriage)

   (1) Nancy Thornton Williams, b. 6/30/1928, m. 6/29/1947, Thomas Stevenson Leitch, no issue.

   Children: (2nd marriage)

   (2) Winifred Williams, d. in infancy.

   (3) Sue Carol Williams, b. 5/17/1939.

   (4) John Henry Williams, b. 7/9/1945.

III.   Percy Bysshe Thornton Williams, b. 10/1/1872, m. 4/15/1900, Anna S. Anderson, no issue.

IV.   Eva Douglas Thornton Williams, b. 6/10/1874, d. in infancy.

V.   Daisy Douglas Williams, b. 6/27/1875, d. 5/18/1929, m. 6/14/1899, John Leonard Henderson, b. 9/23/1851, d. 1/12/1905.

Children:

1. Douglas Thornton Henderson, b. 5/21/1900, m. 4/3/1930, Belle Gordon Graham, b. 4/23/1907, no issue.

2. Agnes Hare Henderson, b. 12/3/1901, m. 12/19/1925, Joseph White Taylor, b. 7/24/1898.

   Child:

   (1) Douglas Thornton Taylor, b. 12/5/1927.

3. John Leonard Henderson, b. 11/12/1904, m. 9/18/1937, Virginia Crawford.

   Children:

   (1) John Leonard Henderson, III, b. 1/17/1939.

   (2) Alice Vaiden Henderson, b. 3/18/1941.

VI.   Jonas Carr Williams, b. 4/23/1878, m. 11/12/1902, Esther Whitaker, b. 11/1/1877, no issue.

VII.   Sue Garrett Williams, b. 7/23/1880, d. unmarried, 8/13/1947, of injuries sustained in auto accident in which her sister, Alice Vaiden Williams incurred fatal injuries.

VIII.   Hester Grandy Williams, b. 1/22/1883, m. (1)Apr., 1907, Louis Wells Heavner, b. 3/1/1884, (2) Hal Morris.

Children: (1st marriage)

1. Hester Williams Heavner, b. 1/26/1909, m. 10/11/1933, Edward York Smith.

Children:
(1) Edward York Smith, b. 6/10/1934.
(2) William Louis Smith, b. 9/15/1937.
2. William Solomon Heavner, b. 12/19/1910, m.
   12/18/1937, Adele MacMinnis, b. 11/18/1907.
3. Louis Wells Heavner, b. 2/26/1912, m. 10/12/
   1932, Edna Colsey, b. 7/3/1908.
   Child:
   (1) Louis Wells Heavner.
IX. Solomon Buxton Williams, (1886-1889).
X. James Byron Hilliard Williams, (1887-1889).
XI. Alice Vaiden Williams, b. 10/28/1895, d. 7/12/
    1946, unmarried. She was a musician of note, an
    accompanist-coach, composer, and made tours of
    U.S., as accompanist for operatic singers and
    alone.

Jonas Carr Williams, son of Mary Temperance (Hilliard)
and John Buxton Williams, b. 12/24/1850, d. ____, m. 12/27/
1871, Martha (Pattie) Clark Jones, dau. of his first cousin, Lucy Barker Jones and Joseph Speed Jones, and mother
of all his children except the last. He m. (2) Mrs. Anna
Edgerton.

Children: (1st marriage)
I. Eva Thornton Williams, m. Clecy Duke Tharrington.
   Children:
   1. Marvin Speed Tharrington, m. Eva Harper.
      Children:
      (1) Clecy Duke Tharrington.
      (2) Tempie Williams Tharrington.
      (3) William Tharrington.
   2. Tempie Zollicoffer Tharrington, m. William
      Wahman.
      Child:
      (1) Nancy Bidgood Wahman, m. Dr. Marvin M.
          Gibson.
          Children:
          a. Monica Jean Gibson.
          b. John Gibson.
II. Joseph Speed Williams, m. Hattie Hill.
    Children:
    1. Joseph Speed Williams.
    2. Tempie Williams, m. Dr. Ernest W. Franklin,
       Jr.
       Children:
       (1) Ann Franklin.
       (2) Ernest W. Franklin.
    3. Hattie Hill Williams, m. Sidney K. Moorhead.
       Child:

   (1) Sidney K. Moorhead.
  4. Elizabeth Williams, m. Elton Rowland.
   Child:
   (1) Elton Rowland.
III. Lucy Pettway Williams, d. unmarried.
IV. Mary Ann Williams, m. Benjamin Tharrington.
 Child:
  1. Mary Ellen Tharrington, m. George Dorsey.
   Children:
   (1) George Dorsey.
   (2) Clara Williams Dorsey.
V. Tempie Dameron Williams, m. George D. Wheeless, no issue.
VI. John Buxton Williams, m. Maria Williams.
 Children:
  1. Jonas Carr Williams, m. Irene Bohannon.
   Children:
   (1) William Sanford Williams.
   (2) Maria Catherine Williams.
   (3) John Lewis Williams.
  2. Roberta Alston Williams, m. Clayton Everett Smalling.
   Child:
   (1) Clayton Everett Smalling, m. June Cromp-
    ton.
  3. Margaret Mary Williams, m. Carl Clayton Barnes, no issue.
  4. Elizabeth Clark Williams, m. Odell Lee Burkette, no issue.
  5. Eva Pettway Williams, m. Faye Ashby Shannon, no issue.
  6. Anna Williams, m. Thomas Hardy Wilder.
   Child:
   (1) Thomas Hardy Wilder.
  7. Romeo Montague Williams, m. Mildred Jacobs, no issue.
  8. Pattie Jones Williams, m. Jackson Galloway Shannon.
   Child:
   (1) Roberta Gardner Shannon.
  9. John Buxton Williams, m. Grace Jernigan.
   Child:
   (1) John Buxton Williams.
  10. Samuel Ashbury Williams, m. Helen Long, no issue.
VII. Marina Cook Williams, m. Edward S. Paddison.
 Children:
  1. Alfred Paddison, m. Mary Few.

Children:
(1) Edward Simpson Paddison, b. 12/27/1933.
(2) George Marion Paddison, b. 9/29/1940.
2. Lucy Pettway Paddison, m. Carlton Combs.
Child:
(1) Carlton Combs.
VIII.   Mark Pettway Jones Williams, m. Edna Draughn.
Children:
1. Mark Pettway Jones Williams.
2. Frank Draughn Williams.
3. Robert Graham Williams.
4. Joseph Speed Williams.
IX.   Frank Graham Williams, b. 12/29/1886, Warren Co.,
N. C., m. 6/11/1913, in Atlanta, Ga., Fanny
Grier Cook, b. 6/29/1890, dau. of Joseph S. Cook
and wife, Fanny L. Grier.
Child:
1. Virginia Alston Williams, (adopted), b.
1/12/1924, m. 6/16/1944, Russell B. DeCoudres, Jr.
Children:
(1) Barbara Virginia DeCoudres, b. 6/1/1945.
(2) Frank Graham DeCoudres, b. 4/8/1948.
(3) Suzanne DeCoudres, b. 11/18/1952.
X.   Martha (Pattie) Jones Williams, d. unmarried.
Child: (2nd marriage)
XI.   Harry Malvern Williams, m. Isabel Davis.
Children:
1. Harry Malvern Williams.
2. Caroline Williams, m. George Eppes.
Child:
(1) Wayne Eppes.

Leah Hilliard, dau. of James and Mourning (Boddie)
Hilliard, b. at Hilliardston, Nash Co., N. C., 5/2/1819,
and d. at "Cascine," Franklin Co., N. C., 12/7/1892, m.
5/2/1838, at Hilliardston, Algernon Sidney Perry, M.C., b.
11/26/1807, d. at "Cascine," Franklin Co., N. C., 1/26/
1875, son of Captain Jeremiah Perry and wife, Temperance
Boddie, dau. of Nathan and Chloe (Crudup) Boddie of "Rose
Hill," Nash Co., N. C.
Children:
I.   Stella Perry, d.s.p.
II.   Jeremiah Perry, d.s.p.
III.   Sidney Perry, d.s.p.
IV.   Bennett Boddie Perry, M.D., Jefferson Medical
College, b. 10/6/1845, d. 3/11/1880, m. (1)
Josephine Narcissus Mann, dau. of Dr. Joseph H.
Mann, (2) Sallie Alston Crudup.

Children: (1st marriage)
1. Sydney Brooks Perry, (1870-1903), d.s.p.
2. Martha Leah Perry, m. George Anderson Rose, son of George Anderson Rose and wife, Lucy Ann Tunstall.
   Children:
   (1) Bennett Perry Rose, m. Charlotte Beatty Jones.
   (2) John Daniel Rose, m. Frances B. Abbitt.
   (3) Nellie Perry Rose, m. Joseph Harold Conger of Edenton.
   (4) Josephine Mann Rose, m. Herbert W. Jackson, Jr.
   (5) George Anderson Rose, Jr., m. Mary Rolfe Harris.
   (6) Martha Leah Rose, m. Samuel M. Watkins.
   (7) William Brown Rose, d. in infancy.
Children: (2nd marriage)
3. Bennett Boddie Perry, m. Kate Clifton, dau. of J. B. and Annie (Smith) Clifton of Louisburg, N. C.
   Child:
   (1) Willie Clifton Perry, M.D., lives at Louisburg, N. C.
4. Edward Crudup Perry, m. Elinor Lois Tucker.
V. Wiley Perry, d.s.p.
VI. Thomas Perry, d.s.p.
VII. Leah (Nellie) Hilliard Perry, b. 2/23/1852, d. at Henderson, N. C., 1/1/1897, m. 2/23/1876, David Young Cooper, b. 4/21/1847, d. 12/20/1920, at Henderson, N. C.
   Children:
   1. Sidney Perry Cooper, m. Mary Louise Jackson.
   2. Alexander Cooper, m. Ellen Faucette Lassiter.
   3. David Young Cooper, m. Bessie Morgan.
   4. Genevieve Hilliard Cooper, present owner of the Leah Crafford Hilliard miniature portrait, m. Claude Durham Smith, no issue. Residence: Asheville, N. C.
   5. James Allison Cooper, b. 3/7/1894, m. 9/17/1919, Frances Howe Cheatham, b. 11/30/1896, dau. of Frank Howe Cheatham and wife, Cornelia Kearney Alston.
      Child:
      (1) David Young Cooper, M.D., b. 8/14/1924. Lt., U.S.N.R.
VIII. Redding Perry, b. 4/19/1855, d. 2/5/1896, m. 2/23/1881, Frances Cooper Hester, b. 7/15/1861.

Children:
1. Leah Hilliard Perry.
2. Bennett Hester Perry, b. 11/23/1884, m. Katherine Parker Drane.
   Child:
   (1) Bennett Hester Perry, Jr., b. 4/16/1929.
3. Mary M. Perry, m. Robert Gilliam Kittrell.
4. Redding Francis Perry, m. Constance Roberts.
5. Isabella Hester Perry, M.D., m. Louis Kramer.

IX. Henry Perry, b. 12/3/1857, d. 1/15/1934, m. 11/28/1883, Janie Hall, of Oxford, N. C.
Child:
1. Henry Leslie Perry, b. 1/26/1887, d. 6/4/1924, m. 5/18/1920, Flora McKinnon, no issue.
Mr. and Mrs. Henry Perry gave to Henderson and Vance Co., the H. Leslie Perry Library as memorial to their son. Mr. Perry was for 38 years, clerk of Vance Superior Court.

X. Tempie Boddie Perry, b. 5/25/1860, d. 2/24/1934, m. 2/24/1884, Allison Caulincourt Zollicoffer, b. 4/29/1854, d. at Henderson, N. C., 1/27/1922.
Children:
1. Wiley Perry Zollicoffer, (1885-1887).
2. Algernon Augustus Zollicoffer, b. 4/3/1888, m. 10/11/1916, Fannie Spotswood Cooper, b. 9/11/1894.
   Child:
   (1) Algernon Augustus Zollicoffer, Jr., b. 3/6/1924, m. 4/11/1953, Jane Crichton Lewis, b. 4/25/1929, dau. of Jane Crichton (Williams) and Edmund Wilkins Lewis of Jackson, N. C.
      Child:
      a. Jane Crichton Zollicoffer, b. 3/30/1954.
3. Baby, d. in infancy.
4. Jeremiah Perry Zollicoffer, b. 11/30/1890, d. July, 1944, m. 11/15/1919, Julia Bryan Jones.
   Child:
   (1) Julia Bryan Zollicoffer, b. 2/22/1924, m. Kenneth C. Royall, Jr., son of Kenneth C. Royall, Sr., and his wife, Margaret Best.
      Children:
      a. Kenneth C. Royall, III.
      b. Jere Zollicoffer Royall.
      c. Julia Bryan Royall.

     5. John Hilliard Zollicoffer, b. 11/22/1902, m.
         10/16/1934, Helen Summers, dau. of James
         Alexander and Alice (Mountcastle) Summers,
         of Johnson City, Tenn.
         Children:
         (1) John Hilliard Zollicoffer, Jr., b. 4/15/
            1936.
         (2) Jerry Perry Zollicoffer, b. 5/14/1941.
         (3) Alice Mountcastle Zollicoffer, b. 1/4/
            1946.

XI.   Ella Hilliard Perry, d.s.p.
XII.   Marca R. Perry, d.s.p.
XIII.   Genevieve Perry, m. W. H. Nicholson, M.D., no
         issue.

    Robert Carter Hilliard, son of Isaac and Leah (Craf-
ford) Hilliard, was b. at "Woodlawn" plantation, Nash Co.,
N. C., in 1771, and d. at his plantation, "The Meadows,"
Nash Co., N. C. He made his will in Nash Co., dated 1/7/
1828, same recorded Feb. term, 1828. He m. 2/18/1805,
Amaryllis Hunt, dau. of Captain John Hunt and wife, Mary
Jeffreys of Franklin Co., N. C. Amaryllis Hunt was b.
3/16/1784, and d. 7/20/1853, in Monticello, Miss., and
interred in the Fox-Hunt family graveyard.

    Robert Carter Hilliard was educated at the University
of North Carolina. He represented Nash Co., in the N. C.
House of Commons, 1813-14-15; also represented the Co. in
the State Senate, 1817.
         Children:
I.   William Henry Hilliard, m. Sally Dortch. (See
         later)
II.   John Hilliard, m. and settled in Miss. or Tex.,
         untraced.
III.   Mary Hilliard, b. 1810, d. 1840, unmarried.
IV.   Leah Crafford Hilliard, d. 1851, unmarried.
V.   Robert Carter Hilliard, b. 4/23/1824, d. 6/6/
         1883, inherited the home place, "The Meadows,"
         unmarried.
VI.   Rebecca Hilliard, m. Mr. Welborn of Miss. or Tex.
         No issue.
VII.   Amaryllis Hilliard, m. Mr. Price or Prince and
         settled in Miss., or Tex.

    William Henry Hilliard, son of Robert Carter and
Amaryllis (Hunt) Hilliard, was b. at "The Meadows" plan-
tation, Nash Co., N. C., in 1806, and d. 4/17/1886, in
Nash Co., N. C., m. Sallie Dortch, b. 1808, d. 12/15/1872,
Nash Co., N. C., dau. of Louis Dortch and his wife, deWil-
da, of Nash Co., N. C.
         Children:

I.   Alexander Hamilton Hilliard, m. Elizabeth Jane
        Hilliard, dau. of Elijah Boddie Hilliard and
        wife, Rebecca Powell. (See later)
II.   David Hilliard, b. 6/22/1833, d. 2/17/1856, while
        a student at the University of N. C.
III.   Richard Johnston Hilliard, b. 7/4/1835, settled
        in Tex., untraced.
IV.   Louis Hilliard, m. (1) Claudia Gorham, (2) Nellie
        Cherry. (See later)
V.   Mary (Molly) Carter Hilliard, m. Samuel B. Hyman.
        (See later)
VI.   William Henry Hilliard, m. Lucy King Harrison.
        (See later)

   Louis Hilliard, son of William Henry and Sally (Dortch) Hilliard, was b. 12/24/1837, Nash Co., N. C., and d.
8/20/1894, at Norfolk, Va. He attended the University of
N. C., where he graduated with an A.B. degree in 1859,
after which he entered the Law School and graduated with
his L.L.B. degree. He was Solicitor of his district and
was appointed Judge of the second Judicial District, following the Civil War. He was also a member of the board
of trustees of the University of N. C. About 1880, Judge
Hilliard moved to Norfolk, Va., where he entered the cotton
commission business. He m. (1) Claudia Gorham, (2) Nellie
Cherry, dau. of William and Mary (Gorham) Cherry.

        Children: (1st marriage)
I.   Churchill Hilliard, d. unmarried.
II.   Emma Hilliard, d. unmarried.
III.   David Hilliard, m. Anne Turner.
        Children:
        1. David Hilliard, killed on the "Roma"
            dirigible.
        2. Irene Hilliard.
        3. Claude Hilliard.
        4. Sterling Hilliard.
IV.   Lillie Hilliard, m. Samuel Bowen.
        Children: (2nd marriage)
V.   Melissa Hilliard, b. 11/1/1877, d. 6/24/1907,
        unmarried.
VI.   Louis Hilliard, d. in infancy.
VII.   Llewellyn Hilliard, b. 12/24/1881.
VIII.   Logan Hilliard, b. 4/19/1885.
IX.   Elinor Hilliard, m. Richard Blackburn Tucker.
        (See later)
X.   Landon Hilliard, b. 5/8/1892, m. Page Shelburne.
        Child:
        1. Landon Hilliard, Jr., b. 6/10/1911.
            Educated at V.M.I.

Elinor Hilliard, dau. of Judge Louis Hilliard and his second wife, Nellie Cherry, was b. 6/24/1889, at Norfolk, Va. She m. Richard Blackburn Tucker, b. 6/3/1886, son of Rt. Rev. Beverley Dandridge Tucker, D.D. Bishop of Southern Va., and his wife, Anna Maria Washington, dau. of John Augustine Washington and wife, Eleanor Love Seldon. Anna Maria Washington was the last of the Washington family to be born at Mount Vernon. Elinor (Hilliard) and Richard Blackburn Tucker resided at Pittsburg, Pa.

Children:

I. Elinor Hilliard Tucker, b. 10/10/1910.
II. Richard Blackburn Tucker, b. 5/8/1914.
III. Isota Ashe Tucker, b. 10/20/1918.

Alexander Hamilton Hilliard, son of William Henry and Sally (Dortch) Hilliard, was b. 11/16/1831, Nash Co., N.C., and d. 4/28/1880, in Nash Co., N. C., m. 11/4/1863, at Hilliardston, Nash Co., N. C.. his cousin, Elizabeth Jane Hilliard, b. 11/25/1840, Hilliardston, Nash Co., N. C., d. 5/21/1914, Rocky Mount, N. C., dau. of Elijah Boddie and Rebecca (Powell) Hilliard.

Children:

I. Elijah Boddie Hilliard, b. 10/8/1864, d. 6/30/1930, at Birmingham, Ala., m. 4/29/1889, Nina Webb, no issue.

II. deWilda Hilliard, b. 1/17/1867, and d. 5/5/1931, at Washington, D. C., m. 4/29/1897, John Henry Edwards, b. 1867, d. 9/21/1905.
Children:
1. Hilliard Webb Edwards, b. 12/10/1898, m. Alma Christensen.
Child:
(1) Hilliard Webb Edwards, Jr.
2. Mary Elizabeth Edwards, b. 3/7/1902, m. 5/31/1921, John Simpson Abbott, Jr., b. 9/21/1899; divorced him, and m. (2) Fred Arlington Wetzel, Washington, D. C., 12/8/1937.
Child: (1st marriage)
(1) John Simpson Abbott, III, b. 3/4/1922.
3. John Marriott Edwards, b. 1/1/1904, m. 3/12/1922, Marguerite Piner Newnam, b. 7/8/1904.
Children:
(1) Emilie Jean Edwards, b. 12/23/1926, m. Louis James Nolan.
Child:
a. Lina Jeanne Nolan, b. 2/13/1953.
(2) John Marriott Edwards, Jr., b. 7/17/1929.

III. Jerry Hilliard, twin brother of Robert Carter

Hilliard, b. 1/13/1873, d. 1900, unmarried.

IV. Robert Carter Hilliard, b. 1/13/1873, d. 4/11/
1954, Blytheville, m. 6/17/1906, Josephine Lynch,
b. 3/24/1889, dau. of Dudley and Jennie (Lock)
Lynch of Luxora, Ark. Mr. Hilliard was engaged
in farming in Ark., for many years and he was an
insurance salesman.
Children:
1. Robert Carter Hilliard, Jr., b. 5/13/1907,
m. Hazel Leasure.
Children:
(1) Robert Carter Hilliard, III, b. 8/10/
1928.
(2) Mary Elizabeth Hilliard, b. 1/15/1930.
(3) Jean Hilliard, b. 12/5/1931.
(4) Jerry Hilliard, b. 10/18/1933.
Residence: Royal Oak, Michigan.
2. Dortch Hilliard, b. 7/30/1909, d. 7/5/1949,
m. 8/29/1928, Claude Faught, d. 9/21/1932,
no issue. She m. (2) 1/23/1934, William
Jester of Market Tree, Ark., and by her
second marriage, she left 3 boys and 3 girls.
3. Amaryllis Hilliard, b. 6/18/1911, d. 11/7/
1918.
4. Jerry Hilliard, b. 6/27/1913, m. 5/26/1934,
Mary Louise Morgan, b. 1/3/1910, dau. of
Samuel Right Morgan and wife, Anna Paul of
Enterprise Coffee Co., Ala. U.S. Navy, WW
II, 2/12/1942-10/30/1945. Residence: Opeli-
ka, Ala.
Children:
(1) Jerre Louise Hilliard, b. 5/26/1941.
(2) Henry Morgan Hilliard, b. 4/11/1946.
5. Patrick Liston Hilliard, b. 3/2/1917, d.
11/10/1920.
6. Patrick Liston Hilliard, b. 1/1/1920, name
changed to Patrick Liston, after the death
of Patrick Liston Hilliard, I. He m. 11/22/
1940, Christine Brittain. Residence: Blytheville, Ark.
Children:
(1) Shannon Hilliard, b. 7/21/1941.
(2) Fay Hilliard, b. 12/26/1945.
(3) Jack Hilliard, b. 5/26/1947, (twin).
(4) Jill Hilliard, b. 5/26/1947, (twin).
(5) Phil Hilliard, b. 4/21/1951.
7. Betsy Hilliard, b. 9/3/1923, d. 2/24/1939.
V. Jesse Hilliard, b. 9/3/1923, d. 11/10/1919, at

Macon Ga., m. Mrs. Annie Clark, widow, at Macon, Ga.

Child:

1. Harrold Hilliard, b. 8/10/1907, Lt. Commander, U.S. Navy, WW II.

VI. Alexander Hamilton Hilliard, Jr., b. 9/26/1879, Nash Co., N. C., d. 5/23/1944, Wilmington, N.C., m. 10/14/1915, Neva Beatrice Croom, b. 10/7/1887, d. 2/15/1941, Wilmington, N. C., dau. of Rotheus Caswell and Mary (Waters) Croom of LaGrange, N.C.

Children:

1. Alexander Hamilton Hilliard, III, b. 11/18/ 1919, m. 4/10/1942, Wilmington, N. C., Emmaline Lewis Smith, b. 3/31/1921, dau. of Norvin Cliffe Smith and wife, Ruth Adelle Burrows. WW II service, Naval Reserve, 1/27/ 1939, called to active duty, 2/1/1941, discharged 10/21/1945.

   Children:

   (1) Alexander Hamilton Hilliard, IV.

   (2) Neva Louise Hilliard.

2. Betsy Jane Hilliard, b. 8/10/1929, m. 9/21/ 1947, Paul Edward Donnelly, Major, U.S.A. Entered service as 2nd Lt. F.A. (ROTC), St. Bonaventure College, St. Bonaventure, N. Y., 7/25/1941. Promoted to 1st Lt., July, 1942. Attended parachute school, Sept., 1942, and joined the 82 Alen. Div. in Oct., 1942. Promoted to Captain in April, 1943, served as Battery Commander of Hqs. Battery, 376 parachute F.A. Bn. of the 82 Alen. Div. In the following campaigns: Sicily, Naples-Foggie, Rome-Arno, Anzio, Ardennes, Rhineland and Central Europe. Served with Army of occupation in Berlin until Jan., 1946. Decorations: Bronze Star, Bronze Arrowhead (mission), Seven Campaign Stars, Belgian Forragers and Netherlands Orange Langard. He was b. 11/9/1919, at Estlin Saskatchewan, Canada, son of William Cyril Donnelly and wife, Anna Cecilia Shea. Major Donnelly stationed at Fort Sill, Oklahoma (1952).

   Children:

   (1) Marian Ruth Donnelly, b. 10/6/1948.

   (2) Shela Marie Donnelly, b. 7/13/1950.

   (3) Paula Elizabeth Donnelly, b. 2/21/1964.

3. Ruth Hilliard, b. 9/12/1930.

Mary (Molly) Carter Hilliard, dau. of William Henry

and Sally (Dortch) Hilliard, was b. 1/17/1845, in Nash Co.,
N. C., and d. 7/18/1906, at Rocky Mount, N. C. She m.
1/18/1873, Samuel B. Hyman of Scotland Neck, N. C., b.
6/13/1832, d. 10/20/1877, at Scotland Neck, N. C., son of
John Llewellyn Hyman and wife, Elizabeth Wheatley of Scotland Neck, N. C.

        Children:
- I.   Hilliard Hyman, d.s.p.
- II.   Sally Dortch Hyman, m. Thomas Hall Battle. (See later)

    Sally Dortch Hyman, dau. of Mary Carter (Hilliard) and
Samuel B. Hyman, b. 11/3/1876, at Scotland Neck, N. C., and
d.4/17/1917, at Rocky Mount, N. C. She m. 10/23/1895,
Thomas Hall Battle of Rocky Mount, N. C., b. 8/2/1860, d.
1/23/1936, at Rocky Mount, N. C., son of Dr. Kemp Plummer
Battle and wife, Martha Ann Battle. Children were born at
Rocky Mount, N. C.

        Children:
- I.   Hyman Llewellyn Battle, b. 8/11/1896, m. 6/22/
1921, Mamie Louise Braswell, b. 3/20/1898, at
Rocky Mount, N. C., dau. of Mark Russell Bras-
well, M.D., and wife, Mamie Hackney of Rocky
Mount, N. C.
  Children:
  1. Hyman Llewellyn Battle, Jr., b. 1/19/1925,
     m. Peggy Harrison.
     Children:
     (1) Craige Llewellyn Battle.
     (2) David Harrison Battle.
     (3) John Martin Battle.
  2. Thomas Braswell Battle, b. 7/16/1929, m.
     Charlotte Timberlake.
     Child:
     (1) Charlotte Battle.
- II.   Annie Lamb Battle, (1900-1905).
- III.   Ethel Hall Battle, b. 9/26/1903, m. 10/23/1925,(1)
A. W. Peters of Tarboro, N. C., b. 5/28/1903, d.
10/24/1928, son of R. Brooks Peters and wife,
Sallie Brown of Tarboro, N. C., m. (2) 2/28/1935,
William Colter Paxton of Wilson, N. C., b. 4/7/
1899, at Danville Va., son of Walter Thomas Pax-
ton and wife, Elizabeth Williams of Danville, Va.
  Child: (1st marriage)
  1. A. W. Peters, Jr., b. 3/27/1927.
  Children: (2nd marriage)
  2. William Colter Paxton, Jr., b. 9/25/1936.
  3. Sally Battle Paxton, b. 11/7/1940.
- IV.   Josephine Battle, b. 11/27/1908, m. Austin F.

Comer of Rocky Mount, N. C., no issue.

William Henry Hilliard, Jr., son of William Henry and
Sally (Dortch) Hilliard, b. in Nash Co., N. C., 8/13/1848,
and d. 4/2/1925, at Morehead City, N. C., m. 6/19/1878,
Lucy King Harrison.

Children:

I. Mary Carter Hilliard, m. Mr. Newberry of South-
port, N. C.

II. Nellie Hilliard, m. Col. Covington, M.D., surgeon, U.S.A. (Retired)

Child:

1. Harry Covington.

III. Emma Hilliard, (1884-1922), m. Joseph David Taylor, (1877-1915), son of Jesse Macon and Sarah
Elizabeth (Barbee) Taylor, of Wilson, N. C.

Children:

1. Joseph David Taylor.
2. Hyman Taylor, (1906-1909).
3. William Hubert Taylor, m. Vivian Harris.

John Hilliard, son of Isaac and Leah (Crafford) Hil-
liard, was b. at "Woodlawn" plantation, Nash Co., N. C.,
in 1773, and d. at his plantation, "Black Jack," Nash Co.,
N. C., 4/11/1814, buried at "Woodlawn", (grave not marked).
He m. 1/5/1807, Elizabeth Tunstall, b. 1787, dau. of Edmund
and Ann Eliza (Nancy) Tunstall, his first cousin. (Edmund
Tunstall was the son of Thomas Edmund Tunstall. Ann Eliza
(Nancy) Tunstall was the dau. of Lt. Col. William Tunstall
who married Betsy Barker, dau. of Hon. Thomas Barker of
Edenton.) After the death of John Hilliard, his widow m.
(2) Dr. Joseph Arrington, 12/31/1822, son of Joseph and
his wife, Mourning (Ricks) and grandson of Arthur Arrington and his wife, Mary (Sandeford). John Hilliard was
educated at the University of N. C., and represented Nash
Co. in the N. C. House of Commons, 1802-03. Children of
first marriage were born at "Black Jack," Nash Co., N. C.

Children: (1st marriage)

I. Dr. Robert Carter Hilliard, m. Mary Rebecca Harrison Walker. (See later)

II. Betsy Kearney Hilliard, b. _____, d. 2/20/1836,
m. Robert Allan Burton, b. 1810, d. 1838, at
"Rocky Hill" plantation, Halifax Co., N. C., son
of Gov. Hutchins Gordon Burton and wife, Sally
Jones, dau. of Hon. Willie Jones and wife, Mary
Montfort of "The Grove," Halifax, N. C.

Child:

1. Betsy Kearney Burton. (See later)

III. Lucy Emily Hilliard, m. her cousin, Isaac Hilliard, son of James and Mourning (Boddie)

Hilliard.

IV.   John Tunstall Hilliard, M.D., d. in Nash Co., N. C., 1837, unmarried.

Children: (2nd marriage)

V.   Edmund Arrington.

VI.   Thomas C. Arrington.

VII.   Felecia Arrington.

Betsy Kearney Burton, only child of Betsy Kearney (Hilliard) and Robert Allan Burton, was b. 2/20/1835, at "Rocky Hill" plantation, Halifax Co., N. C., and d. at "Woodlawn" plantation, Halifax Co., N. C., 7/15/1875. She m. 3/1/1853, William Henry Wiggins, b. at "Woodlawn," Halifax Co., N. C., 11/11/1830, and d. there 11/7/1867, son of Mason Lee Wiggins and wife, Elizabeth Slade.

Children:

I.   Sarah Elizabeth Wiggins, b. 1/7/1854, m. Oscar Harris.

II.   Mary Roberta Wiggins, b. 12/10/1856, m. Joseph John Williams Harris.

III.   Jessie Gordon Wiggins, b. 12/10/1858, d. at Raleigh, N. C., 2/10/1947, m. 12/9/1880, James McNeill Leach, b. 3/9/1850, d. at Raleigh, N.C., 5/5/1906.

Children:

1. Edgar Leach, d. unmarried.
2. John Robert Leach, d. unmarried.
3. James Mason Leach, d. unmarried.
4. William Wiggins Leach, d. unmarried.
5. Eliza Thompson Leach, b. 5/31/1897, at Raleigh, N. C., m. 5/14/1921, Robert Timberlake Newcombe, b. 2/26/1895, at Raleigh, N. C., son of Charles William Newcombe and wife, Anne Timberlake of Raleigh, N. C. Residence: Raleigh, N. C. (Newcombe)

Children:

(1) Robert Timberlake Newcombe, b. 4/2/1923, m. 2/8/1948, Randolph Mason Gardner.

Children:

a. Robert Timberlake Newcombe, III, b. 2/16/1949.

b. Allan Randolph Newcombe, b. 12/23/1951. Residence: Spring Hope, N. C.

(2) Charles Allan Newcombe, b. 10/17/1925.

6. Allan DeMontfort Leach, b. 11/5/1900, d. unmarried.

IV.   Winifred Wiggins, b. 12/7/1860, m. Ferdinand Harris.

V.   Allene Lee Wiggins, (1863-1926), m. 1882,

Leonidas Alston, (1863-1904), son of Charles
Julien Poydras Alston and wife, Mary Janet Clark,
dau. of William McKenzie Clark and wife, Martha
Boddie Williams, dau. of Gen. William Williams
and Elizabeth Williams, dau. of Capt. Solomon
Williams and Temperance Boddie.
Children:
1. John Patterson Alston, m. Mrs. Leona Leoda
   (House) Langley, no issue.
2. Jesse Gordon Alston, (1886-1928), d.s.p.
3. William Wiggins Alston, (1888-1926), m.1915,
   Lucy Lillian Patton.
4. Edgar Leonidas Alston, m. 1923, Carrie Clark.
5. Mary Elizabeth Alston, m. 1921, Charles
   Thompson Mabry.
6. Roberta Harris Alston, m. 1919, John Milton
   Rose.
7. Harriet Lucy Alston, m. 1922, William Bailey.
8. Sallie Burton Alston, m. 1919, Clifford
   Rudolph Woodward.
9. Allene Lee Alston, m. 1923, Stuart Rhodes
   Moffit.
VI. William Henry Wiggins, (dau.), b. 3/7/1866, m.
     Sol. W. Cooper of Fayetteville, N. C.
     Children:
     1. Crawford James Cooper, m. Georgia Dixon.
     2. Allene Lee Cooper.
     3. Elizabeth Burton Cooper.
     4. Sol. W. Cooper, Jr.

Dr. Robert Carter Hilliard, son of John and Elizabeth
(Tunstall) Hilliard, was b. at "Black Jack" plantation,
Nash Co., N. C., 12/31/1808, and d. 9/10/1867, at New
Iberia, La. He m. 12/20/1837, Mary Rebecca Harrison Walker, b. 12/2/1819, in Brunswick Co., Va., and d. at New
Iberia, La., 9/3/1897, dau. of Dr. John Mumford Walker and
wife, Lucy Cargill Jones of Brunswick Co., Va. Dr. Hil-
liard was educated at the University of N. C., and the
Baltimore Medical College, Baltimore, Maryland. He repre-
sented Nash Co., in the N. C. House of Commons, 1830. He
sold "Black Jack" plantation about 1850, and with his
family, he settled in New Iberia, La.
     Children:
I.   John Tunstall Hilliard, b. 1841, killed 4/6/
      1862 at Shiloh.
II.   Robert Lucy Hilliard, b. 6/22/1843, m. Charles
      McVea. (See later)
III. William Walker Hilliard, b. 1845, d. 1849.
IV.   Edmund Thorne Hilliard, b. 9/29/1849, d. 1882,

m. 1880, Ina Graham, of Graham, Tex., and was
District Judge for Eastland and adjacent coun-
ties.
V. Baby, d. in infancy.
VI. Audibun Hilliard, b. 7/8/1854, in St. Martin's
Parish, La., d. 3/16/1889, at New Orleans, Treas.
of U. S. Mint of New Orleans, m. at New Iberia,
La., 2/8/1877, Ida Campbell, b. 4/6/1856, in New
Iberia Parish, La., d. 2/3/1894, at New Iberia,
dau. of John T. Campbell and wife, Sophie Taylor
Lee.
Children:
1. Beverly Campbell Hilliard, b. 2/16/1878, at
New Iberia, d. 6/22/1931, at Chicago, Ill.,
a veteran of Spanish-American and WW I, m.
(1) Estelle Black, 5/20/1902, in New York
City, and (2) Maurine Ely, in July, 1924.
Child: (1st marriage)
(1) Beverly Campbell Hilliard, b. 4/23/1903,
at Philadelphia, Pa., m. 6/10/1944, at Alden,
Pa., Aleta Wilson, b. 11/18/1905.
2. Ethel May Hilliard, b. 1/1/1880, unmarried,
assistant principal of New Jersey School for
the Deaf.
3. Sophie Lee Hilliard, b. 11/23/1881, at New
Iberia, m. at Philadelphia, Pa., 9/11/1906,
Thomas J. Murphy, b. 8/12/1878, in St.Landry
Parish, La., teacher of the deaf at Colorado
Springs, Colorado.
Children:
(1) Donaldson Murphy, b. 9/11/1911, d. 2/16/
1912.
(2) Beverly Hilliard Murphy, b. 7/1/1913, in
Iberia Parish, La., m. at Bernalillo,
N. M., 1/8/1940, William B. Witkind, b.
10/1/1913, at Colorado Springs, Colo.
Children:
a. Beverly Alice Witkind, b. 3/20/1941.
b. William Max Witkind, b. 7/28/1943.
c. Jane Christine Witkind, b. 5/24/1948.
4. Mary Walker Hilliard, b. 3/27/1885, in St.
Martin's Parish, La., m. in Philadelphia,
Pa., 6/26/1909, Max Hermann Bickler, b. 6/21/
1881, at Austin, Tex., teacher of the deaf
at Austin, Tex.
Children:
(1) Ethel Hilliard Bickler, b. at Austin,
Tex., 12/18/1911, m. at Austin,12/22/1932,

Stuart Buckley, b. 8/5/1908, at Eagle
Pass, Tex.
Children:
a. Eileen Ethel Buckley, b. 1/13/1934,
at Houston, Tex.
b. John Stuart Buckley, b. 6/21/1946, at
Houston, Tex.
c. Mary Hilliard Buckley, b. 2/11/1948,
at Houston, Tex.
(2) Jane Harriet Bickler, b. 9/29/1917, at
Austin, Tex., m. at Austin, 7/3/1939,
Arthur Sylvester Grenier, b. 8/24/1914,
in New York City.
Child:
a. Sally Duncan Grenier, b. 9/27/1947.
VII. Susan Douglas Hilliard, b. 1856, d. 1859.
VIII. Henry Peebles Hilliard, b. 2/8/1859, d. 1945,
banker at Austin, Tex., and afterwards receiver
for banks at Fresno, Calif., m. (1) Estelle Bre-
mond, of Austin, Tex., no issue; m. (2) 1/10/
1910, Elizabeth Bissell, b. 1/17/1888, of St.
Louis, Mo.
Child: (2nd marriage)
1. Henri Hilliard, (dau.), b. 6/8/1912, m.
5/10/1945, Pieter Dirksz, from Amsterdam,
Holland.
IX. Mary Hilliard, b. 2/25/1865, d. at Oklahoma City,
Oklahoma, 1945, m. 9/18/1882, Charles Winter
Trader, physician, b. 1/17/1857, d. in 1908, son
of John Trader of Baltimore, Md., and resided in
Oklahoma City, Okla.
Children:
1. Ina Trader, b. 7/14/1884, m. 1/17/1905, John
L. T. Sneed, b. 7/24/1873, and live in Oklahoma City, Okla.
Children:
(1) Marjorie Sneed, b. 8/22/1906, m. 9/18/
1929, Dr. Charles R. Moon, no issue.
(2) Hilliard Bulluck Sneed, b. 1/2/1919, m.
6/25/1936, Susanne Knox.
Children:
a. John Roger Sneed, b. 10/5/1939.
b. Susan Beverly Sneed, b. 6/17/1944.
2. Curtis Winter Trader, (dau.), b. 1/21/1891,
m. 7/24/1912, Daniel Bissell, Jr., b. 1881,
of St. Louis, Mo., (his second wife).
Children:
(1) Daniel Bissell, III, b. in 1914, m.

6/28/1947, Lucille LaMont, b. in 1927.
(2) Evelyn May Bissell, b. 9/26/1916, m.
3/23/1940, Richard W. Horner, b. 2/1/
1915.
Children:
a. Daniel Bissell Horner, b. 3/5/1941.
b. Wesley W. Horner, b. 2/18/1944.
c. Douglas DuBose Horner, b. 2/5/1947.
(3) Beverly Bissell, b. 6/18/1922, m. Robert
Monroe Smith, b. 9/11/1914.
Children:
a. Geoffrey Moore Smith, b. in 1945.
b. Carter Bissell Smith, b. in 1947.
(4) Martha Bissell, b. in 1929, unmarried.

Robert Lucy Hilliard, dau. of Dr. Robert Carter Hilliard and wife, Mary Rebecca Harrison Walker, was b. 6/22/
1843, in Brunswick Co., Va., and d. 8/13/1875, at San
Antonio, Tex. She m. 12/4/1866, at New Iberia, La., Charles McVea, Circuit Judge, b. March, 1832, at Bayou, Sara,
La., and d. 10/4/1886, at Baton Rouge, La.
Children:
I.   Robert Hilliard McVea, b. 12/4/1867, d. 1868.
II.   Charles McVea, physician, b. 2/2/1869, at Clinton, La., d. 7/5/1920, at Baton Rouge, m. at
Baton Rouge, 2/5/1894, Pearl Winifred Lobdell,
b. 9/5/1871, dau. of James L. Lobdell and wife,
Angelina Bird of "Bell Vale" plantation, West
Baton Rouge Parish, La. Dr. Charles McVea was
educated at La. State and Tulane University.
Lived at Baton Rouge, La.
Children:
1. Pearl McVea, b. 4/13/1898, m. Ivy Morris,
(1892-1953), no issue.
2. Charles McVea, Jr., b. 12/22/1909, physician,
m. 4/25/1938, Mildred Lamoreaux, b. 7/21/
1910. Educated, La.State,Tulane University.
Children:
(1) Mary Worthington McVea, b. 11/7/1939.
(2) Jane Lobdell McVea, b. 6/2/1943.
(3) Charles McVea, III, b. 7/18/1946.
Lives at Baton Rouge, La.
3. Bena McVea, b. 10/29/1911, m. 11/21/1934,
John Alexander Chambliss, b. 10/21/1910,
lawyer. Residence: 200 Fairy Trail, Lookout
Mountain, Chattanooga, Tennessee.
Children:
(1) Ann McVea Chambliss, b. 9/8/1935.
(2) John Alexander Chambliss, Jr., b. 5/19/

1938.

(3) Betsy Jane Chambliss, b. 3/13/1943.

III. William Walker McVea, b. 3/3/1871, d. 2/9/1928,
m. Sadie Connor Link, no issue.

IV. Mary Virginia McVea, b. 1/26/1873, at Clinton,
La., m. at Baton Rouge, La., 2/2/1898, Dr. Edward
Dunbar Newell, surgeon, at Chattanooga, Tenn.,
b. 2/2/1873, at Newell's Ridge, La., d. 2/13/
1952, at Chattanooga, Tenn., son of Edward Henry
Newell and wife, Catherine Wade. Mary Virginia
Newell d. 4/3/1955.
Children:

1. Marjorie Newell, b. 1/6/1900, m. 5/8/1924,
Robert Houston Jewell, son of Daniel Ashley
Jewell and wife, Irene Houston of Chicka-
mauga, Ga.
Children:

(1) Robert Houston Jewell, Jr., b. 2/22/1925,
m. June E. Hall. He served in WW II, as
2nd Lt. 30th Div. A.E.F., and attended
Georgia Tech.
Child:

a. Irene Houston Jewell.

(2) Edward Dunbar Jewell, b. 5/9/1928, m.
8/12/1949, Nancy Morgan Carter, b. 6/10/
1928, attended Sweet Briar College, dau.
of Earl Phillip Carter of Chattanooga,
Tenn. Edward Dunbar Jewell attended Ga.
Tech.
Child:

a. Edward Dunbar Jewell, Jr.

(3) William Henry Jewell, b. 5/3/1930, m.
Mary Moore.

2. Bert McVea Newell, b. 10/5/1901, m. at Chattanooga, Tenn., 6/1/1922, Dr. Earl Ray Campbell, b. 4/19/1894, son of George L. Campbell and wife, Nora Davis.
Children:

(1) Mary Virginia Campbell, b. 7/1/1923, m.
6/7/1946, Frederick M. Williams, Jr., b.
5/10/1923.
Children:

a. Frederick M. Williams, III, b. 8/18/
1948.

b. Bert Campbell Williams, b. 3/20/1951.

(2) Earl Ray Campbell, b. 2/2/1929, m. 8/28/
1951, Donna Lauverne Dobbs, b. 4/10/1929,
dau. of Raymond Dobbs and wife, Elizabeth

Hicks of Chattanooga, Tenn.
Child:
a. Mary Elizabeth Campbell, b. 8/10/1953.
3. Catherine Wade Newell, b. 10/7/1903, m.
10/16/1923, Edward West Oehmig, b. 8/26/1894,
son of William Gallupe and wife, Frances
Howard West of Chattanooga, Tenn.
Children:
(1) Frances West Oehmig, b. 1/14/1925, m.
4/10/1948, Preston Milo Collins, b.
2/13/1923, of Macon, Ga.
Children:
a. Preston Milo Collins, Jr., b. 3/19/
1949.
b. Mary Catherine Collins.
(2) Catherine Newell Oehmig, b. 5/18/1926,
m. Dr. Harry Alfred Stone of Chattanooga,
Tenn.
Child:
a. Harry Alfred Stone, Jr.
(3) Elizabeth Dunbar Oehmig, b. 10/20/1927,
m. 6/11/1949, Dr. Richard Jennings
Field, Jr., son of Dr. Richard Jennings
Field of Centerville, Miss.
Child:
a. Richard Jennings Field, III.
(4) Edward West Oehmig, b. 5/10/1930, m.
Carolyn Miller.
Child:
a. Edward West Oehmig, III.
(5) Dunbar Newell Oehmig, b. 7/22/1931.
    Isaac Hilliard, son of Isaac and Leah (Crafford)
Hilliard of "Woodlawn" plantation, Nash Co., N. C., born
there 5/19/1775, and d. at his plantation "The Retreat",
near Franklin, Williamson Co., Tenn., 4/18/1832, m. 3/9/
1803, Mary Moore Murfree, b. 3/9/1786, d. 3/1/1848, dau.
of Col. Hardy Murfree and wife, Sally Brickell of Murfrees-
boro, N. C., and Tenn.
    Isaac Hilliard and his wife, Mary Moore Murfree,
built "Mill Brook," in Halifax Co., N. C., said to have
been the handsomest home in N. C. About 1828, Isaac Hilliard sold his N. C. holdings to his brother, James Hilliard of Hilliardston and settled in Williamson Co., Tenn.
He was educated at the University of N. C., and represented Halifax Town in the N. C. House of Commons, 1801.
Their children were born at "Mill Brook," Halifax Co.,N.C.
        Children:
I.   Elizabeth Caroline Hilliard, b. 2/3/1804,d.s.p.

II.   Mary Moore Murfree Hilliard, b. 12/1/1805, m.
        William Hardeman, no issue.
III.   Fannie Julia Ann Hilliard, b. 11/15/1807, d.s.p.
IV.   William Harry Hilliard, b. 10/20/1809, d.s.p.
V.   Isaac Henry Hilliard, b. 9/7/1811, d. in June,
        1868, at his plantation in Ark. He m. 5/26/
        1836, Lavina H. Linor, b. in 1817, d. Aug.,1837,
        dau. of Daniel and Eliza (Jordon) Linor of Mur-
        freesboro, Tenn. He m. (2) Mirream Brannon of
        Louisville, Ky., 7/28/1847.
        Child: (1st marriage)
        1. Lavina LaFayette Hilliard, b. 4/15/1837, d.
            at Nashville, Tenn., 6/30/1872, m. at Mobile,
            Ala., 3/22/1856, William Dickson Shute, b.
            8/9/1834, d. at Nashville, Tenn., 3/20/1916.
            Children:
            (1) Margaret Shute, d.s.p.
            (2) Isaac Hilliard Shute, d.s.p.
            (3) Mary Hardeman Shute, d.s.p.
            (4) William Dickson Shute, d.s.p.
            (5) Kate Kearney Shute, m. William Craft.
            (6) Lavina Hilliard Shute, b. 9/22/1870, m.
                at Christ Church, Nashville, Tenn., 12/
                5/1900, Marshall Hotchkiss, son of Eli
                Hall and Mary (Marshall) Hotchkiss.
                Child:
                a. Mirream Hotchkiss, b. 2/2/1914.
        Children: (2nd marriage)
        2. Isaac Henry Hilliard, Jr., b. 3/25/1849, d.
            6/16/1882, m. his first cousin, Caroline
            Polk.
            Child:
            (1) Isaac Henry Hilliard, III, d. in infancy.
        3. Edwin Summers Hilliard, (1850-1920), d.s.p.
        4. Mary Hardeman Hilliard, d. in infancy.
VI.   Henry Crafford Hilliard, b. 7/24/1813, d.s.p.
VII.   John Mathias Murfree Hilliard, b. 4/16/1815,
        d.s.p.
VIII.   James Crafford Hilliard, b. 6/2/1816, d.s.p.
IX.   Sallie Leah Hilliard, b. 11/26/1819, m. George
        Washington Polk. (See later)
X.   George W. Hilliard, b. 4/17/1822, d.s.p.
XI.   Lavinia LaFayette Hilliard, b. 8/25/1824,d.s.p.
        Sallie Leah Hilliard, dau. of Isaac and Mary Moore
(Murfree) Hilliard, b. at "Mill Brook," Halifax Co., N.C.,
11/26/1819, d. 7/2/1894, m. 11/24/1817, George Washington
Polk, b. at Raleigh, N. C., 7/12/1817, and d. in Maury
Co., Tenn., near Columbia. Their plantation was called

"Rattle & Snap." They are buried at St. John's Episcopal
Church in Maury Co., Tenn. Children:
  I.   James Hilliard Polk, b. 1/8/1842, d. at Fort
         Worth, Tex., 11/27/1926. He m. 11/24/1885, at
         Nashville, Tenn., Mary Demonville Harding, b.
         10/18/1859, d. at Fort Worth, Tex. James Hilliard
         Polk, Captain (C.S.A.) captured and imprisoned
         at Camp Chase, Fort Delaware, Morris Island, and
         later under fire of his own guns for six weeks
         off coast of Charleston, S. C. Last of "Immor-
         tal Six Hundred."
         Children:
         1. Harding Polk, U.S.A., b. at Nashville, Tenn.,
             3/16/1887, graduated, 1910, U. S. Military
             Academy, West Point, N. Y. Served as com-
             mission officer in U.S., Mexico, Philippines
             and France during WW I. He m. at Burlington,
             Iowa, 12/29/1910, Marie Ester, dau. of John
             Joseph Fleming and his wife, Mollie (Bracken).
             They reside at 1001 N. 7th St., Burlington,
             Iowa.
             Children:
             (1) James Hilliard Polk, b. 12/13/1911.
             (2) John Fleming Polk, b. 8/11/1914.
             (3) Mary Gertrude Polk, b. 12/29/1916.
             (4) Harding Polk, b. 4/18/1921.
             (5) Thomas Harding Polk, b. 7/20/1922.
         2. George Washington Polk, Fort Worth Texas,
             Lawyer, b. Fort Worth, Texas, 11/18/1888,
             graduated V.M.I., University of Texas,
             attended Columbia University, N. Y. City.
             Captain Artillery, WW I. He m. in Chicago,
             Ill., 12/28/1912, Adelaide Elizabeth Roe, b.
             at Fort Worth, Tex., 9/22/1889, dau. of
             Addison John Roe and wife, Jenny Henry
             Scranton. Issue b. at Fort Worth, Texas.
             Children:
             (1)George W. Polk, b. 10/17/1913.
             (2) Adelaide Elizabeth Polk, b. 9/2/1915.
             (3) Milbrey Catherine Polk, b. 3/16/1919.
             (4) Jennie Marie Polk, b. 8/8/1922.
             (5) William Roe Polk, b. 3/7/1929.
  II.   Rufus King Polk, b. 10/31/1843, d. 8/27/1902,
         m. 4/28/1881, at Nashville, Tenn., Margaret
         Phillips, b. 9/11/1842, and d. 11/18/1909, dau.
         of William Duncan Phillips and wife, Eliza Dwyer.
         Child:
         1. Mary Elizabeth Polk, b. 7/30/1883, m. at

Nashville, Tenn., 4/26/1911, John White
Moore, b. at Nashville, Tenn., 8/4/1878, son
of James Henry Moore and wife, Anna Patrick.
Children:

(1) Margaret Philips Moore, b. 12/27/1913.
(2) John Polk Moore, b. 10/24/1918.

III.   Sallie Hawkins Polk, b. 6/18/1845, d. unmarried,
11/18/1914.

IV.   Mary Murfree Polk, b. 6/25/1847, d. ___, m.
11/29/1870, Col. J. J. DuBose.
Children:

1. Juliet Brevard DuBose, b. 11/29/1871, d. in
   infancy.
2. Tasker Polk DuBose, b. 1/4/1873.
3. Mary Hilliard DuBose, b. 12/26/1875.
4. Alfred Bishop DuBose, b. 9/30/1877.
5. Jessie McIver DuBose, b. 11/24/1879.
6. George W. Polk DuBose, b. 7/4/1881.
7. Sarah Camilla DuBose, b. 6/17/1883.
8. Julius Jesse DuBose, b. 8/18/1889.

V.   Susan Spratt Polk, b. 6/23/1851, d. ___, m.
3/7/1877, James Yeatman Player.
Children:

1. Susan Polk Player, b. 10/25/1879.
2. George Polk Player, b. 1/21/1881.
3. James Yeatman Player, b. 3/30/1882.
4. Susan Trezevant Player, b. 8/8/1884.
5. Thomas Trezevant Player, b. 9/7/1886.
6. Sallie Hilliard Player, b. 3/28/1889.

VI.   Lucius Junius Polk, b. 4/13/1853, d. unmarried,
2/22/1922.

VII.   Isaac Hilliard Polk, b. 8/8/1854, d. ___, m. (1)
4/13/1889, Ella Martha Cook, m. (2) 4/19/1897,
Minerva J. Bradbury.
Child: (1st marriage)
1. Sallie Hilliard Polk, b. 2/24/1891.
Children: (2nd marriage)
2. Isaac Hilliard Polk, b. 4/6/1898.
3. Lewis Bradbury Polk, b. 7/30/1899.

VIII.   William Hardy Polk, b. 1/27/1859, d. 3/26/1896,
m. Mable Vanderbogart.
Child:
1. Anna Leah Polk.

IX.   Caroline Polk, b. 6/26/1861, at Nashville, Tenn.,
m. (1) her cousin, Isaac Henry Hilliard, child
d. in infancy, m. (2) Joseph Horton of Nashville,
Tenn., no issue.

*****

HILLIARD - HUNT OF TENNESSEE

Martha Hilliard, dau. of Isaac and Leah (Crafford) Hilliard, was b. at "Woodlawn" plantation, Nash Co., N.C., 10/25/1788, and d. in Tipton Co., Tenn., 8/10/1847. The text of the sermon at her funeral service, preached by the Rev. James W. Rodgers, was from the 64th Chapter of Isaiah - "and all do fade as a leaf." She m. (1) James Branch of Halifax Co., N. C., and (2) 3/10/1810, Nathaniel Macon Hunt, son of Mary Jeffreys and Capt. John Hunt of Franklin Co., N. C. Mary Jeffreys was the dau. of Osborne Jeffreys, Jr., son of Capt. Osborne Jeffreys, m. Patience Spear, dau. of Capt. John Spear of the Revolution. Nathaniel Macon Hunt was b. 12/7/1782, in Franklin Co., N. C., and d. in Tipton Co., Tenn., 12/27/1866, educated at the University of N. C., and represented Franklin Co., in the N. C. House of Commons, 1814-1816. In 1828, he removed from Franklin Co., and settled in Tipton Co., Tenn.

Child: (1st marriage)

I. Martha Branch, d. in infancy.

Children: (2nd marriage)

II. Martha Ann Matilda Hunt, b. 1/17/1811, d. 10/4/1875, m. William Turberville, 10/20/1836.

III. Elizabeth Hunt, b. 1/2/1813, d. 12/24/1872, m. George Hooper Elcan, 3/30/1836.

IV. John Hilliard Hunt, b. 7/12/1814, d. 9/14/1841, m. Elizabeth Hunt, 2/18/1839.

V. Nathaniel Macon Hunt, b. 6/8/1816.

VI. JAMES HENRY HUNT. (See later)

VII. Mary Leah Hunt, b. 10/6/1820, d. 6/3/1843, m. William Hay, 2/21/1839.

VIII. Archibald Davis Hunt, b. 8/30/1823, d. 7/15/1867, m. Sallie Nelson.

IX. George Washington Hunt, b.5/7/1825, d.7/24/1836.

X. William Isaac Hunt, b. 4/15/1827, (Capt. C.S.A.), killed in battle at Shiloh battleground, m. Sarah Gray.

XI. Thomas Edward Hunt, b. 11/30/1829, d. 7/20/1830.

XII. Christopher Stanton Hunt, b. 2/16/1832, d. 6/20/1849.

James Henry Hunt, b. 9/6/1818, d. 1/30/1897, at Mason, Tipton Co., Tenn., m. Ann Elizabeth Oslyn, 12/19/1838. He was educated privately and operated a plantation in Tipton Co., Tenn. Issue b. in Tipton Co., Tenn.

Children:
I. Martha Amaryllis Hunt, b. 10/14/1839, m. Herbert Hilliard Elcan.
II. John Hilliard Hunt, b. 10/30/1841, m. Sarah Frances (Fannie) Cotten. (See later)
III. James Fletcher Hunt, b. 9/2/1843, m. Sallie Elizabeth Williams.
IV. Fannie Serena Hunt, b. 7/10/1845, m. Nathaniel Henry Kimbrough. (See later)
V. Ann Elizabeth Hunt, b. 1/27/1848, m. Dr. Marmaduke Bell. (See later)
VI. Sallie Rebecca Hunt, b. 12/7/1849, m. Thomas Hilliard Poindexter, (a cousin).
VII. Fenton Edward Hunt, b. 12/17/1851, m. Mary Eliza Black.
VIII. Madora Oslyn Hunt, b. 12/13/1853, m. Gabriel Poindexter, (a cousin).
IX. Nathaniel Henry Hunt, b. 10/10/1856, m. Hannah Moore Webster.
X. Mary Iola Hunt, b. 6/23/1860, m. James T. Meek.

DR. JOHN HILLIARD HUNT, b. 10/30/1841, d. 3/21/1891, was educated in the county schools of his neighborhood until 1858, at which time, he entered the High School of Prof. James Byars at Covington, Tenn. After which, he studied medicine under Dr. W. L. Terry, then attended the Medical School at Louisville, Ky., where he graduated. He settled in Miss., and commenced the practice of medicine. The war coming on, he returned to Tipton Co., Tenn., and assisted Capt. Sam Taylor in raising a calvary company which became a part of the 7th Tenn. Calvary. After a short service, as private, he was promoted to the post of assistant surgeon of the regiment where he served with skill and ability until 1863, at which time, he was taken down with camp fever, erroneously reported as dead and military burial honors were conferred on him. As soon as sufficiently recovered, on hearing that the report of his death had reached his parents, he returned to Tenn., to relieve their distress. Dr. Hunt continued his medical practice in Tipton Co., Tenn., until his death in 1891. He m. Sarah Frances (Fannie) Cotten.

Children:
I. Fannie Rob Hunt, b. 8/24/1878, m. 12/26/1905, John William Perry Hall.
Children:

1. Francis Hilliard Hall, b. 5/4/1909.
2. Letitia May Hall, b. 3/30/1912, d. 6/2/1927.
3. Mary Alice Hall, b. 7/31/1913, m. Vernon D. Murrell of Memphis, Tenn., 12/23/1932.
4. James Hunt Hall, b. 6/8/1915.
5. John Cotten Hall, b. 11/4/1919.)
6. David Preston Hall, b. 11/4/1919.) twins
7. Elizabeth Ann Hall, b. 3/18/1923, d. 6/23/ 1931.

II. MAGGIE HILLIARD HUNT, b. 9/3/1884, m. James A. Holmes, 2/25/1903.
Children:
1. James A. Holmes, Jr., b. 8/5/1904, m. Bessie Bishop.
Children:
(1) Jamie Virginia Holmes, b. 11/19/1926, m. Robert Maupin.
Children:
a. Robert Lynn Maupin.
b. Robyn Maupin.
(2) Margaret Rose Holmes, b. 9/6/1928, m. Bobbie Joe Kinney.
Child:
a. Ronnie Kinney, educated at Memphis State University.
(3) Jack Allen Holmes, b. 6/2/1930, m.Roslyn Lewis. Children: 1. Thersa Holmes, 2. Jacquelyn Holmes, 3. Elna Holmes, 4.John Holmes, 5. Michael Holmes, 6. Charles Holmes, and 7. an infant.
(4) Joseph Nicholas Holmes, b. Dec. 1931, m. Evelyn Rusher, and have two daughters.
(5) Charles Franklyn Holmes, m. Joanne Thompson and have two children.
2. Margaret Jacquelyn Holmes, b. 4/21/1906, d. 3/11/1948.
3. Horace Cotten Holmes, b. 9/5/1908, m. (2) Evelyn Savage of Bolivar, Tenn., (she had a son by a former marriage).
Children: (1st marriage)
(1) Horace Cotten Holmes, II, b. 11/12/1931, m. Mary C. Brown, 9/28/1957.
Children:
a. Sharon Holmes, b. 12/10/1959.
b. Leslie Carol Holmes, b. 12/2/1961.
(2) David Eugene Holmes, m. Mollie O'Neal.
(3) Richard Gordon Holmes, m. Mary Neil Hollis, 8/11/1963.

4. Pauline Mae Holmes, (Polly), b. 8/12/1916,
   m. Kenneth Shellabarger.
   Children:
   (1) Phyllis Annette Shellabarger, m. George
       Washington Walls.
   (2) Cheryl Jane Shellabarger, m. James H.
       Shellabarger, Jr., (a cousin).

FANNIE SERENA HUNT, b. 7/16/1845, d. 10/14/1932, m.
5/22/1867, Nathaniel M. Kimbrough.
   Children:
I.   Anna Elizabeth Kimbrough, b. 2/4/1870, d. 9/18/
      1957, m. Luther Eubank, 2/26/1890.
      Children:
      1. Anna Merle Eubank. (See later)
      2. Lillian Machin Eubank, b. 1/23/1893, m. Jus-
         tus V. Davis, 6/23/1912.
         Children:
         (1) Christine Elizabeth Davis, b. 1/12/1914,
             d. 3/26/1939.
         (2) Lawrence E. Davis, b. 8/14/1916, m.Mary
             Ruth Bishop, 12/4/1939. Children:
             a. Lawrence Davis, b. 12/22/1942.
             b. Michael Davis, b. 4/9/1947.
             c. Carolyn Davis, b. 5/8/1952.
         (3) Clyde K. Davis, b. 4/17/1918, d. 10/23/
             1930.
         (4) William F. Davis, b. 9/12/1921, m. Helen
             Ritter, 12/8/1944.
             Children:
             a. Stephen Davis, b. 2/22/1947.
             b. Sandra Davis, b. 10/28/1951.
         (5) Mary Frances Davis, b. 9/2/1926, m. R.
             Jerry Mize, 11/12/1945.
             Children:
             a. Cheral Ann Mize, b. 6/28/1947.
             b. Richard Allen Mize, b. 7/13/1954.
      3. Fannie John Eubank, b. 4/12/1895.
      4. Sammie Kimbrough Eubank, b. 11/6/1901, d.
         7/9/1931, m. Besse Mize in 1920, b. 1902, d.
         1932.
         Children:
         (1) Samuel Clyde Eubank, b. Dec. 1921, m.
             Jane Harris, June, 1953.
             Children:
             a. Sara Ruth Eubank, b. April, 1954.
             b. Sammie Eubank, b. Feb., 1956.
             c. Dorothy Jane Eubank, b. Dec., 1957.
             d. Elizabeth Ann Eubank, b. Dec., 1961.

(2) Janie Eubank, b. 2/9/1929, m. Thurman
      Sage, 10/1/1947. Child: Renea Sage.
(3) Dorothy Eubank, b. 12/17/1931, m. Gene
      Butler. Children: 1. Beverly Kaye But-
      ler, and 2. Ann Butler.

II.   Fenton Hunt, b. 1/24/1874.
III.   William Hunt, b. 8/15/1876.
IV.   C. Moten Hunt, b. 9/10/1881.
V.   Ocie Machin Hunt, b. 12/17/1878, d. 4/20/1900.

BEN W. ROGERS, b. 11/15/1885, m. Anna M. Eubank, b.
3/17/1891, on 12/6/1911.
      Children:
I.   Robert Willis Rogers, b. 8/31/1912, m. Dorothy
      Julia Armstrong, b. 11/15/1912.
II.   Lillian Elizabeth Rogers, b. 9/5/1914, m. Marcus
      Simington Taylor, 2/2/1934.
      Children:
      1. Margaret Elizabeth Taylor, b. 9/26/1935, m.
         Thomas Owen Hayes, 10/14/1953.
      2. Anna Louise Taylor, b. 1/30/1937, m. John
         Buran Studdard, 9/22/1957.
      3. Betty Jean Taylor, b. 2/9/1938, m. David Carl
         Berg, 2/19/1957.
      4. Letty Dian Taylor, b. 2/9/1938, m. Alford
         Price Gossett, 9/5/1964.
III.   Mary Kathryn Rogers, b. 12/31/1916, m. Aubrey L.
      Petty, b. 10/17/1916, on 8/29/1934.
      Children:
      1. Anna Ruth Petty, b. 11/24/1935, m. James A.
         Simpson, 8/3/1952. Two children d. in
         infancy. Son: James Michael Simpson, b. 9/
         26/1957.
      2. Aubrey Royce Petty, b. 2/9/1938, m. Robbie
         Lou Johnson, 6/1/1956.
         Children:
         (1) Audrey Leigh Petty, b. 2/10/1958.
         (2) Charles Lewis Petty, b. 9/26/1959.
      3. Charles Rogers Petty, b. 5/20/1939, m. Clara
         Adkins, 3/24/1962, attended school in Tipton
         Co., Tenn., graduated from Byars Hall High
         School in Covington, Tenn., June, 1957; he
         spent five years at Memphis State University
         and graduated June, 1962, majored in mathe-
         matics. Clara Adkins graduated from Forrest
         City High School and attended Business Col-
         lege in Memphis, Tenn., where they now live.
         Child:
         (1) Aubrey Scott Petty, b. 12/19/1962.

IV.   Paul Woodrow Rogers, b. 1/24/1919, m. Mary
Rogers, b. 12/20/1920.
Children:
1. Paul Woodrow Rogers, Jr.,
2. Barbara Elizabeth Rogers,

V.   Anna Margaret Rogers, b. 2/3/1921, m. Lawrence
V. Rike, 5/14/1943.
Children:
1. Beverly June Rike, b. 12/30/1944, m. ___Lewis.
2. Marilyn Rike, b. 12/1/1947.

VI.   Roy Edward Rogers, b. 7/24/1923, m. Mary M.
Diggs, b. 10/24/1924.
Children:
1. Chereyl Ann Rogers, b. 2/10/1946.
2. James Gordon Rogers, b. 6/28/1948.
3. Gary Michael Rogers, b. 1/15/1951.

VII.   Frances Gray Rogers, b. 11/1/1925, m. Bailey L.
Clifton, 3/19/1947.
Children:
1. Ridley Rogers Clifton, b. 2/13/1948.
2. Bailey Willis Clifton, b. 10/16/1949.
3. Mary Sue Clifton, b. 7/22/1951.
4. Anna Kathryn Clifton, b. 12/16/1953.

VIII.   Nell Juniter Rogers, b. 8/12/1929, m. Francis
Herbert Atkeison, b. 5/7/1929, on 8/12/1948.
Children:
1. Nathan Herbert Atkeison, b. 7/1/1951.
2. Virginia Juanita Atkeison, b. 12/19/1952.
3. Amy Marie Atkeison, b. 3/8/1956.
4. Ellen Elizabeth Atkeison, b. 9/12/1958.
5. James Rogers Atkeison, b. 4/20/1964.

****

HALBERT OF ESSEX, VIRGINIA

The Halbert family surname originated in France and was brought to England about the time of the Norman Conquest. It referred to a soldier who carried a halbard, (which is defined as a "weapon in the form of a battle-axe and a pike at the end of a long staff"). Thus, it was of occupational origin, denoting a soldier. The family, according to tradition, were Scots, evidently proficient in the use of the battle-axe or halbert, during the early wars of that country.

The first records, which show the surname, Halbert, are in the Land Rolls of 1265, A.D., which can be examined at the British Museum, London. These Land Rolls were published by Charles Ware in his book "County Estate Rolls of England, 1383." The Rolls show that estates were owned in Hampshire and Yorkshire by several families of Halbert. John or Jon Halberd owned 400 acres near Bishop's Waltham, Hampshire, and held 30 soldiers as King's retainers. At Winchester, Pieter Halberde owned 734 acres and gave feudal service to the king with 25 men-at-arms. At Tadcaster, 8 miles from York, Tomas Halbert owned 654 acres, and at Knaresborough, Walter Halbert owned 285 acres of land.

In 1461, (says Batles, "War with France"), Eduard Halbert led a strong contingent to battle in France and defeated the French near Tours, being killed himself. A Lady Isabella Halberd is recorded in 1520, as marrying the Earl of Kyme . . . parish records of Barnstaple, Bedfordshire, March 18, 1520. Margarethe Halbert is recorded in the town records of Bedford as having sold 548 acres of land to the Duke of Buckingham, the builder of what is now Buckingham Palace in London.

In 1215, A.D., at Sutton in Sussex, the wife (Cecilia) of William Halbert is recorded (Ref: Arch Cant. Vol. II, p. 276) as having sold her manor of Sutton to the monks of Robertsbridge to raise money to ransom her son, William, who had been taken prisoner by the King's forces. The son, William, confirmed the grants of land in Northeye which his mother, Cecilia, then living, had made to Edmund, a

nephew. (Ref: Ms Collection, Arm Vincent, p. 88.) Edmund
also claimed the Manor of Averanche in Kent against the
Duke of Norfolk.

In a Will of 1482, Stephen Halbert, Rector of St.
Martin's, Canterbury, refers to his wife, Joanne - "As to
real estate which lies in the parishes of Ash, St. Martins
and St. Pauls, to his wife absolutely, also, to her lands
in Ash for her life, with remainder at her death to his
grandson, Solomon Houghan Halberd, but if his grandson
dies without heirs, the land is to be sold, and part of
the price laid out in books, vestments, for St. Martin's
Church. He gives legacies to Stephen Halberde and Richard
Halbard, wax chandlers. He desires to be buried before
the High Cross in the nave. To the light of St. Martins,
3s; to the Christopher light, 6d; to the purchase of a
certain book, which Thomas Prettyman named and assigned
for the church, 40/-. To his sisters, Marye and Margaret,
five yards of linen at 3s. 4d. a yard, to be divided
between them and 2s. 6d. in money. To the poor, in bread
on the day of his death, and the same at his month's mind.
A friar from the Dominican House is to be engaged to sing
in St. Martin's for the testator's soul on the principal
feasts of the year, after his death, the executors making
what bargains they can with the Friar for the cost.
Secondly, Richard Halbert, W. Fol. 71. Will dated, Oct.
4, 1479; Proved, Mar. 3, 1480: "My wife, Joanne, sons,
Solomon and Geoffrey, and provides for an unborn child.
Of these I have nothing more." 1503 - the Will of Joanne
Halbert states: "To be buried in St. Martin's Churchyard
beside late husband. To High Altar for neglected dues,
3s. 4d. To St. Christopher light, 2s. To the Crosse
light there in the rode loft, 3s; to Gillys, parson of St.
Martin's, 'my little cuppe, harnessed with silver, and the
cover there-unto belonging, a pilowe of silk and sixe nap-
kins; 15 masses on day of burial and at my month's mind
and my anniversary. She gives her 'household stuff' among
a large number of friends, one article to each, specifying
3 sets of beads, the worst being jet. She had two mes-
suages in the parish, one had a crofte, a barne, and one
acre and yard of land in St. Martin's. Any residue after
legacies, debts and funeral expense are paid, is to be
laid out for her soul - Will 1503.' In 1518, Solomon Halberd of Ash 'bequeaths to Ash Church, a cow to 'keep an
obit once a year, 5th August, from ferme of same to the
value of 16s., and the residue to the church warden to see
it done.'

Another Halbert Will which casts an interesting light
on the lives of the people of these early times is that of

Edmunde Halberde of Rochester, Kent, (Arch Cant. Vol. 35.
W. fol. 211): "to be buried in the churchyard of St. Nicholas. At my burial, 5 masses in honor of the 5 wounds.
My son, Thomas, have the place I dwell in with 5 acres of
land, one acre called 'Longcroft,' five yards in the Close,
but if he dies without issue, to my daughter. To my son,
William, five acres in Newcroft. My wife, Alice, to have
my best black horse, and occupy my messuage and barn; also
2 acres of barley and another piece of land with hemp, and
in the next year following, my wife to have 2 quarters of
wheat and one of barley. My daughter to have my red cow,
six ewes, the middle brass pot and kettle, and my sons
shall pay unto my daughter, 1/4, after the death of my
wife. My son, Henry, to have my best brass pot, with my
messuage called, 'Roodland.' "

In Maunsell's, "Yorkshire Pedigrees", is given the
lineage of a northern branch of the Halbert family, as
follows: "Richard Halbert, who married Adeal Hussye in
1643, was great-grandfather of William Halbert, who was
proprietor of large estates at Boroughbridge, Aldborough,
Minskip, Rowcliff and diverse other places in Yorkshire,
and was steward or seneschal of the Forest of Knaresborough to Richard, Earl of Cornwall. This William's direct
descendant was William Halbert, who married Anne, daughter
of John Palleyne, Esq. of Killinghall and had, among other
issue, Thomas Halbert. This Mr. Halbert was succeeded by
his eldest son, Thomas Halbert, who married Jane, daughter
and co-heir of Bernard Pever, Esq. of Brampton, by whom he
acquired that estate. Thomas Halbert, Esq. of Boroughbridge, was created a Baronet in his old age and was succeeded by his only son, who died without issue."

William Halbert, who with his wife, Mary, lived in
Essex County in 1709, was the FIRST of his name in Va., m.
Mrs. Mary Wood, formerly the wife of Thomas Wood (d.before
2/10/1709), for on that date, William Halbert and Mary
Halbert, his wife, were appointed administrators of the
estate of Thomas Wood. (D.B. 13, -279.) In those days,
widows usually married soon after the death of their husbands and before their estates were settled, for nearly
always their second husbands were appointed administrator
of the first husband's estate. In this case, we have no
doubt but that she was the widow of Thomas Wood, decd.,
for on July 25, 1709, William and Mary Halbert presented
the inventory of Thomas Wood, decd., and at that time, she
is referred to as "Mary Halbert, late Mary Wood." (Id.-296)

On June 10, 1710, William Halbert was a surety on
the bond of Elizabeth Cole as administratrix of the estate
of William Cole. (Id. -342)

Mary Halbert, widow, held land adjacent to Jacob and
Joshua Stepp, on Oct. 18, 1718. This land was formerly
purchased from Edward Moseley by Abraham Stepp, father to
said Jacob. (D.B. 15, -230) The entry is confusing
because the will of William Halbert was not filed in Essex
until 1723, and it is not of record in the County, evidently, therefore, not copied for some reason and the
original will is lost. However, it was not until Feb. 19,
1733, that Joel Halbert was appointed administrator of
William Halbert's estate. He gave bond as follows: "We,
Joel Halberd, Wm. Moseley, and Joseph Leeman are firmly
bound unto the Justices of the County of Essex . . . in
the sum of Ł 200 . . . and to make or cause to be made a
true and perfect inventory of the estate of William Halberd." (W.B. 5-167)

No record of the administration of the estate of William Halbert, who died before Oct. 18, 1718, and whose will
was filed in 1723, has previously been found in Essex. It
seems evident, therefore, that Joel Halbert, whose father
and mother had married in 1709, had become of age. If 21,
about February, 1733, this would place his date of birth
in 1712, and his younger brother, William, would have been
born somewhere between 1714 and 1718.

This is mentioned here because it has been concluded
that Joel was a brother of the William Halbert whose
estate was administered in 1733. (47 V.260) William and
Mary Halbert had issue.

Children:
I.   JOEL[1] HALBERT. (See later)
II.   William[2] Halbert. (See later)

Joel[1] Halbert, m. Elizabeth Frances Jones, dau. of
John Jones and Frances Randolph (dau. of Col. Richard Randolph and Jane Bolling(?)), ca. 1740, in Essex Co., Va.
Joel was living in Caroline Co., 10/28/1754, when he signed
a joint bond with his brother William. Most of the records
of Caroline Co., were destroyed and the date of his death
is not known.

Children:
1. John Halbert, b. ca. 1741, Caroline Co. (?),
    d. after 1810, Stokes Co., N. C. (?), m.
    Peggy Hill, (not related to Elizabeth, Rob-
    ert and William).
2. Elizabeth Halbert, b. ca. 1742, m. 1765,
    William Hill, Jr., b. 1737, d. 1792.
3. WILLIAM ANSON HALBERT. (See later)
4. Martha Halbert, b. 1747, m. ca. 1769, Major
    Robert Hill, b. 1752.
5. Joel[2] Halbert, b. 1749, d. 1819, in Lincoln

Co., Tenn.
6. Frances Halbert, b. ca. 1751, m. 1772, Capt.
Ambrose Blackburn, b. 1750, in Ireland, d.
1820, Maury Co., Tenn., fought in Rev.
WILLIAM ANSON HALBERT, son of Joel[1] and Elizabeth
Halbert, was b. 10/14/1744, in Essex Co., Va., d. 12/28/
1808, in Anderson Co., Va. He seems to have been a resident of Surry Co., N. C., in 1777, when he bought 150 acres
of land in Henrico Co., Va., for the deed then described
him as "of Surry Co., N. C." He m. Elizabeth Hill, b.
Caroline Co., Va., 9/18/1747, dau. of William Hill, Sr.,
and Susannah Smithers, and she d. 1836.

Copied in the Land Grant Office, State Capitol Bldg.,
Richmond, Va., from Virginia Land Grant Book, D.,
p. 820.   486 Acres. No. 268.
Treasury Warrant
QUOTE:
Thomas Jefferson, Esq., Governor of the Commonwealth of Virginia, & c., to all to whom these presents
shall come, Greeting, & c. Know ye that in consideration
of the ancient Composition of fifty shillings sterling
paid by WILLIAM HALBERT into the Treasury of the Commonwealth there is granted by the said Commonwealth unto the
said WILLIAM HALBERT a certain tract or parcel of land
containing Four Hundred and Eighty Six Acres by survey
bearing the date of March 7, 1780, lying and being in the
County of Henry on Russell's Creek waters and bounded as
followeth to wit: BEGINNING at a corner persimmon tree on
a branch on his own line thence with his line North 30
degrees East 16 poles to Corner South 80 degrees East 180
poles crossing a branch to a white Oak corner thence new
line (from) the same Coner (Corner) 28 poles to a Post Oak
North 48 degrees West 107 poles to a post Oak South 74
degrees West 161 poles crossing a branch to a Post Oak
South 20 degrees West 167 poles to a white oak in John
Parr's line thence with his line South 56 degrees East 48
poles to the first station with its appurtenances to have
and to hold the said tract or parcel of land to the said
WILLIAM HALBERT and his heirs forever. In witness whereof
the said Thomas Jefferson Governor of the Commonwealth of
Virginia hath hereunto Set his hand and caused the leser
(lesser) seal of the said Commonwealth to be affixed at
Richmond on the tenth of April, 1781, and of the Commonwealth the fifth.
Signed, Thomas Jefferson

William and Elizabeth Hill Halbert had issue.

Children:
- I.   Joel[3] Halbert. (See later)
- II.   Martha Halbert, b. 3/17/1772, d. 1810. (See later)
- III.   JOHN HALBERT, b. 10/11/1773, in Va. Served several terms in S. C. Legislature, m. ca. 1795, Margaret Harper. Removed, 1818, to Miss., and settled 12 miles below Columbus, on the east side of the Tombigee, d. 7/7/1854, on his plantation. His wife d. 10/8/1842. (See later)
- IV.   Enos Halbert, b. 1/6/1775. (See H.S.F., Vol.V)
- V.   Arthur Halbert, b. 2/17/1777, in Va., m. Elizabeth Cobb.
  Children:
  1. John Halbert.
  2. Henry Halbert.
  3. Linda Halbert.
  4. Arthur Halbert.
- VI.   James Halbert, b. 9/8/1778, in Va., m. Fannie Pepper., emigrated about 1854, to St. Francis Co., Mo., afterwards to Steelville, Crawford Co., Mo., where some of his descendants now live.
- VII.   Susannah Halbert, b. 8/29/1780, in Va., m. Peter Acker, lived in S. C.
  Children:
  1. Halbert Acker.
  2. Frances Acker.
  3. William Acker.
  4. Alexander Acker, (Rev.), lived in S. C.
  5. Elizabeth Acker.
  6. Polly G. Acker.
  7. Tereca Acker.
  8. Peter Newton Acker.
  9. Joel M. Acker, lived in Aberdeen, Miss.
  10. Joshua S. Acker
- VIII.   Frances Halbert, b. 5/30/1782, in Va., d. 1857, m. Charles Garrison and lived in S. C.
  Children:
  1. Elias E. Garrison.
  2. Elizabeth Garrison.
  3. William Barksdale Garrison.
  4. Mourning Caroline Garrison.
  5. Martha A. Garrison.
  6. Mariah Garrison.
  7. May Farley Garrison.
  8. Susannah Acker Garrison.
  9. Frances Garrison.

10. Charles Garrison.
11. Joel M. Garrison.
12. David Vinton Garrison.
13. Matilda Ann Garrison.

IX.   William Anson Halbert, Jr., b. 5/17/1784, in Va.,
       m. Bettie Brown and removed to Ala.
X.   Joshua Halbert, b. 10/4/1785, in Va., m. Matilda
       Nash. He was a Baptist Minister and one of the
       first settlers of Tuscaloosa, Ala., d. in 1842,
       on North River, Tuscaloosa Co., Ala.
       Children:
       1. Lucius Halbert.
       2. Martha Halbert, (1824-1880).
       3. Mary Halbert.
       4. Helen Halbert.
       5. Frances Halbert.
       6. Eliza Halbert, (1814-1868).
       7. Joshua Halbert.
XI.   Elizabeth Halbert, b. 1/6/1788, in Pendleton
       Dist., S. C., d. 7/8/1861, in Tippah Co., Miss.,
       m. William Berry, b. 8/17/1780, in S. C., d.
       6/14/1858, in Tippah Co., Miss., son of Hudson
       Berry and Sarah Anthony.
       Children:
       1. Hudson Berry, b. 8/15/1806, d. 12/13/1813.
       2. Joel H. Berry, b. 2/11/1808, m. (1) Martha
          Elsey Simpson, (2) Mary Louise Cunningham,
          (3) Martha Malinda Simpson.
       3. Sarah Anthony Berry, b. 11/28/1809, m. Tho-
          mas Burress. (See later)
       4. Harriet Elvira Berry, b. 5/29/1812, m.Joseph
          B. Jones.
       5. William Henry Berry, b. 8/1/1814.
       6. James Furman Berry, b. 10/28/1816, m. Mrs.
          Eliza Holmes.
       7. Elizabeth Susan Berry, b. 3/21/1819, m. Wil-
          liam Knox.
       8. Mary Teresa Berry, b. 12/13/1821, m. John C.
          Hiett.
       9. Nathan Manly Berry, b. 4/15/1824, m. Jamima
          Frances Ball.
       10. Micajah Franklin Berry, b. 10/13/1826, m.
           (1) Alethea A. Spencer, (2) Agnes W. Gresham.
       11. Matilda Frances Caroline Berry, b. 5/15/1829,
           m. John D. Rogers.
   SARAH ANTHONY BERRY, d. 11/11/1869, in Prentiss Co.,
Miss., dau. of William and Elizabeth (Halbert) Berry., m.
9/8/1831, Thomas Burress, b. 9/18/1808, in Anderson Co.,

S. C., d. 11/28/1895, in Prentiss Co., Miss., son of John
Burress and Elizabeth Davis.

    Children:
- I.   Susan Elizabeth Anthony Burress, b. 7/30/1832,
  m. Alvis Harper H. Spencer. (See later)
- II.   John William Burress, m. Harriet N. Miller.
- III. Henrietta Louisa Burress, m. William D. Burge.
- IV. Rev. Luther Rice Burress, m. Annie Ball.

SUSAN ELIZABETH ANTHONY BURRESS, b. 7/30/1832, in
Anderson Co., S. C., d. 10/26/1923, at Eutaw, Greene Co.,
Ala., m. 9/23/1852, in Prentiss Co., Miss., Alvis Harper
H. Spencer, b. 7/8/1831, in Pickens Co., Ala. Alvis H.
Spencer was a planter in Greene Co., Ala., and served as
a Lieut., in the C.S.A.

    Children:
1. Thomas Harper Spencer, b. 3/4/1855, m. Sallie
   Ann McGiffert.
2. Samuel Milton Spencer, b. June, 1858, m. (1)
   Florence Stringfellow, (2) Lillian Jones.
3. William Micajah Spencer, b. 7/21/1860, at
   Knoxville, Greene Co., Ala., d. 3/9/1941, at
   Gallion, Ala.

WILL OF WILLIAM HALBERT

In the name of God Amen: I, William Halbert, of Pendleton District, being of perfect mind and memory, Thanks
be to God Almighty, calling to mind the mortality of my
body, knowing that it is appointed for all men once to
die, do make and ordain this my last Will and Testament,
that is to say:

I recommend my Soul into the hands of Almighty God,
who gave it, my body I recommend unto the earth to be
buried in a decent manner at the discretion of my Executors, nothing doubting, but at the General Resurrection,
I shall receive the same by the Mighty Power of God, and
as touching such worthy Estate wherewith it has pleased
God to bless me with. I demise and dispose of the same
in the following manner:

First, My lawful debts to be paid.

I also lend unto my beloved Wife, Elizabeth Halbert,
two hundred acres of land including the plantation whereon I now live, also all my household furniture with all my
old stock of negros and other stock of all kinds during
her natural life or widowhood. Provided that should she
marry then she has one child's part, after all my children
is toted off with what I allow them to have at their set-
ting out or leaving me. My will and desire is that all my
children at their coming of age or marrying shall have as
follows:

I do give my son Joel Halbert, the land I bought from Ralph Owen and Elizah Owen, that he now has in possession, and two negros, Viz: Sal and Mose, with other necessaries that he has in his possession.

I do give my son JOHN HALBERT, two negros, Viz: Gean and Billy, and other goods, he now has in his possession.

I do give my son Enos Halbert, that land he has in possession, including the land I bought from Henry Burdine, one negro, Viz: Rhoda, with other property he has in possession.

I do give my son Arthur's children, two hundred acre of land, the tract whereon he died and fifty of a tract we call Hiroth, to be divided among his children, Viz: Henry, John, Linda, and Arthur, when they come of age.

I do give my son, James Halbert, two hundred acres of land, joining that where Arthur died and running across all the tracts, with one young negro, Viz: Peter, and all the others I gave or put in his possession.

I do give my son, William Halbert, three hundred and thirty-two (332) acres of land, including the mill of Big Creek, and a tract of ninety acres called Datenal, one young negro, horse and bridle, and saddle bed, with stock of different kinds to begin.

I do give my son, Joshua Halbert, two hundred acres of land joining James, across all tracts, and one young negro, also thirty acres and the Mill Shoal of Saluda I purchased from William Acker, and at his Mother's death to have the plantation and tract she lives on, with horse and saddle and bed and furniture and stock of different kinds.

I do give my daughters: Martha Grisham,
                        Susannah Acker,
                        Frankah Garrison, and
                        Elizabeth Acker, two young
negros, with what other property I gave in their possessions.

I do give my daughter, Mary Halbert, two young negros, horse, saddle, bed and furniture with stock of different kinds to house keep it with.

I do give my daughter, Lucinda Halbert, two young negros, horse, saddle, bed and furniture, and stock of different kinds (I don't mean more, but equal to, what the rest of you had).

I do desire that my beloved wife, Elizabeth Halbert, shall enjoy all my personal estate, only what my children take as they come of age, provided she does not destroy or diminish it during her natural life or widowhood. After her death what is remaining of the estate, to be divided among my children, Arthur's children to have a share.

I likewise constitute, ordain, and appoint Joel Halbert, John Halbert, Enos Halbert, and John Grisham executors of this, my Last Will and Testament, and I do hereby disallow, revoke and disannul all and every former testament, wills, legacies, bequeaths, and executions by me in anywise before named and bequeathed, and rectify, confirm this to be my last Will and Testament, in witness whereof I have hereunto set my hand this thirtieth day of July, in the year of our Lord and Savior, Jesus Christ, One Thousand Eight Hundred and Six.

Signed: WILLIAM HALBERT

In The Presence Of:
    William Harper
    James Brown
    David Brown   Will was proven: March 6, 1809.

JOHN HALBERT, b. 10/11/1773, son of William and Elizabeth Hill Halbert, m. Margaret Harper.

Children:

I.   Percival Halbert, b. 2/23/1796, Anderson Dist., S. C., m. Jane Owen, 1822, in Jefferson Co., Ala. He d. on his plantation, Oketibbeha Co., Oct., 1864. Children: 1. Xenophon; 2. Mary; 3. Margaret; 4. Eliza; 5. Isaac; 6. Henry; 7. Alexander; and 8. John.

II.   Xenophon Halbert, b. 2/14/1798, d. 12/27/1863, Lowndes Co., Miss., m. Willie Eddins. Children: 1. Ira; 2. Percival; 3. James; 4. Xenophon; 5. Elizabeth; 6. Mary; 7. Victoria, 8. Rebecca; and 9. Newton.

III.   Francis Halbert, b. 2/7/1800, d. 11/24/1839, Oketibbeha Co., Miss., m. John Sitton, d. 1840. Children: 1. Olivia; 2. Margaret; 3. Frances; 4. Sarah; 5. Martha; 6. Bettie; 7. Eliza; 8. Octavia; 9. Susan; and 10. William.

IV.   WILLIAM HALBERT, (Uncle Billie), b. 2/22/1802, Anderson Co., S. C., d. 2/26/1885, Lowndes Co., Miss., m. Nancy McClannahan, b. 11/14/1807, d. 3/28/1868, on 1/10/1822. The Rev. William Halbert united with the Baptist Church in Lowndes Co., 8/23/1823, and was ordained in 1825. Mt. Zion Church was organized in 1843, and the first Church was built in 1849 with Rev. Halbert as the Pastor. He built his plantation home at New Hope, in 1826, and later gave each of his six sons 120 acres of land, known as Pane Place, Quinn Place, Frances Place, two on Ala. State Line, and Simpson Place. Children:

The Rev. William (Uncle Billie) Halbert
1802-1885

James Monroe Halbert
("Paw") 1826-1913

1. Mary Ann Halbert, ("Aunt Polly,"), b. 3/10/1823, d. 11/26/1912.
2. John Halbert, b. 11/18/1824, d. 6/1/1902.
3. JAMES MONROE HALBERT, ("Paw"), b. 10/4/1826, Lowndes Co., d. 12/18/1913, m. Sarah Edmundson, b. 2/19/1834, d. 4/2/1870. He was a member of the Masonic Lodge, and a Confederate Veteran.
   Children:
   (1) William Halbert, b. 6/16/1858. (See later)
   (2) Ezra Halbert.
   (3) Laura Halbert.
   (4) Margaret Halbert, ("Aunt Mag"), b. 3/14/1862, d. 9/9/1932. (See later)
   (5) Mary Halbert, ("Aunt Mollie"), b. 8/29/1855, d. 10/8/1933.
   (6) Sallie Halbert. (See later)
   (7) JAMES LEMUEL HALBERT, b. 7/24/1866, in Lowndes Co., d. 3/8/1936, served with the Riflemen after the Civil War, elected Justice of the Peace, Lowndes Co., 1935, m. (1) Mattie Fergerson, d. 7/3/1900, (2) Etta Wooten, (3) Jessie Gordon Land, dau. of James L. and Sallie Gordon Land, b. 8/12/1886, Pickens Co., Ala., d. 3/2/1959, Lake City, Florida.
      Children: (3rd marriage)
      a. James Lemuel Halbert, b. 7/5/1912, d. 10/4/1914.
      b. William Halbert, b. 2/28/1914, d. 8/5/1940.
      c. Kirby Smith Halbert, b. 5/19/1925, in New Hope Community, about ten miles from Columbus, Miss., enlisted in the Navy, 7/10/1942, completed boat training and Hospital Corps School in San Diego, Calif., discharged, 11/26/1945, with the rank of PHM 2/C, attended the Guyton-Jones College of Mortuary Science at Nashville, Tenn., m. Lucy Jane Guyton, b. 1/17/1939, dau. of Moses and Margaret McKay Guyton. Address: 6517 Harlow Blvd., Jacksonville, 10, Fla.
         Children:
         (a) Mary Margaret Halbert, b. 1/6/1957.

James Lemuel Halbert (1866-1936)

William Halbert
(1914-1940)

Kirby Smith Halbert
(b. 1925)

      (b) James McKay Halbert, b. 12/30/
         1963.

4. Thomas Jefferson Halbert, b. 2/12/1829, d. 7/4/1837.

5. Franklin Halbert, b. 5/10/1831, Lowndes Co., Miss., d. 1862, from wounds at second Battle of Bull Run.

6. Anna Eliza Halbert, b. 3/8/1834, d. 1855, m. John Weaver in 1851. Children: 1. Jessie Weaver, and 2. Idella Weaver.

7. Frances Halbert, b. 7/29/1836, d. 1870, m. Col. A. S. Payne, 10/5/1852. Children: 1. Lewis Payne, 2. Woodruffe Payne, 3. Blanche Payne, 4. Frances Payne, 5. Dr. Guy Payne, and 6. Dr. Winter Payne.

8. Joel Joshua Halbert, b. 5/1/1839, d. 1855.

9. Margaret Halbert. (See later)

10. Arthur Calhoun Halbert, (Dr.), b. 2/21/1843, d. 1908, m. Donie Yeager. Children: 1. Harris Halbert, 2. Alice Halbert, 3. William Halbert, 4. Nancy Halbert, 5. Arthur Halbert, 6. Mary Foote Halbert, and 7. Laura Halbert.

11. Ezra Halbert, b. 8/25/1945, d. 2/20/1916, m. Ann McReynolds, served with Co. 1, 43rd Miss. Infantry, C.S.A. Children: 1. Lou Halbert, and 2. Mary Eliza Halbert.

12. Zachary Halbert, b. 3/2/1849, d. 6/30/1907, m. (1) Lura Ellis, b. 1/5/1859, d. 1/14/1891, (2) Claudia Cox.
    Children: (1st marriage)
    (1) Nancy Halbert, b. 3/28/1880, Lowndes Co., Miss., m. Sidney A. Cox, 10/28/1909.
        Children:
        a. Tyllman Cox, b. 6/8/1911, m. Virginia R. Whitlock, 8/30/1934.
           Children:
           (a) Tillman Reed Cox, b. 6/30/1936, New Hope, m. Nancy C. Craig, 9/13/1957. Child: Steven Reed Cox, b. 7/11/1959, Huntsville, Ala.
           (b) Robert Taylor Cox, b. 8/17/1941.
           (c) Carol Cox, b. 10/5/1958, West Point, Clay Co., Miss.
        b. Halbert Earl Cox, b. 2/4/1917, d. 4/27/1919.
    (2) Norma Halbert, b. 1/6/1882, Lowndes Co., m. John F. Taggart.
    (3) Zachary Taylor Halbert, b. 10/10/1883,

d. 10/12/1959, m. Nina Payne.
- (4) James Dudley Halbert, b. 7/30/1886, d. 7/20/1889.
- (5) Samuel Dyer Halbert, b. 7/23/1889, m. Serella Simmons

Children: (2nd marriage)
- (6) Grace Halbert, b. 8/28/1892, in Lowndes Co. .
- (7) Mary Lucille Halbert, b. 3/1/1894, m. Willis Sparks Montgomery, d. 8/29/1960.

V. Arthur Clarke Halbert, b. 2/25/1805, d. Dec., 1861, m. (1) Parmelia Arnold, (2) Mrs. Sophia Crigler.

Children: (1st marriage)
1. John Bently Halbert, b. 1825, Columbus, Miss., d. 1858, m. Catherine B. Bostic of Nashville, Tenn.

    Children:
    - (1) John Bentley Halbert, Jr., b. 9/23/1850, d. 3/18/1924.
    - (2) Hardin Bostic Halbert, b. 1856, d. 1907, m. Cassie J. Halbert (dau. of Rev. Joel Halbert),b. 9/18/1858. Children:(a) Hardin Bostic, Jr., b. 7/25/1887, m. Ethel Moon;(b) Joel Bentley, b. 4/15/1896.

2. Wiley Halbert.
3. Elizabeth Halbert.
4. Joel Halbert.
5. Margaret Halbert.
6. Clementine Halbert.
7. Henry Halbert.

Children: (2nd marriage)
8. Jefferson Davis Halbert, b. 8/15/1854, d. 2/11/1934, m. Amelia Jordan McGee, b. 2/22/1863, d. 9/16/1909, on 5/10/1882.

    Children:
    - (1) Clemmie Lucile Halbert, b. 5/29/1884, d. 3/31/1929, m. Alexander Wayland Nickerson, 11/17/1914.

        Child:
        a. Ruth McGee Nickerson, b. 3/27/1917, m. William F. Leffler, 8/27/1939. Children: 1. Paul Leffler, 2. Margaret Faye Leffler, 3. Barbara Lynn Leffler, and 4. Alexa Leffler.
    - (2) Lulu Augusta Halbert, b. 6/4/1885, d. 12/3/1902.
    - (3) Hattie Sue Halbert, b. 6/11/1888, d.

9/15/1904.

(4) Bettie Dee Halbert, b. 10/15/1891, d. 10/1/1918.

(5) Edgar James Halbert, b. 12/18/1895, d. 3/9/1941, m. Frances Austin, 3/9/1934. Child:

a. James Austin Halbert, b. 12/9/1939.

(6) Amelia McGee Halbert, b. 8/5/1897, m. Guy Werter Thaxton, 12/21/1916. Children:

a. Werter Edgar Thaxton, b. 9/1/1918, m. Margaret McCon, 8/31/1940. Children: 1. Robert Thaxton, 2. Dennis Thaxton, and 3. Gary Thaxton.

b. Halbert Colclough Thaxton, b. 12/5/ 1921, m. (1) Helen Thomason, 1/10/ 1946. Child: Donna Ruth Thaxton, b. 4/14/1950. M. (2) Barbara Gallett Fowler, 6/22/1957.

9. Burt Vincent Halbert, b. 8/15/1854, d. 12/31/ 1925, m. Annie Laura Nance, 10/9/1879, b. 6/25/1857, d. 4/2/1931, dau. of James Nance and Emily Toland. Children:

(1) Minnie Lee Halbert, ("Mimpie"), b. 3/3/ 1882, m. Dr. Henry Harrison Smith, Jr., in 1906. Children:

a. Henry Harrison Smith, III, b. 5/5/ 1907, m. Rubilee Moore. Children:

(a) Martha Smith, b. 12/6/1942.

(b) Suzanne Smith, b. 3/10/1946.

(c) Michael Smith, b. 12/20/1957.

b. Burt Halbert Smith, b. 7/25/1912.

c. Carolyn Nance Smith, b. 1/19/1916, m. Thomas Andrew Hamill, b. 2/27/1903, on 5/10/1937. Child:

(a) Thomas Andrew Hammill, II, b. 2/26/1938, m. Doris Boyed, 11/1/ 1958. Child: Thomas Andrew Hammill, III, b. 11/13/1959.

(2) Nellie Blanche Halbert, ("Sistee"), b. 1/1/1886, m. Joe Russell Howarth, b. 2/ 15/1876, d. 7/23/1930, on 2/15/1916. Children:

a. Ruth Fleming Howarth, b. 7/16/1918,

           m. Thomas Graham Wells, b. 9/20/1916,
on 5/18/1945.
Children:
(a) Rebecca Lynn Wells, b. 5/16/1946.
(b) Linda Blanche Wells, b. 3/4/1948.
   b. Virginia Nance Howarth, b. 12/24/1921,
m. Jack Mims, b. 12/5/1918.
Children:
(a) William Joseph Mims, b. 5/26/1949.
(b) Stephen Halbert Mims, b. 10/30/
1953.
(3) William Halbert, deceased.
(4) Burt Vincent Halbert, Jr., b. 1/14/1901,
m. Marie Stuart Goodwin, b. 6/28/1906,
on 6/19/1924.
Children:
   a. Burt Vincent Halbert, III, b. 9/13/
1925, m. Martha Jean Allen, b. 8/17/
1928, on 9/25/1948.
Children:
(a) Kathleen Halbert, b. 10/24/1955.
(b) Burt Vincent Halbert, IV, b. 3/
26/1959.
   b. William Edward Goodwin Halbert, b.
3/3/1931, m. Sally Ellen Bowling, b.
3/30/1932, on 11/9/1956.
Children:
(a) William E. G. Halbert, II, b. 1/
7/1958.
(b) Stuart Lee Weaver Halbert, b. 2/
28/1960.
10. James Halbert.
11. Emma Halbert.
12. Arthur Halbert.

VI.   Annie Halbert, b. 6/22/1807, d. 5/10/1837, m.
Gabriel Nash. Children: 1. Evans Nash, 2. Reuben
Nash, 3. Margaret Nash, 4. James Nash, 5. John
Nash, 6. Bettie Nash, and 7. Frances Nash.

VII.   Elizabeth Halbert, b. 3/26/1810, d. 6/5/1850, m.
Thomas Mullin. Children: 1. Arthur Mullin, 2.
Margaret Mullin, 3. John Mullin, 4. Thomas Mullin, 5. Lucy Mullin, 6. Elizabeth Mullin, and
twins, 7. & 8. Thomas and Newton Mullin.

VIII.   James Halbert, b. 2/3/1812, d. 8/22/1828.

IX.   John Hill Halbert, b. 4/5/1814, d. 1858, m.Levey
Campbell. Children: 1. Margaret Halbert, 2.
James Halbert, 3. Arthur Halbert, 4. Joel Hal-
bert, 5. Ansavilla Halbert.....list incomplete.

X.   Rachael Halbert, b. 2/20/1817, d. 8/19/1822.
XI.   Mary Halbert, b. 3/25/1819, d. 3/27/1867, m.
        John Pertwood. Children: 1. Hilary Pertwood, 2.
        William Pertwood, 3. John Pertwood, 4. & 5.twins,
        unnamed, and 6. Leonidas Pertwood.
XII.   Joel Joshua Halbert, (Rev.), b. 10/29/1821, d.
        3/17/1875, m.(1) Martha Taylor, b. 12/7/1820, d.
        11/4/1864, (2) Susan Harrison.
        Children: (1st marriage) 1. Melissa Halbert, 2.
        Mary Halbert, 3. Charles Halbert, 4. Calvin Hal-
        bert, 5. Thomas Halbert, 6. Joseph Halbert, 7.
        Perry Halbert, 8. Lilly Halbert, 9. Cassie Hal-
        bert, 10. Lula Halbert, and 11. Martha Halbert.
        Child: (2nd marriage) Sudie Josie Halbert, b.
        10/8/1869, d. 2/28/1870.

JOEL[3] HALBERT,son of William and Elizabeth Halbert,
was b. 6/13/1767, in Caroline Co., Va., d. 6/24/1848, at
the home of his son, Elihu, Hancock Co., Ill. He served
in the War of 1812, under Jackson, m. Mary Lindsey, b. 9/
27/1772, dau. of John and Sarah Lindsey. Joel owned 1303
acres in Martin's Co., Md., called, "Halbert's Bluff."
Children: 1. Sarah Halbert, 2. Lizzie Halbert, 3. Seth Halbert, 4. Enos Halbert, 5. Elihu Halbert, 6. Ruth Halbert,
7. Martha Halbert, 8. Pallas Halbert, 9. Susan Halbert,
10. Mary Halbert, 11. John Halbert and 12. Silas Halbert.

ELIZABETH HALBERT, ("Lizzie"), b. 2/13/1793, in
Anderson Co., S. C., d. 2/9/1879, dau. of Joel and Mary
Halbert, m. 1816, Thomas Evans, who is believed to have
come to America from Wales at the age of ten years. Among
their 13 children, was JOHN, b. 2/21/1820, d. 2/6/1897. He
was a Judge for many years in MacDonald Co., Mo., and died
in Southwest City, Mo. He m. (1) Mrs. Elizabeth Vandeveer,
a widow; their fourth child was ELBERT ALBRE EVANS, b. 10/
16/1853, d. 5/27/1925, who m. Angie Applewhite on 8/16/
1876, in Wise Co., Texas; their fifth child was RUTH EVANS,
b. 7/6/1886, d. 2/28/1963, who m. Charles Ward Hooper, b.
1/20/1876, son of Joseph and Susan Bennett Hooper. Charles
and Ruth Hooper had issue.
        Children:
        1. FLORA EALA HOOPER, b. 9/12/1904, in Cotton
            Co., Hastings, Okla., m. (1) Glenn Strange,
            b. 8/16/1899, son of William Russell Strange
            and his wife, Sarah Byrd, (2) Horace Collier,
            b. 3/17/1900, in Newton Co., Mo., d. 3/16/
            1956, in Springfield, Mo.
            Children: (1st marriage)
            (1) Vera Strange, b. 2/13/1921, m. Maurice
                Lastfogel, 6/11/1948.

      (2) Eva Strange, b. 4/15/1923, m. Edward M.
         Miller, 2/5/1958.
     Child: (2nd marriage)
      (3) Laura Ruth Collier, b. 8/23/1937, St.
         Louis, Mo., m. Howard Wakefield, Jr., b.
         12/19/1936, Chicago, Ill.
         Children:
         a. Kimberly Sunnita Wakefield, b. 8/14/
           1957, Tucson, Arizona.
         b. Howard Wakefield, III, b. 7/17/1959.
         c. Anthony Collier Wakefield, b. 12/3/
           1960.
   MARTHA HALBERT, dau. of William and Elizabeth Halbert,
(sister of Joel[3] Halbert), was b. 3/17/1772, in Va., m.
11/13/1788, John Gresham, Esq., b. 3/14/1761, d. 6/22/1835,
in Culpepper Co., Va., son of John Gresham[1] and Barbara
Burdyne Gresham, and was a private in the Revolution and
died "7 miles from old Pickens Court House, S. C."
        Children:
  I.   Joseph Gresham, (Col.), b. 11/17/1789, m. (1)
         Nancy Watt, (2) Nancy (or Mary) Love Steele.
  II.   Elizabeth Gresham, b. 11/12/1791, m. James Mc-
         Daniel.
 III.   Susan Gresham, b. 4/19/1794, d. in infancy.
  IV.   Lucinda Gresham, b. 12/5/1795, m. Arthur Craig.
   V.   Frances Gresham, b. 2/6/1798, m. Jno. B. Hammond.
  VI.   John Ridge Gresham, b. 9/4/1800, m. Julia Finch.
 VII.   WILLIAM GRESHAM, b. 3/6/1803, m. Susan Bradford.
         (See later)
VIII.   Malinda Caroline Gresham, b. 7/25/1805, m. Thom.
         Watson.
  IX.   Reuben Gresham, b. 2/4/1808, m. Susan ___.
   WILLIAM GRESHAM, b. 3/6/1803, Pendleton Dist., S. C.,
d. 5/10/1876, in Canton, Ga., m. 11/6/1825, Greenville,
Green Co., S. C., Susan Bradford, dau. of Philemon Brad-
ford. William Gresham's name was erroneously spelled
Grisham by an early schoolmaster and the spelling con-
tinued through his life.
        Children:
  I.   Elizabeth Susan Gresham, b. 10/17/1826, m. Prof.
         Jn. Dorsey Collins.
  II.   MALINDA CAROLINE GRESHAM, b. 4/11/1829, m. Joel
         Lewis Galt. (See later)
 III.   Joseph Lemuel Gresham, b. 2/9/1832, m. Sarah
         Cain.
   MALINDA CAROLINE GRESHAM, b. 4/11/1829, Decatur,

DeKalb Co., Ga., d. 4/17/1902, in Canton, Ga., m. 10/6/
1844, Canton, Ga., Joel Lewis Galt, b. 6/26/1817, Spartan-
burg Dist., S. C., d. 3/18/1873, in Canton, Ga., son of
Jabez Galt and Frances Machen.
Children:
   I.   Susan Elizabeth Galt, b. 3/3/1846, m. Milton
          Tuggle.
  II.   Margaret Amanda Galt, b. 12/22/1848, m. Dr. Jas.
          Speir.
 III.   Jabez Galt, II, b. 5/30/1851, m. (1) Martha Speir,
          (2) Lizzie Teasley.
  IV.   Ada Collins Galt, b. 2/21/1854, m. John Prince
          Lewis.
   V.   Frances Galt, b. 9/5/1856, m. George Headen.
  VI.   MILDRED GALT, b. 12/19/1855, m. Henry Lamar
          Roberts. (See later)
 VII.   William Galt, b. 9/8/1861, m. Lucy Putnam.
VIII.   May (Mary) Galt, b. 7/20/1864, d. in infancy.
      MILDRED GALT, b. 12/19/1855, Canton, Cherokee Co.,
Ga., d. 2/4/1941, in Canton, Ga., m. 1/26/1892, Canton,
Henry Lamar Roberts, b. 10/7/1853, at Stylesboro, Pauling
Co., Ga., d. 11/26/1919, in Canton, son of Griffin Lamar
Roberts and Martha Adelaide Rogers.
Children:
   I.   Nancy Glenn Roberts, b. 12/5/1892.
  II.   Malinda Adelaide Roberts, b. 4/5/1894, d. single.
 III.   Griffin Lamar Roberts, II, b. 1/24/1897, m. Sara
         Hudson, 10/23/1924, and he d. 4/27/1933.
        Child:
        1. Lamar Hudson Roberts.
  IV.   Joel Galt Roberts, b. 12/14/1899, d. in infancy.
    WILLIAM[2] HALBERT, son of William and Mary Halbert,
and brother of Joel[1] Halbert was b. ca 1716. He made his
will 11/18/1760, probated 4/20/1761. He bequeathed to his
son James Halbert, "the Plantation whereon I now live."
This son James[1] Halbert served in the Militia, during the
Rev. (Rev. Soldiers of Va., p. 196.) He m. Sarah Shadduck
and d. on the plantation given him by his father. James[1]
Halbert made his will 12/11/1811, probated 5/17/1819. He
mentions seven children: John, James[2], Thomas, Anthony,
Lewis, William (see later), and dau. Mary. John and James
were appointed Executors. (See later)
    JOHN HALBERT, son of James[1] Halbert, was the ancestor
of the Halberts of St. Clair Co. He m. Martha Ross in Va.,
1/8/1807, dau. of William Ross, who d. in the War of 1812.
In 1810, James[2] Halbert and his wife Sarah, deeded John Halbert a tract of land in St. Anne's Parish, Essex Co. On
5/6/1830, John conveyed all his real estate, including his

father's gift, to Wm. Gray, and was thus in a position to leave for his new home in what was then the far west. He freed his slaves, and moved in slow stages through Ohio into Illinois. He finally settled on uncleared land close to the Kaskakia River, three miles east of the present town of New Athens. He d. in 1844. He and his wife, Martha, were deeply religious, and the Bible they carried with them then is still preserved in the family.

Children:
I.   David Halbert.
II. James Halbert.
III. Joseph Halbert.
IV. Thomas Halbert.
V.   Catherine Halbert, ("Aunt Kate McGuire"), m. Joseph McGuire, grandmother of Mrs. Goodnight of Harristown.
VI. Mary Ann Halbert, m. _____ Marshall.
VII. Sarah Halbert, m. Wm. James, near Belleville.

DR. JAMES[2] HALBERT, brother of John Halbert, was b. 8/19/1785, d. 11/5/1858, m. Nancy Rennolds, b. 12/24/1816, d. 11/10/1858. They moved to Ross Co., Ohio, ca 1831. Later the family moved to Ill. Dr. Halbert was famed for his medicines, and presented the first Medical Bill ever offered to the Ill. State Legislature. He was also an ordained minister in the Baptist Church.

Child:
I.   Mary Lindsay Halbert, b. 11/5/1817, Essex Co., Va., m. (1) Eli Harbert, d. 1839, (2) R. H. Constant, b. 1809, d. 1887.
     Children: (1st marriage) 1. Samuel Harbert, 2. Nancy Harbert, and 3. Eli Harbert.
              (2nd marriage) 4. Cordelia Constant, 5. Lila Constant, 6. William Constant, and 7. Grace Constant.

- RECORDS -

HALBERT

Copied in Court House, Essex Co., Va.
Deed Book 44, pp. 1-3, with pictured plot of ground.

JAMES AND NANCY HALBERT deeded 284 Acres of land to James Kay, May 26, 1832. This land was owned jointly by JAMES AND ANN (NANCY) HALBERT and Andrew Rennolds, who sold it to James Kay; 206 Acres belonging to the Halberts, and 78 to Andrew Rennolds.

While the name Ann appears in the body of the deed, her signature is as below: James Halbert
     All signed by <u>seal</u>,   Nancy Halbert
     not by mark X.   Andrew Rennolds
(Andrew Rennolds was probably brother of Nancy Halbert)

RENNOLDS

Deed Book 39, p. 604.

James Rennolds and Martha, his wife, sold 138 Acres to WM. HALBERT. It was bounded by lands of Capt. Wm. Thomas, Wm. Noel, Mark Andrews and James Hunter. Sold for L200.

Signed: James Rennolds

About 1817-18.   Martha Rennolds

RENNOLDS

Deed Book 39, p. 400.

Andrew Rennolds bought 30 Acres - part of the land of John Dishman which was being sold. It was partly bounded by the lands of John Dishman, JAMES HALBERT, JR., the heirs of John Micon, Sarah Rennolds, Samuel Dishman, John and Obed Gray. May 12, 1817.

HALBERT

Copied in Court House, Essex Co., Va.

Will Book 19, p. 358.

JAMES HALBERT, SR.'S estate was settled Feb. 7, 1823, by John Halbert, one of the executors. Among other items in final account are:

Jan. 1, 1819 - Paid for coffin: 7..63.

Sept. 28, 1819 - Paid for brandy used at sale: 2..00.

Total amt. to be divided as shown by execs.: 213..08.

RENNOLDS

Copied in Court House, Essex Co., Va.

Will Book 15, p. 125-7. Appraisers bond, $6,000, p. 297.

Appraisers return, L1121-6-9, p. 356.

John Rennolds' will was drawn Oct. 26, 1791, and proved Dec. 15, 1794. He mentions wife, Elizabeth (Betty), children: Sally (Hipkins), John, Sthreshley. He willed away 26 slaves, and "all the rest of my slaves I give to my beloved wife." JOHN RENNOLDS was given Phill, Peter, Simon, Dinah, Cate, Nanny, and Milly. Sthreshley was given Scipio, Dick, Frank, Tamar, Harry, Winney, Sukey and Bill. To his daughter, Nancy, mother of James Halbert, he willed one eighth of the negroes belonging to his estate, and names two of them - Titus, and Winney. Titus was valued at L90.

ADAM LINDSAY - beginning with . . .

Mary Lindsay Halbert, b.11/15/1817, d.5/18/1863, dau. of James Halbert, Jr., b.8/19/1785, d.11/5/1858, and Nancy Rennolds, b.ca 1790, d.11/10/1834, dau. of John Rennolds, b.ca 1740, d.1794, and Elizabeth Sthreshley, d.1807-14. John Rennolds, son of James Rennolds, III, d.1771, and Sukie Lindsay, b.ca 1748. She was dau. of Col. James Lindsay, b.1700, d.1782, and Sarah Daniel, b. Middlesex Co.,Va., he was son of ADAM LINDSAY, Va.,ca 1700.

JAMES REYNOLDS (RENNOLDS) - from . . .

Mary Lindsay Halbert, b. 11/15/1817, d. 5/18/1863, dau. of
James Halbert, Jr., b. 8/19/1785, d. 11/5/1858, and
Nancy Rennolds, b. ca. 1790, d. 11/10/1834, dau. of
John Rennolds, b. ca. 1740, d. 1794, and
Elizabeth Sthreshley, d. between 1807-14. John Rennolds,
            son of
James Rennolds, III, d. 1771, and
Sukie Lindsay, b. ca. 1748. James Rennolds, III, son of
James Rennolds, II, d.1750, and Sarah __. James Rennolds,
            II, son of
James Rennolds, I, d.1724. He was son of
Cornelius Reynolds, d.1685. He was son of
James Reynolds the 1st, d. between 1650-60, presumably in
            England, and Marjery ____.
    Spelling of name from REYNOLDS to RENNOLDS was by Act
    of Parliament between 1685-1724, for benefit of the
    Va. family.

ANTHONY SAMUEL, SR. - beginning . . .

Dr. James Halbert, Jr., b. 8/19/1785, d. 11/5/1858, son of
James Halbert, Sr., b. ante 1760, d. 5/8/1819, and
Sarah Shaddock, d. post 7/30/1823, dau of
James Shaddock, b. ca. 1735-37, d. 1795, and
Hannah Samuel, b. 1741, d. post 1795, dau. of
James Samuel, b. ca. 1715, d. 5/10/1759, and
Sarah Boulware, b. 1739, d. post 1759. James Samuel, son of
Anthony Samuel, Jr., d. 1761, (after his son), son of
Anthony Samuel, Sr., d. 6/10/1731, and
Mary _____.
    Ref: Will Book 5, Essex Co., Va., pp. 26-28.

JAMES BOULWARE - beginning with . . .

Hannah Samuel, b. ca. 1715, d. post 1798, dau. of
James Samuel, b. ca. 1715, d. 5/10/1759, and
Sarah Boulware, b. 1739, d. post 1759, dau. of
James Boulware (Bowler), d. 2/10/1718 (?), and
Margery (jory) Gray, d. post 1718. James Boulware, son of
Thomas Boulware (Bowler), d. 1679, and
Tabitha _Edlow_.
    Will Book 2, p. 134 - Thomas Boulware's Will.

WILLIAM GRAY - beginning with . . .

Sarah Boulware, b. ante 1699, d. post 1759, dau. of
James Boulware, d. 1718, and
Margery (jory) Gray, d. post 1718, dau. of
William G. Gray, d. 1673, and
Elizabeth ___, second to Mrs. Magdalen (Maudlin) Ingram, _m_
            but Elizabeth was apparently mother of
            Margery.
    William Gray was captain of a sailing vessel in which

he brought from England a number of "headrights" whose fare he paid.

Ref: "Va. Hist. Mag.", Vol. 4, p. 255, et seq.

William Franklin Halbert, son of James and Sarah Halbert, was b. 6/16/1858, at New Hope, Miss., d. 11/19/1939, in Texarkana, Ark., m. 6/30/1878, in Denton, Tex., Emma Elizabeth Stigall, b. 8/10/1860, d. 8/20/1939.

Children:

I. Sarah Rozana Halbert, b. 11/5/1882, m. J. H. Oden.
   Children:
   1. George Oden.
   2. Bessie Oden. (Mrs. George Graham, Shreveport, La.)
   3. Cleo Oden. (Mrs. Cherry Wallace, Shreveport, La.)
   4. Glynn Oden. (Mrs. Connie Lowe, Shreveport, La.)
   5. Olin Oden.
   6. Roxie Oden. (Mrs. H. L. Shover, Houston, Tex.)
   7. Thomas Oden. (Houston, Tex.)
   8. John Oden. (Spring, Tex.)

II. John Monrow Halbert, b. 3/20/1884, m. Salina Eaton.
    Child:
    1. Jack E. Halbert. (216 Hickory St., Texarkana, Ark.)

III. Lena Elizabeth Halbert, b. 9/25/1885, m. Earl Eaton, (brother to Salina).
     Child:
     1. Lena Bell Eaton. (Mrs. Robert Piland, Va.)

IV. Mary Willie Halbert, b. 6/26/1889, m. Roy E. Robison.
    Children:
    1. Mary Robison. (Mrs. Mary Robison Smith, Creve Coeur, Mo.)
    2. Roy E. Robison, Jr., Mount Olive, Ill.
       Children:
       (1) John Halbert Robison.
       (2) Roy E. Robison, III.

V. Maggie Halbert, b. 3/21/1895, m. J. C. Bankston.
   Children:
   1. Margaret Bankston. (Mrs. Alford Munroe, Houston, Tex.)
   2. Bessie Bankston. (Mrs. W. E. Thomas, 2626 Valley Ridge Road, Shreveport, La.)

Sallie J. Halbert, b. 7/24/1864, d. 5/21/1893, dau. of James and Sarah Halbert, m. R. E. Baxter, 2/3/1887.

Child:

I. Lucy Imogene Baxter, b. 10/13/1887, (premature baby), d. 8/2/1958, m. James Henry Waggoner, 3/8/1905.
   Children:
   1. Myrtle Ophelia Waggoner, b. 3/4/1906, m. Warren Caryl Sanders, 6/10/1953.
   2. James Robert Chambers Waggoner, b. 12/3/1907, d. 4/13/1953.

Margaret Halbert, dau. of Rev. William Halbert (Uncle Billy), and his wife, Nancy McClannahan, was b. 2/28/1841, d. 2/3/1908, in Columbus, Miss., m. Thomas Benton McCracken, 12/28/1864, b. 8/29/1834, d. 7/24/1904.

   Children:
I. Bessie McCracken, b. 11/17/1865, d. 1938, m. Robert Ernest Baxter, 10/3/1893, in New Hope, Miss.
   Children:
   1. Inez Elizabeth Baxter, b. 8/6/1894, d. 1938, m. Jud J. Smith.
   2. Lizzie Esther Baxter, b. 3/7/1897, m. Herman Asher of Yazoo City, Miss., b. 1878, d. 1957.
      Child:
      (1) Herman Asher, Jr.
II. William Halbert McCracken, b. 12/17/1867, (Dr.), m. Mollie Parter of Alligator, Miss.
   Children:
   1. William McCracken.
   2. Mary McCracken.
   3. Marguerite McCracken.
   4. Joseph McCracken.
   5. Hilda McCracken.
III. Margaret Elizabeth McCracken, b. 12/2/1869, d. 12/25/1949, m. Robert Franklin Weaver, 11/7/1888, in New Hope, Miss., b. 3/9/1866, d. 8/10/1941.
   Children:
   1. John Benton Weaver, b. 2/10/1890, m. Esther F. Jewell, 8/15/1926, in Columbus, Miss.
      Children:
      (1) Esther Weaver, b. 4/12/1927, m. Albert Pippen, 9/2/1949.
      (2) Mary Jane Weaver, b. 8/13/1933, m. William E. Still, 6/23/1956.
         Children:
         a. John Rayford Still, b. 1/24/1958.
         b. Stephen Still, b. 2/25/1961.
      (3) John Benton Weaver, Jr., b. 2/5/1935.
   2. Infant, d. at birth.

3. Bessie Jane Weaver, b. 1/4/1892.
4. William Robin Weaver, b. 1/4/1899, m. Grace
    Hazel Martins of Augusta, Ga., 6/17/1930.
    Children:
    (1) Margaret Ann Weaver, b. 5/3/1931, in
        Memphis, Tenn., m. William Claude San-
        ders, in Columbus, Miss., 6/17/1953.
        Children:
        a. Stephanie Sanders, b. 3/16/1956.
        b. Margaret Sanders, b. 2/2/1958.
        c. William Claude Sanders, Jr., b. 11/
           30/1959.
        d. Bruce Sanders, b. 9/30/1961.
        e. John Sanders, b. 8/12/1964.
    (2) William Robin Weaver, Jr., b. 3/1/1933,
        m. Bettie Joyce Greenhaw, at Columbus,
        Miss., 6/2/1962.
        Child:
        a. William Robin Weaver, III., b. 6/23/
           1963.

                        ****


```
X X X X X X X X X X X X X X X X X X X X X X X X X X
X                                                  X
X              HALBERT  COAT  OF  ARMS             X
X                                                  X
X       Arms: Gules, a chevron between three       X
X             Halbards argent.                      X
X       Crest: A Wolf Rampant reguardant ppr.       X
X       Motto: None recorded, often the case        X
X             with the older arms.                  X
X       Authority: Burke's Armory, 1878 edition,    X
X                  p. 440, (this furnished by        X
X                  International Ancestry Guild,     X
X                  Co. Dublin, Ireland.)            X
X       Tinctures as indicated by description:      X
X       The Shield is of Red (Gules).  The chev-    X
X       ron and Halbards are of Silver. The Wolf    X
X       is natural Color.  The Gentleman's Helmet   X
X       is of Steel Gray lined with Red.            X
X                                                  X
X X X X X X X X X X X X X X X X X X X X X X X X X X
```

ABSTRACTS from the records of Essex Co., Va., were
kindly obtained by Mr. and Mrs. Kenneth Waddell of
Washington, D. C.

                        ****

Lineage from WILLIAM HALBERT
of
Eugenia Hodge Lawton

1. William Halbert,(1744-1808), m. 1765, Elizabeth Hill,
   (1747-1836).
2. Susanna Halbert,(1780-1868), m. 1798, Peter Acker, Jr.,
   (1780-1820).
3. Peter Newton Acker,(1813-1881), m. 1840, Harriet
   Shumate, d. 1850.
4. Harriet Lucinda Acker,(1843-1919), m. 1859, Richmond
   R. McDavid,(1837-1864), k. Battle Sabine Cross Roads,
   Mansfield, La.
5. Annie Eugenia McDavid,(1860-1939), m. 1881, John
   Thomas McWilliams,(1849-1912).
6. Dovie McWilliam, (1882-living,1965), m. 1907, Robert
   Hickman Hodge, (1879-1949).
7. EUGENIA FLORENCE HODGE, b. 1911, m. 1932, Robert
   Gillam Lawton, Jr., b. 1908.
8. Diane Lawton, b. 1934, m. 1956, Don Mack Mayer, b.
   1932.
   9. Marianne Mayer, b. 1958.
   9. Robert Michael Mayer, b. 1961.
8. Robert Gillam Lawton, III, b. 1937.
8. Linda Eugenia Lawton, b. 1943.

****

SAUNDERS OF CAROLINE COUNTY, VIRGINIA

Richard Wren Saunders, son of Reuben Saunders and his wife, Leanah (?), was b. 9/5/1762, and d. 6/19/1838.(Family Bible Records.) He served in the Rev. War, (State of Va. Records), from 1779-1781, and was taken prisoner by the British on the surrender of Charleston, S. C. He remained a prisoner in the barracks for five months, and then in the prison ship, "Fidelity", for a further nine months. In 1781, he was landed at Old James Town, and was discharged at Williamsburg, Va.

He m. (1) Leanah Gravett, b. 3/16/1766, d. 1/30/1830, on 12/16/1784. They settled for a time on a plantation called, "Goose Pond", in Caroline Co., Va. The Caroline Co. Land Tax Lists record that in 1785, James Bowie transferred 285 acres to Richard Saunders, later sold to Richard Taylor in 1788. As Richard Saunders does not appear again on the tax list, it is believed that he removed from Caroline Co. He m. (2) Ann Puller Wharton, b. 1800, on 6/12/1834.

Children: (1st marriage)

I. Wesley Saunders, b. (?), d. prior to 1844. Ellis G. Saunders, Administrator. Later, in 1858, Wesley W. Wright, Sheriff of Caroline, Admr. His wife is mentioned sometimes as Mildred. He was survived by his widow, Sarah Ann Saunders, of Henrico Co. (Later the wife of Ellis G. Saunders.)
Children:
1. William Wallace Saunders.
2. Robert Bruce Saunders.
3. Frances Ellen Saunders.
4. John Wesley Saunders.
5. Christopher Walthall Saunders.
6. George Waverly Saunders.

II. Ellis G. Saunders, b. 12/23/1801, of Caroline Co. Francis W. Scott, Admr., in 1858. Survived by his wife, Sarah Ann Saunders.
Children:

218

1. William Ellis Saunders, resident of King &
   Queen Co., 1858. (See later)
2. Elizabeth Saunders, m. Thomas C. McClelland,
   resident of King & Queen Co., 1858.
3. Richard Wren Saunders, b. 6/24/1837, of Ash-
   land, Hanover Co., 1858. Killed in Battle
   of Manassas in the Civil War, 7/21/1861,
   buried where he fell, d.s.p. (Bible Records)
4. Lucy Saunders, infant in Caroline Co., 1858.
5. Mildred C. Saunders, m. a Mr. Evans. She
   deceased in 1858. (Records taken from
   Hanover Co. Chancery Wills and Notes, p.152,
   Cocke.)
   Children:
   (1) Charles E. Evans.
   (2) John W. Evans.
   Children: (2nd marriage)
III.   Catherine Virginia Saunders, b. 1835.
IV.   John Wharton Saunders, b. 1836.
   WILLIAM ELLIS SAUNDERS, son of Ellis G. Saunders, b.
9/3/1829, on a plantation, Pamunkey River, Va., educated in
King William Co., m. (1) Martha Hesseltine Cross, b. 4/26/
1832, in Va., on 11/4/1852, m. (2) Agnes Dorothy McDowell,
at Starkville, Miss.
         Children: (1st marriage)
1. Marie Elizabeth Saunders, b. 8/30/1854, in
   King William Co.
2. William Ellis Saunders, Jr., b. 5/23/1856.
3. William LeRoy Saunders, b. 9/26/1858, d. 8/
   19/1865.
4. Richard Ellis Saunders, b. 3/5/1862, in Miss.
   The family removed from Va., in 1860.
   Children: (2nd marriage)
5. Charles Evans Saunders, b. 9/7/1870, d. Nov.,
   1941. (See later)
   CHARLES EVANS SAUNDERS, m. Anna Stovall, b. 3/4/1873,
d. July, 1926, in 1894, dau. of William Gilbert Stovall of
Miss., and his wife, Eleanor Lagrene. William G. Stovall
served in the Miss. Legislature for several years, and held
other posts of responsibility, particularly in the field of
education. He was Superintendent of City Schools for 54
years. He and his wife are buried in Greenwood, Miss.
         Children:
I.   William B. Saunders, b. 1896, in Greenwood, Miss.
         m. Margaret Johnson, b. 1903, in Dec., 1923.
         Child:
1. Lois Ann Saunders, b. 6/1/1926, m. Richard
   Horner, 6/1/1944, in Columbus, Miss. No

issue.
2. Charles Evans Saunders, Jr., b. 9/4/1901, m.
Grace McLean, dau. of Charles Earl McLean
and his wife, Sarah Britt McLean. Charles
E. McLean was b. in New York State in the
1860's, graduated from Cornell University,
and came to Miss., 1892.
Children:
(1) Jane Earliane Saunders, b. 5/4/1929, in
Jackson, Miss., m. Marion Gordon Stewart,
Jr., of Natchez, Miss., 4/9/1949.
Children:
a. Sarah Anne Stewart, b. 5/15/1950.
b. Jennifer Dixon Stewart, b. 10/13/1954.
c. Marion Gordon Stewart, III, b. 2/19/
1959.
(2) Charles Evans Saunders, III, b. 3/23/
1932, m. Connie Reimer of Minneapolis,
Miss.
Children:
a. Britt McLean Saunders.
b. Charles Evans Saunders, IV.

*****

HAYNES OF NORTH CAROLINA

(Further data since the publication of H.S.F., Vol. IV.)

     Bruce C. Powell, of Fair Bluff, N. C., interviewed
Mrs. Marshall Sealey of Barnesville, N. C., in January,
1962. She told him she was descended from Lawrence Haynes
(Francis Lawrence Haynes), and that his children were:
(Compare p. 98, H.S.F., Vol. IV)

I.   Francis L. Haynes (called by many in the family
       - "Frank"). He was no doubt Francis Lawrence
       Haynes, Jr. He m. Eliza Byrd Worley of Fair
       Bluff, December 4, 1856. (Bible Record) Their
       home was near Princess Anne, eight miles from
       Fair Bluff in Robeson Co., N. C., and was built
       immediately after their marriage. A great-grand-
       son, Lawrence Edwards, lives in the old home now.
       Bruce Powell was at this home when Mrs. Bealey,
       a sister of Lawrence Edwards, gave him the Haynes
       data and showed him the old Francis Haynes Bible.
       Francis is buried about four miles from Fair
       Bluff, in the old Spring Hill Cemetery. A grand-
       daughter, Mrs. Lou Byrd of Orrum, N. C., put a
       marker on the grave, but she was unable to locate
       any birth or death dates to put on it. Eliza
       Byrd Worley Haynes is buried in the family ceme-
       tery near the old home. Lawrence, (father of
       Francis), is buried on the Haynes land near Prin-
       cess Anne, also. Mrs. Sealey said that Lawrence
       first owned the land which later belonged to
       Francis.
       Children: (data from Francis Haynes Bible and
              cemetery records)
      1. Alexander, b. 12/30/1857, d. 5/11/1937, m.
         Jane Strickland, b. 6/15/1863, d. 2/7/1936.
         Lived about five miles from Fair Bluff in
         Columbus Co.
      2. Lucinda, b. 1/24/1860, m. John S. Herring,
         lived at Fair Bluff at one time.

3. Mary Ann Charity Byrd, b. 9/3/1862, d. 11/12/1940, was sometimes called "Chattie," m. W. H. Edwards and lived in the old Francis Haynes home. Her son, Lawrence Edwards lives there today. Mrs. Marshall Sealey, (Gertrude Edwards), is her daughter.

4. Elizah Lawrence, b. 10/18/1866, d. 2/4/1940, m. Anna Surles, b. 6/26/1872, d. 10/18/1952. At Bloomingdale Baptist Church, there is a plate near the entrance which says: "This House of God is a testimony of faith in God, and love for mankind." Elizah and his wife are buried in a family cemetery between Orrum and Barnesville, N. C., in Robeson Co.

5. Carrie Francis, b. 5/9/1870, d. 8/29/1958, m. J. A. McColsky.

6. Clinton, b. 10/1/1872.

II. A daughter, m. a Nye.
III. A daughter, m. a Sellers.
IV. A daughter, m. Allen Waters.
V. Rose, never married.
VI. Martha, (Patsy), unmarried.

In the Haynes Chapter, (Vol. IV, p. 91), it is stated that Bythell Haynes, (1755-1833), m. Lucy _____. It is not known whom he married, but as he named his eldest son, Armistead, it is thought that his wife may have been an Armistead, and that his son, Armistead, m. Nancy, dau. of Capt. Anthony Armistead, (who d. Wilkinson Co., Miss., 1841).

The will of Lucy Haynes, (mentioned on the same page), was that of Nancy Haynes, widow of Armistead, the eldest son of Bythell Haynes. (Wilkinson Co. W.B. 2, p. 4, 1/2/1842) Francis Bythell Haynes was her son.

*****

HARRISON OF JAMES RIVER
(See H.S.F., Volume V, p. 74, revised as follows:)

Robert Harrison, son of Benjamin[4] Harrison and his wife, Anne Carter Harrison, was b. ca 1732, Charles City Co., and d. 1788. He attended William & Mary College with his brothers, Carter, Henry, and Nathaniel. He m. 1754, Elizabeth Hill. He removed from Charles City Co., ca 1765, with his young family, and established a residence on a six hundred acre tract known as Bicars and Curetons on Tar Bay of the James River in Prince George Co., directly across the river from Berkeley, which his father, Benjamin Harrison, had purchased in 1733, and where he d. in 1788. The Bicars tract continued to be held and occupied by his descendents until 1926.

Children:
1. Robert Harrison, Jr., b. Charles City Co., 2/11/1755, d. Prince George Co., 7/8/1797. Pvt. 15th, and 5th and 11th Va. Reg. of Foot, 1777-1779, Rev. War. He m. 4/12/1777, Henrietta Maria Hardyman, b. 2/14/1751, d. 8/17/1836, dau. of William and Angelica Epes Hardyman. Issue: Seven children.
2. Sally Harrison, m. 11/13/1780, Thomas Mattox. Issue: Nine children.
3. Susanna Harrison, m. Jesse Binford.
4. Mary Harrison, assumed d.s.p. post 1792.
5. Duke Harrison, assumed d.s.p. ante 1811.

NOTE: This revision shows Robert Harrison, ca 1732-1788, as being the son of Benjamin Harrison of Berkeley, and not the York River Robert Harrison, of the same era, so placed by Keith, Stanard, and Boddie.

****

NOTES ON THE YORK RIVER HARRISONS

The York River Harrison family was founded by Robert Harrison, b. 1603, in London, and who settled in York Co., in the early 1600's, about the same time that Benjamin Harrison, founder of the James River Harrison family appeared in Surry Co., and Jamestown. The will of Robert Harrison was proved in York Co. Court, 4/10/1667. The early generations of the York River family seem to have intermarried with the Braxton family of King William, and with the Minge and Collier families in the Weyanoke area, in the eastern part of James City and Charles City Counties, where these families were large land holders.

There seems to have been a Robert in each succeeding generation of the York River Harrisons. Robert Harrison of Charles City Co., m. Elizabeth Collier and had two sons: Collier Harrison and Braxton Harrison.

Collier Harrison of "Kittewan", m. Christiana Shields, widow of David Minge, from whom came "Kittewan," long a Minge holding. Issue: one dau., Elizabeth Collier Harrison. He m. (2) Bersheba Bryant. Issue: Braxton Harrison and Robert Carter Harrison. In his will, (proven Charles City Co., 7/20/1808), Braxton Harrison, d.s.p., bequeathed his place, "Farmer's Rest," several miles east of "Kittewan," to his namesake nephew, Braxton Harrison, II.

In his will, (proven Charles City Co., 2/15/1810), Collier Harrison of "Kittewan" bequeathed slaves, etc., to his daughter, Elizabeth, recognized his son, Braxton, as having inherited "Farmer's Rest," and bequeathed "Kittewan" to his son, Robert. He named among the executors, and guardian of his children, "my friend Mr. Benj. Harrison of Berkeley." This was Benjamin Harrison, VI, father of Benjamin Carter Harrison, who married Elizabeth Collier Harrison about the time of the will of Collier Harrison. So far as is known, this was the first intermarriage between the James River and the York River Harrisons.

****

HORTON and MORRISON
of
VIRGINIA and OKLAHOMA

John Horton, Jr., b. 12/23/1749, in Stafford Co.,
Va., d. 7/1/1817, in Russell Co., Va., was the son of John
Horton, Sr., and his wife, Sarah. He m. Isabell Kendrick
(b. 10/13/1754) in Stafford Co. She was the dau. of Patrick Kendrick, a farmer, and his wife, Jane. Patrick was
the son of Thomas Kendrick (d. 1770) and his wife, Marian.
A connection between the Kendricks of Gloucester Co., Va.,
(see H.S.F., Vol. I) has not been established.
    John Horton, III, son of John and Isabell, b. ca
1777, in South West Va., d. after 1850, in Lee Co., Va.,
m. ca 1800, in Russell Co., Jane Sargent, b. ca 1782, in
Russell Co., dau. of James (?) Sargent, a farmer, and his
2nd wife, Jane Love (?).
    Children:
    1. Thomas Horton, b. 10/19/1801, m. (1) Patsy Wil-
        son, (2) Martha Stewart Edwards.
    2. Cynthia Horton, b. 6/16/1804, m. John Skaggs.
    3. Mary (Polly) Horton, b. 1812, m. Wm. Richmond.
    4. Daniel Horton, b. 1816, m. Cynthia Ann Mitchell.
    5. Sarah (Sallie), b. 1823, m. Dr. Aaron Collier.
    6. Henderson Horton. (See later)
    7. Harvey Nelson Horton, b. 5/20/1825, m. Ellen
        McAfee.
    8. Jane Horton, m. Jo. Heyl Davidson.
Other children: William, John, and probably others not
listed.
    Major Henderson Horton, b. 5/1/1821, in Russell Co.,
Va., d. 9/22/1890, at Midland, Texas, fought in the Civil
War, m. 8/24/1843, Arminda Jane Mitchell, b. 1827, at Rye
Cove, Scott Co., Va., d. 3/24/1914, at Vinita, Craig Co.,
Okla., dau. of William Mitchell, a farmer, and his wife,
Agnes Carter. Major Horton was buried in Midland Co.,Tex.
    Children:
    1. Elizabeth Horton. (See later)
    2. Thomas Horton, b. 4/14/1857, m. Alwine Specht.

225

3. Henderson Horton.
4. Sarah Horton, m. S. W. Easton.
5. Daughter, m. Eugene Sage.

Elizabeth Horton, b. 9/17/1847, at Rye Cove, Va., d. 10/21/1927, at Vinita, Okla., m. Leroy Ladd Crutchfield, b. 10/25/1844, Collins Co., Texas, d. 3/5/1897, at Vinita, on 8/12/1868, in Collins Co., Texas. Leroy L. Crutchfield was a merchant, and lived at Jacksboro, Texas, and Vinita, Okla. He was a member of the Methodist Church.

Children:
1. Annie Elizabeth Crutchfield. (See later)
2. Josephine Crutchfield, b. 11/30/1875, m. W. E. Hallsel.
3. John Crutchfield, d.s.p.

Annie Eliza Crutchfield, b. 5/23/1869, at Jacksboro, Jack Co., Texas, d. 4/21/1950, at Vinita, Okla., m. William Henry Morrison, b. 11/7/1862, at Prairie Grove, Washington Co., Arkansas, d. 2/23/1923, at Vinita, Okla., on 12/12/1887, at Jacksboro, Texas.

Children:
1. Elsie Lee Morrison, b. 10/1/1889, m. John W. Nichols.
2. Ruth Morrison, b. 9/8/1891, unmarried.
3. Elizabeth Morrison. (See later)
4. Henry Clinton Morrison, b. 10/4/1897, m. Anna Melton.
5. Leroy Ladd, b. 12/8/1899, m. Patricia Smith.

Elizabeth Morrison, b. 8/9/1894, at Vinita, Craig Co., Okla., m. Jasper Eugene Smith, b. 7/4/1894 at Vinita, on 6/25/1930. Jasper and his wife, Elizabeth, live at Vinita, Oklahoma.

The Morrison family has been traced back to Amos Morrison, b. 1/17/1774, son of John Morrison, who came from Virginia to Kentucky, and fought in the Revolution. (Family Bible Records.)

****

RUFFIN and DE LOACH
of
VIRGINIA, NORTH CAROLINA, AND MISSISSIPPI
(Continued from "Virginia Historical Genealogies", p. 264)

William[4] Ruffin, (ca 1708-1781), son of William[3] Ruffin and his wife, Faith Gray, dau. of William Gray, (for Gray, see V.H.G. - 309), m. ca 1742. The name of his wife is unknown. She d. prior to the date of his will. He was b. in Bertie Co., N. C., in that section which was made into Northampton Co., in 1741.

On 1/12/1773, he bought from Shadrack Stevenson of Edgecombe Co., N. C., for £100 Proclamation money, 100 acres of land in Northampton, on the south side of Bridger's Creek at Cashy Road, the said land given by Charles Stevenson.

William[4] Ruffin's will was dated 3/1/1779, probated November Term of Court 1781. Children mentioned in the will were:

1. William [5] Ruffin.
2. Richard Ruffin, m. Avarilla DeLoach, sister to William DeLoach.
3. Purity Ruffin, b. 1746, m. William DeLoach. (See later)
4. Faith Ruffin, m. (1) John Bridgers of Northampton Co., N. C., 1764, (D. & M. Bk. 5, p. 72) m. (2) Joseph Pender.

William[4] Ruffin lived in Northampton Co., but due to county boundary dispute, his will was probated in Bertie Co., N. C. His will names his daughters as "Purity DeLoach and Faith Pender."

William DeLoach m. 1763, Purity Ruffin, dau. of William Ruffin of Northampton Co., N. C., as shown by joint deed given by William DeLoach and his wife, Purity; also, by will of William Ruffin and by will of her brother, Richard Ruffin of Wayne Co., N. C. William DeLoach was father of Ruffin DeLoach, as shown by Power-of-Attorney given by William DeLoach in 1792, to "my son", Ruffin DeLoach, on record at Tarboro, Edgecombe Co., N. C. He

removed from Edgecombe Co., to Sumner Co., Tenn., and from
thence to Logan Co., Kentucky.
Children:
1. Ruffin DeLoach. (See later)
2. William DeLoach.
3. Samuel[6] DeLoach, d. ca 1791, m. Elizabeth Hopper.
    Child:
    a. Mary DeLoach, m. William Sneed. They had a
       dau., Mary DeLoach Sneed who m. her cousin,
       George Sneed.
4. Thomas DeLoach.
5. Mary DeLoach, b. 8/9/1777, d. 7/9/1837, Ky., m.
    ca 1795, John Sutton, b. 9/15/1772, d. 6/21/1826.
    Child:
    a. William DeLoach Sutton, (1803-1875), m. 1839,
       Eliza McReynolds, (1803-1873).
       Child:
       (1) Eliza Williston Sutton, (1845-1900), m.
           George Strother Browning, (1834-1910).
           Child:
           (a) George Francis Browning, b. 1881, m.
               Blanche Davidson. Child: George
               Francis Browning, Jr., b. 1914, and
               and two daughters: Cynthia and Brenda
               Browning.
6. Sarah DeLoach, m. Glidewell Killebrew.
7. Celia DeLoach, m. Isaac Pennington.
    Ruffin DeLoach m. Abba Mercer, Oct. 1783, dau. of
John Mercer of Norfolk Co., Va., and Mary Thompson. He
removed from Edgecombe Co., N. C., and settled in Sumner
Co., Tenn., and from there he and his family floated down
the Mississippi River on a "Kentucky Boat," in the same
caravan as Admiral Farragut's father and his family, and
landed at Fort Adams, Wilkinson Co., Miss., where his will
and that of his wife, Abba Mercer are on record at Woodville, Wilkinson Co., Miss. Ruffin and his family removed
from Fort Adams and settled at Pinckneyville, Miss., on
the plantation called "Meteraire." John Mercer was a
Lieutenant in the Rev. War.
Children:
1. John Mercer DeLoach, known as Capt. Jack DeLoach.
2. William Ruffin DeLoach, fought in War of 1812,
    and d. shortly thereafter of wounds.
3. Jesse DeLoach.
4. Elizabeth DeLoach. (See later)
5. Olivia DeLoach, m. John McElrath, 1808, in Tenn.
    Elizabeth DeLoach m. Dr. James Orr and moved with her
father to Wilkinson Co., Miss. Dr. James Orr enlisted in

War of 1812 as a private, 9/24/1812, was promoted to Surgeon's Mate and served throughout the war. (Report Adjutant General's Office.)

Children:

1. Evelina DeLoach Orr. (See later)
2. Mary Orr, m. ___ Trimley.
3. Ruffin H. Orr.
4. Wright B. Orr.
5. John Orr, d. in infancy.

Evelina (Evelyn) DeLoach Orr, b. ca 1810, d. 3/7/1875, m. John McNulty from near Philadelphia, Penn., on 3/29/1827. They lived and died at Ft. Adams, Wilkinson Co.

Children:

1. Thomas McNulty, d. in infancy.
2. Mary Ann McNulty, d. at school at Pascagoula, Miss., age 17.
3. Elizabeth Ellen McNulty, m. Benj. Rowe of West Feliciana Parish, La. (See later)
4. John Wall McNulty, k. in action during the Civil War, m. Augusta Pressley of La.
   Children:
   a. Ida Augusta McNulty, d. in childhood.
   b. Mary Evelyn McNulty, d. in infancy.

Elizabeth Ellen McNulty, b. 1835, d. March, 1855, m. Benjamin Rowe, 3/27/1851. They lived on Rose Hill Plantation, Wilkinson Co., Miss.

Children:

1. A son who d. in infancy.
2. Ella Evelyn Rowe, b. 1853, d. 1941, d.s.p.
3. Sarah Elizabeth Rowe, b. April, 1855, d. 1927, m. Darling Babers, 10/11/1876, son of John Babers, of S. C. John and his son, Darling, later settled in Bienville Parish, La. Darling Babers served in the Civil War, first under General Stonewall Jackson in the Valley Campaign, and later under General Lee at the Battle of Gettysburg, where he was taken prisoner and sent to Ft. Delaware. After the Civil War, he settled at Ft. Adams, Miss., as a planter.
   Children:
   a. Elwyn Babers, d. in infancy.
   b. Evelyn DeLoach McNulty Babers, b. 6/21/1879, d. March, 1923, m. George L. Roger.
   c. Bertram Ferman Babers, b. Sept., 1880. (See later.
   d. Edith Alpha Babers, b. 11/2/1881, m. James Chas. St. Germain.
      Children:

      (1) Elise L. St. Germain, d.s.p.
      (2) Aimee Mercer St. Germain, m. Louis
          Broussard.
      (3) Edith Alpha St. Germain.
    e. Lenore leBaron Babers, b. 10/20/1883. (See
       later)
    f. Sarah Elise Babers, b. 1/2/1890, m. Harold
       Beresford White. Child: Harold Beresford
       White, Jr.

Bertram Ferman Babers, son of Sarah Elizabeth Rowe
and Darling Babers, m. Lucille Walsh Jackson, 12/23/1903.
Children:
1. Vincent Darling Babers, b. 10/26/1904, d. young.
2. Bertram Ferman Babers, Jr., b. 6/14/1906, m. Vida
   Pelayo, 8/24/1929.
   Children:
   a. Bertram Ferman Babers, III.
   b. Sharon Miskell Babers.
3. Hannah Eldredge Babers, b. 5/2/1908, at Rosemound
   Plantation, West Feliciana Parish, La., m. 12/23/
   1929, St. Francisville, West Feliciana Parish, to
   Montrose Hamilton Barrow, son of Ruffin Bennett
   and Eliza Amanda (Hamilton) Barrow. He was educated at the University of Tulsa and the Colo.
   School of Mines. He is district manager of the
   Foster Wheeler Corp., in Houston, Texas. He is
   a member of the Protestant Episcopal Church. Mrs.
   Barrow is a member of the United Daughters of the
   Confederacy, D.A.R., and Colonial Dames. Address:
   901 Kirby Drive; Houston, Texas.
   Children:
   a. William Ruffin Barrow, b. 10/3/1942.
   b. Mary Anne Barrow, b. 11/15/1948.
4. Horatio Jackson Babers, b. 1910, m. Ruth McGhee
   (Marsalis) Savage.

Lenore Babers, dau. of Sarah Elizabeth (Rowe) and Dar-
ling Babers, b. 10/20/1883 at Ft. Adams, Wilkinson Co.,
Miss., m. 7/7/1916 at Des Plaines, Cook Co., Ill., James
Edward O'Donnell, b. 7/16/1883, Chicago. Mrs. O'Donnell
was educated at Sacred Heart College, Newcomb College,
Tulane College, New Orleans, La. She is a member of the
United Daughters of the Confederacy, D.A.R., Colonial Dames
XVII Century, Daughters of Founders and Patriots of America,
National Society Magna Carta Dames, and the Sovereign
Colonial Society Americans of Royal Descent. Address: Box
282, Woodville, Miss.

****

WILL OF THOMAS WARREN
SURRY CO., VIRGINIA
(See Warren Chapter in H.S.F., Vol. VII)

Will Book, 1754-68, p. 197:

    IN THE NAME OF GOD AMEN: I, Thomas Warren, of Surry County being very sick and weak but of perfect mind memory do make constitute and appoint this my last Will and Testament in manner following:

IMPREMIS: I give and bequeath my Soul to God my Saviour in sure and certain hope of a joyfull resurrection at the day of judgment.

Item: I give and bequeath to my Dear and Loving wife Lucy Warren the use of the plantation whereon I now live during her natural life it being one hundred and sixty acres.

Item: I give and bequeath to my son John Warren the old Plantation whereon my father lived it being one hundred and thirty acres and after my wifes decease I give to my said son John the plantation whereon I now live it being one hundred and sixty acres bought of William Warren to him and his heirs forever.

Item: I give and bequeath to my son Thomas Warren two hundred and eighty acres of land bought of John Debury and one hundred give to my mother by her father laying on the fork of Long Branch and Pigion Swamp. I give to my said son Thomas all my lands in North Carolina.

Item: I give and bequeath one hundred acres of land whereon William Savidge formerly lived to the Church wardens of Southwark Parish their successors to be applied for the Education of such poor children as they think most in need of charity.

Item: I give and bequeath to my dear and loving wife one negro woman named Nanny.

Item: I give and bequeath to my son Thomas Warren one negro man named Bristol. I give him all my

Smiths tools and my smooth bored gun.

Item: I give and bequeath to my son John Warren one negro boy named Dick.

Item: I give and bequeath to my daughter Mary Warren one negro girl named Kate.

Item: I give and bequeath to my daughter Lucy Warren one negro girl named Dinah.

Item: I give and bequeath to my daughter Rebecca Warren one negro girl named Betty.

Item: I give and bequeath to my son in law Richard Rowell my rifle gun.

Item: I give and bequeath to my dear and loving wife all the remainder of my personal estate after my just debts are paid and lastly I do appoint dear and loving wife Lucy Warren whole and sole Executrix of this my Last Will and Testament. My desire is that my estate may not be inventoried nor appraised. Witness my hand and seal the twenty-fifth day of April 1759.

Thomas Warren   (L.S.)

John Warren
John Judkins Jun[r]
John Harris

At a Court held for Surry County June the 19th 1759.

The afore written last will and testament of Thomas Warren deceased was presented in Court by Lucy Warren the Executrix therein named who made oath thereto according to law and the same was proved by the oaths of the witnesses thereto and by the Court ordered to be recorded and on the motion of the said Executrix certificate is granted for her obtaining a probate thereof in due form.

Teste: Wm. Nelson Cl. Cur.

Examined
Copy   Teste: V. E. Savidge, Clerk

WILL OF LUCY WARREN, his wife.

Will Book #12, p. 86:

IN THE NAME OF GOD AMEN, I, Lucy Warren, tho weak and low in Body yet blessed be God of sound mind and memory, likewise of perfect understanding do make and ordain this my last Will and Testament in manner and forme as follows:

Item: I give and bequeath to my daughter Mary Batts twenty shillings current money of Virginia to her and her Heirs forever.

Item: I give and bequeath to my Daughter Rebeckah Davis twenty shillings current money of Virginia to her and her Heirs forever.

Item: I give and bequeath to my Son Thomas Warren twenty shillings current money of Virginia to him and his Heirs forever.

Item: I give and bequeath to my Daughter Charity Smith one Negro girl named Nan to her and her Heirs forever.

Item: I give and bequeath to my Son in Law Richard Rowell one Book by the name of Burket to him and his Heirs forever.

Item: I give and bequeath all the rest of my Estate to my son John Warren to him and his Heirs forever, but if my son John Warren should die without Heirs my Will is then that my Daughter Charity Smith should have my Desk, my will is that this my Will should not be inventoried nor appraised. Lastly I do appoint my Son John Warren and Richard Rowel Executors of this my last Will and Testament revoking and making void all former Wills by me made in witness hereof I have set my hand and fixe my Seal this 29th day of March in the year of our Lord Christ 1783.

her

Lucy X Warren   Seal

mark

Signed sealed and acknowledged in the presence of
Joseph Warren
John Carroll

At a Court held for Surry County November 22, 1785.
The afore written last Will and Testament of the within named Lucy Warren, deceased was presented in Court by John Warren the Exec. therein named who made oath thereto and gave bond according to Law. The same was proved by the oaths of Joseph Warren and John Carroll Witness and ordered to be recorded. And on the motion of the said Exec. certificate is granted him for obtaining a probate thereof in due form.

Teste: Jacob Faulcon, Cl.Cur.

Examined
Copy

Teste: V. E. Savidge, Clerk

THE BODDIE FAMILY
of
SOUTH CAROLINA and ALABAMA

John Boddie, II, the second son of John Boddie and his wife, Elizabeth Thomas of Isle of Wight Co., Va., moved to Northampton Co., N. C., in 1734. He m. Elizabeth Jeffrys, the dau. of Capt. Simon Jeffrys of Bertie Co., N. C., and his wife, Elizabeth Pottle. By 1771, he had moved to Granville Co., N. C., as a deed dated 5/8/1771, transferring some land in Isle of Wight Co., Va., at that time recorded his residence there. In this deed, he stated that the property was devised to him by his father, John Boddie, to whom it had been devised by his father, William Boddie. He moved to S. C., about 1780, settling, it is believed, in Lexington Co., near the Edgefield line. Two of his children were Elizabeth and John Boddie.

John Boddie, III, the son of John Boddie, II, and Elizabeth Jeffreys, was in the Colonial Militia for Granville Co., N. C., in 1771. He fought in the American Rev. and may have been residing in S. C., by this time as the N. C. Rev. Army Accounts indicate he was paid 40 pounds as a soldier of the N. C. and S. C. Militia. Also, he patented land in Lexington Co., S. C., in 1774, on the West side of Messers Branch of Cloud Creek. John Boddie, III, (referred to in the records as John Boddie, Sr., and in the 1790 S. C. Census as John Boddie, Sr.)d. between 1790 and 1800. He appeared in the 1790 Census records with one son over sixteen, three under sixteen, and four females in the family. The children of John Boddie, III, (or John Boddie, Sr.) and Hannah established by census records, were the following: John IV, m. Sallie Mitchell about 1802; Obidiah, b. 1786, S. C., d. 1864, m. Margaret Durham; Joshua, d. 1839; Nathan, m. secondly, Elizabeth Warren; and Allen, m. first, Penelope and second, Elizabeth (of whom later).

Allen Boddie appears in the 1800 census and in 1811, he made a deed transferring land situated near Cloud's Creek, bounded by lands of William Fluker, Obidiah Boddie,

Nathan Boddie and Martin Foutz to William Fluker. Evidently, Nathan, Allen, Obidiah, John IV (or John, Jr.), Martin Foutz who m. Sarah Boddie, and Hannah had adjoining
lands, consisting probably of the original grant to John
Boddie, Sr. He d. in 1826 and letters of administration
on his estate were granted to his widow, Elizabeth, and
his son Abijah Boddie on 3/20/1826. He had the following
children: Abijah, b. 1804, in S. C., (of whom later); William; Simeon; Alison (Alcey); Elizabeth, m. Richard Duncan
of Bibb Co., Ala.; Nancy m. Elisha Whittle of Crawford Co.,
Ga.; Sarah m. James Newton; Sarah m. Mark Haviard; John,
d. before 1832; Charon; Althia m. William Vaughn; Jane;
and Hester.

Abijah Boddie, b. 1804, S. C., m. Elizabeth, b.1810,
S. C. He was in Edgefield Co., S. C., in 1830, and moved
to Ala., where they were in Lowndes Co., in 1850 and in
Dale Co., in 1860. Abijah Boddie was a planter. Abijah
and Elizabeth Boddie had the following children: Elizabeth,
b. 1832, S. C., m. James Parrish, in Ala.; Mahala, b.1832,
S. C., twin to Elizabeth; Nancy, b. 1836, in Ala. Abijah
Boddie is buried at Dairy Ann Church in Dale Co., Ala.

Elizabeth Boddie, the dau. of Abijah and Elizabeth
Boddie, was b. in 1832, in Edgefield Co., S. C., m. James
Parrish, a widower, about 1857, in Ala. James Parrish was
b. 7/24/1818, at Darlington, S. C., the son of Samuel, b.
1765, Va., and Elizabeth Parrish, b. 1785, N. C. James
Parrish moved with his father to Ozark, Dale Co., Ala.,
about 1835. He m. (1) Mary Ann Dowling, b. 1823, in S.C.,
the dau. of Dempsey Dowling (1783-1865), about 1840, and
they had the following children: Chapman, b. 1842, Ala.;
Marcellus, b. 1843, Ala.; Savanna, b. 1845, Ala., m. Philip
Clark; Rosa Burr Parrish, b. 1847, Ala., m. John Holley
11/27/1867, and lived at "Solitude," their farm near Waco,
Texas; James Young, b. 1850, Ala., m. Martha Bird; Lawrence, b. 1852, Ala., m. Martha Bird, widow of his brother;
and Mary Ann, b. 1854, Ala., m. Joseph G. Deveny. Mary
Ann Dowling Parrish d. about 1856, in Dale Co., Ala.

James Parrish and his wife, Elizabeth Boddie, moved
from Dale Co., Ala., to Waco, Texas, in 1865, traveling
in covered wagons drawn by oxen. They settled in the
Brazos River Valley, eight miles east of Waco at the old
Pleasant Hill Community, now known as Concord Community,
on the banks of Tehuacana Creek. This area was part of
the Thomas de la Vega grant and was wild and unsettled at
the time the Parrishes arrived.

In 1866, James and Elizabeth Boddie Parrish purchased
a farm on which they built a typical pioneer Texas ranch
house. The lumber for this house was brought to Waco by

ox drawn wagons from East Texas and one room was notable
for its interior of red cedar wood. They set out a grove
of cottonwood trees about the place and called it Cottonwood Grove Plantation. It consisted of about 800 acres.

Elizabeth Boddie was well known for her singularly
good, kind, and gracious disposition. As the young mother
of several step-children, she had a particularly delicate
role to play, but she was held in high esteem by her step-
children as well as her own children, and the descendants
of both, as has been attested to her granddaughter, Mrs.
Elizabeth Torrance, many times through the years by various relatives who knew her and knew of her. She was an
excellent horsewoman, always, of course, riding side saddle. Once, while riding on the road near her home, her
horse, about to cross a bridge on Tehuacana Creek, stopped,
shimied, neighed, and refused to cross. She nevertheless
spurred him on and, on reaching the other side, was
startled by the cries of a panther coming from under the
bridge. She fled and the panther followed in pursuit.
Despite the distressing circumstances of the situation,
she remained calm and in an attempt to distract the panther
from its prey, threw down her apron. The panther stopped
and sniffed around as she on her horse continued to flee.
Soon the panther was in pursuit again and she tried again
to delay him by throwing down her bonnet. This time the
panther stopped and was distracted long enough for her to
get back to the house where she called her husband to do
away with the panther.

Elizabeth Boddie Parrish d. 11/11/1869, at Cottonwood Grove Plantation, near Waco, McLennan Co., Texas. It
was her request to be buried beside a small church building in the Pleasant Hill Community not far from her home.
She was buried beside the little country church building
and became the first person to be buried in the Concord
Cemetery, east of Waco, in McLennan Co., Texas. A brick
tomb was built above her grave, but this deteriorated
through the years and has disappeared. She died at the
birth of triplets who, also, died at birth. They were
buried on either side of her and at her foot.

James and Elizabeth Boddie Parrish were Methodists.
James Parrish was a planter and miller, operating a mill
in Dale Co., Ala. In Texas, he was a farmer and rancher.
He married a third time and had one daughter, named Elizabeth, who died young. He d. 2/24/1884, at Cottonwood
Grove Plantation, near Waco, McLennan Co., Texas, and is
buried at Concord Cemetery. James and Elizabeth Boddie
Parrish had the following children:
1. Emma Frances Parrish, b. 4/2/1858, in Dale Co.,

Ala., m. Benjamin Franklin Deveny, 11/2/1876, at
Cottonwood Grove Plantation, McLennan Co., Tex.,
and d. 12/2/1911, at her home near Waco, McLennan Co., Tex., and is buried at Concord Cemetery.
She left a large family. (See the Deveny Family
of North Carolina and Alabama, this Volume, for
a discussion of her and a list of children and
descendants.)

2. James A. Parrish, b. 1859, Ala., m. Molly
Buchanan.
3. Bartholomew Parrish, b. 1862, Ala.
4. Alabama Parrish, b. 1865, Ala., m. John Laxon.
5. Abijah B. Parrish, b. 1866, Tex., d. unmarried.

****

This Chapter contributed by: Harold T. Purvis
600 North 33rd Street
Waco, Texas

THE DEVENY FAMILY
of
NORTH CAROLINA, ALABAMA, and TEXAS

Jenkins Deveny - Divin - O'Devin, Gentleman of Dungannon, County Tyrone, Ireland, took up arms against the state in 1649, and his estates were confiscated. After Cromwell's conquest, he was allowed to keep 60 acres and pay quit-rents to the English. He was b. ca 1620, and m. ca 1640. The evidence points to the fact that he was a Protestant. He was probably the father of the following.

William Deveny who was b. ca 1680, came to America and d. in Monmouth Co., N. J. His wife was Mary and his children probably were: Aaron, b. 1710, (of whom later); John, will dated 1770, Salem Co., N. J.; Phoebe, m. John Lock, 1735; Andrew, m. Lucretia Guffey, Philadelphia, 10/8/1751; George; and William, Jr., d. 1821, Monmouth Co., N. J. The first two generations of this pedigree have not been definitely established, but the similarity of names used in sucessive generations seems to indicate their authenticity.

Aaron Deveny, b. ca 1710, m. Margaret Stuart (or Stuerde) in 1736, at Wilmington, Delaware, and settled in York Co., Pa., by 1747. His will, dated 1775, in York Co., was proved in Bedford Co., Pa. Aaron and Margaret Deveny had the following children: John; Jenkins, who moved to Franklin Co., N. C.; Hannah; Aaron, b. in 1747, (of whom later); Mary; Jean; Andrew, a Major in the American Rev.; and William.

Aaron Deveny, Jr., was b. 4/16/1747, in York Co., Pa. He m. Sarah Black, b. 10/26/1748, the dau. of Robert and Ann Black. Robert Black left a will dated 6/3/1799, and proved 6/27/1799, in York Co., Pa., in which he named his daughter, Sarah, "intermarried to Aaron Deveny." He was a planter and belonged to the Presbyterian Church. In 1772, Aaron Deveny and his wife moved from York Co., Pa., to the Frontier of N. C., settling in Tryon, now Rutherford Co. He was living there when in 1775, he volunteered for service in the militia against the British in the American

Rev. War. In 1775, he was commissioned a Lieutenant in the company commanded by Capt. Robert Raiskins and of the regiment commanded by Col. William Graham. In the fall of 1776, his home was plundered and burned by the Tories, and in that year he was stationed at the Fort at Montford's Cove, N. C., where his company protected the settlers from the Indians and Tories. In 1777, upon Capt. Raiskin's removal from the country, he was elected Captain of the company and was commissioned by Col. Andrew Hampton. In 1780, shortly before the Battle of King's Mountain, he was taken prisoner by British soldiers under the command of Col. Ferguson. He was released about two weeks later and was put in charge of the Forts at Montford's Cove. This information was taken from records submitted by Aaron Deveny in his Revolutionary Claim for a pension, dated 1832, number S 8321.

The following Bible record lists the names and birth-dates of Aaron and Sarah Black Deveny and his children and is a copy of the original record on file in his Rev. Claim in the National Archives in Washington, D. C.

THE BIRTH OF AARON DEVENY, HIS WIFE AND CHILDREN

Aaron Deveny Born April ye 16th 1747
Sarah Deveny Wife of Aaron Deveny Born October ye 26th 1748
Robert Deveny Son to Aaron Born April 14. 1773
Margaret Deveny Born October ye 29. 1774
Ann Deveny Born June ye 26. 1776
Aaron Deveny Born January ye 26. 1778
Jane Deveny Born November ye 1. 1780
Rachel Deveny Born March 7. 1782
Mary Deveny Born March ye 26. 1784
Sarah Deveny Born February ye 24. 1786
Elizabeth Deveny Born February ye 1. 1788
Sarah Black Deveny Born February ye 1. 1791
Sussanah Grayson Deveny Born May ye 25. 1777
Aaron Deveny Born July ye 5. 1800

ROBERT BLACK DEVENY was b. 4/14/1773, in Rutherford Co., N. C. He evidently m. Sussanah Grayson who was listed in Aaron Deveny's Bible record as b. 5/25/1777. In the 1810 Census of Rutherford Co., N. C., Joseph Grayson and his wife were listed, both over age 45, and in the 1820 Census, Joseph Grayson and Benjamin Grayson, both age 26 - 45 were listed. Sussanah was probably the dau. of the older Joseph Grayson, as this was the name of one of her sons, and the sister of the younger Joseph and Benjamin Grayson, as the name Benjamin was also introduced into the Deveny family. Robert Deveny appears to have left Ruther-ford Co., by 1810, but he was still living in N. C. in 1818

when his son, Robert Black Deveny, Jr., was born. Robert
Deveny had the following children: Jane, m. a Bracket;
William; Jenkins; Joseph G., in Rutherford Co., in 1840;
Benjamin, in Rutherford Co., in 1840 and 1850; Aaron J.;
Sarah, m. a Pruet; Robert Black Deveny, Jr., b. 12/25/1818,
in N. C., (of whom later). Robert Deveny, Sr., was a
planter and he d. before 1854. A list of his children
appears in the will of Aaron Deveny, dated 2/15/1832, and
proved in 1842, in Rutherford Co., N. C.

Robert Black Deveny, Jr., was b. 12/25/1818, in N. C.
He m. Frances Champion, 1/2/1840, in Benton Co., now Calhoun Co., Ala. He was a builder and miller by trade and
built several of the old mills, with their old fashioned
water wheels, in Tenn., and Ala. He was also a builder of
bridges. He owned and operated an old fashioned water mill
in Bradley Co., Tenn., where he and his family lived during
the Civil War Period. The Deveny family experienced many
deprivations during the Civil War, and hard times came
upon them as a result of this war. Robert B. Deveny was
often harrassed by the Yankees and at one time was taken
into the wilds of the Tennessee mountains and left. It
took him twenty days to make his way back home. His oldest
son, Joseph Grayson Deveny, was taken into the Confederate
Army at the tender age of 16 and served the last two years
of that war under General Joe Wheeler. Robert Black Deveny
d. 1/22/1873, in Elmore Co., Ala. A list of his children
and the Bible records will follow.

Frances Champion who m. Robert Black Deveny was b.
1/4/1824, in Franklin Co., Tenn. She was the dau. of
Willis Champion and his wife, Abigail Duncan. Willis Champion was the son of John Champion whose will, dated 1818,
in Franklin Co., Tenn., lists his children: Randolph; Elizabeth; Stanley; Frances; Polly; Charlotte; William; Ginny;
Jefferson; and James. John Champion, originally from Granville Co., N. C., was among those men over 45 of Winchester,
Tenn., who formed a group "for the purpose of defending the
frontiers and property of our younger brethren when fight-
ing our battles abroad, and to suppress and put down any
combination which may manifest itself inimicable to our
beloved Country." He was descended from the Champion
Family of Isle of Wright Co., Va.

William Champion and his wife were in the 1820 Census
of Franklin Co., Tenn., both with ages 26 to 45, and among
other children, one son was listed as 16 to 18 years of age;
this would have been 17 year old Willis Champion. Between
1830 and 1840, both William Champion and Willis Champion
emigrated to Benton Co., now Calhoun Co., Ala., where they
are listed in the 1840 Census. In 1840, a very bad typhoid

epidemic occured in that country during which both Willis
and Abigail Champion died. William and Frances Champion,
having survived this epidemic, moved to Bradley Co., Tenn.,
by 1850, and later Robert Black and Frances Champion
Deveny also moved to Bradley Co., Tenn.

Willis Champion m. Abigail Duncan on 10/31/1820, in
Franklin Co., Tenn. Abigail Duncan was b. 11/1/1800, and
was the dau. of Charles Duncan and his wife, Mary Ann
Woods. Charles Duncan d. about 1840, and there is a record
of the settlement of his estate. Mary Ann Woods, Abigail
Duncan Champion's mother, was the dau. of John Woods and
Abigail Estill. The will of John Woods, proved 4/19/1815,
in Franklin Co., Tenn., listed his wife, Abigail, and among
others, his dau. Mary Ann Woods Duncan and his son-in-law,
Charles Duncan.

John Woods was b. in 1751, and d. in 1815, in Franklin
Co., Tenn. He m. Abigail Estill on 4/30/1778, in Rocking-
ham, (Augusta Co., Va.). She was b. 11/22/1762, and d.
8/19/1840. John Woods fought in the American Revolution,
the early Indian Wars, and was a Lieutenant in the Volun-
teer Company of men over 45 in Franklin Co., in the War of
1812. He d. in Franklin Co., Tenn., in 1815.

The father of John Woods was William Woods who was
b. in Ireland in 1707, and came to America with his parents
about 1724. He served as a Colonel in the Colonial Wars
and as a Lieutenant in the American Revolution. He was a
signer of the Albemarle Declaration of Independence. William Woods married his first cousin, Susannah Wallace, the
dau. of Peter and Elizabeth Woods Wallace. He d. in Fin-
castle Co., Va., in 1782, and his will dated 4/12/1776, and
proved 4/16/1782, listed his wife, Susannah Woods; his sons
Peter, Michael, William, Adam, Archibald, John, and Andrew;
and his daughters Mary, Elizabeth, Hannah, and Sarah.

Michael Woods was the father of William Woods. Michael
Woods was b. in 1684, in Ulster, Ireland. He came to
America from the north of Ireland about 1724, with his
brothers William, John, and Andrew, and their sister, Mrs.
Elizabeth (Woods) Wallace, widow of Peter Wallace and
mother of Susannah Wallace who m. William Woods (1707-1784).
They settled first in Lancaster Co., Pa., but in 1732,
moved to Va., and in 1734, settled in Albemarle Co., Va.
He m. Mary Campbell, b. 1690, (strong family tradition
leads us to think she may have been Lady Mary Campbell, the
fifth dau. of Sir James Campbell, 5th Bart. of Auchinbreck
by his wife, Susan, dau. of Sir Alexander Campbell, Bart.
of Cawdor. See Campbell of Auchinbreck, Burke's Peerage
and Baronetage). Their plantation was called Mountain
Plains, but later came to be known as Blair Park and was

located at the southern end of the present Shenandoah
National Park in Va. The Campbells and Woods attended the
Old Derry Church.

Michael Woods was the son of John Woods, b. in Scotland, 1654, who m. Elizabeth Warsup. Elizabeth Warsup was
the dau. of Thomas Warsup and his wife, Elizabeth Parsons
who was the dau. of Richard Parsons, son of Sir William
Parsons of Britt Castle, Ireland, and his wife, Letitia
Loftus. Letitia Loftus was the dau. of Sir Adam Loftus
(b. 1534, Archibishop of Dublin and Lord Chancellor of
Ireland) and his wife, Jane Vaughn. Jane Vaughn was the
dau. of Walter Vaughn of Golden Grove and his wife, Mary
Rice. She was the dau. of Griffith Rice, who was the son
of Rice ap Griffith and Katherine Howard, the dau. of Sir
Thomas Howard, 2nd Duke, Earl of Surrey. (See Burke's
Peerage and Baronetage.)

The children of Michael Woods and Mary Campbell were
the following:

1. Magdalen, b. 1706, d. 1780, m. (1) John McDowell,
   (2) Benjamin Borden, and (3) John Boyer.
2. William, b. 1707, d. 1784, m. Susannah Wallace.
3. Michael, b. 1708, d. 1777, m. Anne ____.
4. Hannah, b. 1710, m. William Wallace.
5. John, b. 1712, d. 1791, m. Susannah Anderson.
6. Margaret, b. 1714, m. Andrew Wallace.
7. Richard, b. 1715, m. Jenny ___.
8. Archibald, b. 1716, d. 1783, m. Isabel Goss.
9. Martha, b. 1720, d. 1790, m. Peter Wallace, Jr.
10. Andrew, b. 1722, d. 1781, m. Martha Poage.
11. Sarah, b. 1724, d. 1792, m. Joseph Lapsley.

Willis Champion and his wife, Abigail Duncan, had a
family Bible in which were recorded the birth, marriage,
and death of members of their family. This Bible was inherited by their daughter Frances Champion Deveny who gave
it to her daughter, Sarah Deveny Williams. Sarah Deveny
Williams gave it to her daughter, Mary Williams Warren
(Mrs. Earle E. Warren of New McGregor Highway, Waco, Tex.),
who owns the Bible at the present time (May, 1965). The
title page of this Bible indicates that it was published
in 1824 at Philadelphia by H. C. Carey and I. Lea. On the
"Family Record" pages of the Bible is written the following
information:

Marriages

Willis Champion & Abigail Duncan were joined in wedlock
October the 31st 1820
William O. Williams & Sarah I. Deveny were joined in wed-
lock November the 2nd 1881
Robert B. Deveny & Frances Champion Deveny was joined in

wedlock January the 2nd 1840

Joseph G. Deveny & Mary A. Parrish were joined in wedlock December the 15th 1872

B. F. Deveny & E. P. Parrish were joined in wedlock November the 2nd 1876

B. D. Gambill & A. E. Deveny were joined in wedlock September the 24th 1879

Births

Willis Champion was born Febraury the 7th 1803

Abigail Champion was born November the 1st 1800

Ages of children born to Willis Champion and Abigail Champion, his wife:

William Champion was born December the 23rd 1821

Frances Champion was born January the 4th 1824

Sarah I. Deveny was born Nov. the 7th 1863
(Note: grandchild)

Charles D. Champion was born April the 15th 1829

John W. Champion was born October the 15th 1829

James E. Champion was born January the 11th 1832

Mary Ann Champion was born December the 15th 1834

Willis Browning Champion was born June the 15th 1836

James Marquis Deveny was born October the 26th 1858
(Note: grandchild)

Frances Elizabeth and Abigail Eliza Deveny were born August the 21st 1862 (Note: grandchildren)

Sarah Isabeler Deveny (Note: Date not listed in Bible, but it was November 7, 1863)

Martha Ann Deveny was born February the 7th day 1843

Mary Jane Deveny was born February the 13th 1843

Joseph G. Deveny was born March the 6th 1847

William Duncan Deveny was born February the 13th 1849

Benjamin F. Deveny was born August the 1st 1851

Nancy Louisa Deveny was born August 13th 1853

Charles Seth Deveny was born November the 25th 1855

Deaths

Willis Browning Champion departed this life September the 4th 1840

Abigail Champion departed this life September 23, 1840

James Estil Champion departed this life October the 1st 1840

Willis Champion departed this life October the 3rd 1840

William Champion departed this life December the 29th 1840

John Woods Champion departed this life February the 16th 1847

William Duncan Deveny departed this life August the 23rd 1855

Charles Seth Deveny departed this life Nov. the 20th 1858

Nancy Louisa Deveny departed this life Nov. the 27th 1858

Mary Jane Deveny departed this life June the 30th 1862
Frances Elizabeth Deveny departed this life January the
9th 1863
Robert B. Deveny departed this life January the 22nd 1873
The children of Robert Black and Frances Champion
Deveny, many of whom were listed in the Champion Deveny
Bible were the following:

1. Martha Ann Deveny, b. 2/7/1843, m. B. K. Gambill
   in 1883, and d. in 1899, in Oklahoma.
2. Mary Jane Deveny, b. 2/13/1845, d. 6/30/1862.
3. Joseph G. Deveny, b. 3/6/1847, m. Mary A. Parrish,
   dau. of James and Mary Ann Dowling Parrish, on
   12/15/1872, and d. in 1899.
4. William Duncan Deveny, b. 2/13/1849, d. 8/23/1855.
5. Benjamin Franklin Deveny, b. 8/1/1851, m. Emma
   Frances Parrish, dau. of James and Elizabeth
   Boddie Parrish, (see Boddie of South Carolina and
   Alabama, this Volume), on 11/2/1876, and d. on
   1/14/1931, of whom later.
6. Nancy Louisa Deveny, b. 8/13/1853, d. 11/27/1858.
7. Charles Seth Deveny, b. 11/25/1855, d. 11/20/1858.
8. James Marcus Deveny, b. 10/26/1858, m. Cinda Florence Morgan on 12/14/1884, and d. 1/8/1929.
9. Frances Elizabeth and Abigail Eliza Deveny, b.
   8/21/1862. Frances Elizabeth Deveny d. 1/9/1863.
   Abigail Eliza Deveny m. B. K. Gambill on 9/24/1879
   and died in the winter of 1882-1883.
10. Sarah I. Deveny, b. 11/7/1863, m. William O. Wil-
    liams on 11/2/1881, and d. about Nov., 1906.

Frances Champion Deveny came to Texas and settled on
a farm eight miles east of Waco, McLennan Co., Tex. She
d. 10/15/1901, at the home of her daughter, Mrs. Sarah
Deveny Williams at Gerald, McLennan Co., Tex., and is
buried at Concord Cemetery, McLennan Co., Tex. She and
her husband, Robert Black Deveny were Baptists.

Benjamin Franklin Deveny was b. 8/1/1851, in Elmore
Co., Ala. He spent much of his childhood in Montgomery,
Ala., "in the shadow of the state capitol." He was a youth
in the Civil War and experienced much hardship during this
conflict, living at this time in Bradley Co., Tenn. He
moved from Elmore Co., Ala., to McLennan Co., Tex., in
January of 1875, traveling by boat across the Gulf of
Mexico from Mobile, Ala., to Galveston, Tex., and settling
at the Pleasant Hill Community, near Waco, McLennan Co.,
Tex. He m. Emma Frances Parrish on 11/2/1876, at Cotten-
wood Grove Plantation, near Waco, McLennan Co., Tex. Emma
Frances Parrish was the dau. of James and Elizabeth Boddie
Parrish (see Boddie of South Carolina and Alabama, this

Volume), and was b. 4/2/1858, in Dale Co., Ala.

Benjamin Franklin and Emma Parrish Deveny lived on a farm on her father's plantation which they called "Elm Grove." He was a farmer and carpenter. They were members of the Church of Christ and he was both an elder and a minister of the gospel, being a thorough Bible scholar.

Emma Frances Parrish Deveny was very young when her parents brought her to Texas, but she always remembered vividly crossing the Mississippi on a ferry. She was also a good rider and rode only side saddle. She had an unusual sense of humor and pleasant disposition. She remembered the high broad steps of her father's home in Alabama and the servants, (never referred to as slaves), sunning the feather mattresses, laying them on the cedars that grew in rows in front of the house.

Benjamin Franklin and Emma Frances Parrish Deveny had the following children:

1. Maud May Deveny, b. 9/12/1877, in McLennan Co., Tex., m.- - Ben Beard on 12/19/1897, in McLennan Co., Tex., and d. 3/25/1950, in Denison, Tex.
2. Ila Edna Deveny, b. 10/24/1879, in McLennan Co., Tex., d. 7/19/1958, in Waco, Tex. She was married but had no children.
3. Charlotte Elizabeth Deveny, b. 11/8/1881, in McLennan Co., Tex., m. Lucius Seals Torrance, on 11/8/1898, in McLennan Co., Tex. (See later)
4. Viola Deveny, b. 11/22/1884, in McLennan Co., Tex., d. 10/22/1886, in McLennan Co., Tex.
5. Alvin Dee Deveny, b. 4/17/1887, in McLennan Co., Tex., d. unmarried, 5/5/1907, in McLennan Co., Tex.
6. Emma Frances Deveny, b. 10/13/1890, in McLennan Co., Tex.
7. Gussie Deveny, b. 2/26/1893, in McLennan Co., Tex., and d. 4/1/1893, in McLennan Co., Tex.
8. Anna Belle Deveny, b. 11/22/1894, in McLennan Co., Tex., and d. 5/13/1926, in McLennan Co., Tex.
9. Nanna Belle Deveny, b. 11/22/1894, in McLennan Co., Tex.
10. Velma Deveny, b. 2/14/1899, in McLennan Co., Tex., was married and had two sons, both of whom died unmarried.
11. Stillborn infant was not named and no record was kept.

Emma Frances Parrish Deveny d. 12/2/1911, at "Elm Grove", near Waco, McLennan Co., Tex., and is buried at Concord Cemetery near Waco, McLennan Co., Tex. Benjamin Franklin Deveny d. 1/14/1931, at Waco, McLennan Co., Tex., and is buried at Concord Cemetery, also.

The "Family Records" pages of the Bible of Benjamin F. and Emma F. Deveny have been preserved by their daughter, Mrs. Elizabeth Torrance and the following records were copied from them:

Births

Benjamin Franklin Deveny was born August the 1 the 1851

Emma Frances Deveny was born April the 2 1858

Maud May Deveny was born Sept the 12 1877

Ila Edna Deveny was born Oct the 24 1879

Lizzie Deveny was born Nov the 8 1881

Viola Deveny was born Nov the 22 1884

Alvin Deveny was born April 17 1887

Emma Frances Deveny was born Oct the 13 1890

Gussie Deveny was born Feb the 26 1893

(Name illegible here)

Velma Deveny was born Feb 14 1899

The twins Anna Belle Deveny and Nanna Belle Deveny were born Nov 22nd 1894

Marriages

Benjamin Franklin Deveny and Emma Frances Parrish were joined in wedlock Nov the 2 1876

Mr. Ben Beard and Miss Maud Deveny were joined in wedlock Dec 19 1879

Mr. Lucius Torrance and Miss Lizzie Deveny were joined in wedlock Nov 8 1898

Mr. Nick Morehead and Miss Ila Deveny were joined in wedlock Dec 24 1900

Mr. Austin Smith and Miss Nannie Deveny were joined in wedlock Feb 18 1912

Mr. Smith Slusher and Miss Annie Deveny were joined in wedlock April 7 1912

Deaths

Mr. James Parrish departed this life at his residence in McLennan Co., Tex., Feb. 24, 1884.

Mrs. Elizabeth Parrish wife of James Parrish departed this life at her residence in McLennan Co., Tex., November 11th 1869.

Bigea Parrish died Feb the 5th 1883.

Viola Deveny departed this life Oct the 22 1886.

Gussie Deveny departed this life April 1, 1893.

Alvin Deveny departed this life May 5, 1907.

Mrs. Emma Frances Deveny departed this life Dec. 2, 1911.

Charlotte Elizabeth Deveny was b. 11/8/1881, at "Elm Grove", her father's farm near Waco, McLennan Co., Tex. She was named Elizabeth for her grandmother, Elizabeth

The Benjamin Franklin Deveny Family, taken about 1891, in Waco, Texas. From left to right, Benjamin Franklin Deveny, Charlotte Elizabeth Deveny, Ila Edna Deveny; standing in front of her, Alvin Deveny, Emma Frances Parrish Deveny; sitting on her lap, Emma Frances Deveny, and standing, Maud May Deveny.

Lucius Seals and Charlotte Elizabeth Deveny Torrance
Taken for their Golden Wedding Anniversary
November 8, 1948, at Waco, Texas

Boddie Parrish. She spent her childhood and youth here growing up in the midst of the large family of seven girls and one boy. The rural areas of Texas were still in a pioneer state at this time and she attended an ungraded pioneer school. She was an excellent equestrian, riding side saddle only. She is a member of the Church of Christ and has been quite active through the years.

She married Lucius Seals Torrance on November 8, 1898, at her father's home near Waco, McLennan Co., Tex. Lucius Seals Torrance was b. 12/21/1876, at Liberty, Amite Co., Miss. He was the son of Robert Blake Torrance and his wife, Jeannette Elivira Silliman Dixon, who moved with their children to Waco, McLennan Co., Tex., in 1881. Lucius Seals and Elizabeth Deveny Torrance celebrated their golden wedding anniversary with an open house at the home of their daughter, Mrs. Mamie Torrance Purvis, at 600 North Thirty-third Street, Waco, Texas, the Sunday preceding November 8, 1948. All the descendants and several brothers and sisters of this couple as well as friends attended. On November 8, 1960, they arrived at their sixty-second wedding anniversary. Elizabeth Torrance is also referred to by the diminutives, "Lottie" for Charlotte and "Lizzie" for Elizabeth, and these names have been used at times in the records.

Lucius Seals and Elizabeth Deveny Torrance moved to Waco in 1908, but spent the years, 1909-1912, on their farm at Granfills Gap in Bosque Co., Tex. They returned to Waco in May, 1912, where they continued to live. Lucius Seals Torrance was a farmer and merchant. He, also, was a member of the Church of Christ. He d. 1/8/1961, in Waco, McLennan Co., Tex., and is buried at Oakwood Cemetery, Waco, Tex.

Charlotte Elizabeth Deveny Torrance now resides in Waco, Tex., with her son, Lucius Seals Torrance, Jr., and his family. At the age of 83, she is still active and attends church services regularly. She has been the source of much of the information regarding her parents and grandparents included in this pedigree as well as the information regarding her husband, children and her own life. She is a thorough and ardent Bible scholar and taught Ladies Bible Classes in her younger days. Her beautiful gray hair brings to mind the passage from Proverbs 16:31, "The hoary head is a crown of glory, if it be found in the way of righteousness."

The children of Lucius Seals and Charlotte Elizabeth Deveny are the following:

1. Jeannette Frances Torrance, b. 10/9/1899, near Elk, McLennan Co., Tex. She m. Benjamin Lincoln

Robinson, 12/26/1918, at Waco, McLennan Co., Tex.
They lived on a farm near Wichita Falls, Wichita
Co., Tex., where she d. 3/21/1957. Benjamin L.
Robinson d. 1/6/1958, in Wichita Falls, Tex.
They were buried at Crestview Cemetery at Wichi-
ta Falls, Tex. They were both members of the
Church of Christ. Their children are the follow-
ing:

A. Jennie Elizabeth Robinson, b. 1/7/1921, at
   Wichita Falls, Tex. She m. James Thomas
   Spray 6/22/1945, at Yuma, Ariz. He graduated
   from Texas A. and M., at College Station,
   Tex., and he is now an electronics instructor
   at Sheppard Air Force Base, Wichita Falls,
   Tex. She is an active member of the Poetry
   Society of Wichita Falls, and has submitted
   many prize winning poems. They are both members of the Church of Christ. They have the
   following children:
   1. Jeanette Frances Spray, b. 8/30/1947, at
      El Campo, Tex.
   2. Nancy Sue Spray, b. 9/27/1953, at Wichita
      Falls, Tex.
B. Benjamin Lincoln Robinson, Jr., b. 7/13/1922,
   at Wichita Falls, Tex. He m. Louise Pray,
   1/23/1944, at Wichita Falls, Tex. He received his B. A. from Oklahoma A. & M., and
   his M. A. from Oklahoma University. She
   also received her B. A. from Oklahoma A. &
   M., and her M. A. from Oklahoma University.
   He is now a major in the U. S. Air Force and
   is stationed in Puerto Rico. They have the
   following children:
   1. Alfred Bennie Robinson, b. 3/24/1945, at
      Wichita Falls, Tex.
   2. Mary Kay Robinson, b. 1/18/1952, at
      Wichita Falls, Tex.
   3. Harvey Lewis Robinson, b. 8/12/1957, at
      Zaragoza, Spain.
C. Robert McCullum Robinson, b. 1/25/1924, at
   Wichita Falls, Tex. He m. Billie Vergene
   Brookshear, 6/24/1944, at Burkburnett,
   Wichita Co., Tex. He received his B. S. and
   M. S., from Texas A. & M. College. She re-
   ceived her B. A. from the University of Tex.
   They are both members of the Church of Christ
   and he is a chemical engineer residing in
   Houston, Texas. They have the following

children:
1. Sharon Elizabeth Robinson, b. 12/14/1945,
   at Bryan, Brazos Co., Tex.
2. ˙Robert McCullum Robinson, Jr., b. 3/3/
   1952, at Great Bend, Barton Co., Kan.
II. Benjamin Franklin Torrance, b. 11/21/1902, near
    Waco, McLennan Co., Tex. He m. Mary Ester Mc-
    Ginty, 12/17/1921, at Waco, McLennan Co., Tex.
    He has an automobile garage in Waco. They are
    both members of the Church of Christ. Their chil-
    dren are the following:
    A. Benjamin Franklin Torrance, Jr., b. 1/22/1923,
       at Waco, Tex. He m. Lula Mae Manuel, 10/2/
       1942, at Houston, Tex. They are both members
       of the Church of Christ. He works for a
       freighting company. Their children are the
       following:
       1. Benjamin Franklin Torrance, III, b. 8/22/
          1943, at Port Barre, La. He m. Deborah
          Ray McPhail, 4/8/1962, at Peidres Neigres,
          Mexico. Their children are the following:
          a. Benjamin Franklin Torrance, IV, b.
             12/31/1962, at Waco, McLennan Co.,
             Tex.
          b. David Todd Torrance, b. 2/27/1964,
             at Waco, Tex.
       2. Luann Torrance, b. 9/17/1944, at Corpus
          Christi, Tex., and d. 9/22/1944, at Cor-
          pus Christi, Tex., and was buried in
          Corpus Christi.
       3. Emily Marie Torrance, b. 7/6/1946, at
          Corpus Christi, Tex., m. Robert Eugene
          Cepak, 11/14/1962, at Marlin, Tex. They
          have one child:
          a. Christi Ann Cepak, b. 9/8/1963, at
             Waco, Tex.
       4. Terrell Ray Torrance, b. 11/7/1953, at
          Waco, Tex.
    B. Dorothy Marie Torrance, b. 1/14/1928, at
       Waco, Tex. She m. (1) Charles Ray Jaynes,
       5/3/1946, at Waco, Tex. Their children are
       the following:
       1. Charles Ray Jaynes, Jr., b. 3/9/1947, at
          Waco, Tex.
       2. Mark Torrance Jaynes, b. 11/21/1956, at
          Waco, Tex.
       She m. (2) John Cabaniss, 3/10/1961, at
       Cameron, Milam Co., Tex.

III. Mamie Alvina Torrance, the dau. of Lucius Seals
and Charlotte Elizabeth Deveny Torrance, was b.
12/12/1904, at "Elm Grove", the Deveny Farm,
near Waco, McLennan Co., Tex. She m. Charles
Ewing Purvis, 9/4/1926, at Waco, Tex. He was b.
10/18/1901, at the Purvis Farm near Proctor,
Commanche Co., Tex., and is the son of George W.
Purvis and his wife, Maggie Boyd Ewing Purvis.
He moved to Waco, Tex., 7/31/1923. He is
Assistant Secretary of the Texas Life Insurance
Company where he has worked for forty years.
They are both members of the Church of Christ
and they live in Waco, Tex. Their children are
the following:
  A. Lillian Adine Purvis, b. 3/22/1930, at Waco,
  Tex. She m. Billy Rex Burleson, 11/11/1950,
  at Waco, Tex. He was the son of Evel Merle
  and Blanche Moseley Burleson. He is an
  insurance claim adjuster in Waco, Texas.
  They are both members of the Church of
  Christ. Their children are the following:
    1. Patricia Kay Burleson, b. 1/30/1953, at
    Waco, Tex.
    2. Pamela Beth Burleson, b. 3/22/1958, at
    Temple, Bell Co., Tex.
  B. Harold Torrance Purvis, b. 6/29/1935, at
  Waco, Tex. He received his B. A. degree
  from Baylor and teaches English in Waco,
  Texas. He is a member of the Church of
  Christ. Compiler of this Chapter.
  C. Charles Ewing Purvis, Jr., b. 2/1/1940, at
  Waco, Tex. He received his B. A. degree
  from Baylor and is an accountant in Waco,
  Tex. He is a member of the Church of Christ.
IV. Robert Blake Torrance, b. 11/14/1906, at Elk,
McLennan Co., Tex. He m. Doris Velda Henderson,
9/16/1930, at Walters, Cotton Co., Okla. He is
a builder. Doris Henderson Torrance d. 1/23/
1964, at Lubbock, Tex.
V. Lucius Seals Torrance, b. 6/8/1910, at Norse,
Bosque Co., Tex. He m. Genevieve Enright, 11/25/
1944, at Waco, Tex. They are members of the
Church of Christ and he is a salesman. They
have one child:
  A. Cynthia Anne Torrance, b. 11/30/1948, at
  Waco, Tex.

****

HILL, HASTY, HARPER
of
NORTH CAROLINA and GEORGIA

We find in Wayne Co., N. C., (Will Book 4, p. 220), the Will of Susannah Hill, dated 2/18/1818, proven Feb., 1819. She named daughters, Jemima Hasty, Delilah Davidson, Rhoda Hasty, Polly, Sally, and Sintha Hill, and grandson, Wills Hasty. The Will was witnessed by Abraham and Sarah Darden. At this time, we do not know the names of either the parents or the husband of Susannah Hill, or just where she lived before settling in Wayne Co., N. C. The first record we find of her in Wayne Co., is a deed recorded in Book 7, p. 228, dated 1789, for land lying on Appletree Swamp. Her daughters, Jemima, Delilah, and Rhoda were buying land on Appletree Swamp as early as 1785, so we assume that they must have come to Wayne Co., about that time, and that Susannah's husband died some time prior to that. We believe that they came from Va., to N. C. The son of Jemima Hill Hasty was still living in 1880, and gave the birth-place of his mother and father as Va. Delilah Davidson, named in the above Will, was first married to Edwin Hasty, (Wayne Co. Deed Book 7, p. 133), and after his death, she evidently married a Davidson. We do not know if the grandson mentioned in the Will as Wills Hasty, was the son of Delilah and Edwin or the son of Rhoda, who also married a Hasty. Rhoda possibly married John Hasty, (the only other Hasty living in Wayne Co., at the time). Wills Hasty very likely migrated to Ga. We find a Willis Hasty living in Burke Co., Ga., in 1830. The names Wills, and Willis, are very often confused, we have learned to our consternation.

Jemima, daughter of Susannah, was according to Census records, b. about 1760-65, and as we stated previously, we believe, born in Va. She married, very likely in Wayne Co., N. C., William Hasty, a Revolutionary Soldier, born about the same time in Va. William's parents are not definitely proven at this time, but we have wondered if he

could have been the son of James Hasty and wife, Elizabeth
of Southampton Co., Va., who removed to Wayne Co., N. C.
Southampton Co., Va. Deed Book 6, p. 10, dated 3/14/1782,
records a deed of James Hasty and wife, "of Wayne Co.,
N. C." James was selling the land in Southampton Co.,
left to him by the Will of his father, James Hasty. James
Hasty, Sr., left a Will in Southampton Co., (Will Book 2,
p. 263), dated 9/1/1767, proven 11/10/1768. His heirs
were, besides wife, Elizabeth, the following children:

1.	James	6.	Matthew
2.	Benjamin	7.	Moses
3.	Robert	8.	Sarah
4.	John	9.	Isabel
5.	Joshua	10.	Elizabeth

William Hasty d. in Wayne Co., N. C., prior to 1807,
when his estate was settled. (Wayne Co., N. C. Record
Book 1-A, p. 231, 245.) Besides his widow, Jemima, children named, were:

1.	Nowell	5.	Benjamin
2.	William	6.	Robert
3.	John	7.	Delanah
4.	Joseph	8.	Nancy

Among the effects of William Hasty which were sold
after his death, was one item which we thought a little
unusual. It was a trumpet, not an ear trumpet, just a
trumpet. Also sold, were books, Bible and Testament, so
we may assume that William Hasty had some education.

Jemima Hasty sold her land in Wayne Co., N. C., in
1821, (Book 12, p. 150), and removed to Jones Co., Ga.,
where she drew land in the 1827 Land Lottery of Ga., as
the widow of a Revolutionary Soldier. She was granted
land in Muscogee and Coweta Counties. Her sons, Nowell
(Noel), William, John, Benjamin, and Robert, are also of
record in the 1827 Land Lottery while residents of Jones
Co., and Joseph was living at that time in Twiggs Co. We
later find Joseph and Benjamin in the records of Coweta
Co., where the last record we have of Jemima is a deed
dated Dec., 1837, (Book E, p. 235). Benjamin m. Civie
Daniel, 8/20/1833, in Meriwether Co., Ga. Robert m. Elizabeth Hasty, 1/30/1827, in Harris Co., Ga. We have wondered
if she could have been Elizabeth Harper, because Robert
Hasty was the son-in-law of Elizabeth Harper. (See Will
later)

William Hasty, son of William and Jemima Hasty, was
b. 10/26/1797, in Wayne Co., N. C. He moved from Jones
Co., Ga., to Meriwether Co., Ga., where he bought land
from James Hill. Both Hill and Hasty were designated as
of Jones Co., Ga., when the deed was dated 10/27/1827. In

Meriwether Co., Ga., William Hasty m. Elizajane Harper,
5/5/1829. She was b. 10/15/1809, in N. C., and was the
dau. of Elizabeth Harper. We do not know the name of
Elizabeth's husband or just where they lived in N. C.
Elizabeth was living in Harris Co., Ga., in 1830, born
about 1785, in N. C., according to Census records. Her
Will is on file in Harris Co., (Book 2, p. 39), dated
6/25/1837, proven 7/3/1854. Her heirs named, were:
1. Son-in-law, William Hasty
2. Son-in-law, Robert Hasty
3. Son, Collon S. Harper
4. Son, William Y. Harper
5. Son, Durant H. Harper
6. Daughter, Avis H. Harper
7. Daughter, Delaney Harper
8. Daughter, Lovey B. Harper

William Hasty moved to Harris Co., Ga., about 1830-
33. We find recorded to him in Harris Co. Deed Book B, p.
123, a deed dated Jan., 1833, for 405 acres of land on
Shoal Creek. William lived in the community formerly
called Chipley, now known as Pine Mountain, and famous for
the beautiful Callaway Gardens located there. Both William
and his brothers, Robert and John, served in the Creek
Indian War in Harris Co., 67th Regiment, 2nd Division, 9th
Brigade, Ga. Militia. William Hasty d. 8/3/1881, in Harris Co. Elizajane (Harper) Hasty d. 1/16/1850, of child-
birth. Their children were:
1. John Bartis Hasty, b. 3/24/1830, m. Julia Ann
   Webb, 1/8/1854. He was in the Confederate Army,
   Company E, 20th Ga., losing a leg at the Battle
   of Chickamauga. He d. 6/23/1899.
2. William Hasty, b. about 1832.
3. Eliza Ann Hasty, b. 1834, m. James Q. Wills,
   3/17/1854, in Harris Co., Ga. James was in the
   Confederate Army, Company H, 17th Regt., Ga.,
   Vol., and was the son of John W. Wills and wife,
   Sarah (Davis) Wills, who were m. 3/25/1831, in
   Meriwether Co., Ga. John W. Wills was also in
   the Confederate Army, Company G. 20th Ga. Eliza
   Ann d. in 1885, in Chambers Co., Ala. James d.
   during or soon after the war, as a result of the
   war. The date of his death is indefinite. Both
   he and his wife, as were the Hastys, were members
   of Bethany Baptist Church in Harris Co., Ga.
4. Julia Hasty, b. about 1835 or 1836, d. unmarried.
5. Martin Van Buren Hasty, b. about 1840, was in
   20th Ga., also lost a leg at the Battle of the
   Wilderness.

6. Albert Hasty, b. about 1842.
7. Mary Hasty, b. about 1845, m. a Harrelson.
8. Sarah R. Hasty, b. 1850.

Children of John Bartis and Julia (Webb) Hasty: (This family spells the name Hastey. We have found it spelled Haisty, Haysty, etc.)

1. Marenda Frances Hastey, b. 5/8/1855, d. 1/8/1856.
2. William Bunyan Hastey, b. 1/23/1857, m. Curtie Brooks, 11/5/1881, d. 9/9/1888.
3. Martha Cordelia Hastey, b. 10/18/1858, m. R. L. Leath, 7/5/1874.
4. Mary Eliza Hastey, b. 3/20/1860, m. Benjamin F. Hill, 9/5/1880.
5. John Albert Hastey, b. 3/12/1862, m. Mollie Bonner, 12/28/1881, d. 1932.
6. Susan Jane Hastey, b. 10/28/1864, m. J. G. Stanley, 12/30/1883, d. 7/20/1888.
7. Sam Webb Hastey, b. 5/1/1866, m. Susie Mae Sistrunk, 4/5/1914, d. Nov., 1923.
8. Robert Lee Hastey, b. 4/2/1868, d. 8/31/1951.
9. Nancy Elizabeth Hastey, b. 2/25/1870, m. William Edwin Goodman, 10/6/1887, d. 2/4/1956.
10. Joseph Walter Hastey, b. 12/24/1871, d. 5/23/1906.
11. Lula Emma Hastey, b. 5/5/1873, m. Ellsberry Robinson McKee, d. Sept., 1911.
12. Julia Ida Bell Hastey, b. 11/30/1874, m. Henry Maynard Strickland, 2/16/1898, living in Fla.
13. Anna Hastey, b. 5/3/1876, d. 9/9/1878.
14. Minnie Leila Maud Hastey, b. 11/11/1880, m. John Mercer Strickland, 12/24/1903, living in Fla.
15. George Bartley Hastey, b. 6/20/1885, d. 10/1/1885.

Children of Eliza Ann Hasty and husband, James Wills:

1. Anna Wills, b. 1859, m. William Kilgore. They were the parents of six children, all of whom died without issue, in early adulthood. Anna d. in Chambers Co., Ala., in 1932. William Kilgore, b. 1858, d. 1937.
2. William Robert Wills, b. 1/25/1861, Harris Co., Ga., m. Annie Elizabeth Whitten, 2/4/1886, in Chambers Co., Ala. She was b. 11/19/1866, in Randolph Co., Ala., and the dau. of Alfred Whitten and wife, Annie C. (May) Whitten. Alfred Whitten was the son of Lindsey Whitten and the grandson of John Whitten of Laurens Co., S. C. John Whitten was born in 1750, died, 1831. Annie C. May was the dau. of William May and wife, Mary (Polly) Mullins May of Randolph Co., Ala. William Robert Wills and wife, Annie E. moved to Whitfield

Co., Ga., about 1895, where they reared a family of nine children, five having died in infancy. (This Bible record at DAR Library) W. R. Wills d. 4/29/1938, in Whitfield Co., Ga. Annie E., his wife, d. 3/27/1946, in Dalton, Whitfield Co., Ga., at the home of her daughter, Belle, (Mrs. Charles E. Wood). Both are buried in West Hill Cemetery, Dalton, Ga.

3. Virginia Wills, m. Louis Bonner. They lived in LaGrange, Ga., where their daughter, AnnaLou (Mrs. William McDaniel), still makes her home.

Grandchildren of John B. Hastey:

1. Lucile Hill, b. 8/9/1897, m. Dewitt Talmage Gates.
2. John Clifford Hastey, b. 11/13/1887, m. Mary W. Conner, d. 3/24/1961.
3. Thomas W. Hastey, b. 3/15/1893, m. Margaret McGee, d. June, 1964.
4. Bessie W. Hastey, b. 3/11/1895, m. A. D. Cohen.
5. Mary Cathryn McKee, b. 1/26/1898, m. Wm. P. Hall, Jr.
6. Julia Ann McKee, b. 11/18/1899, m. Eugene J. Eames.
7. Jenelle Strickland, b. 6/19/1899, m. Dewey E. Griffin. Their dau., Sibyl Doris, m. Guy Albert McDonald, and they were the parents of Sibyl Dianne McDonald.
8. Sibyl Maynard Strickland, b. 5/9/1903, m. John B. Neuner.
9. Cecile Inez Strickland, b. 11/21/1904, m. Ivan Joel Mitchell.

CHILDREN OF WILLIAM AND ANNIE E. (WHITTEN) WILLS:

1. William T. Wills, b. 12/13/1886, fought in WW I, m. Lena Williams of Chambers Co., Ala. Children: 1) Paul Wills, 2) Wallace Wills.
2. Anna Olee Wills, b. 2/11/1889, m. Charles Gibson of Chambers Co., Ala. Children: 1) Mary Gibson, 2) Anna Gibson, 3) Horace Gibson, 4) Helen Gibson.
3. Mattie Belle Wills, b. 11/5/1890, in Lee Co., Ala., m. Charles Edward Wood, 2/23/1913, in Whitfield Co., Ga., son of William Henry and Ida Ann (Holland) Whaley Wood. Children:
   1) Oris Wheeler Wood, b. 4/6/1916, Dalton, Ga. Postmaster, m. Juanita Swanson. Children:
      a. Carole Ann Wood, b. 12/24/1939, m. David Larry Blaylock. Children:
         a) David Larry Blaylock, b. 7/30/1959.
         b) Alan Scott Blaylock, b. 3/9/1961.
   2) Hazel Virginia Wood, b. 8/9/1926, in Dalton, Ga., m. Charles C. Alexander, living in

Columbia, Tenn.
4. James Wills, b. 10/25/1892, d. 10/27/1892.
5. Charlie Wills, b. 4/11/1894, d. 4/13/1894.
6. Ruth E. Wills, b. 4/26/1895, m. Walter Beck, no issue.
7. Bertha Grace Wills, b. 1/24/1897, m. Lonnie Sargeant, no issue.
8. Ethel Wills, b. 5/9/1899, d. 9/7/1899.
9. Lawson W. Wills, b. 5/19/1900, m. Carnell Anthony in Chambers Co., Ala. Children: 1) Duane Anthony, 2) Doss Anthony, 3) a daughter.
10. Esther M. Wills, b. 5/13/1902, m. Cecil Harden in Whitfield Co., Ga. Children: 1) David Harden, 2) Mildred Harden, 3) Robert Harden, 4) Eunice Harden, 5) Alice Harden, 6) Janet Harden, 7) George Harden, 8) Sandra Harden.
11. Erma Wills, b. 4/17/1904, d. 4/17/1904.
12. Helen Wills, b. 8/22/1905, d. 12/28/1906.
13. Erva Emogene Wills, b. 10/1/1907, unmarried.
14. Thomas Harrison Wills, b. 1/29/1911, m. (1) Myrtle Christopher. Children: 1) Barbara Jean Wills, d. in childhood accident, 2) Robert Wills, 3) Ray Wills, 4) John Alton Wills, m. (2) Jean Boyd, child: 5) Catherine Wills.

****

NOTE: This material compiled by Jenelle (Mrs. Dewey E. Griffin) of Winter Haven, Fla. , and Virginia (Mrs. Charles C. Alexander) of 903 Myers Ave., Columbia, Tenn.

WILL OF GEORGE BOOTH, SUSSEX COUNTY

In the name of God amen March 16, 1763. I George
Booth Senior, of the county of Sussex, being in low estate
of body but of sound and perfect memory thanks be to God
for the same do make and ordain this to be my last will
and testament in manner and form following to wit, I give
my soul to God that gave it; trusting in the merits of my
Lord Jesus Christ for the remission of all sins and my
body to be buried in a christian and decent manner according to the disposition of my executors hereafter mentioned
and _____ such worldly goods as it hath been
pleased for God to bestow upon me, I _____ and
bequeath same as follows.

Item: I give and devise to my grandson George Booth, son
of George Booth, all that part of my land in Sussex
County lying on the south side of Sappony Creek and
southwest side of Stoney Creek, likewise one hundred acres of land on the north of Sappony Creek be
it more or less, bounded as follows (to wit) running
as the middle fence to some marked trees to a pond,
thence down the slough to a couple of marked trees
turning off as the low road goes to a branch called
the Randy branch thence down the branch to Kany
Creek to him and his heirs forever.

Item: I give and devise to my grandson George Parham, son
of John Parham, all the remaining part of my land
in Sussex County situated and being in the fork of
Sappony and the creek and containing two hundred
and seventy acres to him and his heirs forever,
likewise forty pounds in money.

Mary Sue Driver (see Batte of Prince George County,
H.S.F., Vol. II) descends through this line. She is the
daughter of Dr. John D. Driver and his wife, Susan Poyner,
and teaches in Dallas, Texas. Her sister, Miss Dayle
Driver, is a graduate of Texas Christian University, and
also teaches in Dallas Public Schools.

Item: I give and bequeath to my grandson John Parham

forty pounds in money.

Item: I give and devise to my grandson Thomas Parham forty
pounds in money.

Item: I give and devise to my grandson Matthew Parham forty
pounds in money.

Item: I give and devise to my granddaughter Anne Heath
forty pounds in money.

Item: I give and devise to my daughter Mary Parham one hundred pounds in money likewise the lent of one negro
girl called Anna during her natural life and in her
demise the negro to return she and her increase to
my granddaughter Anne Heath to her and her heirs forever.

Item: I give and devise to my grandson Reuben Booth forty
pounds in money.

Item: I give and devise to my grandson Thomas Booth forty
pounds in money.

Item: I give and devise to my grandson Gilliam Booth forty
pounds in money.

Item: I give and devise to my grandson John Booth forty
pounds in money.

Item: I give and devise to my granddaughter Mary Booth
forty pounds in money.

Item: I give and devise to my daughter Ann Malone one hundred pounds in money.

Item: I give and devise to my granddaughter Lucy Jones one
negro girl called Hannah also forty pounds in money
to her and her heirs forever.

Item: I give and devise to my grandson George Malone forty
pounds in money likewise three young cattle.

Item: I give and devise to my granddaughter Winifred
Robertson forty pounds in money.

Item: I give and devise to my grandson Booth Malone forty
pounds in money.

Item: I give and devise to my grandson William Malone forty
pounds in money.

Item: I give and devise to my friend Lucy Hill forty pounds
in gold or silver coin, a piece of double Irish
linnen, a saddle and bridle the one she usually rides
with, and twenty yards of check linen.

Item: I give and devise to my grandson George Booth above
mentioned all my estate not that above mentioned.
Be it of what nature, kind, or quality so over to
him and his heirs or assignes forever. I hereby
appoint my grandson George Booth my whole and sole
executor to fulfill this my last will and testament
hereby revoking and disannuling all former wills
made by me and my desire is that my estate be neither

inventoried nor appraised. In witness whereof have
here unto set my hand and seal the day and year above
written.

George Booth

Signed sealed qualified and pronounced by
the said George Booth to be his last will and testament.
in presence of us.
Teste   Amos Love
        John Malone
        Frederick Smith

***

BRANCH
of
HALIFAX COUNTY, NORTH CAROLINA

The founder of this family was John Branch who appears
in the Bertie Co. records about 1730. He married, as his
second wife, Ann Brown, dau. of William Brown and his wife
Martha Gray, dau. of Richard Gray of Isle of Wight Co.,
Va. William Brown was the son of John Brown of Isle of
Wight, Va., and Chowan, N. C., and his wife, Mary, the
dau. of William Boddie.

It appears from records kindly furnished by Mrs. Rom.
B. Parker of Enfield, N. C., that William Boddie, on June
5, 1683, deeded "to my daughter Mary Browne that plantation which she now dwelleth on and all the houses and
orchards of same, and all the woodland which lieth between
the land I have letten Edmund Windum and the land I have
let John Champion, and to her four children eight head of
Female cattle." (17C-627) (17th Century Isle of Wight,p.
627)

Mary Boddie's husband was John Brown who came over
with William Boddie and was one of his headrights. On
April 10, 1690, John Brown assigned their right to a grant
of 500 acres in Isle of Wight dated Oct. 20, 1688, to
Thomas Reeves, and sometime afterwards moved to Chowan Co.
N. C. (Id. p. 627)

William Boddie, in his will dated 1712 in Isle of
Wight, mentions his grandsons, William and Thomas Brown.
(Id. p. 351)

William Brown m. Martha Gray, dau. of Richard Gray
who made his will in Isle of Wight, Nov. 11, 1724, probated March 27, 1727, and there-in mentions his daughter,
Martha Brown. (W.B. 3-22) On Oct. 11. 1709, William
Brown and his wife, Martha, for divers good causes and
considerations, deeded Thomas Brown of Nansemond, 156
acres granted William Brown on S. Side of Blackwater
Swamp. (BK. 1-401) Thomas Brown was a brother of William.

William Brown moved to Chowan, N. C., soon after
making the above deed and died there with a will dated
Dec. 15, 1718, probated July 21, 1719. (Grimes) He had
three sons and possibly four married daughters to whom he
gave each 150 acres of land which probably enabled them
to make good matches. Sarah married Richard Jackson;
ANN married JOHN BRANCH; Mary married Barnabie McKennie,
Jr.; Martha married William Strickland.

On Aug. 8, 1730, John Branch and Ann, his "NOW WIFE"
of Bertie sold to James Milliken, merchant, of the same
county, 150 acres on the south side of Morratuck River,
bounded according to the Will of William Brown, deceased,
and according to the bounds the law doth Adjudge. Wits.:
John Brooks, John Joyner. (Bertie D.B. p. 247) On Feb.
19, 1747/48, John Branch, Sr., deeded to John Branch, Jr.,
100 acres "being half of the land that I, John Branch,
Sr., took up on Beech Swamp." (Halifax Co., D.B. 3, p.
187) On Oct. 6, 1748, John Branch, Jr., also with a wife,
"ANN" sold this 100 acres on south side of Beech Swamp.
(Id. p. 353) Ann Branch, wife of John Branch, Jr., was
living as late as Jan. 22, 1762, when she signed away her
dower rights in a deed. (BK. 8, p. 62)

There appears to be no further record of John Branch,
Sr. He signed his deeds John (N) Branch, and John Branch,
Jr., signed John (B) Branch.

John Branch, Jr., on Nov. 22, 1749, bought 250 acres
from Richard Street, part of 500 acres granted Edward
Poor in 1740. (BK. 3, p. 519) He also on Feb. 2, 1750,
bought from William Campbell, the other half of land taken
up by John Branch, Sr., on Beech Swamp. (BK. 4, p. 27)

On May 2, 1751, John Branch of Edgecombe sold to William Hendly for ₤. 16, 250 acres part of a tract granted
Edward Poor for 500 acres Aug. 14, 1740, it being the
land on which Thomas Boatright did live. (Book 4, p.900)
This was signed, John (B) Branch.

On Jan. 18, 1755, John Branch, Sr., and John Branch,
Jr., of Edgecombe, Planters, for ₤. 30, sell to Barnaby
Pope all their interest in "100 acres in Edgecombe on the
north side of Beech Swamp, running up to Abraham Hill's
branch to John Branch, Sr., corner tree along line to
Beech Swamp and down it to 1st. station. The aforesaid
tract of land was taken up by the aforesaid John Branch,
Sr." (Signed, John (B) Branch and John (X) Branch) Wits.:
Abraham Hill, William Branch. (DB. 2, -201)

It is difficult to determine whether John Branch, Sr.,
or John Branch, Jr., signed some of these deeds. They
both had a wife, "Ann."

It is certain that the John Branch who made the deed

on Aug. 8, 1730, with "Now Wife Ann" was not the John
Branch of Halifax who died in 1806, for if they were the
same, the John of 1806 would be over 100 years old as
this John Branch had married for the second time by 1730.

Also, it will be shown that William Branch, his son
and also the brother of the John Branch who died in 1806,
was born in 1719. It seems very probable that these two
men were sons of John Branch, Sr., and his unknown first
wife.

On April 17, 1756, William Branch sold to John Branch
for Ł. 10, Va. money, 213 acres on north side of Beaverdam Swamp, being part of land granted William Branch, Oct.
13, 1754, adjacent to Joseph John Alston. (DB. 6, p. 5)
On May 18, 1759, for Ł 15, John Branch, Gent., sold this
213 acres to John Hardy. (DB. 6, p. 128)

John Branch with wife, Ann, on April 4, 1759, for Ł.
25., sold Nathaniel Barrett 157 acres on north side of
Beaverdam Swamp, being a tract granted William Branch,
Oct. 13, 1754, adjacent to Joseph John Alston's line and
Thomas Carn's. (Signed, John (X) Branch and Ann (A)
Branch) Wits.: William Branch, Edward Barrett, George
Dawkins. (D.B. 7, p. 69) On April 10, 1760, John Branch
and wife, Ann, sold to Isaac Strickland for Ł. 2, 56
acres on north side of Beaverdam Swamp, part granted William Branch, Oct. 13, 1754. Wits.; William Branch, Samuel Hardy. (D.B. 7, p. 170)

The last appearance of John Branch, Jr., with first
wife, Ann, in the records seems to have been on Jan. 22,
1762, when "John Branch and wife, Ann", sold to Richard
Standstill for Ł. 70., 151 acres on north side of Beech
Swamp, beginning at Mouth of Abraham Hill's Branch; then
to William Branch's land; then to JOHN BRANCH, SR., land;
then to Beech Swamp. Wits.; George Hawkins, Abraham Hill,
William Duncan. (BK. 8, p. 62)

On Feb. 19, 1777, John Branch (without a wife) sold
to William Hill, 100 acres. (D.B. 13, p. 405) On Aug.
29, 1785, he and wife, REBECCA, sold to Joel Dillard, 150
acres at mouth of Reedy Branch, adjacent Richard Barrett
and Beaverdam Swamp for Ł. 133, signed "J. Branch." (BK.
15, p. 524)

John Branch married, secondly, Rebecca, b. 12/25/1752,
dau. of Col. John Bradford and his first wife, Patience
Reed. (See Bradford in V.H.G., and S.V.F.) His third
wife was Elizabeth, dau. of John Norwood. (See Norwood
in V.H.G.) John Branch was Sheriff of Halifax in 1775;
Colonel of Militia during the Revolution and fought in
numerous engagements. He represented Halifax in the House
of Commons, 1781-82, and 1787-88, (Wheeler). He died Mar.

14, 1806, and he had made two Wills, one dated 11/21/1805, and the other, 1/13/1806, both recorded in the May Court Session, 1806.

Children of first or second marriages:
  I. James Branch, m. (1) Mourning Jackson, (2) Martha Hilliard. No issue.
 II. Martha Branch, m. Eli Benton Whitaker.
III. Gov. John Branch, b. 11/4/1782, d. 1863, m. (1) Elizabeth Fort, (2) Mrs. Mary Bond. (S.V.F. p. 80)
 IV. Joseph Branch, m. Susan Simpson O'Brian and moved to Tenn. (See later)
  V. Patience W. Branch, m. Rev. Daniel Southall.
Children of third marriage:
 VI. William Joseph Branch, m. Rosa William Harris.
VII. Washington Lenoir Branch, m. Martha Ann Lewis.
VIII. Elizabeth Ann Branch, m. (1) Gideon Alston, (2) Rev. William Burges.

William Branch of Edgecombe, brother of John, patented 640 acres in Edgecombe Co., beginning in Joseph John Alston's line and Kearney's line, 10/30/1754. On 11/25/1754, he sold 1/3 of this tract or 213 acres to William Strickland. (P.B. 5-58) (Bk. 1-229) He also sold to JOHN BRANCH for Ł 10. part of this land lying on north side of Beaverdam Swamp, 4/17/1756. (Bk. 615) On 4/20/1763, William Branch and Elizabeth, his wife, of Halifax, sold to Benjamin Wooten 50 acres for Ł 53. (D.B. 8-268) He deeded to beloved son, John Branch in 1775, 200 acres of land and a water grist mill, "being purchased by said Branch from William Short adjacent to Conocanary Swamp and Joseph Lane." (D.B. 13, -290) On 11/21/1786, as William Branch, Sr., he deeded William Branch, Jr., for love and affection, 600 acres on Strickland's Branch on the side of Beech Swamp, adjacent to Solomon Williams, etc. Wits.: J. Branch. (D.B. 16, p. 133)

Halifax County was formed in 1758 from Edgecombe and William Branch's land fell in the new County. He was deputy sheriff of Halifax in 1762, and represented the County in General Assembly in 1762. (Rec. Vol. 6-741) He also was appointed a Justice of Peace for Halifax on 12/23/1778. (State Rec. XXIII-994)

William Branch, on 12/2/1791, petitioned the House of Representatives to relieve him of the duties of a Justice of the Peace, saying, "that whereas the said William Branch is old and infirm being 72 years of age and having served his country for forty years and upwards still being in the commission of the peace desireth to be discharged from the office and to appoint some other or others in my place." This petition was accepted by both the House and

Senate, 12/22/1791. (N. C. Dept. of Archives Legislature
Papers No. 103) In the 1790 Census, William Branch had 16
Negroes and this number is found in his Will. In 1791,
William Branch was granted 5000 acres in Green Co., now in
Tenn., on Bush Creek, Grant No. 2392, Grant No. 2394 was
to John Branch, his brother, for 5000 acres.

John Branch, brother of William, made two Wills,
one dated 11/21/1805, and the other dated 1/13/1806, both
recorded in the May session, 1806, in Halifax. In the
first Will, John Branch does not mention his brother, William, but in the last one, he mentions the above land
grant obtained by William as follows:

"I give and bequeath to my son, Joseph Branch, my
land and plantation known by the name of the "Cellar," containing ten hundred acres or more near Enfield old courthouse and also ten thousand acres of land in Tennessee on
the waters of Duck River agreeable to the deeds now in
possession, 5000 acres which is patented in my own name,
the other was patented in the name of my deceased brother,
WILLIAM BRANCH, whose name only was used by me and with
the court, the existing laws at that day expressly pro-
hibiting my entering my own name for a larger quantity
than 5000 acres."

Joseph Branch, evidently the above mentioned son of
John Branch, moved to his 10000 acres grant on Duck River
in Williamson Co., Tenn., where he died in 1827. His Will
was dated in May and was probated in October of that same
year. His legatees were: dau., Susan; brother, John; son,
JAMES; sister, PATIENCE SOUTHALL. Settlement of his estate
was made October term, 1831. John Branch and R. W. Hill
were executors. (Bk. 4 and 5)

William Branch, as above stated, predeceased his
brother, John. William made his Will, 10/24/1793, proven
Feb. 1794, as William Branch, Sr., as follows: (abstract)
"to beloved wife, ELIZABETH, as long as she shall remain
a widow, the use of the plantation whereon I now live containing 100 acres, and use of negroes, viz., after her
death, to son NICHOLAS; to son, JOHN, boy called George;
dau., ANN FLEWELLEN, 5 sh. exclusive of what I have given
her; dau., ELIZABETH MARSHALL, four negroes; dau., JANE
OVERSTREET, 5 sh. exclusive of what heretofore given; dau.,
MARY SCURLOCK, two negroes; dau., SARAH HILL, three negroes;
to son, NICHOLAS, rest of my land containing 800 acres and
negroes not heretofore given; my worthy friend, John Branch
to be exr." Wits: James Mathews, Wm. Pullen. (W.B. 3, p.
218)

Nicholas Branch, son of William Branch, (1719-1794),
on 4/18/1795, sold to John Branch of Halifax for 152 pounds

10 sh., 635 acres with incumbrances of widows, in Enfield township. (Bk. 18, p. 438) On 1/19/1801, he sold to Wm. C. Hill of Halifax for 150 pounds, 106 acres in Halifax. (Id. 716)

It seems that these two persons, according to his father's Will, were his brother and brother-in-law. In 1801, he sold land to John Taylor and in 1804, he sold 400 acres to William Bailey. He moved afterwards to Williamson Co., Tenn., where on 4/14/1807, he was requested to "lay off a road" to his place. (Vol. I, p. 576) He served in the War of 1812 as a private in Capt. Robert Steele's Co., 2nd Regiment Mounted Gunmen of Tennessee Volunteers between 9/28/1814, and 12/12/1814. This was his second enlistment in the army under Capt. Steele and Col. Williamson, the first being for three months. (War Dept.)

Nicholas Branch m. Elizabeth Hurst and d. 11/1/1846. He did not leave a Will in Williamson Co., and only four of his children are mentioned in the Biographical History of his son, James Wesley Branch, viz: Eliza, b. 1803, m. 8/5/1824, Ezekiah Inman and moved to Williamson Co., Tex., where she d. at the age of 94; Nicholas moved to Tex., in 1840, with his brother, James Wesley. It is stated that he never married; Elizabeth, m. Mr. Culp of Obion Co., Tenn.; James Wesley, youngest son was b. 12/24/1816. (See later)

James Wesley Branch, youngest son of Nicholas and Elizabeth Hurst Branch, was b. 12/24/1816, Williamson Co., Tenn., was raised by relatives after his mother died when he was a year old. He came to Shelby Co., Tex., in 1840. He was married to Miss Nancy Mathews, 12/3/1841. Nancy Mathews was an orphan at an early age. Her mother must have died when she was b. 7/5/1817. Claiborne Co., Miss., records show that Joseph Mathews m. Mrs. Sarah Cummins Culbertson, 10/15/1817, just a few months after Nancy was born. Mrs. Culbertson was the widow of John Culbertson of Pa., a Revolutionary soldier, who died in 1816. Joseph Mathews is shown in the 1820 Census of Claiborne Co., Miss., with wife and ten children under sixteen years of age. Mrs. Culbertson had several children by her first husband. We know none of the names of Nancy's brothers or sisters.

Nancy Mathews came to Tex., with her brother-in-law, Rev. Milton H. Jones, and step-sister, Keziah Culbertson Jones. Rev. Jones was a Methodist preacher. He is mentioned in a book, "Heroes of the Saddlebags," as having a charge at Crockett, Texas, in 1833.

Joseph Mathews d. in Claiborne Co., Miss., in 1826, without leaving a Will. His widow sued for her dower rights and children were mentioned, but their names were not given. We have found that Joseph Mathews was a taxpayer in Miss., as early as 1805.

Bascom Giles, Commissioner of the General Land Office, Austin, Tex., wrote Mrs. Clem Wilson, 5/3/1954, that an examination of their records revealed a land certificate granted to James W. Branch, which recites as follows: "The Republic of Texas, County of Shelby, No. 214, 'This is to certify that James W. Branch is entitled to an unconditional certificate for 320 acres of land by virtue of his emigration, he having proved to us that he has resided in the Republic for the term of three years and performed all the duties required of him as a citizen. Given under our hands and seal of office at Shelbyville, 11/6/1843.'" Mr. Branch appears never to have located land under the certificate. There appears on the reverse side of it a recitation that he transferred it for value to J. W. Flanagan in 1847. This certificate makes the female descendants eligible to become members of the "Daughters of the Republic of Texas." Nicholas and James Branch settled east of Taylor, Tex., on Turkey Creek about 1847.

The Bible records of James W. Branch show that there were four slaves born during the time of the Civil War, which were automatically freed at the end of the War.

After the death of Nancy Branch on 4/17/1876, Mr. Branch m. Mrs. Minerva Spears of Liberty Hill in 1878. No children of this union. James Wesley Branch d. 3/12/1898. They are buried in the cemetery at Old Bagdad, Tex.

Children of Nancy Mathews and James W. Branch:
I. John Wesley Branch, b. 10/16/1842, Shelby Co., Tex., m. 5/25/1870, at Bagdad, Tex., Mary Margaret Sterling, b. 9/17/1851, d. 12/3/1882, at Liberty Hill, Tex. John Wesley Branch d. 8/8/1912, at Mertzon, Tex. He served in the Civil War. Their child was:
    1. Walter Taylor Branch, b. 12/15/1872, at Liberty Hill, Tex., m. 7/18/1894, Caldonie Elizabeth Davis. Children:
        (1) George Wesley Branch, b. 9/1/1895, Sherwood, Tex., m. 1916, Myrtle Davis of Abilene, Tex. Children:
             a. Oquilla Maldene Branch, b. 4/29/1917.
             b. Palm L. Branch, b. 1/6/1921, m. Charles Heard.
             c. George Wesley Branch, b. 7/8/1923. In WW II, d. 1/6/1946, from injuries received in a car accident.
             d. Robert Kenneth Branch, b. 8/17/1928.
        (2) Lorah Amelia Branch, b. 6/16/1898, m. 1920,

W. C. Smith of Abilene, Tex. Children:
a. Lavenia Guendell Smith, b. 6/30/1922.
b. William Branch Smith, b. 12/20/1924.
   In WW II.
c. Amelia Jean Smith, b. 12/5/1930.
d. Lorah Dean Smith, b. 12/5/1930.
e. Sarah Smith, b. 1937, m. W.C. Sherrel.

II. Lizzie Joyce Branch, b. 4/7/1844, m. 1/18/1866,
John Lafayette Rucker, son of John Nelson Rucker.
(Colby Rucker, (Rev. Sol.), Peter Rucker, Thomas
Rucker, (Immigrant to America). J. L. Rucker came
to Tex., from Grainger Co., Tenn. He returned to
Tenn., when the Civil War broke out and enlisted
with his home company, (Morristown, Tenn.). Mrs.
Rucker d. 11/19/1888, and is buried in Georgetown,
Tex. Children:

1. Blanche Rucker, b. 1/21/1867, Leander, Tex., m.
John Mackey of Georgetown, Tex. She was educated in music at Ward's Seminary, Nashville,
Tenn., and taught piano for many years after her
marriage at Dallas, Tex. She m. (2) Mike Rogers
in 1926, and lived at Kyle, Tex., for four
years. Mr. Rogers died in 1930. Four daus. to
live:
   (1) Beulah Mackey, b. 11/22/1893, m. 1910,
        William Franklin Yates of Forney, Tex.,
        just after her graduation from Ursaline
        Academy. Children:
        a. William F. Yates, Jr., b. 7/24/1911.
           Married. He was in the U.S. Navy. Died
           in 1951, and buried in Fla. No children.
        b. Mackey L. Yates, b. 6/11/1913, m. Mary
           Emma Ford. No children.
        c. Betty Yates, b. 1915, was killed by car
           in 1920.
        d. Richard Julian Yates, b. 12/21/1924,
           attended University of Okla. Was in
           U.S. Navy during WW II. He is a Geolo-
           gist for an Oil Co., married and living
           in Texas. Has at least one child.
   (2) Lou Etta Mackey, b. 3/10/1896, m. 6/30/1915
        William Henry Julian, Dallas, Tex.One child:
        a. William Henry Julian, Jr., b. 6/12/1917,
           enlisted in the 8th Army Air Force in
           England and was awarded Distinguished
           Flying Cross for outstanding service.
           Moved to California, where he was in a
           stock exchange. He studied in New

Orleans at the institute of Foreign
Trade, m. 11/8/1946, Penny Milne.
Dau., b. 1948, dau., Jennifer b.
11/20/1952. Mr. Julian, Sr., was
Vice-President of the National Life
& Accident Insurance Co., of Nashville, Tenn., and retired in Calif.
- (3) Harriett Lucille Mackey, b. 1/17/1898,
  m. 12/25/1924, Edward O. McClurg,
  Greenwood, La. Children:
  - a. Claire McClurg, b. 1/14/1926, m.
    Ralph Steward Loveridge. Children:
    - (a) Ralph Steward Loveridge, Jr.,
      b. 11/13/1946.
    - (b) (?)
    - (c) Michael Mackey Loveridge, b.
      8/20/1952.
  - b. Edward O. McClurg, Jr., b. Nov.1930,
    m. 9/9/1949, Betty Lou Wilkerson,
    dau. of Mr. and Mrs. Lewis Wilker-
    son of Greenwood, La. They have
    two children.
- (4) Fay Elizabeth Mackey, b. 9/5/1900, m.
  (1) Roy Wight, (dec'd.), dau. Betty Fay
  Wight, b. 5/8/1921, m. John Brannon,
  m. (2) George Witherspoon.
2. Cora Rucker, b. 8/19/1868, m. Dr. Eugene
   Harris, Navasota, Tex. She d. 3/2/1893.
   No children.
3. James Barton Rucker, b. 7/26/1872, d.
   4/20/1914. Unmarried.
4. Hattie Rucker, b. 8/13/1876, was educated
   at Southwestern University at Georgetown,
   Tex., where she specialized in "elocution."
   She m. 8/4/1897, James Stephen Smith, b.
   12/5/1859, in Jasper Co., Mo., (the son of
   Daniel Smith (1834-1863) of Tenn., son of
   Daniel Smith, b. 1808, N. C., and Ellen
   Lewellyn, (dau. of Robert Lewellyn & Dicie
   Benham, (1817-1902). Mr. and Mrs. Smith
   moved to Mena, Ark., in 1899, and to
   Shreveport, La., in 1910. Mr. Smith was
   an engineer on the Kansas City Railroad.
   Hattie Rucker Smith d. 10/1/1934, and James
   Stephen Smith d. 4/29/1935. They are
   buried at Texarkana, Texas, Cemetery. On
   Mrs. Smith's tombstone are these words:
   "Her many virtues form the noblest monument

memory." And the words on Mr. Smith's
tombstone are: "He lived by the Golden
Rule." Children:

(1) Elizabeth Ellen Smith, b. 5/2/1898,
Paris, Tex., m. in Shreveport, La.,
1/13/1923, Clem B. Wilson, an attorney with the U.S. Dept. of Agriculture. He was the son of Sylvester
Clement Wilson and Frances Ann Arnett
of Marion Co., W. Va. Clem B. Wilson
was a 2nd Lieut., in the Air Corps
during WW I. Children:

a. James Stephen Wilson, b. 11/30/1923
Smithport, Pa. Jimmy attended
North Texas Agriculture College
after graduating from Amarillo
High School. He was in WW II, for
35 months. He attended Harvard
University, was sent overseas and
served in Patton's 3rd Army. Was
in the Battle of the Bulge. Returned home, and entered the Univ. of
Ark. He was a member of the Kappa
Alpha Fraternity. He graduated in
August, 1950, with degree in Indus-
trial Management. In Sept., 1950,
he started to work for Ottenheimer
Factory in Little Rock, Ark. He
m. 10/22/1954, Norma Jean Siler,
dau. of Paul Monroe Siler and Nellie Bell Siler of Bradford, Ark.
Miss Siler graduated from Oklahoma
A & M College. She is a member of
the Phi Mu Sorority.

b. Eugene Garrett Wilson, b. 5/31/
1925, Hot Springs, Ark., was in the
Air Corps during WW II. He atten-
ded the Univ. of Ark., and Little
Rock Jr. College. He m. 1947,
Sarah Hickinbotham, dau. of John
Henry Hickinbotham and Willard F.
Dent. Son:
(a) John Eugene Wilson, b. 1/19/
1948.

c. Roger Clement Wilson, b. 9/29/1927,
Hot Springs, Ark., was in the army
during WW II. He attended Little
Rock Jr. College and graduated from

the Univ. of Ark., Aug., 1950, and
received a degree in Business
Administration. He entered the
insurance field. In 1954-55, he
and his wife attended college at
Phoenix, Ariz., The American Insti-
tute of Foreign Trade. Roger C.
Wilson m. 6/9/1951, Lillian Jane
Lee, b. 1/13/1928, dau. of Everard
Lee (dec'd.), and granddaughter of
J. B. Lee's of Merigold, Miss.,
and Mrs. Arthur Bently Leverett of
Little Rock, Ark., who was Lillian
Hendrix, dau. of J. A. Hendrix of
Marion, Ala., (dec'd) and Mrs. Hen-
drix. Jane Lee attended Judson
College, Marion, Ala., the Univ. of
Miss., at Oxford, and graduated
from Mary Washington College of
Univ. of Va., at Fredericksburg,
Va. She is a member of Delta Gamma
Sorority. They have a daughter,
Courtney Lee Wilson, b. 10/9/1953,
Waco, Tex.

(2) James Rucker Smith, b. 1/1/1902, m.
8/18/1923, Vivian McCain, b. 8/12/1905,
dau. of Edward Lee McCain, (1872-1943)
and Mary Susie Powell, (1873-1953), of
Blanchard, La. Vivian McCain attended
Stephens College, Columbia, Mo. James
Rucker Smith is Rep. Bute Paint Co.,
of Houston, Texas. Home is in Lubbock.
Children:

a. Edward Jackson Smith, b. 7/9/1924,
Oklahoma City, Okla., graduated
from Texarkana, Ark., High School
and the Univ. of Ark. He is a member of the Kappa Sigma Fraternity.
His college education was inter-
rupted by WW II. He served as a
pilot in the Air Corps and was a
2nd Lieut. He has been with the
Commercial National Bank since graduating from the Univ. of Ark.,
June, 1949, and is now Asst. Trust
Officer. He was selected to attend
the graduate school of banking at
Rutgers Univ., New Brunswick, N.J.,

for short courses each summer for
three years. He majored in trusts.
He m. 4/15/1955, Joanne Renshaw,
dau. of Mr. and Mrs. G. Douglas
Renshaw.

b. Robert Cornell Smith, b. 10/10/
1925, was in the U.S. Army during
WW II. He attended the Univ. of
Ark. He is a salesman for U.S.
Steel Co., at New Iberia, La. He
m. 2/18/1949, Mary Frances Teague,
dau. of Mr. and Mrs. R. D. Teague
of Texarkana, Ark. Mary Frances
attended TSCW at Denton, Tex.
Children:
(a) Constance Lynn Smith, b. 1949.
(b) Mary Susannah Smith, b. 1951.

c. Betty Ann Smith, b. 8/9/1929,
attended the Univ. of Ark., where
she was a member of Pi Phi Sorority.
She m. 8/19/1949, Roy William Mor-
ley, son of Mr. and Mrs. Roy Rich-
ard Morley of West Memphis, Ark.
Mr. Morley graduated from the Univ.
of Ark., where he was a member of
Sigma Alpha Epsilon Fraternity. He
is the grandson of the late Mr. and
Mrs. Kirk G. Morley of McGehee, Ark.
Mrs. K. G. Morley was Miss Lillian
Richards of Jerseyville, Ill. Mr.
Morley was b. in Morgan Co., Ill.,
10/21/1858, son of William and
Louise (Kirk) Morley, the former a
native of Pa., and the latter of
Ohio. Roy Morley is in the Ice
Business with his father at West
Memphis, Ark., and other nearby
towns. Children:
(a) William Roy Morley, b. 1951.
(b) Edward James Morley, b. 1953.
(c) (?) Morley, b. 1954.

(3) Helen Lucille Smith, b. 7/18/1904,
Mena, Ark. Attended Stephens College,
Columbia, Mo., and taught school at
Vivian, La., before her marriage,
12/25/1927, to Herbert Benjamin Wren,
Jr., son of Dr. H. B. Wren, Sr., and
Mary Frances Lynch Wren of Shreveport,

La. Dr. Wren was the son of George
Lovic Pierce Wren and Ellen Carr of
Webster Parish, La. He was President
of the Shreveport Medical Society at
the time of his death, 8/12/1938. Mr.
H. B. Wren is Distributor for Pan-Am
Oil Co., at Texarkana. He has held
offices in the First Methodist Church
of Texarkana, Ark., the School Board,
and several Civic Clubs. Mr. Wren
attended Centenary College at Shreveport and Georgia Tech in Atlanta, Ga.
He was born at Rayville, La., May,
1900. Children:

a. Dr. Herbert Benjamin Wren, III,
b. 2/3/1930, was an honor student
in High School. He graduated from
Tulane University receiving B.S.
Degree. He was in the upper five
percent of his class, member of the
Greenbackers, Pan-Helenic Council
and Kappa Sigma Fraternity. He was
elected to membership in Omicron
Delta Kappa, a national honorary
leadership fraternity. He was one
of ten Tulane Univ. students selected out of a student body of 7000.
He graduated from Tulane School of
Medicine, 6/1/1954. He m. 6/12/
1954, Jean Atkinson, dau. of Searcy
Hunter Atkinson, son of Mr. and
Mrs. B. S. Atkinson of Texarkana,
and Edna Mae Andrews, dau. of Mr.
and Mrs. J. D. Andrews of Brooklyn,
Miss.

b. Mary Harriett Wren, b. 5/8/1932,
Texarkana, Ark., attended Sophie
Newcomb College, New Orleans, La.,
two and one half years. She m.
4/6/1953, Ernest Leroy Autrey, son
of Ernest Richard Autrey and Mrs.
Autrey, who is a dau. of Mr. and
Mrs. Oren Sholars. Leroy is the
grandson of Mr. and Mrs. T. M.
Autrey of Castor, La. The Sholars
live at Dubach, La. Leroy saw service in the U.S. Army during WW II.
Leroy is an attorney in private

practice in Texarkana, Ark. Issue:
Rebecca Lucille Autrey, b. 5/8/
1954.

III. Eliza Jane[4] Branch (James Wesley[3] Branch, Nicholas[2],
William[1]), b. 11/1/1845, m. Allen Hawkins Arnold,
b. 1/5/1828, Boonesboro, Ky. A. H. Arnold was the
son of Judge James Arnold and Cassandra Elgin. Mr.
A. H. Arnold d. 1/18/1902. Eliza Jane B. Arnold d.
3/23/1909. Children:

1. Mary Elizabeth Arnold, b. 12/27/1867, Leander,
   Tex., m. (1) 11/28/1889, G. Garland had one son;
   m. (2) 6/16/1906, A. C. Lyon, no issue.
   (1) William Arnold Garland, b. 9/10/1891, Colum-
       bia, Mo., m. 1/12/1923, Laura Erickson. No
       issue.
2. James Arnold, b. 7/20/1869, Columbia, Mo., d.
   6/11/1931, m. Mabel Miller. One dau., Kathryn
   Arnold of St. Louis, Mo., unmarried.
3. Robert Lee Arnold, b. 10/3/1872, Columbia, Mo.,
   m. Rhoda Gibson, moved to Joplin, Mo. Robert
   Lee Arnold, Sr., d. 9/20/1944. Rhoda G. Arnold
   d. 1953. Children:
   (1) Elizabeth Arnold, b. 1/19/1904, m. 12/23/
       1923, Edward Hirt of Minneapolis, Minn.
       Children:
       a. Katherine Ann Hirt, m. Bill Gibbs.
       b. Betty Jane Hirt, m. (?) Richards. Four
          children.
       c. Rosemary Hirt, m. (?) Harold. 1 dau.
       d. Edward Hirt, Jr., unmarried.
   (2) Robert Lee Arnold, Jr., b. 6/1/1906, m.
       Florence Troutman.
   (3) Rhoda Arnold, m. J. W. Bessire of Snyder,
       Tex.
   (4) Roddy Arnold. Killed in action in South
       Pacific, June, 1944, WW II.
4. Nancy Jane Arnold, b. 3/22/1874, d. 4/12/1940.
   Unmarried.
5. Aileen Arnold, b. 8/21/1876, Columbia, Mo., m.
   Thomas Wiswall. Children:
   (1) Mary Wiswall, b. 1899, m. W. Wendell George.
       Children:
       a. Mariana George, b. 1928, m. (1) Mr. Dor-
          ance, (2) _____.
       b. Betty Lou George, b. 1936, m. 11/6/1954,
          Clarence R. Pike.
   (2) Jack Wiswall, b. 1901, m. Mildred Smith,
       had one son, Jack Wiswall, Jr.

    (3)   Thomas William Wiswall, m. Gladys (?).

    (4)   Sarah Jane Wiswall, b. 2/18/1916, m. 10/1/ 1941, Huston Steward, divorced, m. (2) Richard Henry.

6. Ora Arnold, b. 4/14/1880, Columbia. Mo., m. Walter Scott, d. 7/10/1944.

IV. Virginia Ann Branch, dau. of James Wesley Branch and Nancy Mathews, b. 6/18/1848, m. Crockett Collier and had a daughter.

1. Eliza Collier, m. Henry Hill. One child.

    (1)   Everett Hill, d. 1920. No issue.

V. Sarah Frances Branch, dau. of J. W. Branch and Nancy Mathews, was born 1/30/1850. Was probably named for Nancy Mathew's stepmother, Sarah Mathews. This child died when an infant, 7/5/1850.

VI. Martha Kezia Branch was b. 4/17/1854, and d. 11/12/ 1855. Must have been named for Nancy Mathew's stepsister, Keziah Culbertson and maybe another sister named Martha. Her twin was as follows.

VII. James Alexander Branch was b. 4/17/1854, and d. March, 1920. Buried at Leander. He m. (1) Annie Fields of Burnett, Tex., and had children, Maud and Ed, m. (2) Mrs. Grace Ashford of San Angelo, and had Leslie and Victor. Children:

1. Maud Branch, m. Mr. Allen, d. 1931. Residence: Bertram, Tex. Children:

    (1)   Maud Allen.

    (2)   Marion Allen.

    (3)   Bernice Allen, m. J. B. Hightower, Bertram, Tex. Children:

        a. Walter Allen Hightower.

        b. Kay Hightower.

        c. (?) Hightower.

2. Ed Branch, m. Maud Wood of Sherwood, Tex. Res. Big Lake, Tex. Children:

    (1)   Ed Guy Branch, m. Miss Lindly of Stiles, Tex.

    (2)   Riley Branch. Wife deceased.

    (3)   Ione Branch, deceased.

    (4)   Verles Branch.

3. Victor Caryoll Branch, b. 11/10/1889, d. 12/8/ 1941, m. Nellie Alice Catlin, Feb., 1912. She was b. 10/13/1895, d. 9/16/1934. Children:

    (1)   Verlie Caryoll Branch, b. 3/9/1913, m. Donald Orville Wood, b. 8/16/1913, m. 3/15/ 1935. Children:

        a. Caryoll Lynnell Wood, b. 9/18/1937, m. 6/12/1954, have twins, Ricky & Dicky

Rankin, b. 3/27/1955.
b. Karen Le Wood, b. 12/31/1946.
(2) Annell Branch, b. 11/12/1923, m. 4/19/1946,
Lee J. Sandars. Children:
a. Jill Sandars, b. 7/2/1950.
b. Judy Sandars, b. 5/6/1953.
(3) Victor Caryoll Branch, Jr., b. 4/19/1925,
m. 10/15/1949, Marcheta Delores McAnnally,
have a daughter.
a. Donna Kay Branch, b. 4/17/1951.
4. Leslie Branch, m. Cora (?).
VIII. Nicholas Branch, son of J. W. Branch and Nancy
Mathews, was b. 6/24/1857, d. 9/20/1933, m. (1) Lizzie Perkins, d. 2/17/1885, m. (2) Annie Murphy, d.
1/7/1947. Res.: Sherwood, Tex.
Child by 1st marriage:
1. Nancy Louise Branch, b. 10/19/1883, d. 3/9/1953,
m. Stephen Lewis Wright, b. 8/20/1875, d. 3/25/
1930. No issue.
Children by 2nd marriage:
2. Mary Ellen Branch, b. 5/16/1892, m. Finley Sil-
vester Ollis, b. 4/5/1890, d. 4/30/1953.
3. Oscar Jesse Lee Branch, b. Dec., 1896, m. Carrie
Beth Smith. Children:
(1) James Branch, b. 1926, married, was in the
U.S. Navy during WW II.
(2) Michael Alan Branch.
4. James William Branch, b. 7/12/1898, Sherwood,
Tex., m. Vera Ione Potter, 8/17/1922, at Sierra
Blanca, Tex. Children:
(1) Mary Frances Branch, b. 5/16/1923, m.
Clevern Miles Farnum, 2/10/1946, at Pecos,
Tex. Children:
a. William George Farnum, b. 3/27/1947.
b. Ava Jo Farnum, b. 3/1/1948.
c. Mary Louise Farnum, b. 5/3/1949.
d. Judy Kay Farnum, b. 3/30/1951
e. Dee Watters Farnum, b.6/28/1956.
All born at Pecos, Tex.
(2) Vera Elizabeth Branch, b. 10/9/1924, at
Sherwood, Tex., m. Jack Winfield Ford,
11/22/1941, at Crane, Tex. Children:
a. Micky K. Ford, b. 10/18/1942, Pecos,
Tex.
b. Stella Jacquelyn Ford, b. 7/1/1944,
Pecos, Tex.
Vera E. Branch Ford m. (2) Billy Jack Rigdon, 1/28/1951. One son:

c. Billy James Rigdon, b. 12/15/1951.

Joseph Gerald Branch, son of Susan Simpson (O'Bryan) and Joseph Branch, was b. 8/3/1817, in Halifax Co., N. C., and d. 11/22/1867. He m. 3/29/1858, Mary Jones Polk, b. 11/28/1831, in Salisbury, Rowan Co., N. C., d. 12/2/1919, in Nashville, Tenn. She was the dau. of Mary Rebecca Allen Long, b. 3/10/1797, in Halifax Co., N. C., d. 9/20/1885, in Columbia, Tenn., and her husband (and cousin), Dr. William Julian Polk.

Dr. Polk was b. 3/21/1793, in Mecklenburg Co., N. C., and d. 6/27/1860, in Columbia, Tenn. He was the son of Grizelda (Gilchrist) and Col. William J. Polk.

Joseph G. Branch graduated at Princeton in 1835. He moved to Florida, where his uncle, Gov. John Branch had his home "Live Oak", in Tallahasse. There, he and his brother, Lawrence, practiced law, and Joseph became a member of the Legislature at the age of 21. He married (1) Anne Pillow Martin, who died five years after their marriage, leaving two sons, George Martin and Henry. He moved to Arkansas, where he met his second wife. They lived on a large plantation where, after serving as a colonel in the Confederate Army, he was assassinated by a Carpetbagger on 11/22/1867.

Mrs. Mary Polk Branch wrote, "Memoirs of a Southern Woman", in 1911, which is very interesting. Her husband's children by his first wife died young, and of her children only one survived to have descendants. She was Lucia Eugenia Branch, who married John William Howard of Nashville, Tenn., as his second wife.

John William Howard was b. 4/21/1847, in Maury Co., Tenn., d. 10/14/1921, in Nashville, Tenn. He married there 12/11/1888, as his second wife, Lucia Eugenia Branch, the dau. of Mary Jones (Polk) and Joseph Gerald Branch. She was b. 4/6/1864, in Maury Co., Tenn., and d. in Nashville, Tenn., 11/7/1949.

John William Howard served as a soldier in the 9th Batallion C.S.A., 1864-1865. After the war, he farmed his own plantation and later engaged in phosphate mining and fertilizer manufacturing in Nashville, Tenn.

    Child of first marriage:
  I. William Jordan Howard, d.s.p.
    Children of second marriage:
 II. Gerald Branch Howard, b. 1889, m. Annie Craige.
III. Lawrence Branch Howard, b. 8/20/1900, m. Ellen L. Felder.

Gerald Branch Howard was b. 12/29/1889, at Columbia, Tenn., m. 6/15/1930, Anne Elizabeth, the dau. of Mary (Williamson) and Major James Craige. She was b. 9/26/1906.

Gerald B. Howard graduated at Massachusetts Institute of
Technology, in 1912. He was a Lieutenant, U.S. Engineers
(Res.), May, 1917-Mar., 1919; AEF WW I.
    Child:
I. Anne Craige Howard, b. 5/6/1931.

****

MANN OF NORTH CAROLINA and GEORGIA

The name MANN occurs in many counties throughout Virginia, but the following Mann family is believed to have come from King William Co., Va. The name, Arnold Mann, first appears in 1696/97, in King William Co. records as a planter, with Mary, his wife. He was a witness in 1704, King William Co., to the will of George Chapman. The name Arnold Mann also appears in John Mann's will, dated 6/2/1785, Wake Co., N. C., witnessed by David Gill, Isaac Gill, and David Gill, Sr., (Jurat). Thie will names John Mann's wife, Elizabeth, and children, Arnold, Judy, Betty, Avy, Anne, Fanny, John, Zachaeus, David, Peter, Joseph, Agnes, and Nancy.

The following information is taken from Granville Co., N. C., Marriage Bonds:

1. Arnold Mann, m. Rebecca Wright, 11/16/1779. (See later)
2. Judy Mann, m. John Bradford.
3. Betty Mann, m. David Bradford, 1777.
4. Anne Mann, m. (1) Philip White, 2/7/1797, (2) Jordan Moss, 1827.
5. Fanny (Frances) Mann, m. Booker Bradford, 1788.
6. Peter Mann, m. Sarah Freeman, 1796.
7. Nancy Mann, m. Joseph White, 10/24/1799.

The will of David Gill of Wake Co., N. C., dated 5/7/1788, names Arnold Mann, John Mann, and David Mann as witnesses. David Gill states in his will: "Whereas I have a legacy or child's part due me in right of my wife of the estate of Thomas Mann, deceased, now in the hands of Col. Thomas Elliott of King William Co., Va., I hereby authorize my son, Isaac to recover and receive the same with equal power and authority as myself upon his own cost and charges and for his trouble I give and bequeath to my son, Isaac, the said legacy with the interest hereof, to him and his heirs."

Mrs. J. A. Harris, of Wake Forest, N. C., is a descendant of David Gill and his wife, Mary Mann, dau. of Thomas Mann. It is possible that John Mann of Wake Co., N. C.,

whose will was dated 6/2/1785, was either a brother or a
son of Thomas Mann of King William Co., Va., since three
of his sons, Arnold, John, and David Mann, were witnesses
to David Gill, Sr.'s will dated, 1788.

The wife of Dr. William Mann, of Enfield, N. C., is a
descendant of Judy Mann Bradford.

Arnold Mann, b. ca. 1759, in Va., m. 11/16/1779, in
Granville Co., N. C., Rebecca Wright, (b. 1763), dau. of
Winfield and Hannah Wright of Brunswick Co., Va. Rebecca
is buried in the 7th Avenue Cemetery, Rome, Ga. She was
one of the first to be buried in this cemetery.

Arnold Mann served as a Corporal in Captain Samuel
Ashe's 1st. Troop Light Dragoons, N. C., in the Rev. War.
He received land grants in Granville Co., N. C., for ser-
vices; two dated 1781, one dated 1782, and two dated 1785.
Later removed to Cumberland Co., N. C. His will is on
file in Cumberland Co., N. C., dated 1818. After the
death of Arnold Mann in N. C., his wife, Rebecca Wright
Mann and family removed to Ga.

D. B., 41, pp. 52 and 53, Cumberland Co., N. C.,
dated 10/2/1833, lists the following:

Jefse (Jesse) Mann and others of Fayette Co., Ga., to
John M. Dobbin of Cumberland Co., N. C., $500, 500 acres
South side Cape Fear River, Cumberland Co., in three tracts
of 200, 200, and 100 acres each, in estate of Arnold Mann
as follows:

Jefse (Jesse) Mann, Administrator, Fayette Co., Ga.
Young Mann, Administrator, Fayette Co., Ga.
Larkin Campbell, Administrator, Fayette Co., Ga.
Jonathan Mann, decd., Fayette Co., Ga.
John W. Mann, Decatur Co., Ga.
James Mann, Henry Co., Ga.
Jeremiah Davis Mann, Bibb Co., Ga.
Henry H. Vincent, Wilkinson Co., Ga.
Susannah Vincent, Wilkinson Co., Ga.
Daniel R. Mitchell, Cherokee Co., Ga.
Elizabeth Mitchell, Cherokee Co., Ga.

Children of Arnold Mann and Rebecca Wright Mann:

I.   Jonathan Mann, b. 12/25/1782, N. C., m. (1)
Rebecca Davis. Children:

1. Elizabeth Mann, b. 1/29/1807, Cumberland Co.,
   N. C., m. 2/22/1828, George Stewart, b. 1/26/
   1790. They later removed to Fayette Co., Ga.,
   then to Jonesboro, Clayton Co., Ga., and died
   there. Miss Reba Stewart of Jonesboro, a
   Southern Babptist Missionary in China for
   over thirty years, is a descendant of this
   couple. Their sons were David Stewart and

William Stewart, of Jonesboro, Ga.
2. Zachariah Mann, b. 6/6/1813, d. 5/3/1886, m. Mary K. Mangum, b. 3/16/1823, d. 5/6/1882.
3. Ann Mann, m. John Sprouel, 2/24/1836, Fayette Co., Ga.
4. Susan Mann, m. Gabriel Sprouel, 11/20/1834, Fayette Co., Ga.
5. ___ Mann, m. Noah McMullen, Jonesboro, Ga.
6. Allie Mann, m. ___ Campbell, Jonesboro, Ga.
7. Fannie Mann, m. ___ Williams. (No record)
8. Mary Ann (Martha) Mann, m. L. E. Johnson, 2/4/1868.

Jonathan Mann m. (2) Susannah Huckabee, b. 1804, N. C., on 7/6/1827. She was the dau. of Richard Huckabee of Cumberland Co., N. C. Children:
9. John Arnold Mann, b. 7/31/1828, N. C., m. 10/3/1854, Elizabeth DeVaughan, b. 12/24/1833, in Ga. They are buried in the First Methodist Church Pleasant Grove Cemetery, Riverdale, Ga. Elizabeth was the dau. of Samuel and Elizabeth Bailey DeVall DeVaughan. Children:
   (1) Otis Bailey Mann, b. 1857, d. in child-hood.
   (2) A daughter, d. in infancy. Both are bur. in the DeVaughan Cemetery, one mile east of Jonesboro, Ga.
   (3) Oreon Qudellos Mann, b. 8/3/1865, Clayton Co., Ga., d. in accident, Fulton Co., Ga., 8/30/1935, m. Minnie Morris Travis, dau. of Max and Martha Gay Travis, b. 10/7/1872, Clayton Co., Ga., d. 2/16/1956, Fulton Co., Ga. Children:
      a. Otis Earl Mann, b. 10/2/1904, m. Bertha O'Neal, April, 1931, Atlanta, Ga. Earl Mann is owner of the Atlanta Baseball Corp., Atlanta, Ga. One son, Oreon Earl Mann, b. 11/2/1941, m. Pattie Wilson. Two children: Christopher Mann, b. 10/31/1962; Cecilia Elizabeth Mann, b. 3/30/1965. Oreon Mann is working on his Master's Degree at Georgia State College, Atlanta, Ga.
      b. Ena Elizabeth Mann, b. 2/9/1906, Riverdale, Ga., m. 12/24/1931, Karl Thomas Wilson, b. 6/12/1903. He is Director of Purchasing for Delta Air Lines, Atlanta, Ga.

    c. Annis Gay Mann, b. 9/14/1908, m.
9/17/1931, Herman Markey Richardson,
b. 8/21/1905, d. 12/23/1964. He was
with Gulf Oil for thirty-seven years
and was Distributor for the Company
in Blakely, Ga., at the time of his
death. He was a Mason, Shriner,
member of Blakely Baptist Church,
Director of Jackson Tubing & Conduit
Co., member of Blakely Rotary Club,
and was head of Blakely Early Chamber
of Commerce for two successive years.
Under his guidance and leadership
Early County's largest industry came
into operation. He is buried at the
First Methodist Church Pleasant
Grove Cemetery, Riverdale, Ga. No
children. Annis Mann Richardson is
a member of the D.A.R., (with eight
approved lines). She is presently
serving as First Vice-Regent, Ga.
State Society N.S.D.A.R. She is a
member of Daughters of American
Colonists; Sons and Daughters of the
Pilgrims; Huguenot Society of the
Founders of Manakin in the Colony of
Va.; Magna Carta Dames; United Daugh-
ters of the Confederacy; County His-
torian for Early County; Blakely
Baptist Church; and Blakely Study
Club. She was born, reared, and educated in Atlanta, Ga.

    d. John Arnold Mann, b. 2/12/1913. Un-
married.

10. James Richard Mann, b. 2/7/1830, in N. C., m.
(1) Manda Mann, 1/20/1853. They had one son
who d. in infancy. He m. (2) Mary Malinda
Linley, 2/10/1856. They moved to Tex.
Children:

    (1) Joseph Green Mann.
    (2) William Thomas Mann.
    (3) Adeliza Jane Mann, m. Ike Carrell.
    (4) Quintora Mercantile Mann, m. Wade Hamp-
ton Johnson. They had two daughters:
Dr. Ola Johnson, who taught at N. Tex.
State College; and Miss Joe Johnson,
also a teacher. Both are now retired
and unmarried. Residence: Denton, Tex.

JONATHAN MANN is listed in 1830 Federal Census, Fayette, Ga. He d. between 1830-1840, in Fayette Co., Ga. Rebecca Wright Mann, mother of Jonathan, and wife of Arnold Mann, drew land in Cherokee Land Lottery of Fayette Co., Ga., in Gittens, 7th District, 2nd Section, lot No. 134. After the death of Jonathan, Susannah Huckabee Mann m. Reuben Wallis, 7/4/1835. The estate of Jonathan was not settled until after the death of Susannah in 1888. Dr. James Reuben Wallis of Lovejoy, Ga., was a descendant of Susannah Huckabee Mann Wallis and her husband, Reuben Wallis.

II.   John W. Mann, b. 2/8/1785. (Record untraced) Lived in Decatur, Ga., 1833.

III.   James Mann, b. 10/5/1787. The Rev. James Cooper Mann of Arlington, Tex., is a descendant of James Mann. James m. 4/4/1809, Polly Heflin, Granville Co., N. C.

IV.   Susannah (Susan) Mann, b. 2/20/1790, m. Henry H. Vincent, Granville Co., N. C. Lived in Wilkinson Co., Ga.

V.   Jesse Mann, b. 6/4/1792. (Record untraced)

VI.   Jeremiah Davis Mann, b. 3/3/1798, m. Mary Burch Jernigan. He d. 12/16/1863, buried, Monroe Co., Aberdeen, Miss. He was a Methodist Preacher, and Justice of the Inferior Court, Jonesboro, Ga., 1828. Children:

1.   Leanda Fletcher Mann, m. Col. Simmons.

2.   Metsalon Mann, d. 1843.

3.   Nemarius Mann, b. 11/2/1824, Fayette Co., Ga., d. 5/2/1852, Chickasaw Co., Miss., m. Dr. John Bean.

4.   Oreon Mary Summerfield Mann, b. Fayette Co., m. Rufus Wright Smith, 12/2/1856. She taught with her husband almost consecutively for fifty years, from 1857, until her death at LaGrange College, 8/29/1907. The Oreon Mann Smith Building at LaGrange College is named for her. Children:

(1)   Euler B. Smith. He was head of the Department of English in the State Normal School for fourteen years, and then became southern representative of the publishing house of Benjamin H. Sanborn and Company.

(2)   Cecil H. Smith. He was a prominent lawyer in Sherman, Tex.

(3)   Hubert M. Smith. Former Professor of English at LaGrange College. Minister

in the New Mexico Conference.
- (4) Alwyn M. Smith. Was Director of Music at LaGrange College.
- (5) Clifford L. Smith, b. in Greene Co., Ga., 3/25/1867, m. Pearl Long of Greenwood, Fla., 4/2/1893. He attended Emory Univ., and Chicago Univ., and later served as Superintendent of LaGrange Public Schools. He wrote the "History of Troup County, Ga.," 1933. For a number of years he held a responsible position with the New England Southern Mills and the Calloway Mills, rendering valuable service in the research and engineering depts., of those mills. It has been said that Professor Smith was the most versatile man in this part of the state.
- (6) Leon P. Smith. Dean and Professor of Science at LaGrange College. Was also on the staff of Wesleyan College, Macon, Ga. Mrs. Elizabeth Smith Weaver, 1261 Jackson Springs Rd., Macon, is a dau. of Leon P. Smith.
- (7) Maidee Smith. Taught music at LaGrange College. Spent six years in Brazil as a missionary. Principal at LaGrange after her mother's death.
- (8) Claire Lee Smith. Taught music at La-Grange College, m. Frank H. Hill, secretary and treasurer of Atlanta and West Point Railroad, d. 4/19/1907, at College Park, Ga.
5. Parellas Mann, studied at Dickenson College and at Yale. Capt., in the Civil War, taken prisoner.
6. Qudellus (Dell) Mann, went to Alaska, d.s.p.
7. Rasadorius Mann, d. 1853, aged 18.
8. Sideria Mann, m. her cousin, Jack Jernigan. Children: Seaborn, John, Burch, Jerry, Mary, Leanda, Fletcher, and Peyton.
9. Tranquilus (Tip) Mann, m. in Indian Territory.

VII. Young Mann, b. 2/12/1803. (Record untraced) W. S. Graham is a descendant. History of Wilkinson Co., Ga., states that a Young Mann m. Mary Garrison, 10/27/1824.

VIII. Elizabeth Mann, b. 2/24/1806, m. 12/10/1828, Daniel R. Mitchell, Fayetteville, Ga. He was one of the three founders of Rome, Floyd Co., Ga. He

was an outstanding lawyer and was known as the
father of the Rome Bar. He gave the land for the
First Methodist Church. Elizabeth Mann Mitchell
was one of the organizers of that Church in 1840.
She was a second cousin of Jefferson Davis, who
visited them in 1850, at their home in Rome, Ga.
Children:

1. Mary A. Mitchell, b. 8/24/1829, LaGrange, Ga.
2. Georgia Anna Mitchell, b. 10/23/1831, Gaines-
    ville, Ga.
3. Lucius Cornilus Mitchell, b. 6/21/1833, Can-
    ton, Ga.
4. Minerva Elizabeth, b. 5/12/1835, Canton, Ga.
5. Roxanna Rebecca Mitchell, b. 3/29/1837, Rome,
    Ga.
6. Leandas T. Mitchell, b. 3/19/1839, Rome, Ga.,
    twin.
7. Lysander Valeneous Mitchell, b. 3/19/1839,
    Rome, Ga., twin.
8. Lycurgus James Mitchell, b. 9/4/1841, Rome,
    Ga.
9. Daniel Randolph Mitchell, b. 11/14/1843, Rome,
    Ga.
10. Mary Jane Mitchell, b. 8/22/1846, Rome, Ga.
11. Florence Taylor Mitchell, b. 12/14/1848, Rome,
    Ga.

Mr. Yancey Lipscomb, Rome, Ga., and Mr. Charles E.
Terry, Tampa, Fla., are descendants of Elizabeth Mann and
Daniel R. Mitchell.

****

COMPILER: Annis Gay Mann Richardson
            Box 325
            Blakely, Georgia

STOVALL and COOPER
of
VIRGINIA and GEORGIA

The Stovalls were of French descent, and came to England with William the Conqueror. They drifted into Wales, from whence they came to America and settled in Henrico Co., Va.

The Stovalls of Va., descend from the immigrant Bartholomew. His eldest son was George, who married twice. He moved from his home in Powhattan Co., Va., first to Amherst Co., and then to Bedford Co., (later known as Campbell Co.), where he d. 1786. He operated a ferry across the James River to Amherst Co.

Thomas Stovall of Henry Co., Va., son of George Stovall, m. 11/25/1781, Elizabeth Cooper, b. 9/28/1762. (See later) They were the progenitors of the Stovall family in Ga.

Thomas Stovall was a private in the Illinois Regiment and North West Army under Gen. George Rogers Clark. Thomas was b. in Va., and d. in Hancock Co., Ga., Sept., 1806. (Ref: Vol. 1, No. 2, pp. 127-141, "Virginia Historical Magazine", Oct., 1893.)

Thomas Cooper, father of Elizabeth Cooper, was b. in Va., 1733, and d. in Green Co., Ga., 1799. He m. Sarah Anthony in Va., 2/6/1762. He was a member of the House of Burgesses, Frederick Co., Va., 1758, and represented Henry Co., in the Virginia Convention, 1788, with John Mann. (Ref: The Virginia Magazine of History and Biography, Vol. IX, No. 3, Jan., 1902.) He was Captain in the Rev. Army. (Ref: No. 40327: Sand Hill Cemetery, Augusta, Ga.; and Clerk's Office in Va.)

Children of Thomas and Sarah Cooper:
1. Elizabeth Cooper, m. Thomas Stovall. Children:
   (1) George Stovall, b. 1783, m. Elizabeth Jeter.
   (2) Joseph Stovall, b. 6/19/1787, d. 2/4/1848, m. Mary Pleasant Bonner, Ga., 1815.
   (3) Pleasant Stovall, b. 1793, m. (1) Miss Lucas, (2) Miss Trippe, and (3) Mrs. Hill.

    (4) Sallie Stovall, b. 1795, m. Benjamin Simons,
         of Sparta, Ga.
    (5) Ruth Stovall, b. 1797, m. a Mr. Hunt.
    (6) Polly Stovall, m. Mr. Hunt, (after the
         death of Ruth Stovall Hunt).
    Elizabeth Stovall m. (2) John Weeks. She d.
    1843, and is buried in Sand Hill Cemetery,
    Augusta, Ga.

2. Joseph Cooper. (No record)
3. Agnes Cooper, m. George Hamilton.
4. Thomas Cooper, m. Judith Harvey.
5. Polly Cooper, m. Dr. James Nisbet.
6. John Cooper, m. ___ Weeks.
7. Micajah Cooper, m. ___ Lancaster.
8. Penelope Cooper, m. James Nisbet.
9. Sarah Cooper, m. ___ Lancaster.

Copy of letter as received by W. B. Stovall, 1894, and
published in "The Lavonia Times", Georgia:

Mr. W. B. Stovall
Jasper, Ga.

My dear Grandson:

Agreeable to your request I will do the best I can from
the conversations of father, mother, grandmother Farmer
and other old Virginians. My great grandfather Stovall
came from Wales in Great Britain to Virginia a good many
years before the Revolutionary War and married, I don't
know who or where, but they raised a large family of children, some 14 or 15, of whom there were eleven sons. I
will give you their names, as my father would speak fre-
quently of his uncles and aunts.

Names of original Stovall family:

Bartholomew (called Bot), Andrew (called Drudy), Benjamin,
John, George, William, Joshiah, Stephen, Samuel, Peter,
and Thomas.

A few years after the close of the war with Great Britain,
the first named five and two brothers-in-law, by names of
Benjamin Hubbard and Benjamin Fannin, all came to Georgia
with their families and settled in the following named
counties, viz Richmond, Lincoln, Oglethorpe and Wilkes.

They, as a general thing raised large families, and they
were like the army of locusts, they moved westward until

they crossed the continent of North America. George Stovall my grandfather, settled in Wilkes County first, afterwards moved to Elbert County on Clark's Creek near where it comes into Long Creek, but when his children grew up and commenced marrying he sold out and went to West Tennessee, Franklin County, 9 miles from Winchester, the county site, three miles from Salem on Bean Creek. There he bought land and built a fine set of flour mills and raised two or three families of negros and settled his children that went with him all around him. He lived to be very old and died there, leaving nine children and one dead. His youngest daughter, Dorcas, died in her seventeenth year.

As has been stated above, George Stovall married in Virginia to Nancy Ann Newton. My father, the oldest son and his brother Henry went to learn the carpenter's trade. Josiah (my father) and Henry were left in Georgia to finish their apprenticeship. After grandfather died, grandmamma lived about among her children some twenty years or more and died in 1852 or 1853 at the age of 105 years.

Josiah Stovall came to Franklin County about 1795 or 1796 and lived at Robert Walters on Shoal Creek and worked on the farm monthly in the summer and ran a cotton gin part of the time in winter, one of the first gins that was ever in the country. Early in the spring of 1805 he went to Virginia and moved his Aunt Jane Farmer to this country. They got here on the 5th of April and went into a school house on the branch about 300 yards below where Farmer Stovall now lives. In the summer father and Uncle Thomas Farmer built them a house on some land that they had bought from John Mullen near by and they moved into it in the fall. Father stayed on with his Aunt and worked at his trade some, and managed for her. The 3rd of January 1811 my father and mother were married and the 19th of July 1812 your unworthy servant came to see the light of day. My father and mother were both born in Virginia, mother on the 16th of July 1774 and father 26th of December 1774. Mother died Feb. 18, 1840 and father was killed by a limb falling on him Feb. 15, 1849. They left only two children, myself and Jane N. Garner, now in Arkansas. Your grandmother was born Jan. 7, 1814. We were married April 14, 1837. We have lived together quietly nearly 57 years, have nine children, all living a short time ago. We have 58 grandchildren and 14 great-grandchildren living when last heard from.

May the good Lord continue his blessings towards us in the

future as He has in the past. All glory, honor and
praises be to His holy and righteous name forever, Amen.

Henry F. Stovall, Sr.

****

302

- Y -

YARBOROUGH, James 105; Richard
113; Robt. 105; Ruina 105; Wm.
112.
YOUNT, John 12, 24.

ZOLLICOFFER, Algernon 167;
Alison 68, 167; Augustus 68;
Dallas 68; Eugenia 68; Emily
68; George 68, 70; Jerome 68;
Jeremiah 167; John 168; Jul-
ius 68; Marion 68; Mary 68.